Demographic Archaeology

This is a volume in

Studies in Archaeology

A complete list of titles in this series appears at the end of this volume.

Demographic Archaeology

FEKRI A. HASSAN

Department of Anthropology
Washington State University
Pullman, Washington

ACADEMIC PRESS

A Subsidiary of Harcourt Brace Jovanovich, Publishers

New York   London   Toronto   Sydney   San Francisco

ACADEMIC PRESS, INC.
111 Fifth Avenue, New York, New York 10003

United Kingdom Edition published by
ACADEMIC PRESS, INC. (LONDON) LTD.
24/28 Oval Road, London NW1   7DX

Library of Congress Cataloging in Publication Data

Hassan, Fekri A.
    Demographic archaeology.

    (Studies in archaeology)
    Bibliography: p.
    Includes index.
    1. Demographic archaeology.   2. Man, Prehistoric--
Population.   I. Title.
CC79.D46H37   930.1'028   80–1677
ISBN 0–12–331350–3

To the memory of my father
ABDEL-FATTAH HASSAN

عبد الفتاح حسن

Contents

Preface

The horizons of archaeology were expanding rapidly during the 1970s. Although archaeology has always been subsumed under anthropology in the United States, anthropological archaeology is a new phenomenon that has revitalized archaeology and endowed it with a new *raison d'être*. Archaeologists now seek to understand people. Potsherds, flint debris, and food discards are only fragments of the material remains of human populations whose language, songs, myths, and intellectual achievements are now gone. Archaeologists dealing with the mute record of the past have the difficult task of transcending the world of material objects to reach that of behavior and action. Their goal is not merely to provide a narrative of past human events, but also to reach some understanding of the principles of human survival, adaptation, and social interactions.

We are perhaps more aware today than ever of the role of population in society. Julian Huxley considers the problem of population to be *the* problem of our age, and if it is not, it is certainly one of the major problems. Historians, economists, sociologists, and politicians have not lost sight of the importance of population in world affairs, and it is only natural for archaeology, in its search for the cultural past, to turn to population as an element of considerable significance in culture and culture change. The study of population has emerged as one of the most provocative and promising areas of contemporary archaeology. My aim in this work is to bring into focus the studies conducted in the past decade and to present the archaeologist and the advanced student in archaeology with a glimpse of the scope and prospects of population research. The book deals with the determinants and determination of population size and density (Chapters 2–6); prehistoric fertility, mortality, population growth, and population regulation (Chapters 7–9); and the role of demographic variables in cultural evolution (Chapters 10–14).

Demographers, ecologists, and economists may find this book of interest. Many prevalent notions about prehistoric populations are the product of a few earlier studies. Although some of these notions have not been dismissed by the results of recent investigations, others have been modified or disqualified. This phase in the archaeological study of human populations, despite a meager body of data and a methodology in need of much improvement, has already brought prehistoric populations into a new light. The dilemmas of the human population may now be examined in retrospect. The "demographic transition" accompanying industrialization may be compared with another major transition, one that accompanied the emergence of agriculture; and the demographic behavior of modern industrial and agricultural societies may be contrasted with that of Pleistocene hunter–gatherers and Neolithic farmers.

Inasmuch as this work is a synthesis of a young field, it displays both the problems that plague demographic analysis at this stage and the promises that population studies hold for archaeology. The problems, however, are not insurmountable, and the promises are such that they will, I hope, stimulate future studies by archaeologists and demographers.

Acknowledgments

This book is of special significance for me because it brings together the fruits, though some are still green, of my own struggle with an area of research that I strongly believe to be of tremendous importance for understanding prehistoric peoples and cultures. It happened that my involvement with *Demographic Archaeology* started when the field was beginning to take shape, and it was through the stimulation, encouragement, and disagreement with others that my ideas were developed and nutured. I am most grateful to many individuals whom I have been fortunate enough to interact with. I especially wish to mention Lawrence J. Angel, George Armelagos, J. Birdsell, Ester Boserup, Karl W. Butzer, Robert L. Carneiro, J. Desmond Clark, George Cowgill, Don E. Dumond, Michael J. Harner, Marvin Harris, Bernice Kaplan, Solomon Katz, Gabriel Lasker, Steven Polgar, Gordon and Helen Pollard, Charles Reed, P.E.L. Smith, Ronald Wetherington, John Yellen, and Ezra Zubrow. I should also like to mention Mark N. Cohen, with whom I had many stimulating discussions. My students at Washington State University, with their contagious enthusiasm, have been a source of encouragement for which I am grateful.

Various chapters of this book were read by John Bodley, Robert Braidwood, L. L. Cavailli-Sforza, McGuire Gibson, Brian Hayden, Jane Hill, James N. Hill, Nancy Howell, Grover Krantz, and Ann Palkovich. Their comments are most appreciated.

Finally, I am indebted to my family for their understanding and tolerance during the completion of this book. Afifa A. Hassan has been a source of encouragement and support. Mona, my daughter, kept me in good humor.

Demographic Archaeology

1

Introduction

The domain of culture is the life of what ought to belong to death. *

Demographic archaeology is the study of human populations in an archaeological context—their demographic characteristics, temporal trends of growth, decline, or expansion, and causal and processual relationships with cultural variables.

Although interest in the demographic aspects of prehistoric populations had previously been superficial and inconsequential, by the late 1960's, studies of prehistoric populations became popular. Archaeology as a field of investigation became transformed into an anthropological science marked by an avid interest in prehistoric peoples and their behavior, and an equally zealous quest for interpreting the processual dynamics of culture change. The rise of an ecological paradigm within archaeology was to give even greater weight to population studies, especially those concerned with population ecology.

The areas of demographic investigation in archaeology may be subdivided into the following categories:

1. Description of population characteristics: population size, population density, population growth, fertility rate, mortality rate, age and sex composition, and migration pattern and rates of migration
2. Description of population trends

*André Malraux, Anti-Memoirs, translated by T. Kilmartin, Holt, Rinehart and Winston, New York, 1968, p. 243.

1

3. Interpretation of the mechanisms of demographic events, such as the population increase accompanying the transition to agriculture
4. Analysis of the role of demographic variables in cultural systems (e.g., the relationship between population and marriage rules, language, and subsistence)
5. Interpretation of the causal role of demographic variables in culture change and cultural evolution
6. Construction of general population theories for prehistoric populations

Gordon Childe (1936) was among the first to emphasize the importance of obtaining estimates of the density and characteristics of prehistoric populations, and to attempt to investigate the role of human populations in the course of cultural evolution. Julian Steward (1949), who had a deep interest in the relationship between people and their ecological setting, alerted many archaeologists to the need for a better understanding of the ecological determinants of the demographic conditions of prehistoric peoples, and his models of cultural evolution, like those of Childe, incorporated population as a key variable. Leslie White (1949) has similarly linked population changes with urbanization and political developments in prehistoric societies.

Attempts to estimate size and density of prehistoric populations from archaeological remains were pioneered by Hack (1942), Colton (1949), Frankfort (1950), and Cook (1946). Cook and Heizer (1965, 1968) and Naroll (1962) provided rules derived from ethnographic contexts for estimating the size of prehistoric populations. Carneiro and Hilse (1966) made the first attempt to arrive at an estimate of the rate of population growth during the Neolithic.

In the field of physical anthropology, skeletal remains were studied to provide estimates of the longevity of prehistoric man in the pioneer works of Todd (1927), Hooton (1930), Vallois (1937), Weidenreich (1939), and Angel (1947).

Since 1965, publications on prehistoric populations have increased at an exponential rate. Major advances in procedures and methods have been made, and the role of demographic variables in culture change has been highlighted in numerous studies. Among the significant contributions are the studies by Acsádi and Nemeskéri (1970) on the history of human mortality, the monograph by Weiss (1973) on models of mortality, the collections of contributions on population growth and cultural evolution by Spooner (1972), the paper by Binford (1968) on post-Pleistocene adaptations, and Dumond's (1965) analysis of the reciprocal relationship between population and culture.

In 1972, the first review of the nascent field was made by Cook (1972b); this was followed by my reviews (Hassan 1978b, 1979b). The field of demographic archaeology, however, after more than a decade of active research, remains without a general work that brings together the major contributions that have so far been made. It is for that end that I have undertaken the task of writing this book. For a decade, I have been fascinated by the problems of population in prehistory, and have directed a great deal of my research effort toward the solution of some of those problems. It became obvious to me that little could be gained from a narrow approach to demographic archaeology. I also found myself dissatisfied with population estimates that were generated in vacuo and with "demographic explanations" that were lacking both in substance and in theory. It was necessary to become acquainted not only with demography, but also with many other related topics, ranging from ecology to moral philosophy. This book is therefore a product of interdisciplinary research. Its primary commitment is to archaeology, but its roots are in many fields, particularly demography, ecology, and anthropology.

In this book, I have pulled together and evaluated available data, measures, methods, and explanations, and attempted at the same time to generate new data, devise new techniques, and formulate some theoretical models. I have attempted, above all, to present the demography of archaeological populations from anthropological and ecological perspective. My own ideas about cultural evolution also permeates the book. Both in the past (Childe 1936; Steward 1949, 1955; White 1949) and at present a great deal of emphasis has been placed on population increase and culture change. The work by Ester Boserup (1965), an economist, on the causal role of population pressure in agrarian change and Binford's (1968) treatment of post-Pleistocene adaptation have led many archaeologists to regard population increase as a prime mover of cultural change. However, the anthropological investigation of population growth and culture change was pioneered by Dumond (1965).

In a review of the collection of papers on population growth and cultural evolution by Spooner (1972), I (Hassan 1974) expressed skepticism about the validity of population pressure as a causal factor in prehistory. This skepticism is shared with many others, of whom G. L. Cowgill (1975) has presented the most cogent argument against population-pressure models. The reader who wishes to examine the tenets of the population-pressure thesis may consult the pioneer paper by P. E. L. Smith (1972) and the polemic treatise by Cohen (1977).

It is indeed unfortunate that archaeologists have devoted most of their energy to population increase. Kingsley Davis (1959) has been particularly critical of such tendencies among sociologists. Other demographic variables, such as mortality, fertility, age–sex composition, dependency ratio, and spatial arrangement, are of considerable cultural significance; "only when all aspects of demographic change are seen as a system can their connection with the society be understood" [Davis 1959:326]. I have accordingly devoted a number of chapters to various aspects of prehistoric populations. Chapters 2 and 4 focus on the determinants of population density among hunter–gatherers and cultivators. The size of prehistoric populations is discussed in Chapter 5. Prehistoric mortality is reviewed in Chapter 7, and potential prehistoric fertility and population growth are discussed in Chapter 8. The geographic expansion of prehistoric populations is dealt with in Chapter 12. Some aspects of the connections between population and culture are the subject of Chapter 11.

To prepare the stage for the chapters on population and cultural evolution (Chapters 12–14), a discussion on the regulation of prehistoric populations is presented in Chapter 9, and a critical assessment of carrying capacity and population pressure is given in Chapter 10.

Methods and procedures of estimating the demographic parameters of prehistoric populations are presented in Chapter 3 (population density of hunter-gatherers), Chapter 4 (population density of cultivators), Chapter 6 (population size), Chapter 7 (mortality), Chapter 8 (fertility), and Chapter 12 (migration rates).

There is obviously no substitute for good empirical data, not only for an accurate characterization of prehistoric populations, but also for the generation and testing of hypotheses on population and culture change. A great many of the "demographic explanations" in archaeology are verbal generalizations having no factual support. Such a facile approach to theory has been condemned in sociological demography by Kingsley Davis (1959) and in historical demography by Glass (1965). For example, how can we assess the impact of population increase during the Neolithic period if we do not know the rate of increase or the probable mechanisms by which it was achieved?

It is true that the archaeological record is such that demographic estimates cannot be as reliable and as accurate as we would like them to be. However, the lack of a genuine interest in demographic archaeology has in the past been responsible for a very lax attitude toward the collection of demographic data. Luckily this situation is changing, and many archaeologists have committed themselves to the advancement of the procedures and techniques of generating archaeological data on prehistoric populations. Data collection, however, cannot proceed in a theoretical void. For example, if one obtains an empirical relationship between site area and population size from ethnographic contexts and applies such a relationship to archaeological contexts without the benefit of knowing the behavioral or cultural determinants of the empirical relationship, or the transformational history of the archaeological site (cf. Schiffer 1976), the exercise can be meaningless. I have therefore made a special effort to elucidate the basis of demographic methods in archaeology and point out the kinds of data that ought to be obtained for acceptable population estimates.

The archaeologist, however, will not be motivated to spend time, energy, and money collecting archaeological data pertinent to demographic issues if he or she cannot see the potential contribution to archaeological explanation from such data. For that reason, it was necessary to glean population estimates collected accidentally or on purpose for an analysis of the role of demographic variables in prehistory. In some cases, I was forced to generate my own estimates from descriptions of archaeological sites and their contents. As such, this work is provisional and many of the estimates used and the hypotheses generated from such estimates will be, I hope, revised, refined, or discarded as more reliable data become available. It should be made clear, however, that population estimates have many built-in sources of error (Hole and Heizer 1973:363–364) and it would be a long wait indeed if we were to shelve our hypotheses until absolutely accurate and reliable data became available. All sources of demographic data, even census data, have such built-in sources of error (Petersen 1975), and we must be content with estimates having an acceptable margin of error. Confidence in an estimate may be enhanced by cross-checking against estimates made by independent techniques.

Petersen, a demographer, in a discussion of prehistoric demography, has recommended the use of ethnographic analogy (1975:229–230). Unfortunately, ethnographic data on demography are scant, imperfect, and often distorted by cultural contacts (N. Howell 1973; McArther 1970), and we must be very careful in handling such data. Comparing data from different groups, understanding the cultural context of the population, and critically evaluating the sources of the data can minimize some of the potential errors. One should regard ethnographic cases not as fossil survivals of the Stone Age, but as living communities having their own demographic history and peculiarities.

The appeal of demographic studies to the archaeologist lies ultimately in the connections between population and culture. Once the patterns of mortality, fertility, migration, and trends in population in prehistory are detailed, the task of interpreting both the causes of demographic events and trends, and the processual role of demographic variables in cultural adaptation and culture change, must begin.

General theories in demography often deal with the relationship between population and resources, with a consideration of the intermediary mechanisms by which this relationship is established. One of the most celebrated theories is the one first put forward by Thomas Robert Malthus in 1798 and recast in later publications, with a posthumous edition in 1872 (Thomlinson 1965:53–54).

Malthus, moved by moral convictions about human nature and human society, stressed the limitations imposed on population by the means of subsistence. Populations, he thought, increase when subsistence increases unless preventive checks such as epidemics or positive checks such as restraint from marriage lead to a balance between people and resources. He is often credited with highlighting the potential of populations to increase faster than their means of subsistence. Malthus is often criticized for underestimating the ability of man to keep abreast of population increase. Industrialization, improved agrarian technology, and advanced modes of transport have led many critics to believe that Malthus's premise concerning the slow rate of economic growth is untenable. Malthus is also criticized for overlooking the potential of modern contraceptives (of which he would not have approved) to reduce the rate of population growth (Barber 1967).

The ghost of Malthus lingered in the background during the nineteenth century, and is now emerging anew to snicker at his critics as the thrust of industrialization and developments in subsistence technology lag behind the rapid increase in world population. Hundreds of millions suffer from malnutrition, and unprecedented rates of growth are not abating. Malthus may have to retreat again if birth control, family-planning efforts, and industrialization of developing countries can remove the threat of greater misery and starvation. Nevertheless, whether Malthus or his opponents are right, the reality of the conflict between rates of population growth and economic development cannot be dismissed. The warnings issued by Malthus, in fact, may lead to actions that ultimately balance population and subsistence.

One of the basic problems in Malthus' thesis is his neglect of the mechanisms by which a population responds to subsistence or vice versa. The economist David Ricardo (Barber 1967) suggested that population increase results from a shortage of labor, but as population increases surplus labor forces wages down. Another economist, Gary Becker, viewed population growth as a function of the value of children as sources of income to the family (Thomlinson 1965). If prices are low and the family income is high, a greater demand for children ensues. The link between population and economics has been discussed by many others. One of the notable contributions comes from philosopher John Stuart Mill, who viewed population as a function of factors of production: capital, land, and labor. Mill emphasized the need for population control as a means of improving economic conditions (Thomlinson 1965). Karl Marx, who was also aware of the link between population, land, capital, and labor, believed that poverty and overpopulation are closely linked with a capitalist economy based on inequalities and the demand for surplus labor to guarantee low wages (Meek 1971).

Ester Boserup, to whom I referred earlier, has suggested that the Malthusian view of the dependence of the population on developments in the means of subsistence is erroneous, and that population increase can serve as a stimulus to economic change.

These grand theories of population can stir violent emotions between proponents and opponents, but the arguments are often colored by political, moral, and philosophical commitments. Broad interpretations of the relationship between population and resources should perhaps be contingent on a clarification of this relationship in specific case studies on the basis of acceptable empirical data and sound methodology (K. Davis 1959:311–313). The theories must be translated into working models that can be submitted to testing and evaluation (e.g., Zubrow 1975:13). In such models, the demographic and pertinent economic and cultural variables must be spelled out and the mathematical or at least the functional relationship between such variables must be clearly defined. The multiplicity and interdependence of demographic, environmental, and cultural variables are perhaps best examined from a systemic perspective, as in the model by Wrigley (1969:108–115) for demographic and economic variables, Hassan (1973) for the demographic transition during the Neolithic, and Zubrow (1974) for the relationship between population and carrying capacity. Beginning with a conceptual model, which may be represented as a flowchart showing the key variables and functional relationships, mathematical models specifying the equations that express the functional relationships may then be built; ultimately, a simulation model in which data (empirical or hypothetical) may be introduced and calculations of the outcome of the interaction of the variables specified in the model may be generated, often with the help of a computer (Chorley 1964; Clarke 1972; Lehman 1977; Maisel and Gnugnoli 1972; Shannon 1975). Such simulations have been carried out in dealing with demographic variables in anthropological and archaeological contexts by N. Howell (1979b), Kohler (1978), Shantis and Behrens (1973), Thomas (1973), Wobst (1974), and Zubrow (1975).

The ideas and data collected in the following pages underscore the need for adapting standard demographic techniques to the peculiarities of the archaeological record. Data on prehistoric populations should be sought vigorously by field archaeologists, and models and simulations must replace speculative theories. The survival, adaptation, and welfare of human societies are closely linked with demographic conditions, and for this reason demographic archaeology is vital for the interpretation of the archaeological past. The interest evidenced by archaeologists in human societies, behavior, and cultural processes should provide a strong impetus for future work in demographic archaeology.

2

Subsistence and Population Density
of Hunter–Gatherers

*This idea of an optimum density of population is wholly different to that put forward by Malthus. To him the problem was one of the relative increase of population and of food; with us it is one of the density of population and of the productiveness of industry.**

The population density of hunter–gatherers (Table 2.1) is a reflection of the amount of resource yield given certain resource choices and levels of food consumption. Hunter–gatherers are dependent on the natural abundance of wild food resources for their livelihood. Within a given territory, accessible from a base camp within a day roundtrip, for the most part, the hunters and gatherers must supply their food and economic requirements within tolerable levels of labor input.

In any given territory, the abundance and nature of resources will reflect both the place of that territory in world biomes, and the biotopic differentiation within it. Physical obstacles may obstruct full utilization of the territory and the resources exploited must be restricted to those that are accessible. Food resources will be exploited at different rates depending on biomass (density per unit of area × accessible area) and cost of extraction. This cost will be higher for resources that are hard to locate, sparse, isolated, hazardous to harvest, and/or difficult to process for consumption (Figure 2.1). The potential yield of a resource on the basis of its biomass, given a temporal perspective, will not be constant all year round and may fluctuate considerably from one year to the next. The yield will also be a function of the technological and managerial food-extractive potentials.

In this chapter, I will examine those aspects of subsistence that contribute to

---

*A. M. Carr-Saunders, *The population problem*, Oxford Univ. Press, New York and London, 1922, p. 201.

TABLE 2.1
Population Density of Some Hunting–Gathering Populations

Group	Population density (persons/km^2)	Source
Chipewyan	.016[a]	Casteel 1972
Chipewyan	.08	Steward 1955
Algonkian	.08–.12	Steward 1955
Ojibwa	.05	Kroeber 1953
Montagnais	.03[b]	Casteel 1972
Montagnais	.01–.08	Steward 1955
Mt. People	.0103	Burch 1972
Asiagmuit	.010	Burch 1972
Kivallinqiut	.070	Burch 1972
Kuuvakmiut	.040	Burch 1972
Tierra del Fuegans	.05	G.A. Harrison *et al.* 1964
Australian aborigines		
West Australia	.02	Yengoyan 1968
South Australia	.01	Yengoyan 1968
Victoria	.05	Yengoyan 1968
Queensland	.05	Yengoyan 1968
New South Wales	.03	Yengoyan 1968
Northern Territory	.03	Yengoyan 1968
Tasmania	.04	Yengoyan 1968
Diegueño (Northern and Eastern)	.19	Kroeber 1953
Great Basin seed gatherers	.02	Kroeber 1953
Ona	.08–.1	Kroeber 1953
Hadza	.15	Woodburn 1968
Bushmen	.06	Lee 1969
Semang	.05–.19	Steward 1955
Ituri pygmies	.77	Turnbull 1972
California Miwok, Luiseño, Serrano, Cahuilla, Cupeño	.39	Steward 1955
California acorn gatherer–hunters	1.1	Baumhoff 1963
Lower Klamath fishers	1.2	Baumhoff 1963
California acorn/game hunter–gatherers	1.2	Baumhoff 1963
California acorn/game/fish people	3.9	Baumhoff 1963
Andaman Islanders	.85	Radcliffe-Brown 1922
Aleutian Islanders, shoreline	1.8	Yessner 1975
Aleutian Islanders, inland	.65	Yessner 1975
North Alaska	1.2	Yessner 1975
Southeast Alaska, shoreline	1.1	Yessner 1975
Southeast Alaska, inland	.19	Yessner 1975
Greenland, shoreline	.7	Yessner 1975
Labrador, shoreline	.6	Yessner 1975
Central arctic, shoreline	.4	Yessner 1975
Haida	9.5	Kroeber 1953

[a] A.D. 1812.
[b] Nadir × 20.

8

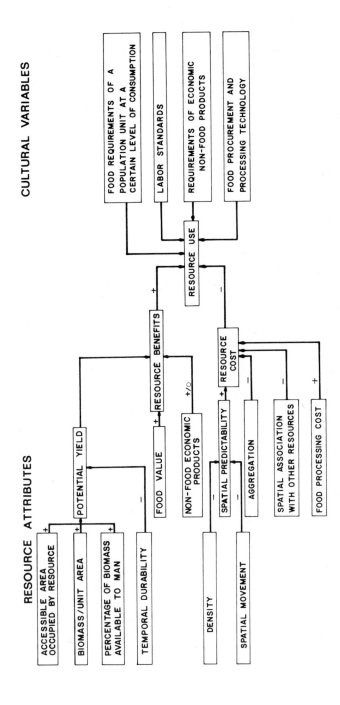

FIGURE 2.1. *A model of the environmental and cultural determinants of resource use* (+ *indicates positive effect;* − *indicates negative effect;* 0 *indicates no effect.*)

9

resource yield under hunting–gathering conditions. I will also review food consumption in order to provide an ecological perspective on the limits to the population density of hunter–gatherers and the variations that should be expected between hunting–gathering populations in different habitats.

Resource Biogeography and Subsistence

Food resources available to hunter–gatherers include a wide variety of wild plants and animals. The abundance and variety of food resources are primarily governed by the ecological setting of the region. Ecologists divide the world into a number of biomes (Table 2.2): tropical forests, temperate deciduous forests, boreal coniferous forests, temperate woodlands, grasslands, tundras, deserts, oceans, estuaries, streams, and so on. Terrestrial biomes vary in their *primary productivity,* that is, in the productivity of their autotrophic plants. Rainfall seems to be a major limiting factor (Figure 2.2). Tropical rain forests supplied with up to 1250 cm annual rain have a range of primary productivity of 1000–5000 dry $gm/m^2/year$. The range for temperate deciduous forests with 60–225 cm precipitation is 600–2500 dry $gm/m^2/year$. Deserts where less than 25 cm rain falls have a maximum primary productivity of 250 $gm/m^2/year$.

The primary productivity sets the limit for the secondary productivity of herbivores, carnivores, and so on. Generally, only about 10% of the energy is transferred from one trophic level to another—for example, from plants (producers) to herbivores (primary consumers). There is, therefore, some correlation among rainfall, primary productivity, and animal biomass. Temperature and seasonal variations seem to be significant factors in governing many aspects of animal life. In the tropics, few species besides ants and termites reach high levels of population density. Cold-blooded forms, especially reptiles and arthropods, reach large sizes, but birds and mammals are generally smaller than their relatives in temperate areas (Kendeigh 1961:340–350). In the tundra, where vegetation is scarce (primary prouctivity 10–400 dry $gm/m^2/year$) the density of animal life is low. Caribou are the most abundant large mammals. Food is generally more abundant in coastal regions.

Ungulates, a major source of food supply, particularly in boreal forests, temperate forests, temperate grasslands, and tropical savannas, show major variations in biomass. Data on animal biomass in pristine environments are unfortunately difficult to obtain and exceedingly rare. Table 2.3 and Figure 2.3 present some of the data available on ungulate biomass (Bourlière 1963).

In many cases, small animals are a secure and stable food supply. In a forest community the number of individuals per hectare for different animal groups is as follows: 1 bird, 3 mammals, 13,000 snails and slugs, and 225,000 large insects (Kendeigh 1961:130). In Alaska, the biomass of small mammals averages about 60 kg/km^2 (Palmer 1941). In the desert scrub biome of New Mexico, the biomass of birds is 40–120 kg/km^2; that of mice and rats is about 25 kg/km^2. In the sagebrush

TABLE 2.2
Principal World Biomes, with Climate, Area, and Productivity[a]

Biome	General climate[b]	Area (millions of km^2)	Range of primary productivity (dry gm/m^2/year)
Forests			
Tropical rain forests	125–1250 cm annual rain, no dry period (18–35°C)	20	1000–5000
Tropical seasonal forests	Marked dry season, generally lower pptn		
Temperate rain forests	125–900 cm pptn nearly even throughout years, some snow (−4–21°C)	18	600–2500
Temperate deciduous	60–225 cm pptn, droughts rare, some snow (−30–38°C)		
Temperate evergreen	35–250 cm pptn, evenly distributed or summer dry season, possible deep snow (−48–27°C)		
Boreal coniferous (taiga)	35–600 cm pptn, evenly distributed; much snow (−54–21°C)	12	400–2000
Reduced forests			
Mediterranean type, broad sclerophyll (chaparral, magius)	25–90 cm pptn, nearly all during cool season (2–40°C)		
Thorn woodlands and scrubs	Dry tropical climates, between seasonal forest and desert	7	200–1200
Temperate woodlands, including pigmy conifers, oak woodlands	Temperate climates between forest and grassland or desert		
Grasslands			
Tropical savanna	25–90 cm rain, warm season thunderstorms, dry during cool season (13–40°C)	15	200–2000
Temperate grasslands	30–200 cm pptn, evenly distributed or high in summer snow	9	150–1500
Tundras (arctic and alpine)	10–50 (arctic) and 75–200 (alpine) cm pptn, snowdrifts and areas blown free of snow (−57–16°C—arctic, −52–22°C—alpine)	8	10–400
Deserts			
Warm (tropical or temperate)	0–25 cm rain; very irregular, long dry seasons (2–57°C with high diurnal fluctuations)	18	10–250
Cold (temperate or arctic)	5–20 cm pptn, most in winter, some snow, long dry season (−40–42°C with diurnal fluctuation)		
Extreme deserts, rock, and ice		24	0–10
Oceans		359	2–600
Estuaries and shores	Wide range of temperatures from arctic	2	500–4000
Lakes and streams	and antarctic cold to tropical warm (with hot springs at one extreme)	2	100–1500
Swamps, marshes, and bogs	Various, from tropical to arctic	2	800–4000

[a] Data from Jensen and Salisbury 1972.

[b] pptn = precipitation.

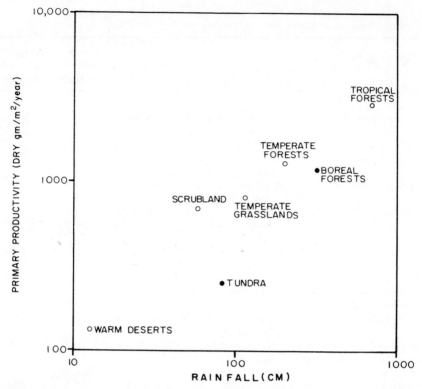

FIGURE 2.2. *Relationship between rainfall and primary productivity for world biomes. Open circle indicates warm to temperate climate. Darkened circle indicates cold climate. (Data from Jensen and Salisbury 1972.)*

desert biome, rodents may make up about 120 kg/km² and birds about 25 kg/km² (calculated after Kendigh 1961:336, 337). In the mixed deciduous–coniferous forest in Europe, the biomass of birds is estimated at about 120 kg/km² (calculated after Kendigh 1961:135).

The biomass of fish, a major source of animal protein food, is high in many streams (Rostlund 1952). In Indiana streams, the standing crop of fish varies from 5.2 to 106 gm/m² (wet weight). The fish crop of warm-water streams is generally higher than that of cool trout streams. Fish are also more abundant in relatively deep streams than in shallower ones.

The distribution of world biomes and the variations in net primary productivity, animal biomass, and abundance of fish resources seem to have a pronounced influence on the general pattern of subsistence among hunter–gatherers.

Lee (1968:42–43) observed that hunting, chiefly of sea mammals, provides more than 50% of the hunter–gatherer diet at high latitudes. The amount of terrestrial mammal hunting is highest in temperate grasslands. Fishing is the most significant subsistence activity in 10 of 17 societies in cold climates (0–10°C). It is also

TABLE 2.3
Biomass of Ungulates per Square Kilometer in a Few Selected Habitats[a]

Habitat	Ungulate biomass (kg/km^2)	Region	Remarks
Arctic tundra	800	Canada	Caribou
Prehistoric European "primitive" forest		Pol'ana Mountain, Slovakia	Red deer (*Cervus elephas*); birds (116.6 kg/km^2 = 302.7)
Deer forest	1000	Scotland	Red deer; habitat severely altered
Open mopane woodland	4418	Southern Rhodesia	Impala (23%), zebra (38%), giraffe (19%)
Pine–oak forest	795–768	Huron National Park	
Oak forest	1043–700	United States	
Scrub oak	3429–2,663	United States	
Dense rain forest	5	Ghana	*Philantomba maxwelli, Cephalophus dorsalis,* and *Neotragus pygmaeus*; scaly anteaters and porcupines (3.5 kg/km^2), primates (67 kg/km^2)
East African savanna, bordering Congolese forest	+23,556	Ewindi-Rutshuru Plain, Alberta National Park, Uganda	Biomass represented mainly by hippopotamus (48–54%)
	+18,795	Queen Elizabeth National Park, Uganda	Elephant (22–24%) and buffalo (19–25%)
Steppe and savanna	+4865	Tanzania, Serengeti–Mara	
Thornbush savanna	+12,261	Tanzania, Tarangire Game Reserve	

(continued)

13

TABLE 2.3 (*continued*)

Habitat	Region	Ungulate biomass (kg/km²)	Remarks
Acacia savanna	Kenya	15,760	Bush country game
Grassland	Tanzania	578.4	Zebra (36%), wildebeest (36%)
Masai steppe	Kenya, Nairobi National Park	13,215	
	Nairobi National Park	12,712–21,656	Herbivorous big game
East African savanna, thornbush	Tanzania, Serengeti	4692	Grant's and Thompson gazelle (17%), wildebeest (42%), zebra (35%)
Grassland	Oregon	175	Antelope (64%), mule deer (36%)
North American prairie	Wyoming	3400	
	Santa Rita Range Reserve, Arizona	5000	Bison (50%), elk, mule deer, whitetail deer
	Montana	2454	Bison (50%), mule deer, elk, bighorn
	Arizona	2979	Bison
	Western United States	3508	Domesticated cattle
Steppe of southern Russia, Khirgiz steppe	U.S.S.R.	350	Large herds of saiga antelope
Aizoon Reg desert		190	Dama gazelle
Subdesertic (Sahellian) steppe	Chad	80	Oryx (54%), Dorcas gazelle (26%), Dama gazelle (17.5%), addax (2.5%)
Erg desert	Sahara, Mauritania	4–17	Addax
Salsola Reg desert	Sahara (Rio del Oro)	.3	Dorcas gazelle

[a] Data from Bourlière 1963; Banfield 1954.

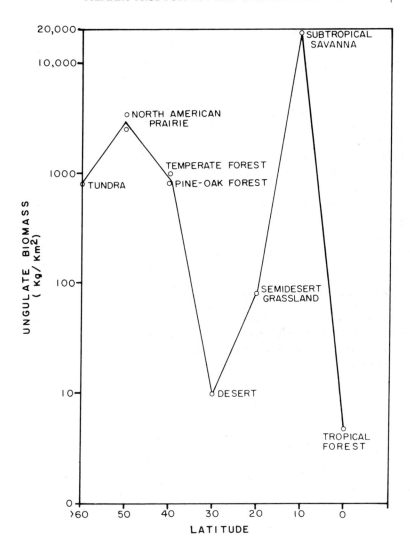

FIGURE 2.3. *Relationship between ungulate biomass and latitude. (See also Table 2.3.)*

common in the tropics. Gathering is most significant in 27 of 36 societies in mild to hot climates (above 10°C). This variation seems to be mainly a function of the density of animal biomass at various latitudes. In the tropic forests ungulate biomass is very low, but in temperate areas it is at its highest (Table 2.3).

Primary Productivity and Optimum Yield to Man

The position of hunter–gatherers in the ecological network as consumers at varying trophic levels makes it impossible for them to override the limitations set by the amount of primary productivity. Primary productivity, however, is a poor index of human population density. For example, the maximum potential population density in a salt marsh, calculated on the basis of primary productivity alone, would be higher than that of a temperate deciduous forest (Casteel 1972). This is evidently erroneous, because the proportion of edible foods available to man is not the same in the two biomes. The kinds of edible resources also are not the same in the different biomes, leading to great variations in the amounts that can be extracted by man. The subsistence regime may also increase the resources within a territory through food exchange, trading, and extraction of resources such as migratory birds and fish (Casteel 1972). The percentage of net productivity that can be extracted by man also depends on the extractive potentials of man.

The utilization of the productivity of those resources actually exploited is the subject of a study by Baumhoff (1963). Baumhoff was able to arrive at the following mathematical approximation, which expresses the relationship between the productivity of acorns, game, and fish in California with aboriginal population density:

Population = 3 (acorn index) + 2(game index) + 3(fish index) − 210

Similarly, Birdsell (1953:200, 1975) has found the following logarithmic relationship between the population density of Australian aboriginal groups (D) and the amount of rainfall (X) in those areas where unearned water (e.g., riverine water) is not available:

$$D = \frac{.703037}{X^{-1.58451}}$$

where D is population density (persons/square mile) and X is rainfall in inches. This relationship is shown in Figure 2.4. Birdsell, however, observed that

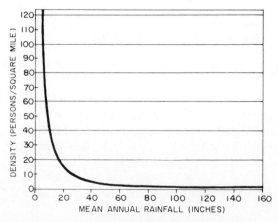

FIGURE 2.4. *Relationship between rainfall and population density of Australian aborigines. (From Birdsell 1975; reproduced by permission of Rand McNally.)*

excess unearned water made available through streams increases the population density by 20–40 times that which might be expected from his equation. Coastal groups also show higher population densities than those suggested by the equation. Birdsell (1972) has indicated that similar relationships between rainfall and population density, with different numerical values, were obtained by his students for areas outside Australia. In this case, the amount of rainfall was taken by Birdsell as an index of the productivity of resources. Although there is certainly a close relationship between the amount of rainfall and primary productivity (Figure 2.2), there may also be a direct relationship between the amount of drinking water and population density, especially in desert areas.

A better index than rainfall of the amount of food potentially available is the *optimum yield to man,* that is, the maximum sustained yield that can be removed from the resource without impairing the ability of the resource to replace the biomass harvested. The optimum yield to man is a function of many factors (Watt 1968:125). For animals, these factors include the degree of interspecific competition, predation, disease, and intraspecific population control. Severe winters may increase natural mortality, particularly of the young and the old. Winter mortality of newborn deer in California, for example, is about 20% (L. Brown 1970:103) and predation by lions, hyenas, cheetahs, and wild dogs in northern Tanzania accounts for the removal of about 10% of the total number of zebras, wildebeest, and hartebeest (L. Brown 1970). Predation on California deer by mountain lions is estimated at about 5.5% (Watt 1968:128). Wolf predation accounts for a 5% loss of caribou and a 5.71% loss of Siberian reindeer (Banfield 1954:51). Disease is also a killer of many large animals. Rinderpest is a particularly significant factor in Africa. The decline of the hartebeest is mainly attributed to this disease, which can reduce the population size drastically. In many cases, disease and predation are age- and/or sex-specific. When females are removed more quickly than males, the biotic potential of the animal population drops and the amount of optimum "catch" by man is adjusted accordingly. In view of the complexity of factors that determine the amount of optimum possible harvest of ungulates, an arbitrary figure of about 5% may be used, unless estimates of natural mortality, loss to predators, reproduction, and the like are available. For example, deer seem to be able to withstand a sustained annual catch of about 10% or more if the kill is appropriately distributed by age and sex (Watt 1968:127). On the other hand, an estimate of the optimum catch of *Bison* amounts only to about 3.2% (Watt 1968:122–123).

When the data are available, the optimum yield (maximum sustained yield) can be estimated from the following equation (Watt 1968:122–123):

$$m = 1 - e^{-M}$$
$$S/N = 1 - e^{-(M+H)}$$
$$O = \frac{NH}{M + H}\ (1 - e^{M+H})$$

Where m is the natural mortality per annum, M is the natural mortality coefficient, S is the number of animals added to the herd each year, N is the size of the herd, H

is the hunting coefficient, and O is the number of animals that can be optimally "caught" each year from the herd. However, this equation does not allow for age-specific and sex-specific mortality. The percentage of the standing crop (biomass) that can optimally be culled annually, y, is equal to $(O/N) \times 100$. The percentage of optimum yield to man, c, will depend on the percentage lost to other predators; that is, $c = y - l$, where l is the percentage of standing crop loss to other predators.

The concept of optimum yield to man is also important for estimating *productive efficiency* of hunter-gatherers (see subsequent discussion on food-extraction).

Food Quality and Consumption

The ranking of foods on the basis of "quality" is perhaps manageable in ethnographic contexts. Universal generalizations, however, pose a more difficult task (cf. Jochim 1976). Tasty, stomach-filling, and nutritional foods are likely to be desired. The nutritional content of food is perhaps the most manageable of the three aspects of food quality. Although people may not immediately recognize the nutritional value of foods when they are first introduced, the effects of the food on health soon become obvious to consumers, and nutritionally sound foods and food combinations are ultimately selected.

The average caloric requirement, according to FAO standards, is 2354 cal per capita per day (Erlich and Erlich 1970:69). In terms of protein, an intake of 1 gm/kg body weight from the time of maturity throughout adult life is considered near the optimum (Dubos 1965). An average adult weighing about 50 kg would thus require about 50 gm/day. Children require more, about 2.2–2.5 gm/kg body weight (Dubos 1965). The requirements also depend on sex, climate, and the type of work the person does. Data on the caloric intake of hunter/gatherers indicate an average slightly below that recommended by the FAO. !Kung Bushmen, for example, have an average intake of about 2140 cal/day (Lee 1969:71). Similar values are recorded for the Australian aborigines (McCarthy and McArthur 1960). The Eskimo show a higher value of 3102 cal/day.

A subsistence intake of about 2200 cal/person/day is thus a likely estimate for hunter/gatherers in temperate areas. This is equivalent to about 803,000 cal/year/person or about 800,000 cal. In colder regions, an average of 3000 or 3100 cal/person/day is a better estimate because of the greater energy requirements.

The amount of meat consumed seems to vary considerably from one group to another. Lee (1969:71) found that the daily allotment per person among the Dobe Bushmen was about 256 gm (34.5 gm per cooked portion) over 28 days. Much higher estimates are given for the American Indian buffalo hunters. Wheat (1972:108–109) surveyed historical accounts and concluded that an average of about 1.36 kg (3 lb) per person is a conservative estimate of the daily consumption. It must be remembered, however, that the amount consumed of a specific nutrient is a function of the proportion contributed by the resource containing that nutrient to the diet. In the case studied by Lee (1969), the Bushmen supplemented their diet with mongongo nuts (33%) and other vegetable foods (30%); meat constituted only about 33% of the diet. The overall protein intake per person per day was thus about 93.1 gm. The Indian buffalo hunters, on the other hand, depended primarily on meat. In terms of protein intake, Wheat's estimate of 1.36 kg/person/day translates into about 293 gm of protein per person, a much higher value than the basic nutritional daily requirements. However, 1.36 kg of meat provides about 3660 cal, compared to a daily requirement of about 2200 cal. Thus, although the amount of meat seems excessive in terms of the amount of protein, it is within reasonable limits of the amount of calories required. The relative deficiency of meat in certain nutrients (vitamins or minerals) that would have been otherwise obtained from other vegetable sources may also account for the consumption of larger amounts of meat. Preferences for certain parts of the animals, for example, brain, tongue, liver, or offal, also may be a function of the variations in the nutritional contents of these parts.

Reference must also be made to the percentage that is usually wasted through spoilage or negligence, as well as the percentage of inedible constituents in the foodstuff. T. E. White (1953) estimates about 50% edible meat in large animals. Food-processing technology (grinding, soaking, etc.) and the type of cooking used can lead to an enrichment or to an impoverishment in certain nutritional components, influencing the amount consumed of the processed food material.

Food Extraction

The term *hunting-gathering* is used here to refer to extractive food-getting strategies. The term thus refers to a wide range of activities including sea mammal hunting, fishing, fowling, shellfish gathering, foraging, big-game hunting, small-game hunting, and insect collecting. The relative dependence on any of these activities varies from one group to another. Hunter–gatherers differ also in their food-extracting strategy, and in the methods and techniques they use.

Generally, the major subsistence activities are conditioned by the most abundant food resources. As noted earlier, in the tundra, where plant food resources are scarce, emphasis is placed on hunting sea mammals and fishing on the coastal areas, and on caribou hunting in the interior. In the tropical forest, at the other end of the spectrum, where the biomass of herbivores is low (Bourlière 1963), a great deal of emphasis is placed on gathering plant resources. The abundance of game in temperate and boreal areas seems to encourage intensive animal hunting, as the evidence from prehistoric Europe suggests.

An abundant food resource, however, may be neglected in favor of another, and specialized subsistence regimes may coexist to avoid conflict or to ensure a more effective exploitation of their habitat.

There is also an element of selectivity in any subsistence regime. For example, of the 223 local species of animals known and named by the Bushmen, 54 are classified as edible, and of these only 17 are hunted on a regular basis. Similarly, although 85 species of edible plants are known, only 23 species contribute 90% of the vegetable diet by weight (Lee 1968:35).

Although the Hadza, as reported by Woodburn (1968), make no attempt at systematic cropping, impala, zebra, eland, and giraffe are the most frequently killed large animals. This "selectivity" may be a function of both conscious selectivity on the part of the hunters and the ease by which a species can be caught (cf. Jochim 1976). The degree of "catchability" is in turn a function of the behavior of the animal, the hunters' technological skills, and the hunting strategy. Gregarious, placid animals can be easier to catch than alert, solitary, and agile ones. Cooperative hunting enhances the chances of catching dangerous and large game. The procedure of hunting (stalking, trapping, or still-hunting) also determines the frequency of a specific catch. For the Hadza, the biomass of the most frequently killed animals represents about 65% of the total biomass of ungulates, using Bourlière's estimates (1963) on ungulate biomass in Tanzanian thornbush savanna.

The impact of trade, as a part of the subsistence regime, on expanding the kind and amount of resources must also be mentioned. Generally, however, the hunting–gathering system is a closed one, especially when compared to the agricultural system, in which trade is a very prominent component. Trade among agriculturalists was probably induced not by the development of surplus but rather by the narrow range of subsistence activity, the development of storage facilities, and the settled mode of life, which limited the farmer's access to distant resources and encouraged the establishment of fixed trade networks. Exchange of resources can also be a mechanism to offset seasonal scarcity (M. G. Smith 1972).

The food-extractive potential can be measured in several ways. M. Harris (1971:205) devised an *index of technoenvironmental efficiency*. The index may be expressed by the formula,

$$e = O/I$$

where e is the value of the index, O is the average energy output in calories and I is the caloric input invested in an average day of subsistence activity. The caloric input invested in an average day of subsistence activity, I equals the number of food producers, m, times the hours of work, t, times the calories expended per hour, r:

$$I = (m \times t \times r)$$

Thus, the formula for the index of technoenvironmental efficiency is

$$e = O/(m \times t \times r)$$

The larger the value of e, the greater the technoenvironmental "advantage" enjoyed by the group.

From the data provided by Lee (1968) on the !Kung Bushmen, Harris arrives at an estimate of 9.6 for e. In a day's work of 6 hours, the labor force consists of 7.4

individuals expending 150 cal/hour each, yielding an average output of 64,200 cal. Hence

$$e = 64,200/(7.4 \times 6 \times 150) = 64,200/6600 = 9.6$$

Variations in the technoenvironmental advantage of different hunting–gathering groups must be expected, but it is interesting to note that the index for the Genieri hoe agriculturalists in Gambia, West Africa, is 11.2, which is not much higher than that of the !Kung Bushmen. The index for the Chinese Lut'un irrigation rice farmers, on the other hand, is 53.5—a much higher index, reflecting the advantage of irrigation farming as an intensive food-producing regime over both hunting–gathering and dry farming.

Harris's index provides an estimate of energy gain per unit of expended energy. This technoenvironmental efficiency must be differentiated from *ecological efficiency* (E. P. Odum 1959:53), which is the ratio between energy levels at different points along the food chain, expressed as a percentage.

Lee (1969) approaches the problem of estimating food-extraction capability from another angle. He devised an *index of subsistence effort* (S). This index is measured by the formula,

$$S = W/C$$

where W is the number of man-days of work and C is the number of man-days of consumption. Lee used the index to indicate how many days are spent in subsistence activity for 100 days of consumption. According to Lee (1969:68), the index for the !Kung Bushmen is 23. Thus, about 1 day of work is required for 4 days of consumption. One can hardly say that the Bushmen are overworked!

In assessing the extractive potential of hunter–gatherers, a useful index would be one that provides a ratio of the amount of a given resource extracted and the optimum yield available to man of that resource. This index (IE) may be estimated from the basic formula,

$$IE = M/Y$$

where M is the total mass extracted from a given resource per person per year and Y is the optimum yield to man per person per year. The absolute value of M equals the number of days invested in subsistence activity per producer per year, D, times the mass produced per day of work per producer, G, times the ratio of producers to nonproducers in the community, F:

$$M = D \times G \times F$$

The Dobe camp of the !Kung Bushmen killed 18 animals with an average live weight of about 23 kg in 28 days (Lee 1969:71). The camp consisted of 31 persons of which hunters numbered 10 ($F = 10/31 = 32\%$). During the 28-day period, about 89 days of work were invested by the hunters (i.e., about 9 workdays by each hunter). Thus, the mass produced per hunter per workday equals the weight of the animals hunted (18 animals $\times$ 23 kg) divided by the total number of workdays invested by the producers (89 workdays); $G = (18 \times 23)/89 = 4.6$ kg. The number of workdays spent hunting per producer per year, D, equals the ratio of hunting workdays to consumption days (9/28) times 365; hence $D = (9/28) = 117$ days. Given these values for G, D, and F,

$$M = 4.6 \times 117 \times .32 = 172 \text{ kg}$$

Unfortunately, we do not have direct estimates of the animal biomass in the area of the !Kung Bushmen. However, on the basis of Bourliére's (1963) estimates of animal biomass in arid or semiarid habitats (Table 2.3), about 500 kg/km^2 may be used to illustrate the application of the formula within the catchment territory of the Dobe camp, an area 10 km in radius (314 km^2). As suggested by Lee (1968), the total animal biomass within the catchment territory would be about 157,000 kg. The optimum yield to man from this total biomass may be placed at 5%. We can thus calculate the amount available to the community as follows:

$$157,000 \text{ kg} \times .05 = 7850 \text{ kg}$$

This amounts to 253 kg/person/year. Our value for M, calculated previously, is 172 kg/person/year. This indicates that at the .5% level of "culling," the extractive efficiency index (IE) would be .64 (i.e., 64% of the optimum yield is actually extracted). It must be recalled that my calculations are only given to show the potential application of this index; the values of the biomass and optimum yield to man are arbitrary, since empirical data are lacking. If the value of IE calculated were truly representative of the actual situation, it would mean a very high level of efficiency. We must also consider that a certain percentage is not culled from the amount optimally available to man to provide a safety margin against periodic shortage, and that additional factors, such as selection and wastage, may reduce the amount of the optimum yield directly available to man. One would suspect that the value of the extractive efficiency index would normally be about .4–.6 or less. Values of IE in excess of 1.0 would mean that the hunters are threatening the biotic potential of the prey animals. An excessively high level of extractive coefficiency could be maladaptive. Thus, firearms may improve extractive efficiency but reduce adaptive potential.

It is interesting to note that this high level of extractive efficiency among the Bushmen does not imply a high rate of hunting success. According to Lee (1969), most hunters kill one large antelope or sometimes two antelopes per year. Also, among the Hadza, Woodburn (1968:54) mentions that perhaps as many as one-half the adult males fail to kill even one large animal a year, and that there are some men who have killed no more than one single large animal during their entire lives.

Overview

The population density of hunter–gatherers is dependent on the biomass of exploitable resources, particularly on the optimum yield to man from these resources under ordinary circumstances. The size of that yield and of periodic and short-term fluctuations set a maximum for the population density. The level of extraction efficiency cannot go above the maximum without endangering the ecological network of which hunter–gatherers are an integral part. These considerations are important to keep in mind if one is to understand the low density of hunting–gathering populations and the regional variations in population density between populations inhabiting different world biomes. They also point to the low growth potential of the hunting–gathering economy. As a result of this low potential and the vulnerability of hunter–gatherers to changes in the availability and abundance of exploitable resources it would appear, first, that regulation of population density via cultural mechanisms was advantageous under ordinary circumstances; second, that ecological conservation was advantageous for long-term survival; and third, that economic growth, in general, was exceedingly slow. Advancements in extractive technology must have been tied in with the search for alternative food resources or an expansion of the subsistence base, otherwise technological advancements could have led to overexploitation and environmental degradation. These issues will be explored in more detail in Chapters 9, 10, and 11.

3

Ecological Models for Estimating Probable Population Density of Hunter–Gatherers

The question of the density of population at different periods has been stressed because of its immense importance as a measure of economic progress, and though the difficulties in the way of reaching even approximately accurate answers are formidable, it is certain that we cannot afford to let slip any opportunity of gaining information on this point.*

The link between population density and resource potentials provides the basis for estimating the population density of hunter–gatherers when resource potentials are established. Sapper (1924) was the first to explore this method. He used it, for example, in estimating the density and the size of the population of North America in aboriginal times. Birdsell's (1953) attempt to relate population density to the amount of annual rainfall and Baumhoff's (1963) trial model linking population density to exploitable resources (see Chapter 2) are sure indications of continued interest in establishing a mathematical relationship that can be used for predicting population density from resource potentials.

In this chapter, I will examine three models—Casteel's (1972), H. P. Thompson's (1966), and my own—designed for estimating population density from resource potentials. All are trial models and will undoubtedly benefit from future refinement and elaboration.

Casteel's Model

Casteel's model (1972, 1973, 1976, 1979a) is based on an estimate of the following variables:

*Grahame Clark, *Archaeology and society,* Barnes & Noble, New York, 1969, p. 245.

1. Net productivity of terrestrial biomes
2. Rate of extraction from net productivity
3. Trophic levels of consumption (primary, secondary, tertiary)
4. Rate of consumption per person per year
5. Annual subsistence cycle

The net productivity of each terrestrial biome (1) expressed in calories is converted to maximum density at various trophic population levels (3). The rate of consumption (4) is placed at 8×10^5 cal/person/year. For example, a temperate deciduous forest biome can support a maximum of 600 persons/km² (1536 persons/ square mile) at a primary consumption level, or 5.9 persons/km² (15.4 persons/ square mile) at a tertiary level of consumption. At the level of primary consumption, only plants are consumed. At the secondary level, herbivores or animals that feed on plants are consumed. At the tertiary level, animals that feed on herbivores and other plant-feeders are consumed. Since there is a reduction in energy flow of about 10% from one level to the next higher level, fewer persons can live at higher consumption levels. As an example, if wheat is converted to feed cattle, more people can survive on the same amount of wheat than can survive on beef.

Casteel calculates the population density for a single year (P_{max}) in a given region (B) by estimating the area of ecosystem i (A_i), the maximum population density (at 100% level of extraction) at a given trophic level j (N_j) of each biome in that region, and the number of days of the annual cycle spent exploiting that specific biome (T_i). This is shown by the formula

$$P_{max} = \left(\frac{\sum_{i=1}^{n} T_i (A_i N_j)}{365} \right) / B$$

where n is the number of biomes[1] utilized; $i = 1, 2, \ldots, n$; and $j = 2, 3, 4$.

Another formula is given by Casteel to estimate the maximum population density from total and/or migratory terrestrial resources (F), if they are not already included in P_{max}:

$$F = \sum_{k=1}^{n'} T''k (BE_k)$$

Here $k = 1, 2, \ldots n$, n' is the total number of aquatic or migratory resources, B is the total area, E is the annual maximum human population density based on any given aquatic or migratory resource, and T'' is the percent of annual cycle spent in exploiting aquatic or migratory resources. A third formula is used to estimate the maximum population density from the energy of food items traded into a given area (S):

$$S = \left(\sum_{q=1}^{n''} \frac{Cq}{D} \right) / B$$

[1]Referred to as ecosystems by Casteel.

where $q = 1, 2, \ldots$ n, C is the total caloric value of traded food, B is the total area, and D is the annual individual energy requirement of 8×10^5 cal, n'' is the total number of traded food items.

The general formula, derived from the foregoing three formulae, is as follows:

$$P_{max} = \left[\left(\sum_{i=1}^{n} \frac{T_i \,(A_i N_i)}{365} \right) /B \right] + F + S$$

A more general version is expressed by

$$P_{max} = \sum_{i=1}^{n} (Z_i N_j) + F + S$$

The only character here that has not been previously defined is Z, which is the percentage of the annual cycle spent in a given "ecosystem".

The maximum population density (P_{max}) obtained from the preceding formulae at 100% level of extraction is then converted into an estimate of probable population density at given levels of extraction. I will denote this by P_x, where x is the level of extraction. Casteel uses an arbitrary level of .5%, and calculates $P_{.005}$ for several hunting–gathering populations (Table 3.1).

The results calculated from Casteel's model are well above those obtained on the basis of ethnographic observations (with corrections for depopulation). Even assuming that $P_{.05}$ derived from Casteel's model is reduced by as much as 20% to allow for a safety margin (see the following discussion), the new estimate $P_{x,y}$, where y stands for the reduction factor is only roughly comparable with the estimate based on ethnographic observations in some cases (Cahuilla, Modoc, and Chilcotin). In other cases (Chipewyan, Montagnais, and Kaska), the estimates are much higher than those derived from the ethnographic observations. What is disturbing is that the estimates are not consistently correlated with those derived from ethnographic in-

TABLE 3.1
Estimates of Population Density of Several Hunting–Gathering Groups[a]

Group	Density (persons/square mile)[b]	Ethnographic nadir *P.D.*	Nadir × 20[b]	Nadir × 25[c]
Cahuilla	3.85 ± .97	.027	.553	.690
Chimariko	7.79 ± 1.93	—	—	—
Chilcotin	4.32 ± 1.05	.008	.163	.204
Modoc	3.18 ± .79	.013	.263	.328
Chipewyan	1.08 ± .27	.0008	.016	.020
Montagnais	4.67 ± 1.17	.0003	.007	.008
Kaska	2.51 ± .63	.0005	.010	.013

[a] From Casteel 1972.
[b] For the first value, $P_{.005}$; for the second, $P_{.005, .2}$.
[c] Based upon depopulation ratio by Dobyns (1966), in persons per square mile.

TABLE 3.2
Discrepancy between Estimates Derived from Casteel's Model of the Probable Density of Some Hunting–Gathering Groups and Estimates of Population Density on the Basis of Historical Records, with Corrections for Depopulation

Group	(A) $P_{.05}$	(B) $P_{.05, .6}$	(C) Nadir × 20	(B/C)
Chilcotin	4.32	.021	.163	.13
Chipewyan	1.08	.005	.016	.30
Montagnais	4.67	.022	.007	3.14
Kaska	2.51	.012	.010	1.20

formation in any way. Casteel suggests, however, that the estimates on the Chilcotin, Chipewyan, Montagnais, and Kaska, whose subsistence consists of 20–30% fishing, may approximate those obtained from the ethnographic records by multiplying $P_{.005}$ by .6 (presumably for the safety margin). Although the significance of the latter factor is not explained, the results do not actually match in all cases (Table 3.2).

In view of the disappointing results, it seems that Casteel's model is in need of major modifications. For example, Casteel assumes that in a given biome at a certain time of the year man is exclusively a primary, secondary, or tertiary consumer. The situation is actually much more complex. Also Casteel uses a figure of .5% for level of extraction, after a vague reference by H. T. Odum (1971:17) to the amount of organic matter that enters the human as food and is metabolized. However, Odum does not specify the trophic level of the food. One is thus led to believe that this is a figure for food that enters the human at all trophic levels, but Deevey (1951:351) estimates the present rate of human ecological efficiency at .1%. Deevey's estimate is based on estimates of world population size, longevity, and rate of population growth. The .1% thus refers to ecological efficiency under *present* agricultural–industrial and demographic conditions. The figure of .5% used by Casteel thus seems to be excessive. However, any single figure masks regional and temporal differences between populations. As we saw in Chapter 2, net productivity in a salt marsh is greater than that in a temperate forest but this does not mean the same ratio of food can be extracted from both biomes.

Food selectivity is another complicating factor. Although *potentially* most plants and animals may serve as human food, the range of edible and favored food items is rather limited. In addition, people are not just limited by the availability of key resources in the leanest season (Liebig's rule). They are also limited by the availability of special components in particular qualitative proportions (Shelford's law of tolerance).

Also, the level of consumption by man influences ecological "equilibrium." Man cannot consume more than a certain percentage of a certain species without damaging the ecological system irrevocably.

Thompson's Model

The regional population (hence the population density) of the Chipewyan has been the subject of a model by H. P. Thompson (1966). Thompson's model differs considerably from Casteel's. It is based on (*a*) the number of caribou required for feeding per tent per year; (*b*) the number of caribou required for hides per tent per year; and (*c*) the proportional dependence on caribou in the subsistence economy of the group. These three factors are in turn related to several other subfactors, such as rate of consumption and biomass of caribou. The general model for the estimation of population size is shown by the following formulae:

$$N_E + N_B - N_{DH} - [(N_{DH}/X)X]K = N_E$$

$$N_{DH}/X = (N_{DH}/X)H + (N_{DH}/X)F$$

where N_E is the yearly "equilibrium" biomass of caribou, N_B is the biomass of caribou born each year, N_{DH} is the biomass of animals dying each year of nonhuman causes, N_{DH}/X is the rate of utilization of caribou per year, X is the number of tents among the Chipewyan (a function of the population size), K is a factor proportional to the dependence on the caribou, $(N_{DH}/X)H$ is the number of caribou required per year for hides per tent, and $(N_{DH}/X)F$ is the number of caribou required for feeding per tent per year. Once all factors are estimated, X can be estimated, and X multiplied by the number of persons per tent provides an estimate of population size. This model is based on the assumption that the number of caribou is at equilibrium from one year to another, which is a risky assumption in view of the documented fluctuations in the number of caribou (Banfield 1954; Burch 1972; Kelsall 1968). The model also does not allow for seasonal and short-term fluctuations. In addition, it is specifically designed for the Chipewyan and cannot be used for other hunter–gatherers.

Hassan's Model

The third model was formulated to estimate the population density of prehistoric hunter–gatherers in the course of an analysis of population dynamics in the Near East and the Nile Valley (Hassan 1973, 1976).

The model is based on the concepts discussed in Chapter 2. Resource potentials and extraction efficiency levels produce a "yield," which is consumed. The amount of the yield from 1 km² is divided by the amount consumed per person per year and provides an approximate estimate of population density. The general model is expressed as follows:

$$D = \frac{\sum_{i=1}^{1-n} F_i N_{ij}}{L_j} \tag{3.1}$$

where D is the population density in persons per square kilometer; F_i is the number of kilograms of the ith food item per square kilometer available to man, which equals the optimum yield to man (Y_i) from that food item per square kilometer, multiplied by a constant (k): N_{ij} is the nutritional content in calories, grams, or milligrams of other units of the jth nutritional element (protein, food energy, a specific vitamin or mineral, etc.) per kilogram of edible portion of the ith food item; L is the average consumption requirement per capita of the jth nutritional element.

Ideally, D would be calculated for all essential nutritional elements, and the lowest D would be the limiting population density on the basis of Shelford's law (see p. 28). Also, in an ideal situation, all the different varieties of food items would be included. In practice, this kind of information is seldom, if ever, available for prehistoric populations. The food items may be subdivided into general classes—meat, plants, fish, milk, and so on. Food energy and protein of the wide spectrum of nutritional elements could, in most cases, be included.

The simplified formula to estimate the population density of a hunting-gathering community (fishing not included) using food energy would be as follows:

$$D = \frac{(F_m \times N_{m,\text{cal}}) \times (F_p \times N_{p,\text{cal}})}{L_{\text{cal}}} \quad (3.2)$$

where F_m is the amount of edible meat available for consumption from 1 km², $N_{m,\text{cal}}$ is the caloric content per kilogram of edible portion of meat, F_p is the amount of edible plant food available for consumption from 1 km², $N_{p,\text{cal}}$ is the caloric content of 1 kg of edible portion of plants, L_{cal} is the caloric requirement per capita per year.

Usually it is more difficult to find estimates of the amount of plant food available in a region than it is to find estimates for animal game. Thus if the ratio of plant food to meat (p/m) in the diet is known or can be estimated, the amount of plant food can be determined from the amount of meat. Equation (3.2) can thus be rewritten as follows:

$$D = \frac{(F_m \times N_{m,\text{cal}}) + [F_m \times (p/m) \times N_{p,\text{cal}}]}{L_{\text{cal}}}$$

To estimate the amount of edible meat available to man from a given catchment territory, the total optimum yield to man from the various biomes included in that territory (Y_m), and the value of the constant (k) must be calculated:

$$F_m = kY_m \quad (3.3)$$

The optimum yield to man of game meat (Y_m) from 1 km² of a given catchment territory can be obtained by the following formula:

$$Y_m = \left(\sum_{i=1}^{1-n} \frac{A_i}{T} \times B_i \right) \times C \quad (3.4)$$

where A_i is the area of the ith biotope in the region, T is the total area of the catchment territory, B_i is the biomass of animal game (in kilograms per square kilometer) in the ith biome within the catchment territory, C is the rate of culling or extraction (i.e., the percentage of the standing crop that can be harvested annually without damaging the ecological network of the biotic potential of the animal game).

The value of the constant k depends on the following:

1. M, the effective percentage of the optimum yield to man that is regularly extracted to allow for a safety margin in order to avoid exposing the population to food shortage as a result of seasonal and short-term violent fluctuations
2. E, the percentage of edible portion of live-weight meat
3. W, the percentage of the portion of the optimum yield that escapes spoilage or waste
4. S, the percentage of the animal game selected from the range of animals available in the catchment territory

The constant k thus equals the product of the foregoing factors:

$$k = M \times W \times E \times S \qquad (3.5)$$

In order to show the application of this model, let us consider a hypothetical case of a group of hunter–gatherers, living in a temperate region, who have a generalized diet. According to the survey made by Lee (1968), the percentage of meat consumed among these groups is about 35% on the average, with a mean, mode, and a median between 25 and 45% of the plant food. The ratio of plant food to meat (p/m) thus equals $65/35 = 1.86$. Animal game in temperate regions generally consists of ungulates. According to Watt (1968), the extraction rate that would not damage the biotic potential or the ecological network of ungulates is between 3 and 10%, with an average of 5%. The edible portion of large mammals, according to T. E. White (1953), is generally about 50% of the live weight. Selectivity of available game among the Hadza amounts to about 70%, according to Woodburn (1968). A selectivity factor of this magnitude may thus be introduced in estimating the constant k. Spoilage and waste perhaps do not eliminate more than 10% of the yield. The value of W may thus be placed at 90%. The safety margin, according to Birdsell (1957, 1968) and others (Lee and DeVore 1968a, *passim*), is between 20 and 60% of the optimum yield or about 40% on the average.

The value of the constant k may be obtained as follows:

$$k = M \times W \times E \times S = .4 \times .9 \times .5 \times .7 = .126$$

The amount of meat available from 1 km^2 of a given catchment territory is expressed by Eq. (3.3),

$$F_m = kY_m$$

which can be written, by substituting .126 for k, as follows:

$$F_m = .126Y_m \qquad (3.6)$$

Also, substituting the value for C in Eq. (3.4), the formula for calculating Y_m may be written as follows:

$$Y_m = .05 \left(\sum_{i=1}^{1-n} \frac{A_i}{T} \times B_i \right) \qquad (3.7)$$

From Eq. (3.6) and (3.7), we get

$$F_m = .126 \times .05 \left(\sum_{i=1}^{1-n} \frac{A_i}{T} \times B_i \right) \qquad (3.8)$$

$$F_m = .0063 \left(\sum_{i=1}^{1-n} \frac{A_i}{T} \times B_i \right) \qquad (3.9)$$

Now let us assume that the catchment territory of a community consists of 64 km² wood savanna, 96 km² thornbush steppe, and 112 km² desert steppe. By inference from Table 2.3 (p. 13) we see that these biotopes would support minimum ungulate biomasses of 5000, 1000, and 10 kg/km², respectively. The maximum would be 10,000, 4000 and 100 kg/km², respectively. Using these figures, the minimum amount of meat directly available for consumption from 1 km² of that territory can be estimated as follows:

$$F_m = .0063 \left(\frac{64}{262} \times 5000 + \frac{96}{262} \times 1000 + \frac{112}{262} \times 10 \right)$$

$$= 10.03$$

Similarly, the maximum can be estimated at 24.89 kg/km². If we assume a ratio of plant food to meat of 1.86 to 1, the amount of plant food would be 18.66–46.30 kg/km².

To estimate the population density according to Eq. (3.2), the food items must be converted into their equivalent caloric content. In general 1 kg of cooked meat will provide about 2700 cal, and a generalized plant diet including legumes, tubers, fruits, and cereals will provide between 1000 and 2000 cal. Plants show a wide range of variation in their caloric content. Nuts provide an average of about 6000 cal/kg; fruits, about 600; fresh legumes, about 300; cooked vegetables, about 400; cereals, about 3500; pulses, about 900; and cooked tubers, about 1000–1500. A generalized plant component with small amounts of nuts and cereals has an average of about 1000 cal/kg, a figure used by Lee (1969:71) for the vegetable portion of the plant diet consisting of roots, melons, gums, bulbs, and dried fruits. The Bushmen's vegetable plant component, however, constitutes only about 48% of the Bushmen's plant diet. About 52% of the plant component is made up of mongongo nuts, the caloric value of which is about 6000 cal/kg. A group with a plant diet consisting of about 50% cereals, 30% legumes, 10% nuts, and 10% fruits would get an average of about 2750 cal/kg of plant food. [Compare the plant diet in the Bus Murdoch phase in Deh Luran (Flannery 1971:62).] Those groups having a generalized plant diet, in which neither nuts or cereals are prominent components, would be expected to attain a much lower energy yield, about 1000–2000 cal. An average of about 1500 may thus be a reasonable estimate. The remaining factor required to estimate population density is the caloric requirement per capita per year. A figure of 8×10^5 for caloric requirements per capita per year seems acceptable (see Chapter 2). Substituting these figures in Eq. (3.2), we obtain the following figure for population density:

$$D = \frac{10.03 \times 2700 + 18.66 \times 1500}{8 \times 10^5}$$

$$= .069 \text{ person/km}^2$$

Similarly, a maximum estimate of .17 person/km² using the maximum biomass figures may be calculated.

The formula used for calculating the foregoing example can be reduced numerically to the following:

$$D = \left[4.3234 \left(\sum_{i=1}^{1-n} \frac{A_i}{T} \times B_i \right) \right] \times 10^{-5} \qquad (3.10)$$

This simplified version is based on a ratio of plant food to meat of 1.86 to 1, a caloric content of 2700 cal/kg for meat and 1500 cal/kg for a generalized plant component, a k of .126, a C of .05, and an L_{cal} of 8×10^5 cal/person/year. The rest of the characters are the same as in Eq. (3.4).

The population size and population density for several hunting/gathering groups have been estimated using this model, and the results were compared with actual figures to test the validity of the model. The groups included the Eastern Hadza and the Caribou Eskimo.

The Eastern Hadza are a small group of 400 persons who lead a mobile hunting and gathering life in the vicinity of Lake Eyasi in Tanzania. The ecology of the Hadza has been studied in detail by Woodburn (1968). The data used here are based on Woodburn's work. The country of the Hadza is about 2590 km² (1000 square miles) of dry, rocky savanna dominated by scrub thorn and acacia trees; it is infested with tsetse flies. Animal life is exceptionally numerous and consists of elephant, rhinoceros, buffalo, giraffe, eland, zebra, wildebeest, waterbuck, impala, Thompson gazelle, and warthog. All except the elephant are hunted and eaten by the Hadza. Impala, giraffe, zebra, and eland are the most frequently killed large animals. However, subsistence depends primarily on gathering activities. Woodburn (1968:51) suggests that probably 80% by weight of Hadza food is vegetable, the bulk of which consists of roots, berries, and fruits. According to Bourlière (1963) and as shown in Table 2.3 (p. 13), the ungulate biomass in the thornbush savanna, Serengeti, Tanzania, is about 4692 kg/km².

Using the simplified formula of Eq. (3.10), under the assumption that the values implied hold for the Hadza, the population density may be estimated as follows:

$$4.3234 \times 10^{-5} (4692) = .20 \text{ person/km}^2$$

This figure compares with an actual population density of .15 person/km² (.4 person/square mile).

The application of the general model may also be illustrated by the case of the Caribou Eskimo. Obviously, the simplified formula for generalized hunter/gatherers does not apply here. The biomass of caribou may be calculated at about 193 kg/km² from Banfield's estimate of 5–6 caribou/square mile. These figures are multiplied by the average weight of mainland caribou, which is about 91 kg, according to Kelsall (1968:29). Considering that 1 kg of raw caribou meat contributes about 4833 cal (H. P. Thompson 1966:423), and that the caloric requirement of the Eskimo is about 3150 cal/day, on the average (G. A. Harrison *et al.* 1964), the value of edible meat available for consumption and the population density on the basis of the food energy obtained may be calculated from Eqs. (3.3), (3.4). The value of the constant k will be changed to .18, since selectivity S would be 1, given the same values for M, E, and W. The value of the F_m, as in Eq. (3.8), would be:

$$F_m = .009 \times 193 = 1.737 \text{ kg/km}^2, \text{ and } F_m = .18 \times .05 \times 193 = 1.737 \text{ kg/km}^2, \text{ and}$$

$$D = \frac{1.737 \times 4833}{3150 \times 365} = .0073 \text{ person/km}^2 \text{ or } .019 \text{ person/square mile}$$

This figure compares satisfactorily with that for the Asiagmuit (.010 person/km²) and the Mt. People (.0103 person/km²), who are primarily caribou hunters (see Table 2.1, p. 8). According to Casteel (1972:27), the subsistence regime of the Chipewyan consists of 60% hunting and 40% fishing. My estimate is close (72%) to the nadir ethnographic estimate multiplied by 20 or 25 (see Casteel 1972). According to Casteel (1972:32), fishing contributes to a population density of .0029 person/km² (.0087 person/square mile) and thus would not significantly alter the population density based on the exploitation of caribou.

These two applications of the model seem to underline its potential for arriving at satisfactory approximations of the population density of hunter–gatherers by reference to the resource potential in their catchment territory, extraction rates, and consumption. However, the model suffers from certain shortcomings. The assumptions concerning optimum yield to man and the level of the safety margin are perhaps the most sensitive areas. It is assumed that the maximum rate of extraction will not exceed the biotic potential of the prey, and that the equilibrium network will not be damaged. It is also assumed that only a certain percentage of the optimum yield to man will in actuality be extracted on a regular basis in order to avoid exposing the population to the stress of food shortage as a result of periodic, seasonal, and short-term fluctuations in the availability of key resources. These two assumptions are legitimate, and indeed necessary, in dealing with hunter–gatherers living under ordinary circumstances. However, disequilibrium must not be ruled out. A population may outstrip its habitat by straining the exploitable resources, by upsetting the ecological network as a result of overexploiting a specific animal, or by disrupting the ecological chain through extensive use of fire. Under these conditions, the rate of extraction in the model would be far in excess of the value of 5% suggested for large animals. Also, the safety margin could either be too narrow or nonexistent. It is unlikely, however, that under these circumstances the population would continue to exist without alternative means of food extraction or other improvements in the subsistence regime.

Although the criticism outlined cannot assail the general model, since the values of C and M (the rate of extraction and the level of the safety margin, respectively) are to be determined by the investigator, the operational model must involve reasonable estimates of the values of these factors in dealing with specific hunting–gathering populations. It may thus be noted that a 5% rate of extraction and a safety margin of 40% are recommended only under "ordinary" circumstances.

The general model is applicable to hunting–gathering populations whose subsistence consists primarily of plant gathering and animal game hunting. In this respect, it does not allow for "unearned" resources (i.e., resources related to animal migrations, aquatic resources, and food items obtained through trade). Casteel's (1972) formulae may be used for estimating such resources.

Among the major limitations of the ecologic models are those related to the values of the variables included. In most cases, adequate, reliable data are lacking or minimal. The quantitative estimates thus must be viewed within a very wide range of error. Considering the tremendous range in population density from less than .01 to more than 10 persons/km², even as much as $\pm$ 50% should be regarded as a satisfactory margin. Even as much as $\pm$ 1 times the "actual" population density would seem permissible. The investigator may also wish to experiment with different values, within an acceptable maximum—minimum range, in order to arrive at a number of estimates from which a mean, median, or mode may be selected and a standard error calculated. A simple computer program can considerably reduce the time spent in calculation. As an example, Table 3.3 shows several "runs" for the estimation of the population density of the Caribou Eskimo via simulation using various values for C, M, and E. The results of 12 runs provided a mode and median

TABLE 3.3
Estimation of Population Density for the Caribou Eskimo

Variables	Runs				
	1	2	3	4	5
B_i (kg/km²)	193	193	193	193	193
C	.05	.10	.05	.05	.10
M	.4	.4	.6	.4	.6
E	.5	.5	.5	.6	.6
W	.9	.9	.9	.9	.9
S	1.0	1.0	1.0	1.0	1.0
L_{cal}	3150	3150	3150	3150	3150
$N_{caribou, cal}$	4833	4833	4833	4833	4833
Population density					
Per square kilometer	.0073	.0146	.0010	.0110	.0260
Per square mile	.019	.038	.028	.280	.068

of .011 person/km² and a mean of .01 person/km² (.027 person/square mile) with a standard deviation of .007. This mean value better matches the ethnographic observations than the single value calculated earlier.

During a detailed investigation of the cultural ecology of the Capsian prehistoric communities by Lubell *et al.* (1976), data useful for estimating population density were collected and may serve here as an example of an application of the model in Archaeology.

The Capsian sites are known from Algeria and Tunisia from about 8000 to 5000 B.C. In the Tebéssa area, about 200 sites are located within a radius of 50 km. Detailed investigation of the archaeological contents of the Ain Mistehyia site in that area, utilizing microarchaeological techniques, revealed that the site, which on the basis of radiocarbon dating spans about 3000 years, was inhabited neither on a year-round basis nor from year to year without interruption (Lubell *et al.* 1976). Since there are about 9 sites within a radius of 5 km from Ain Mistehyia, each of the sites would have been occupied for an average of 3.33 months per year. These sites most probably belonged to a band with a rotating settlement pattern. Since the strategy of the Capsian communities were based partially on the exploitation of land snails, rotation of camps would have eliminated intensive predation stress on the snail populations in the vicinity of the camps. Analysis of the composition of the sites revealed that they consist of habitation and trash disposal areas showing marked lateral shift through time. Therefore, the area of the Ain Mistehyia site (20 × 30 m) does not correspond to the flood area of Capsian camps. The area, on the basis of the analysis of group size from floor area (see Chapter 6) would have accommodated about 40 persons, but since the floor area must have been smaller at any one time, a group size of 20–25 persons, in line with the common size of hunting–gathering bands, seems more acceptable. The territory around Ain Mistehyia within a 5-km radius (other major sites appear outside that area) could have thus been inhabited by about 25 persons, although 9 sites are represented in the area. This amounts to a population density of about .32 person/km².

Environmental analysis revealed that the site region was covered by an open semiarid steppe inhabited by *Alcelaphus buselaphus, Equus mauritanicus,* and *Bos primigenius.* By analogy with similar African habitats a biomass between 2000 and 10,000 kg/km² (Table 2.3, p. 13–14) is probable, with a likely average figure of 5000 kg/km². Using the formula outlined to derive population density from ungulate biomass of generalized hunter–gatherers, we obtain a value of .22 for a probable population density, and a range of .09–.44 person/km². Since the Capsian population complemented its diet with land snails, and the analysis shows that land snails contributed an amount of meat equivalent to one-sixth of the amount contributed by vertebrates, the previously cited figures based on 35% meat from animal game and 65% plant food material are on the conservative side. The actual population density was perhaps close to .29 person/km². This figure is very close to the estimate of .32 obtained from settlement data.

In this example, a good number of the sites had been preserved, a result of the composition of the sites themselves. Yet, without detailed survey of the area for both complete and destroyed sites, and without a detailed analysis of the components of the sites, artifacts, snail shells, megafaunal remains, pollen, radiocarbon dating, and meticulous excavation, an estimation of the population density would have been impossible.

For another example, let us consider the Nile Valley in Upper Egypt during the Final Palaeolithic period (17,000–10,000 B.C.) The number of sites ranged between 20 and 40 sites during successive periods characterized by various lithic industries. Although the archaeological surveys were intensive, much more information is required on the duration of total and seasonal occupancy, rate of destruction, and group size per site for a reliable estimate of the population density. However, one may assume that no more than 10% of the original sites survived, and assuming a group size of 25 persons per site, we can arrive at an estimate of .08–.15 person/ km², a figure not unreasonable considering the range of population densities for hunter–gatherers in temperate regions. To test this figure, a different approach has been taken. About three to five distinct lithic industries are present at any one time during the period. If these lithic industries were connected with regional groups assumed to consist of 500–1000 persons (cf. Birdsell 1968; see also Chapter 5, this volume) the population density would have been within a range of .03–.1 person/ km². In a different study of a single area in the Nile Valley, Upper Egypt, using the aforementioned model, the the population density was estimated to be between .27 and .11 person/km² (Hassan 1973) on the basis of the resource potential of the area (Dishna Plain) and a generalized hunting–gathering economy. A higher figure would be expected if such activities as fishing, fowling, and exploitation of wild cereals were included.

Overview

Ecological models for estimating probable population density of prehistoric hunter–gatherers are based on a consideration of food resources in a region and the number of people who could be adequately supported by those resources. The models make use of primary productivity, yield from a single resource, or the biomass of a class or classes of resources. Each of three models discussed has its specific problems, but certain difficulties apply to all. Not the least of these is the accurate reconstruction of palaeoenvironments. Other major problems include the risk involved in retrodicting rates of food extraction, levels of subsistence below carrying capacity, and rates of food consumption.

One of the models examined in this chapter was developed in conjunction with my work in the Nile Valley on Terminal Palaeolithic hunter–gatherers, in the Near East, and in Algeria. In this model, the biomass of food resources in various biotopes within the catchment territory of a site are used to provide an estimate of yield at a specified rate of culling. Given a certain rate of food consumption, the number of people that can be supported in the area is estimated, providing the basis for an estimate of probable population density. Allowance is made for resource selectivity, percentage of edible portion, and spoilage. Applications of the model to ethnographic and archaeological cases provided satisfactory results. The model by Casteel (1972) is based on estimating population density starting with primary net productivity. The model fails to provide estimates that closely match those of the ethnographic situations to which it has been applied. The serious problems of Casteel's model lie in ignoring the difference between food and nonfood resources, and uncritical application of a rate of extraction based originally on the rate of extraction of human populations today. The model by H. P. Thompson (1966) is more realistic, but it was designed for the specific case of caribou hunting. However, it can be modified for other situations where single resources are exploited, or for situations where more than one resource is exploited but each resource can be dealt with separately.

Ecological models for estimating probable population density are useful in providing figures that can be cross-checked with estimates based on other methods (see Chapter 6). Such models are also indispensable for any empirical attempt to elucidate the dynamics of changing subsistence and population.

4

Food Production and Population Density

Why should we plant, when there are so many mongongo nuts
in the world?
–!Kung of the Kalahari*

Unlike hunting and gathering, food production fosters high human population densities. In addition, its capacity for greater productivity as technological improvements are made allows population densities to continue to increase. During the earliest stages of food production, population densities were most likely quite modest. Hole *et al.* (1969) provide an estimate of about 5 persons/km² for the initial stage of farming in Deh Luran, southwestern Iran. One of the interesting aspects of the shift to food production was the reduction in the area of land used by a group, since subsistence activities were restricted to those areas where arable land was available. In Deh Luran, the area used shrank as the population relied more heavily on food production and irrigation farming (Figure 4.1). Thus, higher population densities were possible in much smaller areas. Food production has enabled the human population to reach densities unprecedented during the Pleistocene, primarily by increasing the biomass of the resources and by eliminating ecological competition between food resources and other biota.

The Population Density of Agricultural Populations

The wide variation in the population densities of agricultural populations (less than 3 persons/km² to more than 2000 persons/km²) reflect the variety of

---

*In R. B. Lee and J. DeVore (editors), *Man the hunter*, Aldine, Chicago, 1968, p. 33.

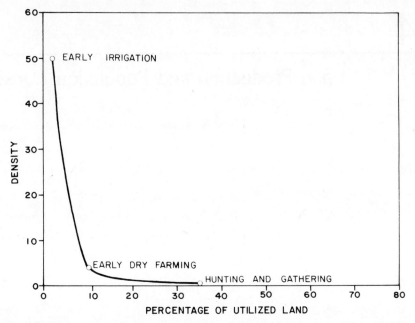

FIGURE 4.1. *Reduction of percentage of land used correlated with increase in population density during the transition from hunting-gathering to dry farming and finally to agriculture in Iran. (Data from Flannery 1969.)*

agricultural practices and the potentials of various agricultural lands (see follow-ing -section).

In Egypt, according to the 1960 census, the population density in rural areas of the Nile Valley averaged 513 persons/km² in the Delta and 755 persons/km² in Upper Egypt (Al-Gihaz al-Markazi lil-Ta'ba' wal'Ihssa' 1966).

In Mesopotamia, the population density of the Lower Diyala region, according to the 1957 census, averaged 33 persons/km², Baghdad not included (R. M. Adams 1965:22). In India, the population density in 1872 was 339 persons/km² (Gilbert 1944). Some estimates are available for Europe before the industrial period (Table 4.1).

Swidden agriculture supports population densities as high as 288 persons/km², as among the Naregu Chimbu, New Guinea (Sahlins 1972:44). Other estimates (Pounds and Roome 1971; Wolf 1966) range from 3 persons/km² to 204 persons/km², with an average of 67 persons/km² (Table 4.2). The above estimates should provide an idea of the range and magnitude of population density under agricultural economy within nonindustrial contexts, and they certainly reflect a stage in the evolution of agricultural production where density was much greater than that of the period of early food production. According to some estimates of population density for the Near East (Hole *et al.* 1969), the population density increased from 5 persons/km² at about 4500 B.C. to 16 persons/km² by 3700 B.C.

TABLE 4.1
Estimated Population Densities for
Preindustrial Europe[a]

Area	Density (persons/km^2)
England, A.D. 1086	78
England, A.D. 1377	135
Holland, A.D. 1514	248
Switzerland, A.D. 1479	93
Central Belgium mid-fifteenth century	30–70
Lorraine, France, mid-fifteenth century	10–25

[a] Data from Pounds and Roome 1971; Wolf 1966.

Food Production: Environmental and Socioeconomic Determinants

Food production differs from hunting and gathering basically in the degree of human control over the resources. In a food-producing system, people exert greater control over the sources of food and their habitat. Selection of cultigens, modification of the genetics of animal and plant species, and relocation of plants and animals are among the major elements of a food-producing system.

The determinants of the population potential under agricultural conditions are for the most part cultural, although natural factors play a significant role. Such factors include climate and suitability of land for agriculture (stoniness, soil fertility, drainage, erosion, and susceptibility to salinization). However, within a natural setting, labor, capital, management, and food-producing strategy can drastically influence the amount of yield and hence population (Figure 4.2).

Under food production, as under hunting and gathering, population density is a

TABLE 4.2
Estimated Population Densities for Groups Engaged in Swidden Agriculture

Group	Density (persons/km^2)
Naregu Chimbu, New Guinea	288
Tsembaga, New Guinea	204
Yagaw Hanaoo, Philippines	30
Lamet, Laos	3
Iban, Borneo	23
Ndembu, Northern Rhodesia	3
Dogomba, Ghana	25–50

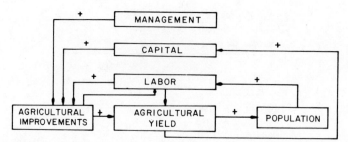

FIGURE 4.2. *Mutual relationships of management, capital, labor, population, and agricultural yield. For two variables X and Y, a positive (+) sign suggests the relationship $X = fY$, whereas a negative (−) sign implies $X = f\frac{1}{Y}$.*

function of the yield from food products and the levels of consumption. The major difference lies in the malleability of the yield and its response to economic management. Yield from wild resources cannot be forced beyond the limits of natural productivity without harming the biotic potential of the resource. Under an agricultural system, the active role played by man allows for selection and improvement of crops for greater yield. Two aspects of the agricultural system that are amenable to change can be discerned (Figure 4.3): the yield per unit of area cultivated, and the size of the area cultivated. Selection and improvement of crops were among the first methods involved in increasing agricultural yield. Flannery (1973), referring to an estimate made by Anne Kirkby, indicates that the earliest maize (ca. 3000 B.C.) from Teotihuacán yielded about 60–80 kg/ha, and that by 2000–1500 B.C. larger cobs of maize were grown, suggesting a yield of 200–250 kg/ha. Other methods of increasing yield involve changing the physical environment (through terracing, irrigation, fertilization, tractor ploughing, land clearance, and even changing the weather by seeding clouds). The yield of certain staple foods, such as wheat, increased dramatically as the result of the use of pesticides, fertilizers, and mechanized farming, along with genetic selection. In the United Kingdom, the wheat yield was as low as .42 ton/ha in the thirteenth century, increasing to 1 ton/ha by the sixteenth century. In 1885–1889 the yield increased to 2.03 tons/ha. In 1934–1938, a slight increase led to a yield of 2.31 tons/ha, but in 1964–1966, the yield rose sharply to 4.05 tons/ha (Clark 1970).

In Egypt, the yield of wheat and barley increased from 260 kg/feddan in A.D. 969–1171 to 742 kg/feddan in 1919, to 1080 kg/feddan in 1949, and to 1430 kg/feddan in 1977 (1 feddan equals 1.083 acres, or 4200 m²).

Modification of the environment is also illustrated in the case of Egypt by the change from basin irrigation to perennial irrigation and by improvments made in waterworks after the early part of the nineteenth century. In 1821 the cropped area was 2.032 million feddans; by 1877 it was enlarged to 4.762 million feddans, and in 1912 it was 7.681 million feddans (Mabro 1974).

Irrigation, land reclamation, fertilization, weeding, and intensive tilling practices and soil management demand both labor and capital. It is in this area that

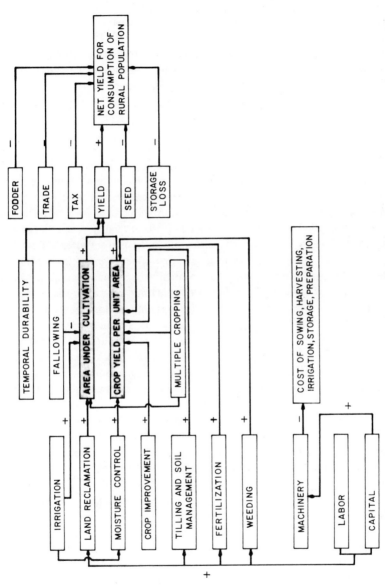

FIGURE 4.3. *A model of agricultural systems illustrating the determinants of agricultural yield. For two variables X and Y, a positive sign (+) suggests the relationship X = fY, whereas a negative sign (−) implies X = f_Y^{\frac{1}{Y}}.*

modern developments in agriculture are most pronounced. The emergence of class differentiation and the control of wealth and labor must be considered critical aspects of the socioeconomic development of agriculture from the later periods of the Neolithic to the present. I will demonstrate in Chapter 15 how such factors were associated with greater agricultural productivity and expanding populations. It is noteworthy that the "agricultural revolution" of A.D. 1750–1880 (Fussell 1958; F. M. L. Thompson 1968) was a managerial revolution. Mechanized agriculture must also be regarded not only as a product of advances in industrial technology, but as a product of the accumulation of capital. Capital, which under nonmonetary systems can be in the form of grain or other products obtained as tax, can be invested in skilled labor for manufacturing agricultural implements or building storage and other cost-saving facilities.

The application of labor to agricultural activity is subject to the law of diminishing returns. For a given area of land under a certain mode of production, the addition of labor can increase yield per capita until the economic optimum population size is reached. Beyond that point (other things remaining the same), the addition of labor provides a less than proportionate increase in yield. The same principle can be applied to the addition of land of poorer quality. The point at which addition of input or land is no longer worthwhile is the *margin of production*. The margin of production, however, can change if the mode of production or the land-use pattern is changed. It is also important to consider labor in agricultural economy in terms of peaks of labor demand during the planting and harvesting season. As much as 35% of a maize crop can be lost if there is not enough manpower to plant within 15 days after the beginning of the rains (Clark 1970).

Agricultural systems are vulnerable because of the simplification of the ecosystem, the susceptibility to major changes in yield as a result of natural or cultural practices, and the sedentariness of the population. The stabilization of an agricultural economy does require pooling of local resources and interregional integration of resources, as well as an emphasis on food storage. As will be argued in Chapter 15, the emergence of a managerial sector and craft specialists, as well as the propensity of agricultural systems to deteriorate under intensive exploitation of local resources, can create a high demand for agricultural labor. This demand can be met by higher labor input per capita, the importing of outside labor, or by population increase. As a result of these dynamics, the labor input is not reduced but increases as people move from hunting–gathering to agriculture, and as more intensive modes of agriculture are introduced, although agricultural production is far more efficient than hunting/gathering as far as calories produced per calories expended.

The role played by agricultural management in controlling productivity and consequently population density is highly significant for interpreting the changes in population during and following the Neolithic period. A strong correlation may be expected between agricultural intensification and population density, as in the case noted by Brown and Podefsky (1976) for the New Guinea Highlands ($r = .845$). Also, estimation of population density from agricultural productivity, given the variety of cultural variables influencing crop yields, is risky. Nevertheless, it can serve as a tool for evaluating the impact of various practices on population density. The next section discusses some of the methods used for estimating population density from agricultural productivity.

Agricultural Potentials and Estimates of Population Density

The population density that can be supported by an agricultural economy is essentially based on the area of arable land, the pattern of land use, cropping practices, net yield of agricultural products, and rate of consumption or number of hectares per family or per capita. The area of arable land can be determined from geomorphological studies and palaeoenvironmental analysis. Ethnohistorical data may be used to determine cropping practices and land-use patterns. Archaeological botanical remains can be used to determine the cultigens. The net yield can be determined from productivity at present or at earlier historical periods. The same applies to the estimation of rates of consumption or number of hectares required per capita. The estimates derived are only suggestive of the probable potential of prehistoric agricultural economy, and should be matched with population estimates from settlement data and palaeodemographic methods.

For the Nile Valley during late Predynastic times, where natural basin irrigation was employed 5500 years ago, we may assume that 25% of the floodplain of the Nile could have been under cultivation. Wheat and barley were sown following the recession of the summer floods in November, and were harvested in April or May. The amount of yield reported since Pharaonic times varies considerably, from 260 kg/feddan during the Fatimid period (Maqrizi n.d.), A.D. 969–1171, to 689 kg/feddan in A.D. 1919 (Audebeau 1919). Kees (1961) reports a figure of about 735 kg/feddan during the Pharaonic period. Using the more conservative figure of grain productivity (260 kg/feddan) and a floodplain area of 1 km² (238 feddans) of which 25% is arable (59.5 feddans), the total yield per year can be placed at 15,473 kg. To obtain the net yield, we must subtract the amount used for seed (65 kg/feddan) and about 10% for storage loss, which amounts to 5415 kg. Thus, the total net yield is 10,058 kg. At a per capita consumption rate of .45 kg/day (164.25 kg/person/year) from ethnographic observations, as many as 61 persons/km² could have been supported.

These figures should not be used as a basis for determining the size of the late Predynastic population without testing against settlement data. However, the figures are significant inasmuch as they indicate the potential of agricultural production for supporting populations. The model can also be used to assess the impact of greater yield and of enlargement of the arable area by irrigation, drainage, and flood controls.

Many attempts have been made to determine the population potential of swidden agriculture. Unlike cultivation in floodplains or under irrigation, the deterioration of the fertility of land plots after a few years of cultivation leads to abandonment and relocation. A plot will lie fallow for many years before it is recultivated. Allan (1949, 1965) developed a formula to estimate potential population density. The same formula and others similar to it were later applied by Brown and Brookfield (1963), Carneiro (1960), Conklin (1959), Cook (1972b), U. M. Cowgill (1962), Gourou (1966), and Rappaport (1968). Allan's formula is as follows:

$$A = CL/P$$

where A is the area required per capita; C is a cultivation factor of the number of plots needed for a full cycle, calculated as the sum of the fallow period and the cultivation period divided by the cultivation period; L is the mean acreage per capita under cultivation; and P is the percentage of arable land available. Thus, an area of 11,380 acres, of which 5% is arable, and where the land is exhausted after 2 years of cultivation, requiring a fallow period of 24 years, possesses a cultivation factor of (2 + 24)/2 = 13. In that area, if 1 acre is maintained under cultivation per person, then

$$A = 100 \times 13 \times 1/5 = 260 \text{ acres/person}$$

This is equivalent to a population density of .95 person/km^2.

One of the factors in this model that is difficult to determine in an archaeological context is the area maintained under cultivation per person. This factor can be regarded as the acreage required to support 1 person for 1 year. Carneiro (1960) uses such a factor (A) to arrive at total population size from the formula

$$P = \left(\frac{TY}{R + Y} \right)/A$$

where T is the total area of arable land, R is the length of the fallow period in years, Y is the productive life span of a plot, and P is the population size. Thus, an area of 13,350 acres, where the plots can remain productive for 3 years and must lie fallow for 25 years, and where .7 acre of manioc can support 1 person for 1 year, can support 2043 persons:

$$P = \left(\frac{13350 \times 3}{25 + 3} \right)/.7 = 2043 \text{ persons}$$

If the arable land is 100% of all available land, then the population density would be 40 persons/km^2.

As a shortcut, the amount of arable land (in acres) required to support one family over a long period of time (A) can be used to determine the population size (P) and hence population density. U. M. Cowgill (1962) uses the following formula for the Lowland Maya:

$$P = (T/A)N$$

where T is the total area of arable land and N is family size. In this calculation the productive span of a plot of land and the fallow period are taken into consideration in the value of A. In applying this model archaeologically, the acreage required per family must be considered in the light of possible changes in yield per acre, as well as in family size. The acreage of arable land must also be estimated from palaeoenvironmental studies. Cook (1972b) provides a method that takes into consideration the yield per acre (Y) and annual consumption per person (C). If the available area of arable land is A, the population size can be calculated as

$$P = AY/C$$

This equation, however, lacks a factor for the fallow period. Generally, a land plot (*milpa*) is exhausted in 2–3 years, and the fallow period is 6–12 years (Cook 1972b) but can be up to 15–20 years (U. M. Cowgill 1962:276). For each acre cultivated, an additional area of fallow land must be available. The area equals the fallow period divided by the life span of a *milpa*. Thus, if the average size of a *milpa* is about 12 acres (11–12 acres according to Cook [1972b]); 13 acres according to U. M. Cowgill [1962]), the area required would be 60 acres. This is close to the estimate of 72 acres reported by E. Wolf (1959:59–60) for the Yucatan Maya.

The average yield of maize in Yucatan is about 450 kg/acre (U. M. Cowgill 1962:277). Using a consumption rate of 390 kg of cob maize/person/year, a fallow period of 10 years, and a *milpa* productive period of 2.5 years, 1 person would require .78 acre/year of land under cultivation and 3.12 acres of fallow land or a total of 3.9 acres, which is equivalent to a population density of .256 person/acre or about 67 persons/km^2.

The addition of other food resources to the diet (Bronson 1966; Puleston 1968; Puleston and Puleston 1971), either from hunting–gathering or from other agricultural activities, fishing, or keeping domestic animals, can increase the population density to be supported in a specific region. B. L. Turner (1974:123), for example, indicates that the prehistoric Lowland Maya were not limited to swidden agriculture. He reports raised fields and terraces under intensive agriculture supporting 150 persons/km^2 (see also R. E. W. Adams 1977). Higher densities were also obtained by Dickson (1978) in estimating the population of the Lowland Maya site of Tikal, and by Rice (1978) for the population of the basins of Yaxha and Sacnab, Peten, from models based on a broad subsistence base. On the other hand, the export of food to urban centers for trade or tax purposes may reduce the population density in rural areas. The urban population can be as much as 10–20% that of the rural population in preindustrial communities. Food from plant resources may also be fed to animals, to convert the plant food into meat or into animal power for addition to the labor force. Also, arable land may be used for cash crops or for fiber plants for textiles instead of for plant foods.

Estimation of the carrying capacity under agricultural production using plant biomass has been attempted by Zubrow (1971), who uses the following model to estimate carrying capacity:

$$K = ABER/C$$

where K is the carrying capacity of an area (A) in square meters, B the biomass per square meter per day in grams, E is the number of kilocalories per gram of biomass, R is the rate of consumption, and C the caloric requirement per person per day. In the lower-grass bottomlands covering an area of 9.92 miles (2.57×10^7 m²) of the Hay Hallow Valley, Zubrow (1971:133) estimates a primary productivity of 2 gm/m²/day. Using an energy content of 4.0 cal/gm of biomass, a rate of consumption of 5% of the total produced biomass, and a caloric requirement of 2500 cal/person/day Zubrow arrives at a total population (carrying capacity) of 4110 persons, equivalent to a population density of 414 persons/square mile (160 persons/km²).

This method is subject to the same criticisms as is Casteel's model of the carrying capacity of hunter–gatherers (see Chapter 3). One of the most serious defects in the model is the rate of consumption of the total produced biomass. Zubrow uses a figure of 5%, a figure he admits is arbitrary but believes to be reasonable. But, the rate of consumption of net productivity by human populations is, in the first place, not constant. In fact, to estimate the rate of consumption of the total net productivity, the number of people must be known. Deevey (1951), for example, uses a world population of 2.1×10^9 persons to arrive at a rate of consumption of .04%, a figure about 13 times smaller than Zubrow's. Zubrow also does not take into consideration the changes in the energy available at various trophic levels (cf. Casteel 1972).

A different approach can be taken in estimating population density from available energy. For example, a pastoral cattle-herding group in East Africa, the Karimojoong, has a herd of 100 animals; the number of people who can be supported can be estimated from the amounts of milk, blood, and meat obtained from that herd. The amounts of these foods are then converted to energy values in calories and totaled. The total divided by the caloric requirement per person yields the number of people who can be supported by a herd of that size. According to Dyson-Hudson (in Little and Morren 1976:58–61), the Karimojoong milk 24 of the 100 cattle, yielding an average of 1 liter/day for 300 days. At 680 cal/liter of milk, this is equivalent to 4,896,000 cal/year. In addition to milk, 400 liters of blood are obtained per year, yielding a total of 200,000 cal/year at 500 cal/liter of blood. Meat consumed amounts to 150 kg/year, yielding a total of 450,000 cal/year, at 3000 cal/kg of meat. The total amount of energy from milk, blood, and meat is 5,546,000 cal/year. At a consumption rate of 1800 cal/day (657,000 cal/year), the cattle can support 8.44 persons. This figure, however, is 34% that of the population size of the herding community (25 persons). Meat from other animals, such as the sheep and goats that are also kept by the cattle herders, and plant foods obtained from cultivation must then support 61% of the population.

This example not only illustrates the use of energy flow in determining carrying capacity, but also indicates the importance of considering resources other than cereal crops or other staple plant foods in estimating the population potential of a food-producing economy under early agricultural conditions, since many of these groups pursued a mixed economy of cultivation and herding.

The estimates of maximum potential population derived through the use of theoretical models are often below those reported from ethnographic observations (Fig. 4.4). In Table 4.3 differences between actual density and potential carrying

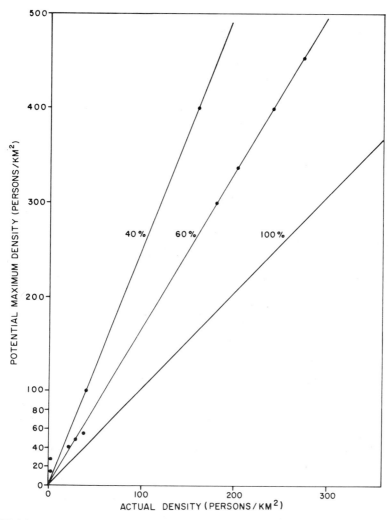

FIGURE 4.4. *Correlation between actual population density and the potential carrying capacity arrived at by means of theoretical models, under conditions of swidden agriculture. Diagonal lines show percentage of maximum potential density. (Data from Sahlins 1972.)*

capacity under conditions of swidden agriculture are presented (Sahlins 1972). The disparity between theoretical values and actual population densities is attributed by Sahlins to a limited labor input and to frequent failure by domestic household units to produce their own livelihood. Such failure can also be a result of stochastic fluctuations in yield. The aforementioned models are deterministic and fail to consider local variations in soil fertility, frequency of adverse climatic conditions, pest infestation, and other factors that are likely to place the effective carrying capacity below the carrying capacity as calculated from average figures of yield, acreage,

TABLE 4.3
Actual and Potential Maximum Population Density of Some Agricultural Groups

Group	Actual density (persons/km^2)	Potential maximum density (persons/km^2)	Percentage of actual density to potential maximum
Naregu Chimbu, New Guinea	288	453	64
Tsembaga, New Guinea	204	313–373	55–65
Yagaw Hanaoo, Philippines	30	48	63
Lamet, Laos	3	11.7–14.4	20–25
Iban, Borneo	23	35–46	50–66
Ndembu, Northern Rhodesia	3	17–38	8–19
West Lala, Northern Rhodesia	<3	4	<75
Dogomba, Ghana	25–50	50–60	42–100

and rates of consumption. People are not likely to subsist at the precarious level of the "mean" carrying capacity. The actual population density will, more often than not, be regulated by the amount of food available during the years of scarcity.

Overview

Food production has had a drastic impact on human population densities. Although the population density at the beginning of the Neolithic was very modest by comparison with some of the modern population densities under advanced food production, there was at least a fivefold increase in world population density by the end of the Neolithic. The increase was greater where agriculture was practiced.

I have attempted to present in this chapter a brief account of some of the major variables that influence agricultural productivity and population density. This is a vast topic and I had to contain my discussion within the scope of this work on population. In my discussion, I hope that the impact of cultural practices on modifying agricultural yield are sufficiently clear. The great potential for an increased agricultural yield through the alteration of crops and livestock, the modification of the environment, and the management of labor and capital must be regarded as a unique aspect of agricultural economy, which places it in a totally different category from hunting and food gathering, in which the potential for economic growth is severely restricted.

5

The Size of Local and Regional
Population Units

*We should note . . . that the size of these hunter groups relative
to their food supply and habits [sic] is very small by primate
standards. A group of 80 monkeys is not large, and groups of
180 baboons are observed frequently. So I think we must look
for social and economic factors that make small hunter groups
of 30–50 efficient.**

The size of local and regional population units in prehistoric times can be determined by a variety of archaeological methods (Chapter 6). Application of these methods to sites from various cultural stages indicates that the population units throughout the Pleistocene, before the introduction of agriculture, were similar in size to ethnographically known hunting–gathering populations.

Generally speaking, hunter–gatherers do not live in large communities, except temporarily and under exceptional conditions. Anthropologists seem to agree that bands, as local groups are commonly referred to, vary between 15 and 50 persons (Table 5.1), with an average of about 20–30 persons (Birdsell 1957; Krzywicki 1934; Lee and DeVore 1968a; Wobst 1974). Regional groups, or band aggregates, on the other hand, show a wider range of variation, with an average of about 500 persons and a modal range of 200–800 persons (Berndt 1959; Birdsell 1957; Krzywicki 1934; Lee and DeVore 1968; Wobst 1974).

Agricultural groups, unlike hunter–gatherers, may consist of large local units and very large regional aggregates. Small local units often range from 50 to 200 persons. There is often a hierarchy of hamlets, villages, and large urban centers. During the Early Dynastic in Mesopotamia, the size of hamlets and villages ranged

S. L. Washburn, in R. B. Lee and I. DeVore (editors), *Man the hunter,* Aldine, Chicago, 1968, pp. 244–245.

TABLE 5.1
Size of Some Hunting–Gathering Bands
(Local Groups)[a]

Population	Band size
Andaman Islanders	30–50[b]
Athabascans (in general)	20–75[b]
Birhor	52[c]
Copper Eskimo	15[c]
Eastern subarctic hunters	25–50[b]
Hadza	25[c]
Iglilingmiut	35[c]
!Kung Bushmen	25[c]
Semang	20–30[b]
Australians	35[c]
Tasmanians	20–50+[b]

[a] Data from Wobst 1974, with additions.
[b] Range.
[c] Mean.

from about 50 to 1000 persons (G. A. Johnson 1972). The average population of hamlets and villages at Ixtapalapa in Mesoamerica, during the Early Formative period is estimated at 80–200 persons, and during the following Middle Formative period at 114–285 persons (Marcus 1976:80–81). The largest early urban centers consisted of as many as 40,000 persons at Uruk in southern Mesopotamia (see Chapter 14); for Teotihuacán, Mexico, in the middle Classic period the figure is 150,000 (Sanders 1972:114). Today large villages in Egypt range from 5000 to 40,000 persons and small villages from a few hundred to 1000 (H. B. Barclay 1971:8).

Local and regional human populations are ultimately limited by the food resources available to the group and by the group's food-procurement technology and patterns of economic distribution (Dyson-Hudson and Smith 1978; Steward 1936). These environmental–economic variables set an upper limit that can be lifted or depressed by natural climatic–environmental changes or by changing cultural practices. The population, however, cannot be reduced beyond a minimum size that guarantees availability of mates and hence biological viability (Wobst 1974). An effective economic policy also requires a minimum population to ensure greater survival potential through cooperation. Beyond survival, the population may be regulated by the optimum economic size of the labor force. Under agricultural conditions, for example, a large group can bring about a higher yield per capita than can a small group, but the addition of people beyond a certain point leads to a decline in the yield per capita. The coherence of the social organization and its effectiveness in maintaining large aggregates may also play a role in regulating the size of groups.

To clarify the foregoing statements, I will now discuss in more detail the relationship between resources, economy, and population size, first for hunter-gatherers and then for agricultural groups.

Hunter-Gatherers

There is little doubt that hunter-gatherers, whether living or extinct, are characterized by small local group (band) size. Judging from ethnographic observations and estimation of group size from site areas (see Chapter 6), 15–50 persons seems to be the modal range for both prehistoric and contemporary hunter-gatherers. This range, with a mean of about 25 persons, is constant regardless of population density, habitat, and time. It is not surprising that 25 is sometimes referred to as the "magic number." Steward (1936) was among the first to observe the prevalence of this group size among hunter-gatherers and to offer tentative explanations. The participants in the symposium on *Man the Hunter* were also impressed by the consistency with which this number appeared among hunter-gatherers, and several explanations were provided (Lee and DeVore 1968a). In general, the prevalence of this number is a reflection of adaptive success.

One way to explore the significance of group size is to consider it as a function of the population density and area. The area that is regularly exploited by a group of hunter-gatherers may be called a *home range* or a *catchment territory* (Vita-Finzi and Higgs 1970). The catchment territory of hunter-gatherers usually lies within 10 km from the base camp (Lee 1968; Vita-Finzi and Higgs 1970), an area of about 314 km² (120 square miles). Steward (1936) arrived at 100 square miles (260 km²) as an average area exploited by hunting-gathering bands. The maximum radius of the catchment territory, according to Lee (1969), is a function of the ratio of food yield to energy cost. The more distant the food resource, the greater the effort required (Figure 5.1). Consequently, as the distance to the resource increases, the ratio of yield to effort diminishes. Thus, beyond a certain distance the exploitation of a resource ceases to be profitable. This is the same principle of diminishing returns

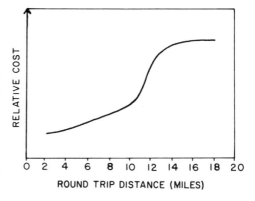

FIGURE 5.1. *Increase in food-procurement cost as distance increases from campsite to the location of food source in the case of the !Kung hunter-gatherers. (From Environment and Cultural Behavior: Ecological Studies in Cultural Anthropology, edited by Andrew P. Vayda. Copright © 1969 by Andrew P. Vayda. Reprinted by permission of Doubleday & Company, Inc.)*

and marginal productivity discussed in Chapter 3. The effort expended in covering a given distance depends, of course, on the mode of transportation and the surface conditions. Factors for the effects that slope, wetness, vegetation, and so on would have on the rate of travel can be used to generate a surface map of travel time. The absence of effort-saving modes of transportation among most hunter–gatherers places physiological limitations on the distances traveled. Trade, food sharing between contiguous groups, and food exchange must be viewed partly as mechanisms to circumvent limitations imposed on subsistence effort. The importance of boats, rafts, and sleds in reducing effort and enlarging the size of the catchment territory is of particular significance in areas with low resource potentials, such as the arctic. One must note, also, that the radius of a catchment territory does not measure the distance actually traveled. This distance is generally greater than the radius, because hunting–gathering activity is not usually carried out along a straight line, and because the terrain is seldom flat. This is particularly important in determining the cost of the subsistence effort. The size of the catchment territory will also vary with the work schedule and the economic seasons.

The 16-mile or 10-m radius from Lee and Steward is perhaps to be regarded as an upper limit for the radius of the group home range. Given a base camp from which an area is exploited, and assuming that the majority of the people will tend to spend their nights in the camp, most subsistence activities will be carried out during a single day. Assuming an average daylight period of 10 hours, at least 2 hours expended in pursuit and capture of food, and a walking rate of 3 km/hour (allowing for a comfortable pace and detours), a return trip cannot be longer than 12 km (7.5 miles) from the base camp. Yellen (1977) has observed that most subsistence activities undertaken by the Bushmen involve not more than a 1-day return trip, and we can safely assume that under conditions of greater food abundance, the actual distance covered would be smaller to reduce effort. However, a group of people may exploit a series of home ranges in the course of a year, changing locations with the seasons or as resources become too scanty to be exploited within the maximum limit of travel. Also, the greater the size of the population, the greater its food requirements. At any given locus, a population may thus be regulated by the yield of resources from no greater than 314 km^2 using the 10-km radius as the maximum travel distance.

The area of the catchment territory increases logarithmically as its radius increases, assuming that the catchment area is circular. As Table 5.2 shows, the area exploited may be, thus, in theory, expanded considerably by a slight increase in the radius of the catchment territory. In most cases, however, the catchment territory is not represented by a circle because of physical barriers and/or the distribution of food resources.

The catchment territory may also be defined by cultural territorial boundaries. Fixed territoriality is not compatible with hunting–gathering regimes, although territorial claims to specific resources are known to exist, particularly when competition for resources is high (Netting 1972:8). Such claims, however, may be short-lived, lasting only for a few generations (Lee 1972a:129).

TABLE 5.2
Radius and Equivalent Areas of Circular Catchment Territories

Radius (km)	Area (km²)
5	78.5
6	113.0
7	153.9
8	201.0
9	254.3
10	314.0
11	380
12	452
13	531
14	616
15	707
16	804

The spatial distribution of the resources, their relative yield, and the effort required to locate and extract them most likely determine the shape and size of the catchment territory. In the Nile Valley, for example, a consideration of these factors indicates that the catchment territory was relatively small and that its shape was predominantly elongate, its long axis parallel to the channel of the Nile (Figure 5.2). The map shown in the figure was generated by gridding the landscape surrounding Terminal Pleistocene sites into 1×1 km cells. For each cell the distance of travel from the site, taking into consideration surface conditions, was calculated and converted to calories required for walking to that cell. The food productivity of the cell and the amount of calories to be obtained from that cell were ascertained and a ratio of yield to travel effort was computed. Values for each cell were then used to draw isolines of catchment value. These values allow us to recognize the degree of attraction or "pull" of various spatial units in the area. The isoline at which the yield was less than the caloric need of the producers and their dependents for the effort expended marks the maximum boundary of the catchment territory. In favorable environments, the people will not be forced to range to that maximum territorial limit and will concentrate on exploiting the resources having the greatest amount of yield per unit of effort expended.

The relationship between a group of 25 persons, population density, and catchment area can be calculated. When, for example, the food potentials dictate low population density, as in the case of Caribou Eskimo, a band of 25 persons requires an area of about 6450 km² with a radius of 45 km (about 2500 square miles and 28 miles, respectively). The Hadza, on the other hand (Woodburn 1968), require an area of about 164 km² with a radius of about 7.2 km (about 63 square miles and 4.5 miles, respectively) for the same size band. For a population with greater density, such as the California aborigines in the Lower Klamath region with a fishing subsistence regime (Baumhoff 1963), the 25-person band needs an area of

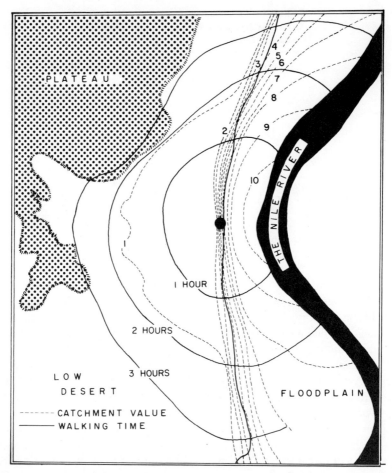

FIGURE 5.2. *Catchment values in the area surrounding a hunting-gathering camp in the Nile Valley during the Terminal Pleistocene. This map is provisional and subject to future modification as a result of ongoing research by the author.*

about 16 km² with a radius of about 2.2 km (about 6 square miles and 1.4 miles, respectively). If no advanced energy-saving mode of transportation exists and great distances must be covered to bring in resources that are scarce and widely dispersed, a small group size may be favored. This may partially explain the smaller size of the bands of the Copper Eskimo and the Reindeer Chukchee. If the resource potentials, such as in arctic and desert regions, are too low (Table 5.3) to permit a group of at least two or three families, it is unlikely that the environment would be inhabited at all. However, frequent relocation may compensate for local scarcities of food. In general, however, given the densities of most hunting-gathering populations, which is between .1 and 1 person/km² in most cases, a group of 25 persons or more can be easily accommodated within a radius of 10 km from the camp.

The size of a hunting–gathering band also seems to be a function of the optimum size required for a stable organizational unit based on daily face-to-face relations, which would be advantageous for cooperation in hunting, locating food, and defense. Calhoun (1970:122) estimates 12 adults as the minimum stable unit, which would amount to a group of 27 persons, if the ratio of dependents to adults is placed at .44. A great deal remains to be learned about the sociological significance of the small size of hunting–gathering local groups. The contributions of sociologists and psychologists to the study of small groups provide a great wealth of information that should be tapped by anthropologists. Some findings indicate that a group size of 21–50 persons is most satisfying to the individuals (R. H. Hall 1972:129). Factors such as cooperation, competition, suspicion, prestige, and conflict are undoubtedly involved in regulating the size of the hunting–gathering group. The observed fluidity of some hunting–gathering local groups is probably a mechanism to offset the impact of negative personal relations on the social stability of the group (Lee 1972a; Netting 1972:7–8). It also may regulate group size in response to seasonal variations in resource potentials. The sociological mechanism, however, may not be separable from the ecological influences, since social conflict may result from declining food yield and a corresponding decline in the standard of living (Netting 1972).

Minimum band size seems to be related to numerous factors. A group consisting of one family, made up of two adults and two or three children (Hallowell 1949), does not seem to be a viable unit on a long-term basis because of its low chances of discovering or having access to widely dispersed resources, low hunting success, low defense capacity, and precarious genetic viability. Martin (1972) estimates four adult males as an optimum number for a work group among Pai Indians of the southwestern United States. A theoretical model based on that estimate and the ratio of hunters to other persons in the group provides a mode of 28 persons as the mean size of the band (Figure 5.3).

A group size of 15–50 persons may not be unique to hunter–gatherers. A preliminary analysis based on the data assembled by Jolly (1972) indicates that the

TABLE 5.3
Estimated Population Density and Size for a Catchment Territory of 314 km² in Different World Biomes

Size of catchment territory (km²)	Biome	Biomass (kg/km²)	Population density (persons/km²)[a]	Number of persons
314	Arctic	200	.0086	3
314	Subtropical savanna	10,000	.43	136
314	Grassland	4,000	.17	54
314	Semidesert	800	.035	11

[a] Estimated based on Hassan's model (see Chapter 3).

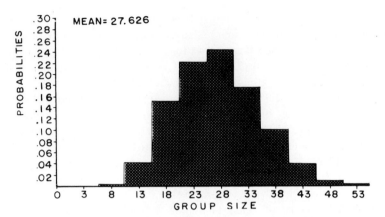

FIGURE 5.3. *Probability of the size of hunting–gathering bands on the basis of the model formulated by Martin (1972). Note that 28 persons is the most probable size. (Data from Martin 1972.)*

distribution of mean group size of various semiterrestrial primate species is polymodal. Groups having an average size of 15–20 are the most common. Groups having an average size of 2–4 are also common (Figure 5.4).

The prevalence of an average group size of 15–20 individuals among semiterrestrial primates suggests that the terrestrial habitat may have some influence on group size. For example, the formation of multimale social groups for defense against terrestrial predators (Eisenberg *et al.* 1972) should be considered. Early Pleistocene hominids were perhaps faced with the dangers of terrestrial predators, and having a group that included several male adults would have been advantageous.

It is also illuminating to illustrate here the importance of diet and habitat on the home range of primates. The primates, arranged according to the grades suggested by Jolly (1972) as arboreal leaf-eaters, arboreal omnivores, semiterrestrial leaf-

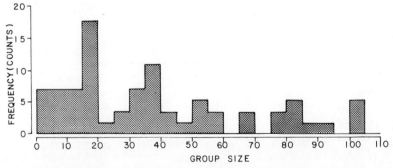

FIGURE 5.4. *Frequency distribution of the size of nonhuman primate groups. Note that the most common size is 15–20 individuals, and that distribution is polymodal, with the modes following the rule: $M_k - M_j = M_l$, where M_k is the modal size next to the modal size M_j, and M_l is the first modal size (about 17.5 persons). (Data from Jolly 1972.)*

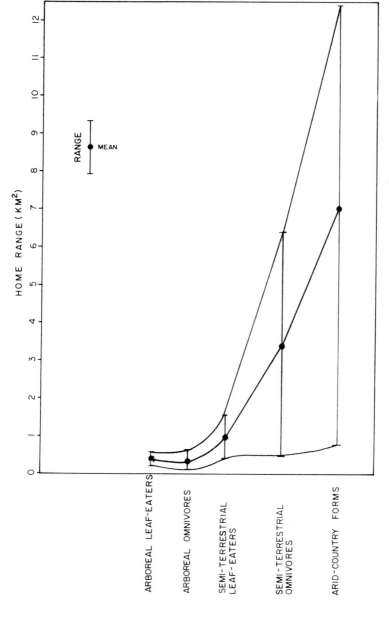

FIGURE 5.5. *Home range of nonhuman primates showing an increase in area as a function of diet and habitat. (Data from Jolly 1972.)*

eaters, and semiterrestrial omnivores, show a geometric increase in the size of their home range (Figure 5.5). Terrestrial life and an omnivorous diet seem to be associated with larger home ranges.

The question of biological viability as a determinant of the minimum size of hunting–gathering bands has been dealt with by Wobst (1974). Given prehistoric patterns of fertility and mortality, Wobst concluded from a Monte Carlo simulation that the minimum equilibrium size is 175–475 persons, or about 7–19 bands of 25 people each. The minimum "equilibrium" population unit (MES) describes the number of people that can constantly provide members of the population with mates upon reaching maturity. The size of the minimal equilibrium population unit is also affected by the sex ratio and the cultural rules of mating. Adult life expectancy is negatively correlated with the MES, whereas juvenile mortality is positively correlated. Restrictive mating tends to increase the MES. Under environmental conditions leading to low population density, restrictive mating rules would be expected to be minimal.

Cultivators

Cultivators are often sedentary and their economic system permits a high population density (Chapter 3), which removes the threat of a lack of mates. In fact, because the availability of mates is not a limiting factor under such circumstances, restrictions on mating may be instituted in order to maintain constant and predictable (stable) reciprocal social relations among the members of the population (Wobst 1974). A stable social organization is crucial for the maintenance of the agricultural group, given the social and interpersonal conflicts that must be ironed out without recourse to spatial mobility. The diversity of economic endeavors and the necessity of coordinating production and distribution are some of the factors that encourage the development of coherent forms of social organization.

The size of regional units thus appears to be mostly a function of the degree of social integration and the stability of the agricultural system. Variations in agricultural productivity will, of course, influence population density, but cultural management can play a definite role in developing agricultural resources.

The size of local agricultural units (villages and hamlets) is to be viewed as the optimum group size for a number of families (mating units) that will function cooperatively as a more or less semiautonomous productive economic unit.

Overview

The size of the hunting–gathering band is a function of environmental, cultural, and biological factors (Figure 5.6). Spatiotemporal variability of resources

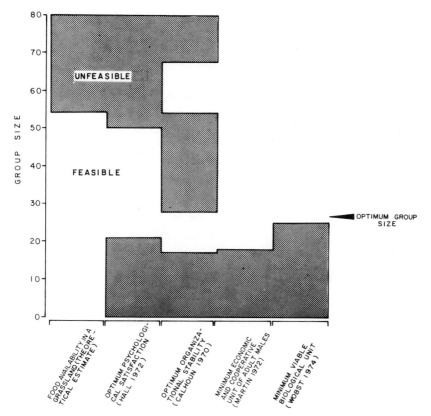

FIGURE 5.6. *A model of the determinants of the size of hunting-gathering bands. The unshaded area shows the group size feasible for various determinants. Twenty-five to 28 persons is the only size feasible for all determinants combined and thus represents the optimum group size.*

demands a fluid demographic composition and enhances intergroup movement of individuals, thus inhibiting the emergence of formal group-integrative social mechanisms. The yield from natural food resources would not on the average support more than about 50 persons, assuming a catchment territory within a feasible travel distance from the campsite. The size of a band seems also to be determined by the advantages of having at least four adult male hunters. This provides a work force for cooperative endeavors and increases the changes of food procurement. Psychological satisfaction and stable social organization are served by a small group size. The band, however, cannot be maintained as an economic or a biological unit for a number of generations if it falls below 25 persons. Therefore, where resources within the catchment territory are not sufficient to provide for a group of this size for a full season or a whole year, the group must move to another territory.

The size of the regional units of hunter-gatherers is perhaps influenced most by the size of the mating pool, which is set at a minimum of 175 persons (Wobst 1974), and by the decay of linguistic and social affinity with distance (Howells 1966).

The large size of local agricultural groups is made possible by the greater carrying capacity of food production. The maximum size is set both by the maximum possible density and by the social integrative mechanisms that minimize fission. There is evidence for urban centers (actually agro-urban centers made up predominantly of farmers in association with a high concentration of food non-producers) of as many as 150,000 persons, which may represent the limits of both productivity and social coherence under early farming and urban conditions.[1] Maximum regional agricultural population units under early agricultural conditions were perhaps less than a few hundred thousand because of relatively low yield and limited food transport facilities.

---

[1]The population of New York in 1800 was 60,000 and that of Paris was 547,000 in 1801 (P. Hall 1966:22); the population of Roman London was less than 20,000 (Briggs 1957:278).

6

Determination of Population Size from Archaeological Data

Accurate demographic data are hard to obtain even today; yet they are vital if we are to understand trends of stability or change, and they are very useful in helping to assess the nature of a particular society. Accordingly, demographic data are one aspect of archaeology that needs a good deal more emphasis in the future so that better techniques and more accurate estimates can be developed.

The size of population units that once occupied a site or a region can be determined from a careful analysis of settlement data, artifacts, food refuse, burials, and ethnohistorical data. In this chapter I will review the various methods devised by archaeologists for this purpose and offer criticisms and suggestions for improvements.

Determination of Population Size from Settlement Data

Archaeological settlements can provide information on the size of residential population units. In a survey of the prehistoric sites near Flagstaff, Arizona, Colton (1932) attempted to estimate regional population size. Colton's work, which he continued (Colton 1936, 1949), was followed by that of many others in the southwestern United States (Hack 1942; Plog 1975) and in other parts of the world (Frankfort 1948, 1950). In another pioneering study, Naroll (1962) focused on the relationship between dwelling space and population. His study was followed by another important work, by Cook and Heizer (1965, 1968).

*Frank Hole and Robert F. Heizer, *An introduction to prehistoric archaeology* (third ed.), Holt, Rinehart and Winston, New York, 1973, p. 367.

The use of regional surveys and the application of certain rules of thumb developed by Naroll and by Cook and Heizer are now widely accepted by archaeologists and serve as the basis for many estimates available on archaeological groups.

To examine the potentials and problems of these approaches to the determination of the size of prehistoric populations, it would be worthwhile to examine the basis for such approaches. The underlying assumption is that there is a correlation between population size and settlement space. Although it would be difficult to quarrel with this assumption, there is a problem in determining the nature of the correlation (linear, logistic, exponential?). Also, given that factors other than population influence settlement space, we need to know the coefficient of correlation between population and settlement space.

Figure 6.1 is a model of the variables that are likely to influence those aspects of a settlement that may be used for population estimates: number of dwelling units, dwelling space, and site area. In addition to the number of families, family size, and changes in population size through time, behavioral factors such as spatial patterning of activities, social organization, duration of occupation, continuity of occupation, and pattern of reoccupation are known to influence settlement space. Moreover, the rate of decay of dwellings (life expectancy of dwellings) is an intrinsic factor that must be considered in sites where occupations last for long periods. Lastly, the destruction, burial, or differential preservation of whole settlements or parts thereof alters the original pattern and area of settlement. The adequacy of the archaeological sampling strategy is another key factor in translating archaeological data into numbers of persons.

Attempts to estimate the size of population units from settlement data are based on the length of a site (Hack 1942), the area of a site as determined from the scatter of artifacts (R. M. Adams 1965; Blanton 1972; Marcus 1976; Parsons 1971; Sanders 1965), the number of dwellings (Frankfort 1950; J. N. Hill 1970; Longacre 1976; Plog 1975), and the volume of site deposits (Ammerman et al. 1976).

Site Length

Hack's (1942) attempt was oriented toward arriving at an index of population size rather than the absolute size of the population. For example, he used a site 10 yards long as equivalent to two population units, and a site 18.3m (20 yards) long as equivalent to five population units.

Site Volume

Ammerman et al. (1976) approach the problem of estimating population size from settlement remains of village sites through the determination of the volume of site deposits (V), the life span of a site (T), the duration of site occupation (P), and the compacted volume of house materials (H). These variables are used to estimate

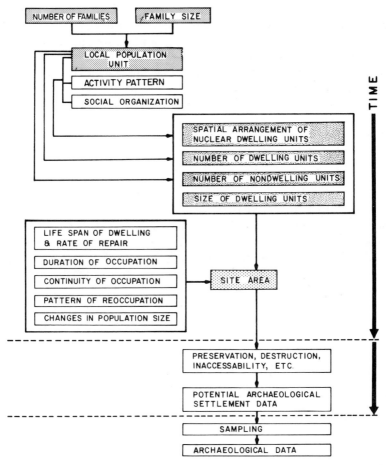

FIGURE 6.1. *A model of the variables influencing the determination of population size from settlement data. Note especially the role of nondemographic variables.*

the number of houses at any one time (*N*), from which the number of persons can be estimated using number of persons per family. Their equation is as follows:

$$N = VT/HP$$

Applying the equation to a site consisting of 15,000 m³ of deposits that was continuously occupied for 750 years and is made up of the remains of houses that lasted for 15 years and collapsed to a volume of 20 m³ provides the following number of houses at any one time of occupation:

$$N = 1500 \times 15/20 \times 750 = 15 \text{ houses}$$

Assuming five persons per house, the number of persons comes to 15 × 5 = 75.

To obtain reliable results from this method, we need (a) archaeological information on the duration of the sites by tree-ring dating or other dating methods; (b) an analysis of the construction of the houses, in which size, thickness of walls, and other attributes are examined and compared with ethnographically known houses of similar construction; (c) a determination of the life span of houses of similar construction from ethnographic cases; and (d) estimates of the number of persons per house, arrived at from ethnic analogy or one of the formulae correlating dwelling space and number of household members. The effects of deflation, sheetwash erosion, and gaps in occupation should be carefully scrutinized.

Site Area

Robert M. Adams (1965) estimated the area of the archaeological sites in Mesopotamia by employing a figure of 200 persons/ha to arrive at the size of ancient populations. His 200 persons/ha figure was derived from modern data on the old quarters of Baghdad (216 persons/ha) and other Middle Eastern towns and villages in the Susiana Plain and Kur Basin, Iran (223 persons/ha and 137 persons/ha, respectively).

In an earlier study Frankfort (1950) measured house sizes, estimated the number of persons per house, and counted the number of houses per hectare, to arrive at an estimate of 297–494 persons/ha, or 20–34 m²/person. He compared this estimate with the number of persons per acre in Aleppo and Damascus, which he calculated at 160. Braidwood and Reed (1957) took the size of the present population of the mound of Erbil to arrive at an estimate of 213 persons/per acre (19 m²/person) of town area. Colin Renfrew (1972b) has suggested that the population in the late Bronze Age in the Aegean was probably not so dense as that in a Sumerian town. Accordingly, he used an estimate of 300 persons/ha (30 m²/person). For the Neolithic period he used a figure of 200 persons/ha (50 m²/person), a figure close to that used by R. M. Adams (1965).

Kramer (1978), on the basis of her study at Shahabad, Iran, and estimates of population density of other rural settlements in Southwest Asia, concludes that the density in most cases is well below 200 persons/ha (Table 6.1). The average density is 119.6 ± 54/ha. Kramer notes that differences might result from the degree of nucleation of settlements.

An alternative to determining population size from a constant figure for population density is to determine a mathematical relationship between population size and site area. The formula for estimating population (P) from site area (A), employing a constant figure for population density (k), is

$$P = k A$$

For example, if a density of 100 persons/ha is employed and the site area is measured in hectares, the formula is

$$P = 100 A$$

TABLE 6.1

Population Density of Some Rural Settlements in Southwest Asia [a]

Settlements in Southwest Asia	Density (persons/ha)
Shahabad ($N = 30$)	106.8
Marv Dasht ($N = 110$)	147.0
Central Tauran ($N = 13$)	52.3
Dez Pilot area ($N = 54$)	208.8
Other areas ($N = 22$)	82.9 ± 58

[a] Kramer 1978.

The relationship between site area and population size may also be examined in the light of the data on rural settlements in Southwest Asia compiled by Kramer (1978). Excluding questionable data, the mathematical relationship can be expressed as follows (see Figure 6.2):

$$P = 146.15 \, A^{.51}$$

where P is again population and A is area, in hectares. This can be simplified to the following formula, without any significant deviation from the empirical relationship:

$$P = 146\sqrt{A}$$

The correlation coefficient, r, is .62.

It seems, therefore, that correlations between site area and population drawn from modern contexts cannot be applied to archaeological contexts without reservations. The area of a site will vary for the same population size depending on whether the settlement is walled or open (Wenke 1975). Higher densities are often observed in walled settlements. The area of a site is a function of the spatial arrangement of the dwelling units (linear, stellar, ring-type, axial, checkered) and the spacing between dwelling units. Kramer (1978) also notes that in a case study only 60% of the site area was actually used for habitation.

The relationship between size of campsite area and population size of hunting–gathering groups was examined by Wiessner (1974), who used the data on the !Kung Bushmen collected by John Yellen (1977). According to Wiessner (1974), the camps had a standard hut–hearth relation, a prerequisite for obtaining a consistent relationship between population size and a habitation space that may consist of more than a single hut/hearth unit. According to Wiessner, for the first 10 inhabitants about 5.9 m² of campsite area are alloted per person (29.5 m² for the first 5 persons and 59 m² for the first 10 persons). In a camp of 25 persons, the area per person increases to 10.2 m²/person:

$$A = .23P^{1.96}$$

where P is population size and A is area. (The value .23 in the equation is misprinted as $-.23$ in the article by Wiessner.)

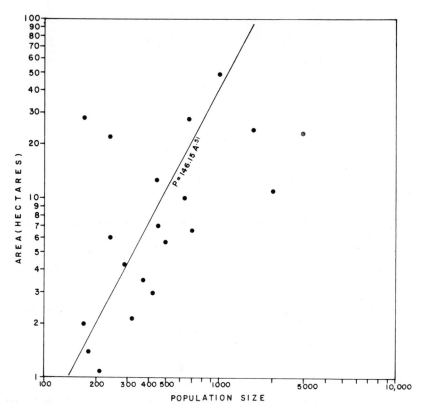

FIGURE 6.2. *Correlation between settlement area and population size, Southwest Asia. (Data from Kramer 1978.)*

Casteel (1979) reexamined the relationship between the population size and the area of the Bushmen campsites, using the data published by Yellen (1977). The mathematical relationship obtained by Casteel is as follows:

$$A = .1542 \ P^{2.3201}$$

The correlation coefficient is as high as .93. The area (in square meters) is that described by Yellen as the LNAT, the area of all huts, their associated hearths, and debris surrounding the hearth. The power curve $A = .1542P^{2.321}$ fits the published data by Yellen better than Wiessner's $A = .23 \ P^{1.96}$ (see Figure 6.3). The curve used by Wiessner underestimates the area for a given population size. The data provided by Yellen, however, can be equally fitted by an exponential curve of the following form:

$$A = 8.9584 \ e^{.1414P}$$

where A is area, P is population, and e is the base of the natural logarithm. The correlation coefficient for this relationship is as high as .9223, accounting for 85% of the variance compared with 86% for the relationship as obtained by Casteel.

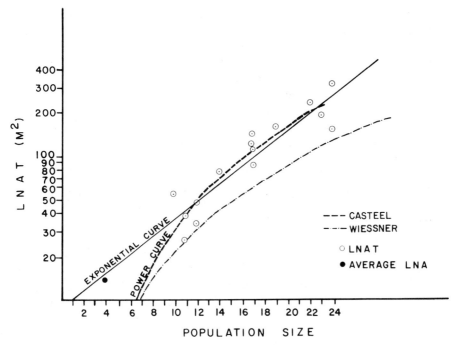

FIGURE 6.3. *Correlation between site area (LNAT) and population size of !Kung Bushmen camps. The data are fitted with an exponential curve, a power curve calculated by Casteel (1979), and another curve by Wiessner (1974). (Data from Yellen 1977.)*

The curve that is used (power or exponential) makes a great difference in estimates of population size if the relationship is extrapolated to determine the area occupied by large population units (Figure 6.3).

The lesson to be learned here is that we must find out the reasons for the pattern of increase in the area of a site. Norbeck (1971) indicates that, for an urban area, population density is low in peripheral rural areas, increases very rapidly in suburban areas, and decreases in the downtown center where residential areas are comparatively rare. He compares this with the shape of a longitudinal section of a volcano. Using the relationship between the area of a volcano and its volume (2/3), he hypothesized that the relationship between urban population and urban area is expressed by the formula

$$A = a P^{2/3}$$

where a is a constant.

Norbeck's formula expresses a growth pattern that follows a power function similar to the one used by Casteel and Wiessner. This pattern of growth is referred to as *allometric growth*; the area required as individuals are added to the population is not constant.

Norbeck's observation on the density distribution of population in an urban area does not of course apply to hunting–gathering camps, but it does indicate that the application of an empirical relationship without an understanding of the behavioral pattern of population activities can lead to serious problems. Wiessner (1974) and Yellen (1977) proposed that the allometric growth of hunting–gathering campsites is a function of a spatial arrangement of huts in a ring (Figure 6.4) Read (1978) attempted to provide a theoretical model to explain the relationship obtained by Wiessner (1974) and a ring model of settlement. Read arrived at the conclusion that the growth pattern is governed by a constant distance between points of tangency with the camp boundary of adjacent residence locations, L (Figure 6.4). The theoretical equation obtained by Read is as follows:

$$A = (L^2/4N^2\pi)P^2$$

where A is camp area, N is the number of persons per residence unit (hut), and P is population. According to Read, the value of L is a constant of 10 m. According to Yellen (1976:106) the value of N is 3.66 persons.

Read's equation thus may be rewritten as

$$A = .5941\ P^2$$

The shape of the curve seems to fit the curve obtained by Casteel, except that the values for site area are larger for those estimated from the curve by Casteel. How-

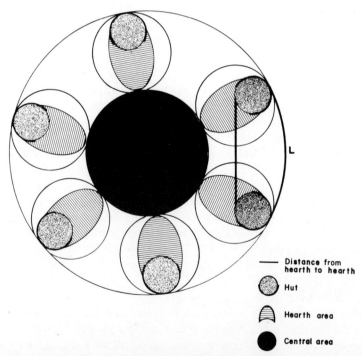

FIGURE 6.4. *A ring model of !Kung Bushmen campsites. Huts are arranged in a ring surrounding a central area. Each hut opens to an activity area where the hearth is located.*

ever, if we lower the value of L to 8 m, instead of 10, the fit is very satisfactory (Figure 6.5).

As Read (1978:317) remarks, this theoretical model takes us back to the realm of anthropology. The question must be asked if this relationship is justifiable; that is, whether the relationship is causal or spurious. This can be answered only if the cultural factors determining the spatial arrangement of settlements are known.

From the data by Yellen (1977 and personal communication), I gained the impression that the distance between the points of tangency with the camp boundary of adjacent residence location (L in Read's equation) is not of much behavioral significance to the Bushmen. Instead, the central area inside the ring is the one that has cultural significance, because it is an area of communal activity. Thus, as the number of people increases, the demand for a larger area increases. Starting with the average area of campsites associated with certain population numbers, an oval area of huts and hearths has a long axis of 4 m, the central area where the campsite consisted of four huts was found to be 1.04 m, increasing to 2.1 m for a campsite with five households, and 3.7 m for a camp of six huts. Using the average of 3.66 persons/hut, I obtained the following relationship:

$$A = .71015 \; P^{1.76}$$

This relationship fits the data very well. On the recommendation of Yellen (personal communication), I plotted the distance between hearths against population size as a

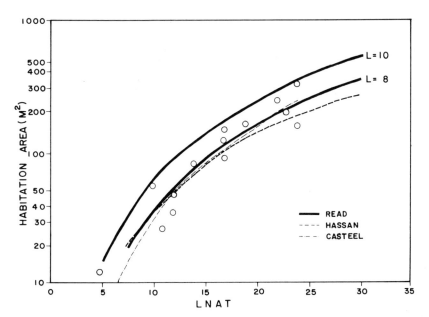

FIGURE 6.5. *Diagram showing the fit between theoretical models of the relationship between population size and site area (LNAT) by Read (1978) and Hassan (this volume), as compared with empirical correlation by Casteel (1979). (Data from Yellen 1977.)*

test of this relationship (Figure 6.6). The increase in the average distance as population increased is in agreement with the model of expanding central locus of communal activities as population increases. Also, a camp made up of a large number of people may consist of distantly related individuals who may place their huts farther apart. Where the population size is small, people will tend to camp close to each other for a sense of social and psychological security.

The formula $A = .71015\ P^{1.76}$ provides both a good fit to the data and an anthropological explanation for the factors underlying the empirical relationship between population and site area. The formula may thus be used for hunting-gathering campsites where huts are arranged in a ring.

Number and Size of Dwelling Units

The number of houses or rooms and their area obtained from archaeological investigations may be converted to population size by an estimate of the number of persons per room or per house. This approach, pioneered by Frankfort (1950) and applied in many other contexts, is much more promising than estimating population from site area. However, certain problems must be considered. First, the estimate of number of persons per room or per house must be obtained from ethnographic analogs. James N. Hill (1970), for example, used a mean of 6.1 persons/house for his estimate of population size at Broken K Pueblo. This led to a figure of 1.7 persons/room. Longacre (1976), noting that the rooms at Grasshopper Pueblo were larger than those at Broken K Pueblo, used a figure of 2.88 persons/room, on the

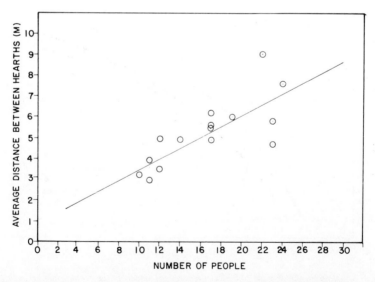

FIGURE 6.6. *Correlation between the number of people in a camp (population size) and average distance between hearth. (Data from Yellen 1977.)*

basis of ethnographic data. In certain areas in California, Cook (1972b) noted, the family size (number of persons per house) is about 7–7.5 persons. Cheyenne villages in North Dakota also contained 8–9 persons/house. In general, however, the size of a household is about 4–5 persons—2 adults and 2–3 younger individuals (Blanton 1972; Braidwood and Reed 1957; Butzer 1959; Parsons 1971; Steward 1937; Winter 1972). The Illinois Indians in 1680 had a family size of 4.17 persons (Cook 1972b), and the ethnographic Maya (Cozumel Island) in 1492 had an average of 4.9 persons per nuclear family (Haviland 1972:138).

The relationship between population size and habitation space, as distinct from total site area, has been employed to arrive at estimates of prehistoric population size. For example, Naroll (1962) derives the following equation from data on 18 societies from different parts of the world:

$$A = 21.7 \ P^{.84195}$$

Naroll, however, simplifies this formula to:

$$P = \frac{A}{10\text{m}^2}$$

The empirical finding does not justify this simplification, since the value of the exponent (.84195) is less than 1 (Wiessner 1974).

In another attempt, Cook and Heizer (1965, 1968) and Cook (1972b) estimate population size from habitation space by means of a procedure that is in concordance with the logarithmic relationship between the two. Cook's formula, however, is based on a different set of original data. His rule of thumb is to allow 13.92m² for the first six persons (2.32 m²/person) and 9.29 m² for each additional person.

The ekistic and anthropological factors underlying the empirical relationship obtained by Naroll can be understood from a theoretical model where spatial units (dwelling space per person or household) are packed as in Figure 6.4. This settlement pattern yields an equation of $A = 3.497 \ P^{1.169}$, which provides a satisfactory fit with the equation obtained by Naroll (Figure 6.7). However, Binford et al. (1970:84–87) note that the application of Naroll's formula to the Hatchery West site yields a very low population size estimate compared to the population size obtained from the number of houses and pits at the site. The theoretical equation does show that Naroll's formula underestimates population size for dwelling spaces that are less than 1000 m². LeBlanc (1971) has commented on the inadequacy of the data used by Naroll. Using additional data, LeBlanc shows that the standard deviation of floor habitation areas of family units is large, undermining the reliability of determining population size from floor area.

The application of any formulae correlating habitation space of dwellings to population size should take into consideration the number of rooms or areas with functions other than habitation (see LeBlanc 1971), such as storage cells and kivas. Table 6.2 gives data for two houses inhabited by settled nomads in Upper Egypt, near Nagada.

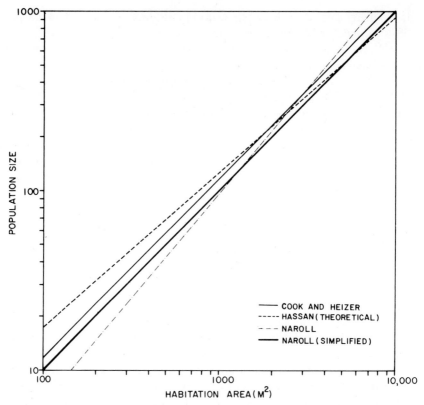

FIGURE 6.7. *Comparison of various models of the relationship between population size and habitation area.*

No more than 35% of the total dwelling space was used for human habitation, 54% was reserved for animals! Note that the formula gives $A = 3.5\ P^{1.17}$ for a family of 6–7 persons, a habitation area of 28–34 m². The total average area of the dwellings, 114 m², would indicate a household unit of about 20 persons, a highly inflated figure.)

Another major problem in estimating population size, especially when a site is occupied for a long time, is the ratio of the sites occupied to those that have been abandoned as a result of decay and collapse. In his study of Broken K Pueblo, Hill (1970) used a figure of 22% for the percentage of the site that consisted of abandoned rooms. The figure was based on ethnographic observations of modern pueblos in the U.S. Southwest.

Plog (1975), in order to determine the number of pueblo rooms occupied in the sites of the Upper Little Colorado, used the following relationship, which he obtained from ethnographic observations:

$$N = .1\ A + 4$$

TABLE 6.2
Dwelling Space of Two Households of Settled Bedouins, Nagada, Upper Egypt

	Dwelling area (m²)			
	House I	House II	Average	Percentage
Sheep, goat, and cattle enclosures	39	86	62	54
Storage	17	6	12	11
Habitation	45	35	40	35
Total	101	127	114	100

where N is the number of pueblo rooms and A is the area of the rubble mound in square meters.

To overcome the problem of changes in the number of rooms through time, Plog also estimated that 78% of the dwellings were occupied during the period of maximum occupancy. At 50-year intervals before and after the peak period of occupancy, the number of dwellings occupied is regarded as half that of the previous period. This approach is based on a logistic growth of sites and seems to be inspired by the logistic pattern of population growth. Initially, since the number of people is small, the increase in the number of rooms is small. As the population increases, more rooms will be required. Following the zenith of occupation, as population declines the number of rooms occupied declines. However, assuming that at peak occupation the number of occupied dwellings is 78% of the total number of dwellings, we would expect the ratio of abandoned rooms to occupied rooms to increase as population declines.

The change in the number of rooms at a site and the rate of abandonment may be examined as a function of population size and life span of a dwelling. For a constant population and a life span of 50 years for a dwelling, we obtain the relationship shown in Figure 6.8. If we start with 10 families, each living in a single dwelling, the 10 dwellings will be replaced every 50 years. After 350 years of occupation, the number of dwellings occupied represents about 11% of all the site dwellings that were ever constructed and may be uncovered by archaeological excavations or surveys (Figure 6.9). Thus, to use the total number of rooms without considering the duration of occupation and the rate of replacement of dwellings can lead to very misleading results.

When a population is changing in size through time as a result of population growth, decline, or migration, in addition to replacing collapsed houses, new dwellings must be added for new occupants. At times of population decline, the number of rooms replaced will be commensurate with that of the surviving number of families (Figure 6.10). The percentage of occupied dwellings of the cumulative number of dwellings through time shows a pattern similar to that of constant population (Figure 6.9). However, during a period of population increase the percentage of occupied houses is greater than it would be if the population was constant, and during periods of population decline, the percentage is lower.

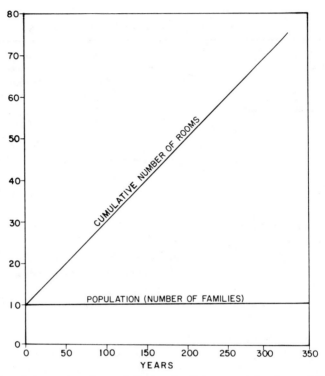

FIGURE 6.8. *Cumulative number of rooms built on a site. (It is assumed that the population remains constant and that rooms have a life span of 50 years.)*

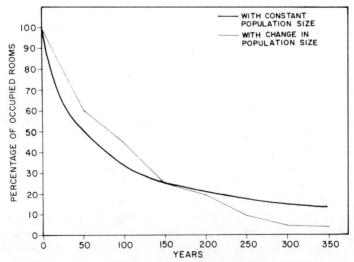

FIGURE 6.9. *Percentage of rooms actually occupied at any one time under conditions of both constant and changing population. This graph is derived from Figures 6.6 and 6.7.*

76

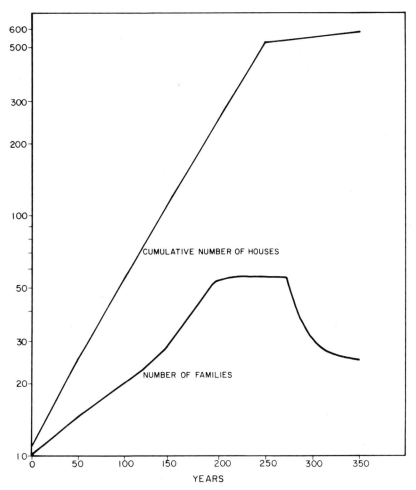

FIGURE 6.10. *Cumulative number of rooms built on a site assuming a changing population size and a 50-year life span for rooms.*

Determination of Population Size from Artifacts and Bioarchaeological Remains

The use of artifacts or food remains to determine population size rests, in most cases, on the assumption that the accumulation of food refuse or artifacts at a site is proportional to the number of persons and an average, constant rate of food consumption or artifact discarding per person.

In 1956, Schwartz used potsherds of the Cohonina, in the southwestern corner of the Colorado Plateau (northwestern Arizona), to estimate population size from the early 600s to about the 1200s A.D. The time range of each site, determined from painted pottery that had previously been dated by dendrochronology, was plotted as a bar on a graph. The bar graphs were then subdivided into 25-year intervals and the number of sites occupied during each interval. The number of sites was taken as a correlate of population. In this method, artifacts were used as time markers to determine the frequency of sites. One of the problems here lies in assuming that each site was occupied by the same number of people.

Artifacts

McMichael (1960) devised an index of relative population size. The index was estimated from the sum of the density of artifacts at a site (component or occurrence), weighted for temporal duration, and subdivided by the number of time units (1 unit = 250 years). McMichael himself noted methodological problems in estimating temporal duration and identifying separable cultural units. There is also the theoretical problem of assuming a constant rate of sherds discarded per person through time.

C. G. Turner and L. Lofgren (1966) used museum collections of ceramics to estimate family size. They first determined the volume of family cooking pots and then subdividing that volume by the volume of the eating bowls used by individuals, arriving at an estimate of 5.3 persons per family with a range of 4.5–7 persons. The number of cooking pots could then be used to determine the number of families. The number of persons per family seems close to that of ethnographic estimates, but we must take into consideration the reliability of determining the number of cooking pots at a site and the rate of pot replacement.

An interesting approach to estimating population size from potsherds, was taken by Cook (1972a), who used the turnover rate of pottery and the number of potsherds found at a site. Published data on the number of sherds at Pecos Pueblo, the George C. Davis site, Snake Town, and the S-U site were used.

In a more sophisticated study, Kohler (1978) employed ceramic-breakage rates in a simulation model to determine probable population size. The study was focused on the McKeithen site in northern Florida (A.D. 150 to A.D. 750). Samples from the site were used to estimate the total weight of ceramics at the site. The average vessel weight (900 gm) was obtained from whole vessels, and the number of vessels per household (30) was obtained from ethnographic sources. Breakage rates (.138 vessel/year for utilitarian vessels and .056 vessel/year for "elite" vessels) were determined by ethnographic analogy. Kohler used Naroll's formula to determine the number of persons per household and assumed that the sites were occupied continuously for 600 years. Simulations were run so that by the end of the runs the total weight of sherds at the site and the ratio of elite to utilitarian ceramics approximated that at the site. In one set of simulations, the population was held constant. In another set, the population was permitted to grow at a constant rate, and in yet another set it was made to increase, then decline. The results were interpreted by Kohler to indicate that the population was not in excess of 300–400 and was not less than 19. Despite this wide range, simulation provides an opportunity to experiment with the influence of variables that are likely to determine the total weight of sherds at a site. It thus promises to provide some understanding of the processes by which sherds are related to the number of persons at a site.

Food Remains

The estimation of group size from the quantity and kind of food remains at archaeological sites is based either on the nutritional value of the foods corresponding to the remains and the annual rate of dietary intake per person, or on the time, labor, and extractive strategy involved in procuring the foods represented by the remains (Ascher 1959; Clark 1954, 1972; Cook 1946; Evans and Renfrew 1968; Klein 1969; Meighan 1959; Müller-Beck 1961; Perkins and Daly 1968; Phillips 1972; Shawcross 1967; Wheat 1972).

The formula that expresses the first approach is

$$N = \left(\sum_{i=1}^{1-n} F_i \times \frac{D_1}{L} \right) / Y$$

where F_i is the amount of the ith food item; D_i is the nutritional content of the ith food item expressed in calories, grams of protein, and so forth; L is the annual rate of consumption of calories, grams of protein, and so forth per person; Y is the total period of occupation; and N is the local group size.

The problems involved in following this approach are as follows:

1. Certain food items, such as plant food remains, are rarely preserved.
2. Differential preservation of various food items makes it very difficult to assess the composition of the diet.
3. The amount of food remains at a site may not correspond to the actual amount of food consumed because certain items may be consumed outside the site area. Also, only a fraction of the food may have been brought to the site. The inhabitants may have discarded these food components that are most useful to us in determining the quantity of food, as in the preliminary processing of animal game and the disposal of skulls, long bones, and other weighty and nutritionally useless items.
4. The total period of occupation is in most cases very difficult to estimate. One needs to know the number of annual occupations and the number of days per year spent at the site.

Some of the problems may be skirted by using ethnographic analogs or by making rough estimates, but the risks involved must not be forgotten.

The study by Ascher (1959) is a good example of this approach. In that study, the goal was to determine the amount of protein contributed by mussels. This amount, divided by the number of years of site occupation, provides the total amount of protein from mussels consumed in a single year. Given the intake of protein from mussels per person per year, the number of site residents may be estimated. To obtain the amount of protein from mussels represented at a midden, Ascher determined the volume of the site, the proportion of mussel shells to other materials in the midden, the density of mussel shell, the weight of mussel meat per gram of mussel shell, and the weight of protein per gram of mussel meat.

Glassow (1967), in a thoughtful discussion of estimating population size through the analysis of prehistoric California middens, notes that to obtain reliable data on the variables utilized by Ascher a special research design must be employed. In such a design, palaeoenvironmental studies, microstratigraphic studies, morphometric studies, and probability sampling should be taken into consideration. A regional view rather than a site-specific orientation is emphasized by Glassow, since subsistence activities are not totally site-specific.

T. E. White (1953) made an attempt to compute the amount of meat intake per person from the quantity of bison bone remains at two sites in South Dakota. A similar approach was used by Müller-Beck (1961) and Phillips (1972:45–46). White made assumptions about the number of persons and the number of annual occupations, arriving at a figure of .2 lb/person/day. We know that the Plains Indians relied heavily on buffalo, so White's figure for consumption appears to be an underestimate. Wheat (1972) indicates that 3 lb/person among the Plains buffalo hunters is a conservative estimate. If we were to redo White's calculation using this figure with the aim of determining the population size, we would arrive at an estimate of 26.9 man-years from the following:

$$M = \frac{NW}{C}$$

$$= \frac{59 \times 500}{3 \times 365}$$

where M is the number of man-years, N is the number of bison, W is the amount of edible meat per bison in pounds, and C is the annual consumption of meat in pounds per person. White assumed that the occupation lasted for 20 years. This means that the site would have been occupied by an average of 1.4 persons! Even if we assume that the consumption rate was about 1 lb/day, we arrive at an estimate of 4 persons. Since the remains come from four houses, it appears either that the number of years of occupation assumed by White is much higher than the actual number, or that the number of bison is underestimated. If information had not been available on the number of houses, the existence of this problem would not have been as clear.

Estimation of population size may also be based on calorie or protein content and rates of consumption. For example, at 2500 cal and 180 gm of protein per kilogram of meat and a consumption rate of 8×10^5 cal and 18.25 kg of protein per person per year, the number of persons would be estimated as 2 using calories and 7 using protein. The discrepancies involved highlight the problem of determining which food provided what percentage of which nutrients. They also indicate the importance of determining the period of occupation.

Not knowing the period of occupation is the major weakness of this approach.

It is for this reason that in attempts where food remains, occupation, and group size are used to estimate the period of occupation a group size of 25–50 persons for hunter–gatherers is hypothesized. For example, R. Klein (1973) has used this method to estimate the duration of occupation at various Kostenki sites (Ukraine), where the remains of wooly mammoth, wooly rhinoceros, wild horse, wild deer, and the like are preserved (Table 6.3).

In the course of a study of the cultural ecology of an Epipalaeolithic Capsian population in Algeria (Lubell *et al.* 1976), it was possible to estimate the total period of occupation assuming a group size of 20 persons. The estimate was about 400 years. However, radiocarbon dating indicated that the site was occupied for 2000–3000 years. This implies that the site was not continuously occupied from year to year and that occupations were most probably limited to a certain part of the year. Other sources of information seem to substantiate this conclusion. It is thus

TABLE 6.3
Area of Some Upper Palaeolithic Sites in the Ukraine (U.S.S.R.)[a]

Site	Dimensions (m)	Area (m²)	Remarks
Berdyzh	9–10 × 3–4	52.2	Ring of mammoth bones around artifactural depression with artifacts and hearth
Dobranichevka	—		Four rings, each 4 × 4 m, site several hundred square meters
Eliseevichi	—	3–4	
	9.4 × 8.8	64.9	Depression with archaeological debris
Gontsy	6 × 4	18.8	Depression
Mezhirich	4–5 (diameter)	63.6	Mammoth bones and artifacts
Mezin			Five concentrations, each with a hearth (one concentration 6 m in diameter)
Radomyshl'	3–6 (diameter)		Six or more concentrations of this size
Yudinovo	7.5 (diameter)	44.2	Inner ring of mammoth skulls
	9.5 (diameter)	70.8	Outer ring of mammoth skulls
Pushkari	12 × 4	48	Quadrangular with three hearths and post-holes
Lipa I	3.6 × 3.65	10.3	One hearth
Avdeeve	500		Now represented by 500 m² of ochre-colored sandy silt with 15 large pits 4–8 m². Seven of the pits are believed to represent caches.
Molodova V, horizon 7	2.6 × 2.1	4.3	Dish-shaped depressions
	4 × 1.6	5	
Voronovitsa I-1	2.5 × 3.8	7.5	Oval depression

[a] Data from Klein 1973.

not sufficient to use the time span between the first and last occupations of the site when estimating group size by means of food remains. If we had relied on the time indicated by radiocarbon dating, we would have arrived at an underestimate of the number of inhabitants. Thus, even when radiocarbon dates are available, calculation of group size cannot be safely attempted without investigating the seasonality of occupation and the ratio of vacancy to occupancy. [For a case study of interpretation of seasonality and frequency of reoccupation, see Shawcross (1967).]

The second approach is based on estimates of the amount of labor involved in procuring food (Cook 1972b). For example, given a certain amount of mussels in a site and the amount of mussels likely to be collected per person per day, the group size can be estimated.

The determination of population size from food refuse, as in the examples mentioned, requires an understanding of the processes by which food refuse accumulates at a site. Factors to be considered include the ratio of foods consumed at a site to those consumed elsewhere; the impact of food preparation, processing, and storage on the mechanical diminution or obliteration of foodstuffs and the discard pattern of food remains; and the modification or destruction of food remains by such forces as scavengers, trodding, and decay, which reduces the original amount of the refuse. The research design and methods of analysis should allow an accurate determination of activity areas, site duration, and number of sites associated with a single group, and should provide adequate samples of food remains, using techniques such as microarchaeological analysis of sediments (Hassan 1978d). The samples should be representative of the whole site.

Ethnohistorical Estimates of Population Size

Ethnohistory consists of the use of primary documents such as library and archival material to gain knowledge of past cultures and the changes they might have undergone (Hickerson 1970:6). This approach to recent "prehistory" has been very fruitful for the study of the aboriginal populations of the Americas, who were observed and commented upon by travelers, missionaries, and traders. In 1910, Mooney compiled the first comprehensive account of the size of aboriginal American Indian populations at the time of European contact. Mooney also prepared material for an extensive study of the topic, which was edited posthumously by Swanton (Mooney 1928). Mooney's 1910 estimate for the total population of Indians in North America was 1,150,000 persons, revised to 1,152,050 persons in 1928. These estimates were adopted with some slight modifications by Rivet (1924), Wilcox (1931), Kroeber (1939), Rosenblat (1945), and Stewart (1973). The estimates range from 900,000 to 1,148,000 persons. Sapper (1924) estimated the carrying capacity of North America at 2–3.5 million persons. I have estimated an average of 1,120,000 persons, with a range of 470,000 to 2.1 million for North America under hunting–gathering conditions (see Chapter 12). A revision of

Mooney's estimate by Ubelacker (1976a, 1976b) provides an estimate of 2,171,125 persons. By contrast, Dobyns (1966), using a depopulation ratio from the point of the greatest decline of the population after contact, arrived at an estimate of 9.8 million.

Estimates for the total population of the Western Hemisphere show a much greater variability, ranging from 8.4 million by Kroeber (1939) to 100 million by Borah (1964). A bibliographic essay on native American populations by Dobyns (1976) may be consulted for additional information, and a forthcoming study by Ubelacker for the *Handbook on North American Indians* will be a welcome contribution to this controversial topic.

Estimates from Mortuary Data

Estimates of population size from burials have been attempted by Howells (1960) for Pecos Pueblo and the Late Archaic Indian Knoll site, by Jamieson (1971) for the Middle Woodland Albany mound group in Illinois, and by Asch (1976) for the middle Woodland population of the lower Illinois Valley. The method is based on determining the total number of years represented by the burials (Y) and the period of occupation (L). Assuming a state of no growth and no migration, as well as demographic stability, the population is estimated from Y/L. In the study by Asch, Y is estimated from the number of burial mounds (M), the mean size of mound group burial population (N), and the average age at death (A); the equation is $Y = M \times N \times A$. The problems inherent in this method are discussed by Asch (1976:19–20) and include undernumeration of certain age and sex classes, the destruction of mounds, assumptions of stability and lack of population increase or migrations. In a monograph-length treatment of the sources of data and attempts to guard against potential errors, Asch arrives at an estimate of less than 3000 persons (less than 2.6 persons/km²). The monograph should be consulted for the details of this method.

Applications in Prehistory

The empirical relationship obtained from the Bushmen camps ($P = 2.9359 A^{.037}$) can be applied to some cases in prehistory to provide some insight into the range of prehistoric group size. I should emphasize here that the figures obtained are only *suggestive* of the range of group size, since we have to assume a ring model of settlement, a similar habitation area per household, and a similar household size for those groups to which this formula may be applied. These assumptions have not been justified for most of the cases in which the formula has been applied.

An interesting application of the relationship between living space and group size was attempted by Isaac (1969:9) for the australopithecines at Flk I, Olduvai, where a central living area of 279 m² (3000 ft²) was exposed. By analogy with the !Kung Bushmen and the formula developed by Cook, Isaac suggests that the group that inhabited the site numbered between 10 and 20 persons. Using the formula $P = 2.9359 \, A^{.037}$ (which will be used from now on), I would estimate 24 persons. The figure matches the range for living hunter–gatherers and is very close to the magic number 25. We must, however, recall that interpersonal space relations, a major factor in space allocation in a site, might not have been the same for both the australopithecines and modern man.

For the site of Torralba in Spain, where a habitation floor of an Acheulian group was exposed, L. Freeman (1968:248) suggests that a figure of 25 persons is a "tentative estimate of the possible minimal number commensurate with the patterned distribution of material in that occupation." Another occupation of Acheulian man is known from Terra Amata on the French Riviera, where De Lumley (1969) uncovered several habitation floors with hearths 26–49 × 13–20 ft in area (about 45 m²). This space could have been inhabited by 12 persons or about three nuclear families. How many of these family groups resided together is not clear. In the Nile Valley, a Lower Palaeolithic site, Arkin 8 (Chmielewski 1968) covered an oval area 15–20 × 40 m (about 550 m²). The site consisted of eight separate occupations 6–8 m in diameter (about 38.5 m² average). On the basis of the overall area of the site, we arrive at an estimate of about 31 persons. If, on the other hand, we estimate the population size on the basis of the eight individual concentrations, each occupied by a single family of about 3.66 persons, using the average size of the social unit among the Bushmen, we obtain a figure of 29 persons. The match between the two figures is remarkable.

If the eight concentrations at Arkin 8 represent the remains of simultaneous habitation by cognate groups, it would indicate that congregations of eight nuclear families were not unknown during the Lower Palaeolithic. We may recall here that Freeman emphasized that his estimate of 25 persons was a *minimal* estimate.

Known Middle Palaeolithic Mousterian settlements in southwestern France consist of caves and rockshelters that rarely exceed 20–25 m in diameter (Mellars 1972). These would accommodate about 25 persons. In the Nile Valley, several sites are about 200 m² in areal extent (Marks 1968). Included are sites 1000, 36B, 1036, and 1038. At site 1000, although the major concentration covers 200 m², the site covers an area of about 1000 m² presumably because of deflation. The areas of these sites suggest a group size of about 21 persons.

Mellars (1972) has collected information on the dimensions of several Upper Palaeolithic sites in southwestern France. The areas of these sites, based on the dimensions given by Mellars, and the inferred probable population sizes are given in Table 6.4. A group size of about 21–31 persons, with an average of about 27 persons, is suggested for most of these sites.

Upper Palaeolithic sites from the Ukraine (Klein 1973) provide a unique opportunity for estimating population size, since many of the sites contain the remains of house foundations represented by rings of mammoth bones surrounding artificially

TABLE 6.4
Area and Probable Population Size of Some Upper Palaeolithic Settlements in Southwestern France[a]

Site	Area (m²)	Probable population size
La Quina		
(Aurignacian)	408	27
Laussel		
(Aurignacian)	471	29
Abri Pataud		
(Aurignacian to Upper Perigordian)	393	27
Laussel		
(Upper Perigordian)	565	31
Les Vachonsq		
(Upper Perigordian)	196	21

[a]Data from Mellars 1972.

dug depressions. The dimensions and structural features at some of these sites, as given by Klein (1973), are listed in Table 6.5. Among the Bushmen, a single residential unit (3.66 persons) inhabits an area of 13.33 m², that is, 3.64 m²/person. Using this relationship and the formula used earlier, it appears that in six cases the houses contained 12–14 persons. In two or three cases the habitation areas correspond to a single family unit. In three cases the habitation area does not seem to have accommodated more than 1–3 persons.

Since the sites belong to different "cultural" groups (Klein 1973), the differences may reflect culturally dictated preferences. At Avdeeve, where seven large

TABLE 6.5
Estimates of the Population Size of Some Upper Palaeolithic Settlements in the Ukraine (U.S.S.R.)[a]

Site	Area (m²)	Number of areas	Population size
Molodova V	4.3	1	1
Voronovitsa	7.5	1	2
Lipa I	10.3	1	2
Dobranichevka	12.6	4	4
Radomyshl'	7–28	6	2–8
Avedeeve	12.6–50	7	4–13
Gontsy	18.8	1	5
Yudinovo	44.2	1	12
Pushkari	48.0	1	12
Berdyzh	52.2	1	13
Mezihirich	63.6	1	14
Eliseevichi	64.9	1	14

[a]Original data on site area from Klein 1973.

depressions, believed to be sleeping chambers, were found, an area of 500 m²
demarcates the extent of the site, which could have accommodated about 27 persons. The original area of the site, however, could have been larger. In this case,
there would be some disparity between the two estimates.

The remains of two Middle Palaeolithic huts are also known from the Ukraine
(Klein 1973). At Molodova I, horizon 4, an oval arrangement of mammoth bones
encloses an area of 31.2 m². At Molodova V, horizon 11, a rough arc of mammoth
bones encloses an inner area of 49.5 m². These two areas suggest a population of
11–13 persons, which is within the range of some of the Upper Palaeolithic sites, as
shown earlier.

The estimates of the number of inhabitants of Lower, Middle, and Upper
Palaeolithic sites presented so far suggest that the local group size of prehistoric
hunter–gatherers of the Pleistocene was probably within the range of living hunter-
gatherers. The areas of some Upper Palaeolithic sites and many Final Palaeolithic,
Mesolithic, and Epipalaeolithic sites, however, pose some problems.

In southwestern France, Laugerie Haute (Solutrean–Magdalenian) and La
Madeleine (Magdalenian) are each about 5000 m² in area. The area of the Solvieux
site (Magdalenian) is 10,000 m² (Mellars 1972). In the Nile Valley, two sites
associated with the Khormusan industry (ca. 25,000–16,000 B.C.) measure about
7000 and 9000 m² (Marks 1968). Two sites associated with the Isnan industry (ca.
12,000–10,000 B.C.) measure 11,300 and 15,386 m². Several other sites associated
with various industries between 16,000 and 12,000 B.C., are more than 2000 m² in
area. In the Levant, several Natufian sites are in excess of 1000 m² and in the
Northwest European Plain, some Mesolithic sites are 5000–5500 m² in area.

If we apply the rules of population size estimation from site area without any
qualifications, we will obtain figures of population size in the range of scores or
hundreds and in some cases more than 1000 persons. Obviously, these figures are
unacceptable. To gain an understanding of the factors that undermine the estimates,
I will consider in some detail the relationship of the large sites to other sites in the
region in which they are located.

The Nile Valley has been the subject of numerous intensive archaeological
surveys, mainly by teams headed by F. Wendorf (see Wendorf 1968; Wendorf et al.
1970; Wendorf and Schild 1976). The surveys provide adequate information on the
size and the archaeological contents of more than 60 sites from ca. 25,000 to 12,000
B.C. Most of the sites are from ca. 16,000 to 12,000 B.C. Table 6.6 gives information on sites associated with the various Final Palaeolithic Nilotic industries, including their dimensions.

Sixteen of the Terminal Palaeolithic sites are less than 114 m², 11 sites are
between 157 and 314 m², and 7 sites are between 400 and 589 m². Thirty-four sites
are less than 589 m². Using our formula ($P = 2.9359 \, A^{.37}$), we may infer that many
sites—about 65%—were inhabited by groups of between 9 and 29 persons (Table
6.7). The population of the additional 35% is difficult to evaluate. It is, however,
doubtful that Wiessner's rule is applicable beyond 50 persons and it is highly
probable that the site areas of these very large sites represent not single occupations

TABLE 6.6

Area and Dimensions of Terminal Palaeolithic Sites in Egypt[a,b]

Site	Dimensions (m)	Area (m²)	Remarks
Halfan			
1020	40 × 50	1570	Deflated
1018		20	
624	25 × 18	450	Dense concentration Deflated area
443		250	
2014		15	
1028		160	
Idufan			
E71P1	110 × 58	4836	
E71P2	25 × 30	589	
E71P6	20 × 10	157	
E71P7A	12 × 12	450	
E71P7B	18 × 14	200	
E71P7C	10 × 6	47	
E71K9	120 × 30	2826	Dense
E71K9x	15 × 25	295	Dense
Fakhurian			
K1-K5	30 × 30	700	
Ballanan			
8956	30 × 40	940	
8957	5 × 5	20	
8863	8 × 20	160	
Affian			
E71K18	15 × 15	176	One of five concentrations
E71K6A	20 × 20	314	
E71K6B	45 × 60	2120	
E71K6C, Area 1	18 × 6	114	
E71K6C, Area 2	6 × 7	35	
E71K6D	35 × 40	1099	Deflated
Unit D			
K13	60 × 65	3000	
Unit E			
K12	60 × 60	2835	
Gemaian			
278	50 × 300	11,775	
2009	25 × 25	490	
1025	50 × 30	942	
1026	25 × 10	196	
412	10 × 10	78.5	
Sebilian			
1024A		60	
1024C		70	
2013		60	
83		200	

TABLE 6.6 (*continued*)

Site	Dimensions (m)	Area (m²)	Remarks
2010A		300	
2010B		400	
1042		5000	Deflated
8899B		66	Area excavated
8888A		22	
8898	20 × 20	314	
8866A	40 × 40	1256	
8888		100	
E61M1A		110	
E61M1B		75	
Isnan			
K14	140 × 140	15386	Site consists of three dense occupations
K15	40 × 40	1256	
E61M2		534	
E61M3A–B		706	
E61M3C		157	
E61M5A		177	
E61M5B		177	
E61M6		1256	
E61M7		706	
E61M8		1256	
E61M9		11,300	
E61M10		1236	
Qadan			
1046	3–5 × 20	62.5	
609	350 × 400	109,900	Entirely deflated
2012	55 × 20	863.5	
1023	25 × 25	490	

[a] Data from Wendorf 1968; Wendorf and Schild 1976.
[b] Blank space indicates missing data.

but rather numerous overlapping occupations with considerable lateral shift through time.

Let us now consider the situation in a different area, where a detailed study of Mesolithic sites has been attempted by Newell (1973). The area is the Northwest European Plain. According to Newell, 44 sites were classified into four types on the basis of statistically significant differences in their dimensions. In addition, by investigating the total number of flint tools, tool density, and intersite variability in functional tool classes (Table 6.8), Newell was able to conclude that these four dimensional types are different residential units. The first type (A) is the most common, consisting of 22 sites or 50% of all sites, and has an average area of about 400 m². The area covered by the second and third types (B and C) measures about 27 and 6 m², respectively. In contrast, the fourth type (D) covers an area in excess of 2000 m² on the average.

TABLE 6.7
Estimates of Probable Population Size of Terminal Palaeolithic Settlements in Egypt[a]

Site area (m²)		Number	Probable population
Range	Mean	of sites	size[b]
15–35	22.4	5	9.3
47–114	72.4	11	14.3
157–176	166.0	5	19.5
196–314	250.0	6	22.6
400–589	486.1	7	29.0
700–863.5	743.8	4	
900–942	941.0	2	
1236–1256	1252.0	5	
	2120.0	1	
2826–3000	2887.0	3	
	4836.0	1	
	11,775.0	1	
	15,386.0	1	

[a] See Table 6.6 for source of data.
[b] Based on average site area.

Newell suggests that the Type A site is a "maintenance camp." All functional tool classes are present, and intersite variability in the frequency of these classes is minimal. On the basis of Naroll's figure of 10 m²/person, Newell suggests that the camps were occupied by bands of 15–50 persons (about 28 persons if $P = 2.9379 A^{.37}$). The smaller sites (B and C), situated within the same spatial zone are considered ancillary, subordinate extraction camps. Newell notes that the intersite variability in the frequency of functional tool classes, in variance with that of Type A sites, is great. According to Newell, this reflects a wide divergence in the function

TABLE 6.8
Characteristics of Mesolithic Sites from Northwest Europe[a]

Site type	Average dimensions (m)	Site shape	Average number of tools	Functional tool classes	Average tool density/m²
A	24.2 × 19.4	Trapezoidal	243.3	All present; inter-site uniformity.	.6
B	8.3 × 4.2	Oval	37.0	Great intersite variability in	1.4
C	3.4 × 2.4	Rounded	18.3	presence and frequency.	2.8
D	78 × 35	Elliptical	5000–5500[b]		2.3

[a] Data from Newell 1973.
[b] Predicted range.

and range of activities performed at these sites, suggesting that the small sites represent single activities. Although Newell's suggestions would have been tremendously strengthened by evidence for variations in the food remains in these sites, such remains are unfortunately lacking. Type A settlements definitely appear to be base-camp settlements. The smaller sites, however, may represent either ancillary base camps or small seasonal encampments by one or two families. The smallest sites (Type C) occur as single, double, and treble concentrations. The great variations in the frequency of functional tool classes could be, as Newell contends, connected with different seasonal activities or specialized food-getting activities, but the small numbers of tools retrieved from these sites—37 tools for Type B sites and 18.3 for Type C sites on the average—should not be overlooked. Tremendous random variability is inevitable in the case of such small samples.

The fourth type (D) is of later chronological age. It belongs to the De Leien-Wertena Complex. Newell provides no clues to the probable size of the population of the large sites of this type (5000–5500 m²). He notes, however, that unlike earlier sites, which are associated with small ponds, bogs, kettle holes, pingos, and the like, the De Leien–Wertena sites are concentrated along river systems or around open bodies of water. The number of inhabitants could not have exceeded 50–100. A change in the residential pattern concomitant with a change in subsistence strategy is not unlikely. The repeated occupation of a favored locality for long periods is perhaps responsible for the enlargement of the site area.

The two cases of the Nile Valley and the Northwest European Plain during the Final Palaeolithic and Mesolithic may be contrasted with the case of the Levantine Epipalaeolithic. The Levant is one of the areas where the first steps toward agriculture were undertaken at an early date. Prior to the emergence of Neolithic villages, sites associated with a lithic industry called the Natufian show evidence of permanent residential structures, including houses, storage pits, and nonportable food-processing equipment. The Natufian most probably was associated with a semisedentary residential pattern and an economy based on the exploitation of a variety of resources, including wild cereals. The Natufian was preceded by the Kebaran complex, which was associated with hunting and gathering. Wild cereals were apparently first exploited in association with that complex. The areas of Kebaran sites (Table 6.9), with the exception of one site, are small, and applying the formula $P = 2.9379\ A^{.37}$ results in an estimated group size of 10–27, with an average of 22. Although many small sites are associated with the Natufian (Table 6.9), some of the sites are more than 1000 m². Fortunately, information is available on the number of huts included in two of these sites. At Eynan, 50 huts were presumably in use (Flannery 1972). The huts belong to two categories, one about 5–7 m² in area and the second about 20–28 m². At Nahal Oren, 13 huts ranging in size from 4 to 15 m² are recorded; most are 6–9 m² in area.

We may estimate population size by multiplying the number of huts by the average number of inhabitants. The number of persons per hut ranges from 1 to 5, and we assume about 2.32 m²/person; given the small size of the huts, we may assume an average of 3 persons/hut. If this were the case at Eynan, the figure

TABLE 6.9

Area and Probable Population Size of Epipalaeolithic Settlements from the Near East[a]

Sites	Area (m²)	Probable population size
Kebaran		
Ksar Akil		16–19
Jaita II		27
Hayonim		10
Irq Barud		
Kebara		21
Ein Gev		19
Kefr Darow		21
El Khiam		48
Ramat		
Matred		13–16
Natufian		
Eynan	>2000	
El-Wad B1	>250	>23
El-Wad B2	>350	>26
Hayonim Cave	?	
Hayonim Terrace	>1000	
Kebara B	>200	>21
Nahal Oren	>1000	
Abu Usba	>140	>18
Shubkah B	>1000	
Erq el Ahmar A2	>50	>13
Oumm ez-Zeoueitina	<50	<13
Tor Abu Sif	<50	<13
Ain Sakhri	<50	<13
Rosh Zin	>800	>35
Rosh Horshea	>7000	
Ala Safat	<50	<13

[a]Data on area from Bar-Yosef 1970 and D. O. Henry 1973.

obtained is 150 persons. The major problem with these estimates, however, is that we do not know how many huts were inhabited at any one time. The number of huts at Nahal Oren is much smaller and the area of the site is about 500 m². Using the area of the site, a population of about 27 may be inferred. Using the number of huts and assuming 3 inhabitants per hut, we get an estimate of 35–65 persons, or an average of 39 persons. Again, it is not known how many of the 13 sites were inhabited at any one time. Thus, the estimate given is a maximum one. Estimates of population based on the area of sites less than 500 m² indicate that the population might have ranged from <13 to >26. Settlements more than 500 m² in area may reflect large residential groups with lateral site growth.

The appearance of large sites in considerable numbers by the end of the Palaeolithic period may be the result of two contrasting residential patterns: mobility within a limited territory, or fixed settlements with lateral growth. The first pattern is illustrated by the Natufian settlements, whereas the second is illustrated by the large settlements in the Nile Valley. The changes were probably tied in with the changes in subsistence strategies that emerged by the end of the Palaeolithic.

The first type of pattern, which we may call *tethered mobility,* was present before the end of the Palaeolithic. However, it differs from mobility without more or less fixed territorial boundaries. Territory-bound communities were perhaps more common by the end of the Palaeolithic because of the considerable increase in population density. The limitations against free territorial mobility would have led to greater reoccupation of favored places.

Under a residential pattern of tethered mobility, where favorable camping grounds are abundant we would expect the same spot to have a lower chance of being reoccupied than if favorable camping localities were scarce. Also, if the chances for lateral movement of the camp are obstructed, it is likely that the camps would be reestablished more or less on the same spot previously occupied. If, on the other hand, the later relocation of a camp is not obstructed, the location of the camp will shift considerably through time in a lateral direction.

Overview

Reliable estimates of archaeological populations demand a careful consideration of both field procedures and the theoretical basis of assumptions made in converting archaeological data into population figures. The point that should be stressed here is that collecting archaeological data for the purpose of generating population estimates must be based on a clear understanding of the method to be used in arriving at the estimate.

In addition, the empirical relationship derived from ethnographic contexts should not be applied blindly. The limitation of ethnographic analogy must be very carefully evaluated and the behavioral factors responsible for the empirical relationships must be elucidated.

The area of archaeological sites during the Palaeolithic was small and the residential population units these sites accommodated was perhaps comparable to that of contemporary small bands of hunter–gatherers. Application of a formula based on a theoretical model of site spatial arrangement and an empirical relationship between site area and group size for the !Kung Bushmen indicates that the residential population units were in most cases between 11 and 31 persons, with an average of 22 persons (3 persons short of the magic 25!). During the Mesolithic/ Epipalaeolithic period large sites emerge, reflecting a change in settlement strategy that might have been associated with socioeconomic changes. The smaller sites of that period, however, reflect an average of about 23 persons. The population size of the larger sites is difficult to determine, but at least in one case the population could have been as large as 150 (Table 6.10).

TABLE 6.10

Average Population Size of Basal Pleistocene to Early Farming Settlements[a]

Period	Approximate average number of persons
Basal Pleistocene	
FlK I, Olduvai	24
Lower Paleolithic	
Torralba, Spain	25
Terra Amata, France	12
Arkin 8, Egypt	29–31
Middle Palaeolithic	
Southwestern France	25
Egypt	21
Molodova I, Ukraine	11–13
Upper Palaeolithic	
Southwestern France	21–31
Ukraine	1–8, 12–14, 27
Mesolithic/Epipalaeolithic	
Nile Valley, small sites	9–39 (19)
Northwest Europe, small sites	28
Kebaran	10–48 (22)
Natufian	
Small sites	<13->26
Large sites	≤150
Early Farming	
Mesoamerica	
Ixtapalapa, Valley of Mexico	
1150–650 B.C.	80 min, 200 max
850–550 B.C.	114 min, 285 max
Texcoco, Valley of Mexico	
850–550 B.C.	
Hamlets	10 min, 53 max
Nucleated center	600 min, 1200 max
Valley of Oaxaca	
1300–1150 B.C.	30–150
1000–850 B.C.	
Hamlets–villages	15–50
Nucleated center	400–600
600 B.C.	
Hamlets–villages	48–55
Guatemala, Pacific coast	
1350–850 B.C.	ca. 28 min, ca. 55 max
850–500 B.C.	50–60

[a] Data from Marcus 1976; Isaac 1969: Tables 9, 11, 13, 15; L. Freeman 1968; and Chmielewski 1968.

7

Prehistoric Mortality: The Palaeodemographic Approach

Utnapishtim said, "There is no permanence.... From the days of old there is no permanence." *

The aims of palaeodemography consist primarily of determining estimates of vital statistics from "populations" of skeletal remains. The statistics often include age at death, life expectancy, survivorship, probability of death at successive years, and death rates. Because of the nature of the material the focus is primarily on mortality statistics. However, given certain assumptions, inferences can be made on birth rates, population growth rates, and population size. Two major problems are often encountered in palaeodemographic analysis. These are problems of sampling and sex and age estimation. I will briefly discuss these here. [For additional material see Palkovich (1978) and Ubelacker (1978).]

Census and historical data, which serve as the basis for arriving at the vital statistics of contemporary and historic populations, are, of course, not available for prehistoric groups. The methodology developed to deal with prehistoric populations is therefore, by necessity, different from that employed in the study of contemporary and historic groups. The term *palaeodemography* is generally used to refer to the study of prehistoric and protohistoric populations through the examination of skeletal remains (Acsádi and Nemeskéri 1957; Angel 1969a; Brothwell 1971).

The nature of the evidence used to obtain the vital statistics for the dead precludes the attainment of the degree of reliability and accuracy possible for living populations. Unfortunately, it is seldom possible to obtain a representative group or

*N. K. Sanders, *The epic of Gilgamesh*, Penguin, Harmondsworth, England, 1960, p. 104.

series of skeletons for a given population. This problem is especially serious in studies of prehistoric hunter–gatherers, who used graveyards only occasionally, during the Final Palaeolithic and the Mesolithic. Consequently, the number of skeletal remains in most cases is pitifully small. An Epipalaeolithic series of 186 individuals from Taforalt (Morocco), for example, is rare occurrence for hunter-gatherers. A series or collection of skeletal remains, in addition, may not be truly representative of the age and sex structure of the population. Dead infants and juveniles may not be disposed of in the same fashion as adults. Likewise, females may not be interred in the same manner as males. Differential preservation according to the age of persons interred may also lead to an underrepresentation of the youngest and oldest individuals (Vallois 1960:186). In addition, the data collector may ignore certain badly preserved or fragmented remains, which might nevertheless be valuable for paleodemographic analysis. Differential burial practices on the basis of social status are not likely to be significant among hunter–gatherers, since differences in status are generally minimal, but they must be taken into consideration for urban populations.

Another problem that besets paleodemographic analysis is related to the analytical methodology of age and sex determination. For example, the error in determining the age of adults, especially old adults, is greater than that for children. Inversely, the error in sex determination is greater for children. For both age and sex determination, the nature of the material available influences the accuracy of the determinations (Acsádi and Nemeskéri 1970, 1974; Brothwell 1971; Genovés 1969a, 1969b; Howells 1960; Lovejoy 1971; Massat 1971, 1973; Ward and Weiss 1976; Weiss 1972b).

However, it would be unfair to dwell on the difficulties involved in palaeodemographic analysis, for it is our only means of developing some understanding of the vital statistics of prehistoric populations. Age estimates on skeletal material can be, in fact, as accurate as those obtained from interviewing living individuals of nonliterate societies (Spuhler 1959). Intrinsic sampling problems cannot be overriden, but sampling and analytical methods can be improved, and it is to these two areas that we should look with optimism for future progress in palaeodemography. We should also be hopeful about improvements in data processing and analysis. The statistical treatment used in the analysis of data on contemporary populations cannot be applied to palaeodemographic data without major modifications. A different set of indices and parameters may be perhaps required to remedy the inadequacies of the palaeodemographic record.

In palaeodemographic analysis the first step consists of the determination of the age and sex of the individuals buried at the site. An average age at death may then be determined and some aspects of the population structure, such as the ratio of males to females or the frequency of old adults, may be examined (Howells 1960; Vallois 1960).

A more sophisticated approach uses the *life table,* which represents the mortality history from birth to death of a *cohort,* a group of people born at the same time (Acsádi and Nemeskéri 1970; Weiss 1972a). From the life table, the life expectancy at various ages can be determined. Other vital statistics can also be generated from the life tables.

In this chapter, the determination of the average age at death of prehistoric populations from the australopithecines to the Upper Palaeolithic *Homo sapiens sapiens* will be reviewed. This will be followed by a discussion of life tables and their application to the study of prehistoric populations. I hope this organization does not pose any difficulties to the reader. The use of life tables, however, is relatively new in this field and the discussion follows the historical developments, by presenting first palaeodemographic data in the framework of traditional approaches to palaeodemography, and then the life table approach and its application. The reader interested in the methods of palaeodemography may skip to the section on life tables before reading the following sections on the traditional approaches to estimating average age at death for prehistoric populations.

Basal Palaeolithic Populations (Australopithecines)

Palaeodemographic analysis of the earliest hominid groups has been attempted by Mann (1974, 1975) and McKinley (1971). The most ancient populations are represented only by incomplete skeletons. Complete skulls and long bones are rare. Isolated teeth, especially molars, are the single most numerous category of specimens. The remains from South Africa were embedded in a hard matrix of breccia, and the probability that skeletal remains were fragmented prior to or during excavation was high enough to induce Mann to estimate a minimum number of individuals using the frequency of particular characters (e.g., left lower molar) and the matching of single fossil pieces.

Mann (1975) has concluded, on the basis of an examination of tooth eruption, that the processes of dental and skeletal maturation in the australopithecines were comparable to those of *Homo sapiens*. Thus he was able to employ the modern human eruption schedule for age determination. According to Mann, the average age at death, as indicated by the two largest samples, Swartkrans ($N = 111$) and Sterkfontein ($N = 42$), was 17.2 years and 22.2 years, respectively. McKinley (1971) has employed the data presented by Mann for the South African and the much smaller samples of East African australopithecines to arrive at an average age at death of 19.8 years. Children (1–5 years of age) are underrepresented in the Swartkrans sample. Likewise, old adults (36 years and older) are only represented by 1%, which might be due to differential preservation, considering the remote age of these specimens. However, this age-group is represented by 7% at Sterkfontein (Table 7.1).

It is noteworthy that the Swartkrans sample belongs to *A. robustus,* whereas the Sterkfontein specimens belong to *A. africanus.* The difference in average age at death does not seem to be intrinsic, as individuals below 5 years of age are underrepresented at Swartkrans. If we calculate the average age at death for adults at

TABLE 7.1

Age Distribution of Australopithecine Specimens from Five South African Sites[a]

Age-group (years)	Swartkrans		Kromdraai		Taung		Makapansgat		Sterkfontein		Sterkfontein extension		Totals	
	Number	Percentage	Number	Percentage	Number	Percentage	Number	Percentage	Number	Percentage	Number	Percentage	Number	Percentage
1–5	8	7	2	33	—	—	1	8	1	2	—	—	12	7
6–10	23	21	2	33	1	100	1	8	7	17	1	100	35	20
11–15	22	20	—	—	—	—	1	8	1	2	—	—	24	14
16–20	20	18	2	33	—	—	1	8	7	17	—	—	30	17
21–25	16	14	—	—	—	—	2	17	9	21	—	—	27	16
26–30	10	9	—	—	—	—	4	33	5	12	—	—	19	11
31–35	11	10	—	—	—	—	2	17	9	21	—	—	22	13
36–40	1	1	—	—	—	—	—	—	3	7	—	—	4	2
Totals	111		6		1		12		42		1		173	

[a]Data from Mann 1975.

Sterkfontein ($N = 26$), we arrive at a figure of 27.1 years, compared with 28.2 years for Swartkrans. However, old adults seem to be underrepresented at Swartkrans, and the sample sizes for adults in both cases are very small. McKinley (1971) provides estimates of average age at death of 22.9 years for *A. africanus* and 19.8 years for *A. robustus*. The estimates include individual specimens from East African sites and very small samples from South Africa. Thus, according to McKinley (1971), the difference in average age at death, though statistically significant, may not reflect an actual demographic difference.

Although it is very likely that sexual dimorphism was marked among the australopithecines, there is as yet no acceptable methodology for differentiating the sexes on the basis of available material. Differences in size of canines and wear patterns might provide information on sexual differences (Mann 1974).

Lower Palaeolithic Populations (*Homo erectus*)

Palaeodemographic information on *Homo erectus* is available through the work of Weidenreich (1943, 1951) on the Choukoutien and Ngandong specimens (Table 7.2). Unfortunately, the data are too scant for a reliable estimate of the average age at death. Juveniles seem to be underrepresented at Ngandong but overrepresented at Choukoutien. Excluding the youngest age-group (<15 years) an estimate of 34.5 and 39 years as average age at death for adults is obtained for Choukoutien and Ngandong[1] specimens respectively. This should be regarded as a *very* rough estimate, given that the sample size was only 7 for the former and 10 for the latter. For both series combined, the average age at death for adults older than 15 years is 37.2 years. For all combined age-groups the average age at death is 22.8 years.

It should be noted here that age determinations for *Homo erectus* were based on the closure of cranial sutures. Acsádi and Nemeskéri (1970:143) have found out, as a result of their study of the Ngandong specimens, that the order of surface closure in Ngandong man was the same as in modern man. They suggest that the process of suture closure might have slowed down in the course of evolution as a result of the thinning of the cranial wall. The difference, however, is not sufficient to undermine the age determinations by Weidenreich (1943), who made his estimates on the assumption that cranial sutures of ancient man closed at an earlier age than those of modern man.

Regardless of the problems involved in estimating the average age at death of *Homo erectus* it is almost certain that the life span (i.e., maximum potential length of life) of this ancient man reached 60–70 years (Acsádi and Nemeskéri 1970:146). The probable ages of the Ngandong specimens as recorded by Acsádi and Nemes-

---

[1]On the basis of probable age at death as calculated by Acsádi and Nemeskéri (1970) the average age at death for adults older than 15 years is 37.3–48.5 years.

TABLE 7.2
Age Distribution of Specimens from Choukoutien and Ngandong[a]

	Choukoutien		Ngandong		Total	
Age-group (years)	Number	Percentage	Number	Percentage	Number	Percentage
0-14 (child)	15	68.2	1	9.1	16	48.4
15-30 (adolescent)	3	13.6	4	36.3	7	21.2
30-50 (young adult)	3	13.6	2	18.2	5	15.2
50-60 (old adult)	1	4.6	4	36.4	5	15.2
Total	22	100.0	11	100.0	33	100.0

[a] Data from Weidenreich 1943 and 1951.

kéri are shown in Table 7.3. Additional data on probable age at death of *Homo erectus* are available on the Sangiran II find (40–80 years or within a narrower range of 56–65 years) and a child and a young adult aged not more than 30 years from Vértesszöllös, Hungary (Acsádi and Nemeskéri 1970:147, 181).

Middle Palaeolithic Populations (*Homo sapiens neanderthalensis*)

The Neanderthal man attained old age as it is known today. Male remains from the Neanderthal site belonged to an individual who died at 57–61 years of age (Acsádi and Nemeskéri 1970:148). Several individuals died between the ages of 40 and 50 years (Table 7.4). The group of finds reported by Vallois (1960) includes 39

TABLE 7.3
Age of Ngandong Specimens

Probable age (years)	Sex
.5-1.5	Male
18-25	Male (?)
20-25	Female
23-39	Male (?)
30-39	Female
35-65	Male (?)
40-49	Female
45-54	Male (?)
50-59	Female
54-63	Female
58-67	Male

TABLE 7.4
Age and Sex Distribution of Neanderthal Specimens[a]

Age-group (years)	Number	Percentage	Number of adult males	Number of adult females
0–11	15	38.5	—	—
12–20	4	10.3	—	—
21–30	6	15.4	1	5
31–40	10	25.6	—	—
41–50	3	7.7	11	3
51–60	1	2.5	—	—
Total	39	100.0	12	8

[a] Data from Vallois 1960.

specimens from Neanderthal, Spy, Banolas, Ehringsdorf, Engis, Gibraltar, La Ferrassie, La Quina, Pech de l'Aze, Spika, La Naulette, Le Moustier, Malarnaud, Galilee, Saccopastore, and La Chapelle-aux-Saints. Additional finds from Hungary include a female, 40–45 years old, and a child, 3–7 years old. The average age at death of all the specimens in Vallois' list amounts to 21 years. For adults older than 20 years, the average age at death is about 34.5 years. Thirty-three years is the average age at death for specimens older than 15 years.

Upper Palaeolithic Populations (*Homo sapiens sapiens*)

The frequencies of age-groups of Upper Palaeolithic modern man are not much different from those of Middle Palaeolithic Neanderthal man (Table 7.5). The specimens come from many sites. Their average age at death is 20 years. For adults older than 20 years, the average age at death is about 34 years. The average age of death for individuals older than 15 years is 31 years.

TABLE 7.5
Age and Sex Distribution of Upper Palaeolithic Specimens[a]

Age-group (years)	Number	Percentage	Adult males	Adult females
0–11	29	38.2	—	—
12–20	12	15.7	—	—
21–30	15	19.7	5	10
31–40	11	14.5	—	—
41–50	7	9.2	15	5
51–60	2	2.6	—	—
Total	76	99.9	20	15

[a] Data from Vallois 1960, recalculated.

Birdsell (1972:342–343) has noted that females are more commonly represented than males between the ages of 21 and 30. Among the Neanderthals in this age group there are 5 females and 1 male. In the Upper Palaeolithic cases 10 females and 5 males are represented in that age-group. If this is not an accident of burial practices, discovery, or methodology, it may indicate, as Birdsell has further noted, that women died more than males during that age period, perhaps as a result of the hazards of childbirth. The difference in mortality between adult males and females is clearly suggested by a higher average age at death of adult males (33.3 years) than females (28.7 years) during the Upper Palaeolithic and later periods (Angel 1972:95), and does seem to suggest a real difference between the mortality of adult males and adult females.

Neolithic and Post-Neolithic Populations

One of the best series from a Neolithic context is of 268 dated skeletons from Catal Hüyük (Angel 1971). The series dates to ca. 6200–5830 B.C. Average adult age at death is estimated as 34.3 years for males and 29.8 years for females. Another skeletal series, from the site of Nea Nikomedia, also analyzed by Angel (1971), reveals adult age at death of 31 years for males and 30 years for females.

The palaeodemographic data also reveal an excess of females over males. The adult sex ratio is 66. In contrast, the child sex ratio is 178, with an excess of male children. The excess of male children may be a result of difficulty in determining the sex of children and perhaps a cultural preference for burying boys.

The greater frequency of adult females relative to males might be in part a result of the hazards of childbirth, as mentioned earlier. There is also a deficiency in the number of newborn infants, which might have resulted from cultural preferences.

A synthesis of the palaeodemographic data on Neolithic populations for the eastern Mediterranean by Angel (1972, 1975) indicates that the average age at death during the early Neolithic (samples from Macedonia and the Konya Plain) is 33.6 years for adult males and 29.8 for females. During the late Neolithic (samples from Macedonia, Leukas, and Acarnania, the average age at death, for adult males is 33.9 years and 28.6 for females (adults include those 15 years and older). During the Bronze Age and early Iron Age in the eastern Mediterranean, an increase in average age at death is found (Table 7.6; see Angel 1972, 1975).

It is interesting to note that during a period of about 8000 years, people gained about 6 years at the most. Only during the last few centuries has longevity increased, becoming almost double that of the Neolithic. The average age of death in the United States in 1960 was 70.1 years for males and 76.7 years for females.

As Table 7.7 shows, the average age at death for a skeletal series from the Illinois Archaic (101 skeletons), Illinois Hopewell (294 skeletons), and Illinois Middle Mississippi (479 skeletons) ranges from 22 to 26.5 years for females and 26

TABLE 7.6

Average Age at Death of Adults from Early Bronze Age to 1750 A.D.[a]

| | Average age at death of adults | |
	Males	Females
Early Bronze Age, 3000 B.C.	33.7	29.5
Middle Bronze Age, 2000 B.C.		
Commoners	36.3	30.8
Royalty	35.9	36.1
Late Bronze Age, 1500 B.C.	39.4	32.1
Early Iron Age, 1150 B.C.	38.6	31.3
Roman Imperial, A.D. 120	40.2	34.6
Byzantine Medieval, A.D. 1400	37.7	31.1
Romantic, A.D. 1750	40.2	37.3

[a] Data from Angel (1972, 1975).

to 33.5 for males (Blakely 1971). The increase in the average age at death for the Illinois Middle Mississippi series, for example, results from an apparent undernumeration of children who died before the age of 10, perhaps as a result of funerary practices (Blakely 1971:47). The large series from Indian Knoll (844 skeletons) provides an average-age-at-death estimate of 18.6 years (Johnston and Snow 1961) but the methods used for estimating age have been criticized (Blakely 1971:44; Stewart 1962).

Life Tables

The life table is a mortality history of a hypothetical group (cohort). Most life tables follow the cohort from the birth to the death of all its members. Through time-successive intervals, (e.g., a year or 5 years) the cohort loses a certain propor-

TABLE 7.7

Average Age at Death of Adults for Skeletal Series from the Illinois Archaic to the Illinois Middle Mississippi

| | Average age at death of adults | |
	Males	Females
Illinois Archaic	27.5	26.5
Illinois Hopewell	26.0	22.0
Illinois Middle Mississippi	33.5	26.5

tion of its members. It is assumed that there are no in- or out-migrations and that people die according to a predetermined schedule. The cohort originates from a standard number of births (100 or 1000) called the *radix* of the life table and normally includes both sexes. Separate tables for males and females, however, may be constructed (G. W. Barclay 1958). The life table includes various functions:

1. Number of deaths between age x and $x + 1$: D_x
2. Proportion of the dead between age x and $x + 1$: d_x
3. Survivors of exact age x: l_x
4. Probability of dying between age x and $x + 1$: q_x
5. Total years (for the cohort) lived after exact age x: T_x
6. Life expectancy, or average number of years lived after exact age x: E_x

The construction of life tables from archaeological material is described by Acsádi and Nemeskéri (1970:60–72). The elements of this method follow.

The basic function (d_x) is the number of people who died between age x and $x + 1$ (d_x) in a cohort of a given size. In the following presentation 100 will be considered the number of people who died during the entire period of burial:

$$d_x = \frac{D_x}{\Sigma D_x} \times 100$$

where D_x is the number of people who died between age x and $x + 1$, and ΣD_x is the number of people who died during the entire period of burial.

The number of survivors (l_x) for each year is obtained as follows:

$$l_x = l_{x-1} - d_{x-1}$$

The value of l_0 is the radix of the life table, which is placed at 100 here.

The probability of death (q_x) is then computed from d_x and l_x, as follows:

$$q_x = d_x/l_x$$

Life expectancy may then be computed from L_x, the number of years lived by survivors between ages x and $x + 1$, and from the number of years that can be lived after exact age x before all have died (T_x):

$$L_x = l_x - (d_x/2)$$

also,

$$L_x = \frac{l_x + l_{x+1}}{2}$$

$$T_x = \Sigma L_x - L_x$$

Life expectancy at birth (E_0), at age 15 (E_{15}), or any other age (E_x) then can be computed as follows:

$$E_x = T_x/l_x$$

The formulae for constructing a life table using 5-year age intervals are

$$d_x = \frac{D_x}{\Sigma D_x} \times 100$$

$$l_x = l_{x-5} - d_{x-5}$$

$$q_x = d_x / l_x$$

$$L_x = \frac{5\,(l_x + l_{x+5})}{2}$$

$$T_x = (\Sigma L_x) - L_x$$

$$E_x \quad \frac{T_x}{l_x}$$

where the age classes are x, $x + 5$, $x + 10$, and $x + 15$.

Acsádi and Nemeskéri (1970) constructed a life table for an Epipalaeolithic skeletal series unearthed on the Mediterranean coast at Taforalt Cave, Morocco. This series was analyzed first by Ferembach (cited in Acsádi and Nemeskéri 1970) and later by Acsádi and Nemeskéri (1970). The results of the analyses were used by the latter to construct an abridged life table (Table 7.8; Acsádi and Nemeskéri 1970:158). Survivorship from birth to successive ages is shown in Figure 7.1. From the table, we see that the expectancy of life at birth is 21.4 years; at the age of 20 it is 23.9 years. A life expectancy at the age of 20 of 21.9 years was calculated from a

TABLE 7.8
Abridged Life Table for the Taforalt Population (Both Sexes)[a,b]

x	D_x	d_x	l_x	q_x	L_x	T_x	E_x
0–4	82.834	44.54	100.00	.445	388.650	2,137.400	21.4
5–9	10.606	5.70	55.46	.103	263.050	1,748.750	31.5
10–14	6.560	3.53	49.76	.071	239.975	1,485.700	29.9
15–19	6.335	3.41	46.23	.074	222.625	1,245.725	26.9
20–24	5.115	2.75	42.82	.064	207.225	1,023.100	23.9
25–29	16.508	8.87	40.07	.221	178.175	815.875	20.4
30–34	14.384	7.73	31.20	.248	136.675	637.700	20.4
35–39	3.382	2.06	23.47	.088	112.200	501.025	21.3
40–44	4.130	2.22	21.41	.104	101.500	388.825	18.2
45–49	4.985	2.68	19.19	.140	89.250	287.325	15.0
50–54	6.250	3.36	16.51	.204	74.150	198.075	12.0
55–59	6.250	3.36	13.15	.256	57.350	123.925	9.4
60–64	6.678	3.59	9.79	.367	39.975	66.575	6.8
65–69	7.381	4.21	6.20	.679	20.475	26.600	4.3
70–74	3.274	1.76	1.99	.884	5.550	6.125	3.1
75–79	0.428	0.23	0.23	1.000	0.575	.575	2.5
Total	186.000	100.00	—	—	2,137.400	—	—

[a] Data from Acsádi and Nemeskéri 1970.
[b] See text for an explanation of symbols.

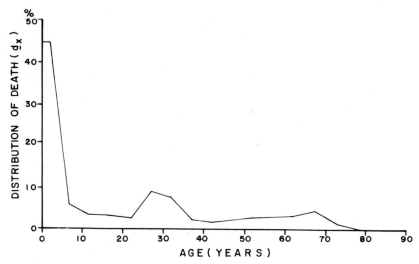

FIGURE 7.1. *Percentage distrubution of deaths for successive age-groups, Taforalt, Epipalaeolithic. (Data from Acsádi and Nemeskéri 1970.)*

series of 57 specimens from another cave, Afalou-Bou-Rommel in Algeria, also located on the Mediterranean coast (Acsádi and Nemeskéri 1970:157).

Because life tables describe mortality for a cohort of 100 persons (or 1000 persons in some tables), comparisons between populations of different size can be readily made (Swedlund and Armelagos 1976). Thus changes in population characteristics such as a decrease in infant mortality and greater survivorship for old adults as a result of advanced health care can be easily detected. Mortality tables may also be constructed, if data are available, for males and females separately; such tables can show the impact of health hazards on the survivorship of mothers by comparison to that of adult males. It should be noted, however, that sex cannot be determined for juveniles.

The life table and graphic representations of its functions (Table 7.8 and Figures 7.1–7.4) provide a clear picture of the changes in mortality with age and thus aid in interpreting the biological and social factors behind the mortality pattern of a population. In the case of the Taforalt population, the distribution of death by age-group (Figure 7.2) shows a high rate of mortality before age 4. The mortality rate declines sharply after that age until age 25. This mortality pattern is also reflected in the high probability of death (Figure 7.3). The probability of dying from birth to age 4 is .445 compared to a probability of .071 for ages 10–14. Such high infant mortality rates are characteristic of preindustrial populations and reflect the inadequacy of health care (Nag 1972). Those who survive the first 4 years of life have a low chance of dying before they reach adulthood. This may be seen in the expectation of life (Figure 7.4). At birth, because of the high probability of dying, any of the infants born can expect to live to age 21.4; at age 5, the life expectancy increases to 31.5 years.

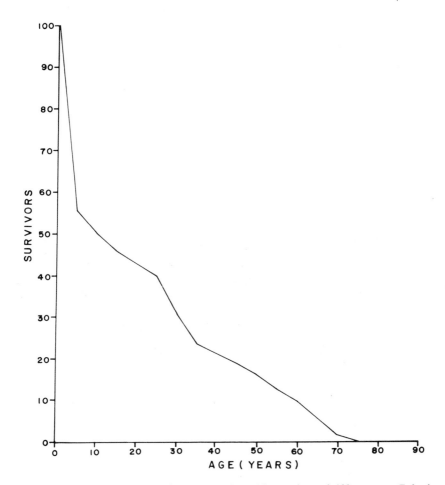

FIGURE 7.2. *Number of survivors by age, starting with a cohort of 100 persons, Taforalt, Epipalaeolithic. (Data from Ascádi and Nemeskéri 1970.)*

Accidents from work, hazards of childbirth, and occupational diseases increase the probability of death for young adults (Figure 7.3) to about three times that of juveniles. After age 50, the deterioration of health and the inadequacy of medical care lead to a progressively higher probability of death, and the number of years a person expects to live begins to drop. A person 60 years of age expects to live an additional 6.8 years (Figure 7.4). A work by Palkovich (1978) on the relationship between disease manifestations and mortality patterns, as revealed in life tables, is useful in elucidating the causes for some of the differences in the vital statistics of prehistoric populations.

The use of life tables in palaeodemography has its dangers (Angel 1969a; Bennett 1973). The assumption is made that the skeletal remains belong to a single population without any migration and with constant age-specific birth and death

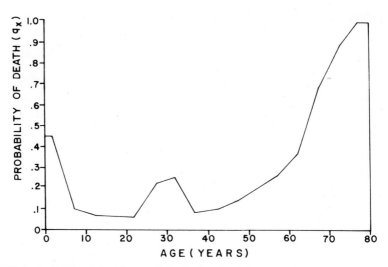

FIGURE 7.3. *Probability of death by age, Taforalt, Epipalaeolithic. (Data from Acsádi and Nemeskéri 1970.)*

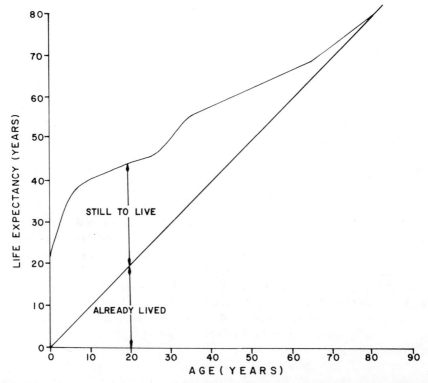

FIGURE 7.4. *Life expectancy by age, Taforalt, Epipalaeolithic. (Data from Acsádi and Nemeskéri 1970.)*

108

rates and therefore an unchanging age–sex distribution (i.e., a stable population). Unfortunately, this assumption does not apply to small hunting–gathering populations, which are characterized by constant demographic flux and frequent fertility–mortality variations (N. Howell 1979a). Nevertheless, in view of the advantages obtained from the use of the life table, the assumption may be considered to hold. But I maintain, in accordance with More and associates (1975), that life tables must be considered hypothetical constructs and should be tested by independent cultural and ecological data.

In addition to the theoretical problems mentioned, the utility and validity of the life table for skeletal material are beset by sampling and age determination problems. The original data may be smoothed (graduated) by certain mathematical formulations to remedy this problem (see, e.g., Weiss 1973). But if the sample is deficient, or overstocked in a certain age-group, graduation does not provide an appropriate solution. Under numeration of infants is often a major problem (Angel 1969a; Weiss 1973). Moore *et al.* (1975) formulated a computer program to construct a life table in which the raw count for infants was increased in steps of 10 until the infants totaled 40% of the sample. Their findings indicate that the effect of errors from infant undernumeration is negligible for the probability of dying and life expectancy outside the infant age bracket, but the effect on the survivorship curve is very strong.

The estimate of life expectancy in a life table is also dependent on the rate of population growth. Bennett (1973), in his study of the Point of Pines, examines this problem, and Swedlund and Armelagos (1976) reexamine it for the Meinarti population (A.D. 1050–1300). For a stationary population having a zero growth rate, life expectancy at age 16 is 15.51 years. At a rate of increase of .012 (1.2%) per year, the life expectancy increases by about 1 year to 16.43 years. The difference does not seem significant for the demographic analysis of prehistoric populations. It should be remembered that there are several inadequacies built in the sources of data, that the absolute numbers obtained in a life table are to be considered within a generous margin of error, and that the figures are suggestive of the approximate levels of mortality.

Life Tables of Prehistoric Populations

A Mesolithic series of 42 specimens from Vassilievka III (U.S.S.R.) has been studied by Acsádi and Nemeskéri (1970:163–166). The age distribution of adults appears balanced. The life expectancy at 20 was estimated at 22.8 years.

The Epipalaeolithic series from the Maghreb and the Vassilievka III Mesolithic series, by comparison to the Neanderthals and the Upper Palaeolithic, are richer in adults over 40 years of age and poorer in younger adults. This may represent a genuine trend in the mortality pattern, but it is suspected that the radiographic method for determining age used by Acsádi and Nemeskéri (1970) for both Taforalt and Vassilievka III is, at least in part, responsible for this result, since Vallois (1960), who studied the Neanderthal and Upper Palaeolithic specimens, used the method of closure of cranial sutures.

The Mesolithic belongs to the cultural stage succeeding the Palaeolithic. In the Near East and North Africa, the Mesolithic is not recognized by many authors. The Epipalaeolithic and Terminal Palaeolithic are the cultural (but not strictly chronological) equivalents. In the Nile Valley, two Terminal Palaeolithic skeletal series dating to ca. 14,000 B.P. were excavated at Sahaba (Anderson 1968a) and Wadi Halfa (Greene and Armelagos 1972). A summary of the age and sex determinations of these two series is shown on Tables 7.9 and 7.10. Unfortunately, the data were originally reported in major age-groups: children, and young, middle, and old adults. The estimation of the life expectancy from life tables is thus complicated by the wide age interval and the assumption that deaths per year within each interval are evenly distributed (Table 7.11). Pending further studies of these two important series, tentative estimates of E_{20} for the Wadi Halfa and Sahaba series are 17.2 and 14.4 years, respectively. The age distribution of the two series is an overrepresentation of middle-aged adults and an underrepresentation of children by comparison to the Upper and Middle Palaeolithic. There is abundant evidence for warfare in both the Wadi Halfa and Sahaba series, and it seems that children were not interred as frequently as adults.

Data are also available on the Natufian (late Epipalaeolithic) from Hayonim Cave (Israel). I have constructed a life table for this series from the data reported by Bar-Yosef and Goren (1973) and summarized in Table 7.12. The series shows an age distribution not unlike that of the Mesolithic series described by Vallois (1960) in the overrepresentation of young adults between 20 and 30 years of age. The frequency of infants and children, however, seems somewhat low. It is very curious

TABLE 7.9

Age and Sex Distribution of the Sahaba Skeletal Remains[a]

Age	Male	Female	Unknown	Total
6 months			1	1
3–5 years			2	2
6 years			2	3
7 years			3	3
10 years			1	1
11 years			1	1
12 years			1	1
17–18 years	0	2	0	2
Young adult	3	3	0	6
Adult	3	3	8	14
Middle-aged adult	8	10	0	18
Old adult	5	4	0	9
Total				60

[a]Data from Anderson 1968.

TABLE 7.10

Age and Sex Distribution of the Wadi Halfa Epipalaeolithic Specimens[a]

Age-group	Number	Percentage	Male	Female	Unknown
Children	3	8.33	—	—	3
Young adults	1	2.77	—	1	—
Adults	21	58.33	9	9	3
Mature adults	11	30.56	4	6	1
Unidentifiable	2	—	—	—	2
Total	36	99.99	13	16	9

[a] Data from Greene and Armelagos 1972.

that the 20–30 group consists exclusively of males, whereas the ratio of males to females in the age-group 10–20 is 1 to 5. Several hypotheses may be generated to explain these anomalies, (e.g., burial distinctions, warfare, maternal mortality, dietary effects associated with the utilization of wild cereals) but further palaeopathological and ecological studies are required. Life expectancy at age 20 is 11.9 years (Table 7.13).

Weiss (1973) estimated the life expectancy of the australopithecines, Neanderthals, and Upper Palaeolithic populations from graduated data, as follows:

	E_0	E_{15}
Australopithecines	ca. 15	12.7
Neanderthals	ca. 18	17.5
Upper Palaeolithic	—	16.9

These figures are derived from collections of diverse specimens, not from a single skeletal series for each population.

The life table constructed from data provided by Angel (1971) on the large sample (268 skeletons) from Catal Hüyük Neolithic shows that the life expectancy at age 15 was 16.9 years (Table 7.14). This series is aged to 5-year intervals and provides excellent data for the construction of a life table. Although infants and children 5 years of age or younger seem to be underrepresented (see foregoing discussion), the series is excellent for the study of adult mortality. At age 50, the survivors represent no more than 2.13% of the cohort. Nemeskéri (1972), by contrast, derives a survivorship of 26.12% for the Terminal Palaeolithic Sahaba population. This estimate is based on raw data where adults older than 16 years are counted as one age-group. Such a high estimate of survivorship at age 50 seems to be inflated, and the estimation of life expectancy based on it may also be too high.

The accurate determination of the age of old individuals in skeletal series is very important for a reliable estimate of life expectancy. If the number of old adults is subdivided into fractions for age-groups from age 40 to 80, a high life expectancy

TABLE 7.11

Life Table for the Sahaba Terminal Palaeolithic Skeletal Series[a,b]

x	d_x	l_x	q_x	T_x	E_x
0–5	5.00	100.00	.05	3445.83	34.45
5–10	10.00	95.00	.11	2958.33	31.14
10–15	3.33	85.00	.04	2508.33	29.51
15–20	3.33	81.67	.04	2091.67	25.60
20–25	9.17	78.33	.12	1691.67	21.60
25–30	9.17	69.17	.13	1322.92	19.13
30–35	10.00	60.00	.17	1000.00	16.67
35–40	9.17	50.00	.18	725.00	14.50
40–45	10.00	40.83	.24	497.92	12.19
45–50	9.17	30.83	.30	318.75	10.34
50–55	7.50	21.67	.35	187.50	8.70
55–60	5.83	14.17	.41	97.92	6.91
60–65	5.00	8.33	.60	41.67	5.00
65–70	2.50	3.33	.75	12.50	3.75
70–75	.83	.83	1.00	2.083	2.50

[a] Young adults were classified as those 20–30 years old; middle-aged adults, 30–40 years old; old adults, 40–70 years old. Adults not classified as young, middle-aged, or old were redistributed among those classes, and the frequency in 5-year intervals was accomplished by constructing a cumulative frequency curve, then subtracting the cumulative frequency of the previous age from the reading.

[b] See text for an explanation of symbols.

TABLE 7.12

Age Distribution of Hayonim Natufian Skeletal Remains[a]

Age	Number
0–5	1
5–10	3
10–15	2
15–20	3
20–25	3
25–30	6
30–35	0
30–40	1
35–40	1
40–45	0
45–50	3
Child	1
Adolescent	1
Adults	2
Total	27

[a] Data from Bar-Yosef and Goren 1973.

TABLE 7.13
Abridged Life Table for the Natufian Population, Hayonim (Both Sexes)^{a,b}

x	D_x	d_x	l_x	q_x	T_x	E_x
0–5	1.25	4.63	100.00	.05	2356.85	23.57
5–10	3.75	13.89	95.37	.15	1868.43	19.59
10–15	2.20	8.15	81.48	.10	1426.30	17.50
15–20	3.80	14.07	73.33	.19	1039.26	14.17
20–25	3.43	12.70	59.26	.21	707.78	11.94
25–30	6.87	25.44	46.56	.55	443.24	9.52
30–35	.57	2.11	21.11	.10	274.07	12.98
35–40	1.72	6.37	19.00	.34	173.80	9.14
40–45	0	0	12.63	0	94.72	7.50
45–40	3.41	12.63	12.63	1.00	31.57	2.50

^{a}Unaged individuals falling in more than one 5-year age class were redistributed among age classes at a ratio proportional to that of the age classes before the redistribution.
^{b}See text for an explanation of symbols.

tends to be produced. Thus, for the same series from Sahaba, Nemeskéri (1972) estimates E_{15} at 31.05 years. The reduction of number of survivors past the age of 50, however, should be taken into consideration, because it has the effect of reducing life expectancy. It is possible that the existing methods of determining age cause the underestimation of the age of old adults. The data by Acsádi and Nemeskéri (1970) and Nemeskéri (1972) do in fact compare well with data on ethnographic hunters and gatherers.

TABLE 7.14
Abridged Life Table for the Catal Hüyük Neolithic Skeletal Series^{a,b}

x	D_x	d_x	l_x	q_x
0–4	29	10.25	100.00	.10
5–9	24	8.48	89.75	.09
10–14	16	5.65	81.27	.07
15–19	18	6.36	75.62	.08
20–24	32	11.31	69.26	.16
25–29	45	15.90	57.95	.27
30–34	48	16.96	42.05	.40
35–39	29	10.25	25.09	.41
40–44	27	9.54	14.84	.64
45–59	9	3.18	5.30	.60
50–54	3	1.06	2.12	.50
55–59	0	0	1.06	.00
60–64	2	.71	1.06	.67
65+	1	.35	.35	1.00
Total	283			

^{a}Data from Angel 1971.
^{b}See text for an explanation of symbols.

Model Life Tables

Life tables constructed for small individual series suffer from statistical and cultural anomalies. Data for a given population may be smoothed, or the smoothed (graduated) data for several populations may be pooled to provide a *model life table*. Acsádi and Nemeskéri (1970) provide a model life table based on the Taforalt and Afalou-Bou-Rommel series, which they refer to as the *Maghreb-type* model life table (Table 7.15). Weiss (1973), on the basis of a large body of data from living and dead anthropological populations, provides a number of model life tables, each characterized by a given value of life expectancy at age 15 and survivorship at the same age. Two of these tables are reproduced here (Tables 7.16 and 7.17). They are

TABLE 7.15
Maghreb-Type Model Life Table (Both Sexes)[a,b]

x	l_x	d_x	q^x	L_x	T_x	E_x
0	100.0	23.1	.23100	88.45	2,114.50	21.145
1	76.9	10.8	.14044	71.50	2,026.05	26.347
2	66.1	7.4	.11195	62.40	1,954.55	29.570
3	58.7	2.7	.04600	57.35	1,892.15	32.234
4	56.0	1.7	.03036	55.15	1,834.80	32.764
5	54.3	1.5	.02762	53.55	1,779.65	32.774
6	52.8	1.4	.02652	52.10	1,726.10	32.691
7	51.4	1.2	.02335	50.80	1,674.00	32.568
8	50.2	.7	.01394	49.85	1,623.20	32.335
9	49.5	.6	.01212	49.20	1,573.35	31.785
10	48.9	.6	.01227	48.60	1,524.15	31.169
11	48.3	.5	.01035	48.05	1,475.55	30.550
12	47.8	.5	.01046	47.55	1,427.50	29.867
13	47.3	.5	.01057	47.05	1,379.95	29.174
14	46.8	.5	.01068	46.55	1,332.90	28.481
15	46.3	.5	.01080	46.05	1,286.35	27.783
16	45.8	.5	.01092	45.55	1,240.30	27.081
17	45.3	.6	.01325	45.00	1,194.75	26.374
18	44.7	.7	.01566	44.35	1,149.75	25.721
19	44.0	.7	.01591	43.65	1,105.40	25.123
20	43.3	.8	.01848	42.90	1,061.75	24.521
21	42.5	.8	.01882	42.10	1,018.85	23.973
22	41.7	.9	.02158	41.25	976.75	23.423
23	40.8	.9	.02206	40.35	935.50	22.929
24	39.9	.9	.02256	39.45	895.15	22.435
25	39.0	1.0	.02564	38.50	855.70	21.941
26	38.0	1.0	.02632	37.50	817.20	21.505
27	37.0	1.0	.02703	36.50	779.70	21.073
28	36.0	1.0	.02778	35.50	743.20	20.644
29	35.0	1.0	.02857	34.50	707.70	20.220
30	34.0	1.0	.02941	33.50	673.20	19.800
31	33.0	1.0	.03030	32.50	639.70	19.385

(continued)

TABLE 7.15 (*continued*)

x	l_x	d_x	q^x	L_x	T_x	E_x
32	32.0	1.0	.03125	31.60	607.20	18.975
33	31.0	1.0	.03226	30.50	575.70	18.571
34	30.0	1.0	.03333	29.50	545.20	18.173
35	29.0	1.0	.03448	28.50	515.70	17.783
36	28.0	1.0	.03571	27.50	487.20	17.400
37	27.0	1.0	.03704	26.50	459.70	17.026
38	26.0	1.0	.03846	25.50	433.20	16.662
39	25.0	·1.0	.04000	24.50	407.70	16.308
40	24.0	.9	.03750	23.55	383.20	15.967
41	23.1	.9	.03896	22.65	359.65	15.569
42	22.2	.9	.04054	21.75	337.00	15.180
43	21.3	.9	.04225	20.85	315.25	14.800
44	20.4	.9	.04412	19.95	294.40	14.431
45	19.5	.9	.04615	18.55	274.45	14.074
46	18.6	.8	.04301	18.20	255.90	13.758
47	17.8	.8	.04494	17.40	237.70	13.354
48	17.0	.8	.04706	16.60	220.30	12.959
49	16.2	.8	.04938	15.80	203.70	12.574
50	15.4	.7	.04545	15.05	187.90	12.201
51	14.7	.7	.04762	14.35	172.85	11.759
52	14.0	.7	.05000	13.65	158.50	11.321
53	13.3	.7	.05263	12.95	144.85	10.891
54	12.6	.7	.05551	12.25	131.90	10.468
55	11.9	.7	.05785	11.55	119.65	10.055
56	11.2	.6	.05263	10.90	108.10	9.652
57	10.6	.6	.05556	10.30	97.20	9.170
58	10.0	.6	.05882	9.70	86.90	8.690
59	9.4	.6	.06250	9.10	77.20	8.213
60	8.8	.6	.06667	8.50	68.10	7.739
61	8.2	.6	.07143	7.90	59.60	7.268
62	7.6	.6	.07692	7.30	51.70	6.803
63	7.0	.6	.08333	6.70	44.40	6.343
64	6.4	.6	.09091	6.10	37.70	5.891
65	5.8	.6	.10000	5.50	31.60	5.448
66	5.2	.6	.11111	4.90	26.10	5.019
67	4.6	.6	.12500	4.30	21.20	4.609
68	4.0	.6	.14286	3.70	16.90	4.225
69	3.4	.5	.13889	3.15	13.20	3.882
70	2.9	.5	.17241	2.65	10.05	3.466
71	2.4	.4	.16667	2.20	7.40	3.083
72	2.0	.4	.20000	1.80	5.20	2.600
73	1.6	.4	.25000	1.40	3.40	2.125
74	1.2	.4	.33333	1.00	2.00	1.667
75	.8	.4	.50000	.60	1.00	1.250
76	.4	.2	.50000	.30	.40	1.000
77	.2	.2	1.00000	.10	.10	.500
Total				2114.50		

[a] Data from Acsádi and Nemeskéri 1970.
[b] See text for an explanation of symbols.

TABLE 7.16
Model Life Table A[a,b]

x	q^x	l_x	L_x	T_x	E_x
0	.2670	100.0	83	1896	19.0
1	.1600	73.3	262	1813	24.7
5	.1100	61.6	291	1551	25.2
10	.0876	54.8	262	1260	23.0
15	.1905	50.0	226	998	20.0
20	.1970	40.5	182	773	19.1
25	.2038	32.5	145	591	18.2
30	.2108	25.9	115	445	17.2
35	.2180	20.4	91	330	16.2
40	.2254	16.0	71	240	15.0
45	.2330	12.4	54	169	13.7
50	.2409	9.5	42	115	12.1
55	.2812	7.2	31	73	10.2
60	.3646	5.2	21	42	8.1
65	.4546	3.3	13	21	6.4
70	.5738	1.8	6	8	4.6
75	1.0000	0.8	2	2	2.5
80	0	0	0	0	0

[a] From *Memoirs of the Society for American Archaeology* 27:119, 1973. Reproduced with permission of the Society for American Archaeology.
[b] l_{15} = 50%; E_{15} = 20 years. See text for explanation of symbols.

TABLE 7.17
Model Life Table B[a,b]

x	q_x	l_x	L_x	T_x	E_x
0	.2670	100.0	83	1645	16.5
1	.1600	73.3	262	1563	21.3
5	.1100	61.6	291	1300	21.1
10	.0876	54.8	262	1009	18.4
15	.2547	50.0	217	748	15.0
20	.2666	37.3	160	531	14.2
25	.2789	27.3	117	370	13.5
30	.2917	19.7	84	253	12.9
35	.3049	14.0	59	170	12.2
40	.3186	9.7	40	111	11.5
45	.3328	6.6	27	71	10.7
50	.3474	4.4	18	44	9.9
55	.3625	2.9	12	26	8.9
60	.3780	1.8	7	14	7.5
65	.3940	1.1	5	6	5.5
70	1.0000	.7	2	2	2.5
75	0	0	0	0	0
80	0	0	0	0	0

[a] From *Memoirs of the Society for American Archaeology* 27:128, 1973. Reproduced with permission of the Society of American Archaeology.
[b] l_{15} = 50%; E_{15} = 15 years. See text for explanation of symbols.

based on life expectancies at age 15 of 15 and 20 years, and a survivorship at age 15 (l_{15}) of 50%.

Overview

Certain demographic characteristics of prehistoric hunter–gatherers are clearly shown by the age and sex structure of their skeletal remains. Unfortunately, the analysis of these remains cannot yield data comparable to those available from censuses or historical records, except in rare circumstances. Methodological problems in age and sex determination are not altogether absent. Nevertheless, the results so far available are of extreme significance in revealing some aspects of the demographic life of prehistoric man.

A summary of the available data on skeletal series and collections from the Middle Paleolithic to the Neolithic (Figure 7.5) indicates that E_{15} was about 17–30 years (Table 7.18), with an average of about 21.2 years. It is risky to make statements about trends in the change in mortality of prehistoric populations at this moment because the differences between estimates for different populations result in part from sample size, the composition of the collections, lack of detailed data on the age of old adults, preferential interment, and methodological differences in determining age.

The estimates on the Middle Palaeolithic and the Upper Palaeolithic are based on collections of specimens from different localities and thus do not constitute a skeletal series adequate for the construction of life tables. It should be noted, however, that Weiss (1973) has graduated the raw data to arrive at his estimates.

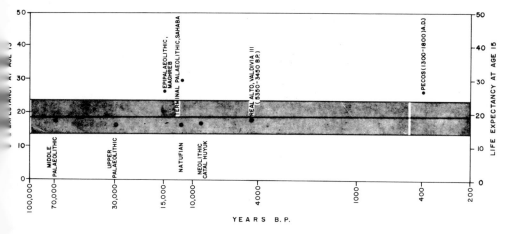

FIGURE 7.5. *Trend in the life expectancy at age 15. (Data from Acsádi and Nemeskéri 1970; Angel 1971; Klepinger 1979; Mobley 1978; Weiss 1973; also Hassan, this volume.)*

TABLE 7.18

Adult Life Expectancy (E$_{15}$) of Some Prehistoric Populations[a]

Population	E$_{15}$ (years)
1. Australopithecines	12.7
2. Neanderthals	17.5
3. Upper Palaeolithic *H. sapiens sapiens*	16.9
4. Epipalaeolithic, Maghreb	26.6
5. Terminal Palaeolithic, Sahaba	29.5
6. Late Epipalaeolithic (Natufian)	17.5
7. Neolithic, Catal Hÿük	17.0
8. Ethnographic hunter–gatherers	26.4
9. Pecos Pueblo	26.5
10. Real Alto, Valdivia III	17.75
11. England, 1301–1400 A.D.	25.8
Mean of 2, 3, 4, 5, 6, 7, 9, 10	21.2

[a] Data from Acsádi and Nemeskéri 1970; Klepinger 1979; Mobley 1980; Russell 1958; Weiss 1973; also Hassan, this volume.

TABLE 7.19

Adult Life Expectancy (E$_{15}$) of Some Living Hunting–Gathering Populations

Population	E$_{15}$ (years)
Baker Lake Eskimo	27.7
Birhor	24.0
Australians, Groote Eylandt	23.3
Angamgssalik	19.2
East Greenlanders	23.5
Australians, Northern Territory	34.0
Australians, Tiwi	33.1

[a] From Weiss 1973.

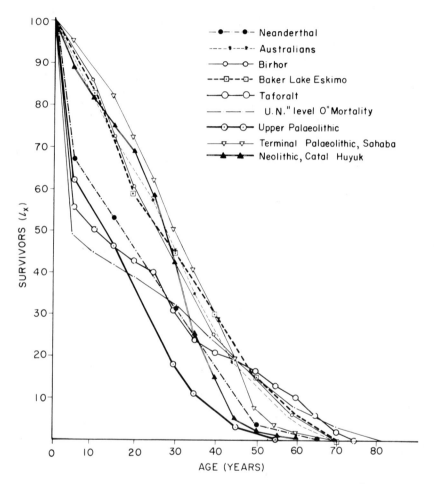

FIGURE 7.6. *Survivorship curves of Neanderthals, Upper Palaeolithic* Homo sapiens, *Taforalt Epipalaeolithic, Australian aboriginies, Birhor, Baker Lake Eskimo, and U.N. "level 0" mortality hypothetical population. (Data from Acsádi and Nemeskéri 1970 and Weiss 1973.)*

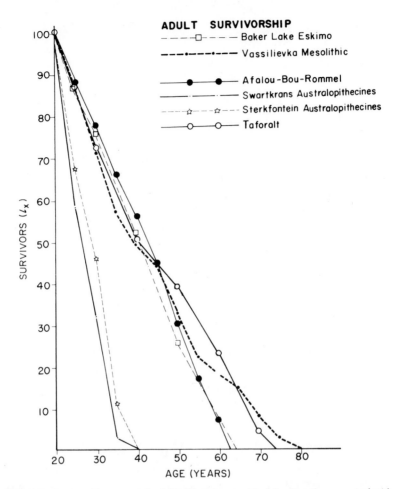

FIGURE 7.7. *Survivorship curves of adults (20 years or older) for Swartkrans australopithecines, Sterkfontein australopithecines, Taforalt Epipalaeolithic, Afalou-Bou-Rommel Epipalaeolithic, Vassilievka Mesolithic, and Baker Lake Eskimo. (Data from Acsádi and Nemeskéri 1970; and Mann 1975; and Weiss 1973.)*

The data on Epipalaeolithic populations from the Maghreb present a case where methodological differences in determining age illustrate the great discrepancy between the estimates of life expectancy for those populations and those from other skeletal series from Nubia and Palestine (Terminal Palaeolithic at Sahaba and Natufian at Hayonim Cave). Age determinations made by Ferembach, who did the initial analysis of the Taforalt collection from the Maghreb, lead to an estimate of 12.5 years as the life expectancy at age 15 (Acsádi and Nemeskéri (1970:155). However, a restudy of the series by Acsádi and Nemeskéri of old adults led to an estimate of 26.9 years, a figure more than double that of Ferembach.

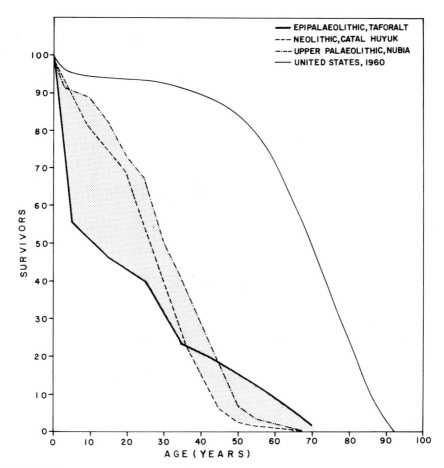

FIGURE 7.8. *Survivorship curves of Upper Palaeolithic, Epipalaeolithic, and Neolithic populations compared with survivorship curve of the United States, 1960. (Data from Acsádi and Nemeskéri 1970; Thomlinson 1965; Weiss 1973; and Hassan, this volume.)*

It is premature, pending further evaluation of the age distribution of prehistoric skeletal populations, to affirm that prehistoric mortality was greater than that for ethnographic hunter–gatherers. The data on the life expectancy of Maghreb Epipalaeolithic and the Sahaba Terminal Palaeolithic populations are very close to those of ethnographic hunter–gatherers, but other prehistoric hunter–gatherers show a lower life expectancy (Table 7.19). However, in the light of the estimates available for prehistoric populations, it can be stated that prehistoric mortality was not less than that of ethnographic populations, and that an upper limit of about 26–27 years as the life expectancy at age 15 is most likely.

With this cautionary note we may proceed to compare the survivorship curves of the prehistoric populations with those of ethnographic populations. In Figure 7.6,

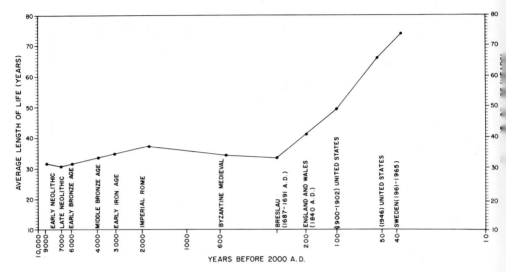

FIGURE 7.9. *Trend of average length of life. (Data from Angel 1972, 1975; Pressat 1971.)*

where the survivorship of living hunter–gatherers and that of the Taforalt series are presented, the curves of three living hunting–gathering populations (Birhor, Baker Lake Eskimo, and Groote Eylandt Australians) are remarkably similar. However, the curve of the Taforalt series shows a lower number of survivors after the first 5 years and a higher number of old adult survivors. When the children are removed and survivorship is recalculated starting with a group of 100 at age 20 (Figure 7.7), the Taforalt curve shows a close resemblance to that of living hunting–gathering groups, represented on this curve by the Baker Lake Eskimo, for the age period from 20 to 50 years. Still, a greater number of old adult survivors appear in the Taforalt series. However, this is not the case when the Afalou series is compared.

Although the Taforalt series may be partially skewed toward low survivorship of infants and high survivorship of old adults, the survivorship of the Taforalt series closely matches the U.N. "level 0" mortality model (males), which corresponds to the highest contemporary mortality rate (Figure 7.6; Acsádi and Nemeskéri 1970:172). Thus, living hunter–gatherers may not be representative of Mesolithic/ Epipalaeolithic groups. However, problems of census and difficulty in obtaining exact figures on infanticide must be considered.

The survivorship curves for the Terminal Palaeolithic (Sahaba) and the Neolithic (Catal Hüyük) are similar to those of the Baker Lake Eskimo and the Birhor up to age 35 (Figure 7.8). The similarity, however, is closer to that of the U.N. "level 0" mortality after that age. Again, this may be due to problems of determining age.

With regard to the survivorship of the australopithecines, the curves for both *A. africanus* from Sterkfontein and *A. robustus* from Swartkrans closely match (Figure 7.7). Both are distinctly different from that of both the Mesolithic/ Epipalaeolithic populations and living hunter–gatherers.

One of the most significant results of palaeodemographic analysis concerns the greater frequency of young women (20–30 years) among the dead, which seems to be connected with the hazards of childbirth. It should also be noted that juveniles are usually represented by a smaller number of cases than either infants or adults, indicating that once the vulnerable age of infancy is passed, the chances of survivorship became greater until adulthood was reached. During adulthood, occupational hazards and progressive lowering of "resistance" to death lowered survivorship.

It should also be of interest to compare the mortality pattern of prehistoric populations with that of more recent populations. As Table 7.18 shows, life expectancy at age 15 in England during the thirteenth century as determined from tombstones by Russell (1958) was 25.8 years, not much different than that of the Maghreb Epipalaeolithic populations or contemporary hunter–gatherers (26.6 and 26.4 years, respectively). The average age at death for several populations from the Middle Ages to 1965 (Figure 7.9) indicates that up to the eighteenth century the average length of life was not that much different from that of the Middle Bronze Age to the Early Iron Age, with a gain of no more than 2–3 years over that of the Neolithic populations. The average length of human life in Sweden in 1961–1965 was 73.6 years (Pressat 1971:38), more than double the life span before the eighteenth century. The increase in the length of life after the eighteenth century was rapid and has no parallel in prehistory. There is, however, a slight gain in the length of life from the Neolithic to Roman times, followed by a decline.

The pattern of survivorship has also changed radically (Figure 7.8). The greater divergence between the "archaic" survivorship curve and that of modern populations in developed countries lies in the high survivorship of children to age 15 and of adults older than 60 years of age, reflecting the impact of health care.

8

Prehistoric Fertility and Population Growth

Of the dark past
A child is born;
With joy and grief
My heart is torn.

Calm in his cradle
The living lies.
May love and mercy
Unclose his eyes!

Young life is breathed
On the glass;
The world that was not
Comes to pass.

A child is sleeping;
An old man gone.
O father forsaken,
Forgive your son!

—James Joyce, *Ecce Puer**

The transition from hunting–gathering to food production was associated with a dramatic increase in the size of world population. Prior to the transition, the world human population was perhaps no larger than 10 million (Hassan 1978b:78). During the period of early food production the world population soared to about 50 million (Brothwell 1971; Deevey 1960).

The small size of the world population by the end of the Pleistocene reflects a very slow *average* rate of population growth, considering the more than 2 million years over which it took place. The rate was less than .001% per year (Hassan 1973; Polgar 1972). During the period of early food production, the growth rate rose to an average of about .1% (Carneiro and Hilse 1966; G. L. Cowgill 1975; Hassan 1973). Although this is very low compared with the 2–3% of many contemporary populations, it was far greater than that of the Palaeolithic. Since these rates may reflect either low intrinsic rates of growth or cultural regulation of population, it is important to explore the most probable causes of the slow rate of growth because of their significance in interpreting the dynamics of cultural change and evolution.

The present chapter deals with the potential fertility of prehistoric human populations. The reader may also wish to examine the thoughtful treatment of this topic by Dumond (1975), and for a historical perspective the reader may refer to Wolfe (1933) for one of the earliest discussions of the subject. The comprehensive, yet concise survey of human fertility by Leridon (1977) may be also consulted. Unfortunately the excellent treatment of the demography of the Dobe !Kung by N. Howell (1979a) appeared after the present work had been completed and submitted for publication. The interested reader is strongly advised to consult this important work, from which much can be learned about the demography of hunter– gatherers and the methods of collecting and analyzing data in ethnographic contexts.

Determinants of Human Fertility

To examine the potential fertility pattern of prehistoric populations it would be advantageous to outline the major biological variables that influence human fertility. These variables are included in the model presented in Figure 8.1. Basically, fertility is related to the length of the reproductive span of adult females and the interval between successive live births. The length of the reproductive span is determined by the age at which females are capable of conceiving (nubility) and by menopause or death before menopause is reached. Nubility, in turn, is influenced by the age at menarche and adolescent sterility. The natural interval between successive live births is a function of amenorrhea, gestation period, sterility, and fetal death. In this section I will examine the parameters of each of these variables in prehistoric contexts.

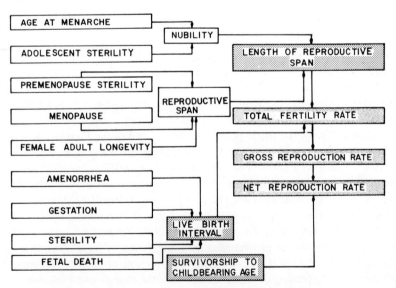

FIGURE 8.1. *A model of the determinants of human fertility. The key variables are length of reproductive span, live-birth interval, and survivorship to childbearing age. Secondary variables are both biological and cultural.*

Natural Live-Birth Interval

According to Wrigley (1969:92), the birth interval, which is a major determinant of fecundity (the biological potential for reproduction), is about 22 months on the average, allowing for an average of 10 months for amenorrhea, 3 months for the interval before new conception, and 9 months for conception to delivery. The live-birth interval, however, is somewhat longer. Starting with a birth interval of 22 months and allowing for a 12% incidence of fetal death, as well as sterility (Hassan 1975a), we arrive at an estimate of about 27.3 months. A survey of numerous nonindustrial societies by Nag (1962) indicates wide variability in fetal death and sterility, with an average of about 12% for each. A close estimate of 13.2% sterility for six European nations (seventeenth to nineteenth centuries) was obtained by L. Henry (1961). The relationship between age and sterility for females in these nations is given in Table 8.1.

In a Monte Carlo simulation Barrett (1972) arrived at an average live-interval of 28.4 ± .2 months. A similar interval of 28.7 months was obtained in another experiment (Perrin and Sheps 1964). Several factors may interfere to modify the "natural" birth interval. For example, this interval can be increased by prolonged suckling of the child. Diet also seems to influence the birth interval. A prolonged interval could result from a low fat intake, which leads to irregular ovulation (Coale 1974:48). The role of these variables in population regulation will be examined in the next chapter.

Age At Menarche

Age at menarche, which marks the initiation of the reproductive capacity of human females, seems to vary among human groups, apparently because of dietary differences (Esche and Lee 1975; Nag 1962). The average age at menarche for nonindustrial populations is about 15 years, on the basis of data gathered by Nag (1962). N. Howell (1976:144) estimates an age of 16.5 years as the mean age at menarche for the Bushmen women of the Dobe area. B. G. Campbell (1974) provides an estimate of 13.7 years for women in general. Menarche in western and northern Europe is reached earlier. In addition, average age at menarche has de-

TABLE 8.1
Age-Specific Sterility for Females of Six European Nations[a]

Age of women (years)	Percentage of sterile women
20	3
25	6
30	10
35	16
40	31

[a] Data from L. Henry 1961.

creased in industrial Europe over the last century. For example, there was a drop from over 17 to 13.5 years between 1850 and 1950 in Norway, from 16.5 to 14.5 in Germany, and from 15.5 to 14 in Sweden (Tanner 1955). Nag (1962) has suggested that the age of menarche may be related to nutrition: Females on a high-protein diet reach menarche at an earlier age than those on a largely carbohydrate diet. Indeed, a correlation seems to exist between mean age at menarche and protein intake in the Slovenian regions of Yugoslavia (Kralj-Cercek 1956). This view is now strongly expressed by Frish (1977). Females on a protein diet reached menarche at 12.65 years in contrast with 14.1 years for girls on a carbohydrate diet and 13.42 for girls on a mixed diet.

Esche and Lee (1975), however, argue to the contrary. They associate a higher intake of carbonhydrates and purified sugar with a decrease in the age at menarche and document this for the !Kung Bushmen, Eskimos, and Icelanders. Among acculturated Eskimos, the protein content per capita was only 40% of the protein intake under hunting conditions, whereas sugar consumption quadrupled. This was associated with accelerated growth (Esche and Lee 1975). Since the age at menarche for industrial groups today is 15 years and that of preindustrial Europe was about 17 years, an average of 16 years may be used for prehistoric groups.

Nubility

Nubility is the average age at initiation of the capacity for conception. There is usually a delay, referred to as *adolescent sterility*, between menarche and nubility. The duration of this period varies greatly among individuals and groups (Nag 1962). According to Leathem (1958), it varies from 1 to 4 years, !Kung women, who reach menarche at 16.5 years, are reported to have their first live birth at age 19.5 years (N. Howell 1976a:144–145).

Adult Female Life Expectancy

The longevity of adults, which is influential in determining the length of the reproductive span, is in some societies today very much greater than it was a few centuries ago. On the average, women live well beyond their menopause and can thus have the use of their full potential reproductive span. As shown by the discussion in Chapter 7, throughout the Palaeolitic adult life expectancy at age 15 did not exceed 18 years, which is equivalent to an average adult longevity of 33 years. The data provided by Angel (1969b, 1972, 1975) on Mediterranean populations indicate that adult women had a shorter life than males from 11,000 B.C. to A.D. 1110 (see Chapter 7), and that this had been a consistent trend (Figure 8.2), reversed only in some modern industrial societies. The average difference in the age at death is about 4 years. It can thus be assumed that a figure of 29 years for adult female longevity is a reasonable estimate (33 − 4 = 29). However, this is most likely a conservative figure, since the age of old adults 'may be underestimated for prehistoric skeletal series. For example, the life expectancy at age 15 of ethnographic hunter–gatherers

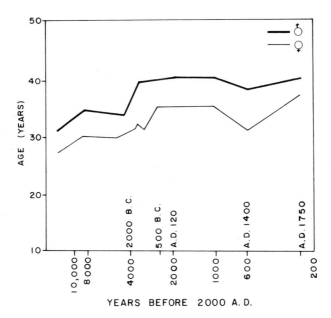

FIGURE 8.2. *Divergence between average length of life of adult males and adult females. (Data from Angel 1972, 1975.)*

is 26.4 years (Weiss 1973). Allowing for a reduction of 4 years, adult longevity would have averaged about 37 years, about 8 years greater than that determined from prehistoric contexts by palaeodemographic methods.

Total Fertility Rate

The total fertility rate is an estimate of the number of live births for each adult female who has lived through her reproductive period. This is estimated on the basis of constant age–specific (or age–group specific) birth rates. It differs from the general fertility ratio, which is the number of births per 1000 women of childbearing age. The total fertility rate is computed by adding the fertility rates for mothers of successive age and dividing the product by the number of mothers,

$$\frac{\Sigma fi}{N}$$

where fi is an age-specific fertility rate, and N is the total number of mothers. A measure of potential fertility, however, when age–specific fertility rates are either not available or unknown could be devised using the length of the reproductive (fertile) period and the "natural" live-birth interval. The average reproductive period, estimated from an average age of nubility of 15–18 years and an average age

TABLE 8.2

Hypothetical Total Fertility Rate at Specified Average Length of Life, Length of Reproductive Period, and a Natural Child-Spacing Interval (28 months)[a]

	Case number								
	(1)	(2)	(3)	(4)	(5)	(6)	(7)	(8)	(9)
Female adult longevity (years)	29	30	31	32	33	34	35	36	37
Reproductive period (years)	11	12	13	14	15	16	17	18	19
Potential total fertility	4.71	5.14	5.57	6.00	6.42	6.85	7.28	7.71	8.14

[a] Mean = 6.42 years; standard deviation = 1.1 years.

of premenopause sterility of 44–47 years, is 32 years. This yields a potential total fertility of 12.2, which is approached by the Hutterites (L. Henry 1961). The calculation of potential total fertility assumes no lack of available mates per fertile woman at any time during her reproductive period and no restrictions on intercourse or interference with conception. If the average age at death of adult females is lower than the onset of premenopause sterility, then that age marks the end of the reproductive period. In the following discussion, I will attempt to present some theoretical estimates of total fertility rates and compare these figures with data on ethnographic cases. In the process, I will refer to the number of surviving children in a family whose mother has completed the childbearing period (size of completed family) and the number of children in a family whose mother has completed the childbearing period (number of children ever born).

Given that the average longevity of adult women in prehistory was about 29 years and the age at menarche was 16, the reproductive span could have lasted as long as 11 years, assuming an adolescent sterility period of 2 years. With a natural live–birth interval of 28 months, the potential total fertility can be estimated at 4.71 children. Assuming a longer reproductive period as a result of a longer female adult longevity (37 years), the potential total fertility can be as high as 8.14 children. The average, assuming an age range of 29–37 years, is 6.42 ± 1.1 (Table 8.2).

In gorilla populations, the fertility rate is approximately four offspring, quite

TABLE 8.3

Prenatal and Postnatal Growth Periods[a]

Primate	Gestation (weeks)	Menarche (years)	Completion of growth (years)
Rhesus monkey (*Macaca*)	2	2	7
Chimpanzee (*P. troglodytes*)	33–32	8.8	11
Orangutan (*Pongo*)	39–37	?	11
Gorilla (*G. gorilla*)	36–37	9	11
Man	38	13–15	20

[a] Data from Campbell 1974; R. Harrison 1967.

TABLE 8.4

Hypothetical Total Fertility Rate at Specified Length of Life, Length of Reproductive Period, and Two Child-Spacing Periods

	Case number								
	(1)	(2)	(3)	(4)	(5)	(6)	(7)	(8)	(9)
Reproductive period (years)	11	12	13	14	15	16	17	18	19
Birth interval of 28 months	4.71	5.14	5.57	6.00	6.42	6.85	7.28	7.71	8.14
Child-spacing interval of 40 months	3.3	3.6	3.9	4.2	4.5	4.8	5.1	5.4	5.7

close to the average of prehistoric humans (Sussman 1972, after Schaller 1963). This is equivalent to a child–spacing interval of 3.5–4.5 years. Gorillas mature sexually at 6–7 years and remain sexually reproductive until the age of 20 years. The life span of captive gorillas is usually no longer than 20 years (Sussman 1972). The child-spacing interval of 3.5–4.5 years among gorillas, according to Sussman, is a consequence of a long period of infant dependence (3–4 years) and the need for the dependent infant to be carried while the troop is moving. Sussman, on the assumption that what is good for gorillas must be good for man, suggests that the actual child-spacing interval in humans was greater than the natural spacing interval of 2.33 years (28 months). Sussman, however, fails to distinguish between the presumably biological spacing mechanisms among gorillas and the sociological mechanisms of early man (Polgar 1972: 260).

It is interesting that the gestation period in man is not significantly longer than it is in other higher primates (Table 8.3). The human infant, however, is far less developed at birth than the infant ape or monkey, because it is born at an earlier developmental stage. This seems to be a function of the greater size of the head of the human infant and the limitations of the birth canal (B. G. Campbell 1974). This pattern of relatively immature birth has some demographic implications, since the child's dependence on the mother is for a longer time than among monkeys and apes and may thus require a prolonged child-spacing period. Also, the immature birth of human infants leads to an increase in the probability of infant mortality because of

TABLE 8.5

Age-Specific Fertility Rates of Women of Some Nonindustrial Ethnographic Populations[a]

	Age-specific rate per 1000 females						
	15–19	20–24	25–29	30–34	35–39	40–44	45–49
Bushmen	46	258	203	172	119	38	25
Australians	175	218	161	151	82	47	1
Average of 13 populations	104	275	275	226	150	52	8

[a] Data from Weiss 1973.

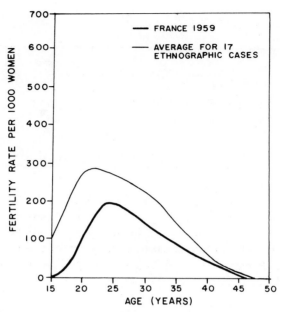

FIGURE 8.3. *Comparison between fertility rate by age of Frenchwomen (1959) and women in 17 ethnographic cases. (Data from Pressat 1972 and Weiss 1973.)*

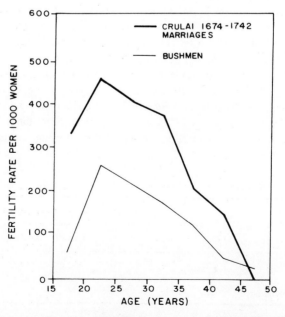

FIGURE 8.4. *Comparison between age-specific fertility rates of Crulai (1674–1742) and Bushmen women. (Data from Pressat 1972 and Weiss 1973.)*

TABLE 8.6

Estimated Fertility Rates for Some of the Most Fertile World Countries, 1955–1960[a]

Country	Total fertility rate per 1000 females	Age-specific rate per 1000 females						
		15–20	20–25	25–30	30–35	34–40	40–45	45–49
Sudan	7496	136.6	315.4	371.7	309.3	234.6	105.2	26.4
Guinea	6605	187.1	315.8	292.7	239.3	177.6	81.9	26.6
Togo	6156	103.1	261.4	293.3	205.8	199.5	97.5	25.7
Guatemala	6510	145.6	272.3	305.4	287.2	189.8	76.9	24.8
Honduras	6962	139.0	328.1	341.0	277.9	205.6	83.2	17.5
Iraq	7243	145.8	347.8	366.8	286.9	202.0	81.7	17.5
Pakistan	6520	184.6	337.7	298.6	230.5	162.1	69.1	21.4
Brunei	7391	152.0	354.0	369.5	290.7	207.8	85.0	19.1
Average	6860	149.2	316.6	329.9	266.0	197.4	85.1	22.4

[a] Data from DeJong 1972.

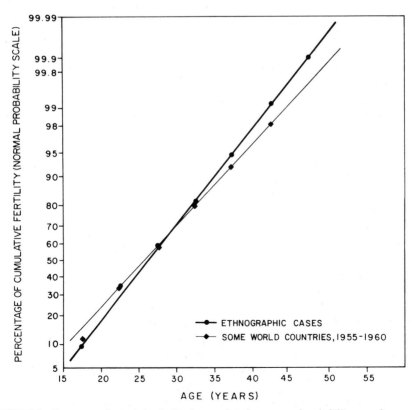

FIGURE 8.5. *Percentage of cumulative fertility by age plotted on a normal probability paper for women from 17 ethnographic cases (Weiss 1973), and women from some of the most fertile populations of the world (DeJong 1972).*

133

the total dependence of the infant on the mother for feeding and its biological vulnerability to predators and disease. A long spacing interval reduces the number of children born per woman. At an average age of death of 29 years (Case 1, Table 8.2) and with nubility reached at age 18, the number of children, as I have indicated, is 4.71. A spacing interval of 3.5 years (42 months) due to resumption of conception following the death of an infant actually amounts to 40 months. Given a child-spacing interval of 40 months, the number of children as calculated from Table 8.2 drops to a range of 3.3–5.7, with an average of 4.5 children (Table 8.4). Among the Australian natives, the highest average limit per woman is cited as five children (Krzywicki 1934). Among the Andaman Islanders, three to four children are reported. A number of four children is recorded for the Sekai and Fuegians (Krzywicki 1934). Among the Bushmen women of the Dobe area, women (15–49 years old) with a life expectancy at birth of 30 years averaged 4.7 live births per woman (N. Howell 1976a:145). Harpending (1976) gives an average of 4.14 for Bushmen women from five other areas. The theoretical figures are thus not unrealistic.

Age-specific fertility rates as constructed in model life tables by Weiss (1973) provide estimates of total fertility of between 3 and 4 children. An example of fertility rates provided by Weiss (1973) is shown in Table 8.5.

It is interesting to note here that the age–specific rate of fertility among the nonindustrial populations is higher than that of Frenchwomen in 1959 (Figure 8.3). The pattern of age-specific fertility, however, is similar, rising from a low point to a peak, followed by gradual decline. The peak in the ethnographic cases is reached at ages 20–25, whereas the peak occurs at 25–30 among the Frenchwomen. This may reflect the tendency toward earlier marriage in the ethnographic cases (Pressat 1972:184), a pattern similar to that for the Crulai population (a non-Malthusian population, i.e., a population unchecked by cultural fertility) (Figure 8.4).

It is also interesting to compare the figures calculated for probable fertility among hunter–gatherers with the figures available on the most fertile nonindustrial (primarily agricultural) nations today (Table 8.6). The average for seven nations is 6.68 children per female. The life expectancy at birth is generally about 40 years. The high fertility is mainly a result of a considerable reduction in infant mortality in comparison with the rates prevalent during earlier centuries. In one case, Guinea, the total fertility is 6.605 children per female, although the female life expectancy at birth is only 28 years. The rate of infant mortality is 21.6%.

It is noteworthy that the percentage of cumulative fertility for the ethnographic cases reported by Weiss (1972a, ,1973) as shown by the normal probability graph approximates a Gaussian distribution (Figure 8.5) that does not differ much from that for the populations of the Sudan and other countries characterized by high fertility (Table 8.6) This distribution seems to be a reflection of changes in fecundity, spontaneous abortion, and so forth with age (Henneberg 1976:43). This regularity in age-specific fertility can be used to arrive at a model of age-specific fertility of nonindustrial populations, which in turn can be used to estimate age-specific fertility rates if the total fertility is known.

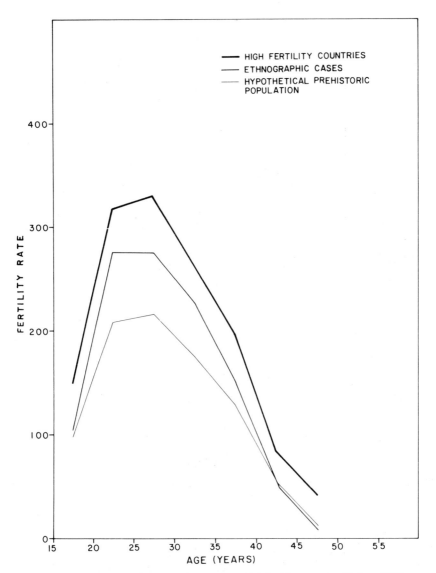

FIGURE 8.6. *Age-specific fertility rates of women from high-fertility countries (DeJong 1972), women from 17 ethnographic cases (Weiss 1973), and women in a hypothetical prehistoric population. The fertility rate for the prehistoric population is calculated from the total fertility rate and a prehistoric fertility model.*

The percentage of cumulative fertility for the high fertility cases and the corresponding percentage of fertility provide the fertility model shown in Table 8.7.

From this model fertility and the estimate of 4.5 children per woman(4500 children per 1000 women), the age-specific fertility rate for a prehistoric population of that fertility rate can be estimated as shown in Table 8.7 and 8.8.

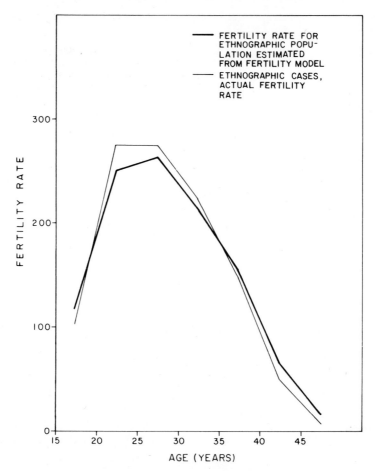

FIGURE 8.7. *Comparison between actual age-specific fertility rates of women from 17 ethnographic cases (Weiss 1973) and age-specific fertility rates calculated from the total fertility rate and a model of human fertility.*

The pattern displayed by the reconstructed age-specific fertility for the hypothetical population (Figure 8.6) matches well that of the ethnographic cases (total fertility rate 5.45 children per woman). The pattern for high fertility countries (with a total fertility rate of 6.86 children per female) resembles that of the ethnographic cases. Application of the fertility model to the ethnographic cases yields specific fertility rates that are very close to actual age-specific fertility rates (Figure 8.7).

Gross Reproduction Rate

The number of female births per female is an estimate of the gross reproduction rate. Since the percentage of female births is a constant of 48.8% of all children

TABLE 8.7
A Model of Age-Specific Fertility for High-Fertility Populations

Age	Percentage of cumulative fertility	Percentage of fertility
15–19	10.9	10.9
20–24	34.1	23.1
25–29	58.0	24.1
30–34	77.7	19.5
35–39	92.1	14.4
40–44	98.3	6.2
45–50	100.0	1.6

born (Pressat 1972) a total fertility of 4.5 (reproductive period of 13 years and child spacing of 28 months) would correspond to a gross reproduction rate of about 4.5 × .488, or 2.22.

Net Reproduction Rate

Net reproduction rate is a measure of the ability of the population to renew itself. It is estimated by reducing the average number of female births per female (gross reproduction rate) by the percentage of women surviving to the mean age of childbearing. In the United States today the proportion of women surviving to childbearing age is 93.8% (Coale 1974). If we assume that the total fertility is four births per female, a generation of 2050 persons (1000 females and 1050 males) will be replaced by a generation of 1000 females × .938 × 4, or 3752 persons. On the other hand, if the proportion of women surviving to childbearing age is only 50%, then the same initial population at the same rate of total fertility will be succeeded by a population of 1000 × .5 × 4, or 2000. Thus, although the same

TABLE 8.8
Reconstructed Age-Specific Fertility for a Hypothetical Population with a 4.5 Children/Woman Fertility Rate Using a Fertility Model (Table 8.7)

Age (years)	Fertility rate
15–19	99.1
20–24	208.8
25–29	216.9
30–34	175.5
35–39	129.5
40–44	55.8
45–49	14.4
Total (for 5-year age classes)	900
Total × 5 years	4500

total fertility is maintained, the first population is growing: the population is declining in the group in which the survivorship of childbearing women is low.

During prehistoric times, and, in fact, up to a very recent time, the survivorship of females, as well as males, was far below the human potential for survivorship that some societies today are fast approaching. The survivorship of human beings is a function of mortality patterns, which are governed by infant mortality, child mortality, and adult mortality. The causes of death for various age-groups are quite different: occupational mortality for adults, maternal mortality for reproductive females, and so on. Infectious, dietary, or accident-related diseases are also age-specific. Among hunter–gatherers and also nonindustrial populations, the infant mortality rates are quite high. Numerous observations indicate that child mortality is responsible for the elimination of 30–50% of all children born (Deevey 1960; Nag 1962). Infant care and improved hygiene could drastically cut down this human wastage and thus increase the proportion of women surviving to childbearing age, as is the case among many human societies today. But the demographic consequences of this cultural interference are very serious, because of the tremendous increase in the rate of population increase. Coale (1974) has indicated that given an adult female survivorship as high as 93.8%, the number of children born per female should not exceed 2.17, which is far below the reproductive potential of 8–10 children. The situation is aggravated by the reduction of the age at menarche and the delay in menopause that accompany better survivorship under modern conditions (Sengel 1973). These changes lead to an increase in the length of reproductive span of the female. It should be noted that improved survivorship of females past childbearing age does not influence population growth because these females are already outside the reproductive pool. The major age-group that would influence population growth is that of prereproductive females. Throughout prehistoric times, human populations were afflicted by a high depletion of that age-group. From ethnographic observation, infant mortality lies between 30 and 50% (Nag 1962). For prehistoric groups infant mortality in the Maghreb Epipalaeolithic is estimated at 41.3% (calculated from Acsádi and Nemeskéri 1970:266). These figures are mostly for the age-groups between 0 and 4 years. A mortality rate of about 10% should be allowed for older children. This would indicate that mortality before adulthood would have removed, on the average, about 50% of the female births. About 50% of the females would survive to childbearing age. This figure is very close to a survivorship figure of 46% for prehistoric populations based on a mortality pattern modeled after the Epipalaeolithic populations of the Maghreb (Acsádi and Nemeskéri 1970:172). Incidently, this figure is close to the model of the worst survivorship in modern populations (U.N. level zero). Also, a figure of about 55% survivorship is obtained for Upper Palaeolitic groups (Weiss 1973:93). We may thus assume an average figure of 50%. These figures are far more realistic than the 32% cited by Acsádi and Nemeskéri based on a dismal mortality type, which they call the *Sinanthropus* type (*Homo erectus*). Thus, with a gross reproduction rate of 2.22, the net reproduction rate would be 1.11 if the survivorship was 50%. The value of 1.33 given by Acsádi and Nemerskéri (1970:175) is close to my estimate.

Rate of Potential Natural Increase

The net reproduction rate measures the replacement of females. Thus it indicates the population potential for survival and growth. If the net reproduction rate is less than 1, the replacement of females is incomplete and the population becomes endangered by extinction if this rate continues. For example, with a figure of .76, derived by Acsádi and Nemeskéri (1970:178) on the basis of minimal survivorship of 32%, there would have been a lack of 24 female children. At that rate prehistoric populations would have died out. At a rate of 1.11, there would be an excess of .11 females, beyond replacement, and the population is likely to grow. A rate of 2 would indicate a population can double itself each generation.

The rate of natural increase or Lotka rate (P) for a stable population reflects the potential of a population to replace itself if existing fertility and mortality rates are continued. Lotka's rate may be derived from the net rate of reproduction (R_0) as follows (Pressat 1972: 350–352):

$$P = (y\sqrt{R_0}) - 1$$

where y is the mean age at childbearing, or approximately 20 years.

If the rate of reproduction is 1.11, the value of the Lotka rate would be 5.23; that is, the population can grow at a rate of about 5.23 persons per 1000 females per year. This figure is only suggestive of the probable rate of intrinsic increase, given the possible values for child spacing and the life expectancy of adult females. For example, with an adult female longevity of 32 years, an age of 18 nubility, and the same child-spacing period of 40 months, the net reproductive rate would be 1.230 and the Lotka rate of natural increase would be 7.4 per 1000 females. Under the same conditions, but with a natural live-birth interval of 28 months, the Lotka rate rises to 20 per 1000 females.

The rate of population growth (r) is obtained from the following equation:

$$r = \ln\left(\frac{N_2}{N_1}\right)/t$$

where N_2 is the population size reached from an initial population N_1 after a time period (t). Since R_0 is a measure of the replacement of women by their daughters, the number of offspring per female, assuming a ratio of 2.05 children for each female, would equal 2.05 R_0. An initial population of 1000 persons consisting of 488 females and 512 men can reach a population of 488 × 2.05 R_0 within a generation. Given a generation span of 20 years, the rate of annual increase can be estimated from the equation:

$$r = \frac{488 \times 2.05\, R_0}{1000}$$

$$= \ln\left(\frac{488 \times 2.05\, R_0}{1000}\right)/20$$

This equation can be simplified to

$$r = \ln R_o/20$$

This equation provides the same results as Lotka's.

Thus, a population with a net reproduction rate of 1.11 would increase at a rate of .0052 per year, about 5.2 per 1000 or .52% per year. At the higher net reproduction rate of 1.758 the rate would be .028 or 28 per 1000 (2.8%) per year. At the net reproduction rate of 2, the population would increase at the more rapid rate of 36 per 1000 (3.5%) per year. At that rate the population would double within one generation. The relationship between growth rate and doubling time (Dt) is expressed by the following equation:

$$Dt = .6931/r$$

For a growth rate of 3.5% per year, the doubling time is 19.8 years. At the rate of .52%, which I estimate as the probable maxium growth rate for prehistoric groups, and a prolonged child-spacing period of 40 months, the doubling time is 133 years or about seven generations.

Overview

The foregoing determination of the potential rate of population growth among prehistoric populations under conditions of high preadult and adult mortality and with a late age at nubility, as well as a long child-spacing period, indicates that prehistoric populations were not incapable of rapid rates of population increase. Populations could double within 130 years. Thus within 2000 years (which approximates the time span of many technological traditions during the Terminal Palaeolithic), an initial regional population unit of 175–500 persons (Wobst 1974) could increase to 3.6–11 million persons![1]

The capacity of prehistoric populations for rapid population increase has been previously expressed by Polgar (1972) and myself (Hassan 1973, 1975) from trial models. Henneberg (1976), using another methodology, also concludes that the capacity of most prehistoric populations for reproduction was great. The impressions gained from the high mortality of prehistoric populations seem alarming and have led many scholars to suspect that prehistoric people were living under the constant threat of extinction. This view was criticized (Polgar 1972), but has been revoiced by N. Howell (1976b).

It is important to note here that the high potential for growth as demostrated by the preceding calculations is only indicative of theoretical potential at the specified

---

[1]The determination of the population size (N_2) after a time period (t) beginning with an initial population (N_1) at a rate of growth (r) is obtained from the equation

$$N_2 = N_1 e^{rt}$$

demographic conditions that seem reasonable. However, assuming conditions that induced malnutrition, the demographic conditions would be worse than those described. Under such conditions, menarche may be delayed, survivorship to childbearing age would be reduced, and the longevity of adult females would also be adversely affected. To simulate the impact of such conditions, age at nubility was placed at 18–19years, the period of adolescent sterility at 2 years, the average age at death for adults at 27–28 years, and the survivorship to childbearing age at .46 (Table 8.9). The results of the simulation runs in all cases indicate that that population under such conditions would show a rapid decline: between -7.2 and -29.1 individuals per 1000 females per year or about -17.5 ± 5.8 individuals per 1000 females per year on the average. In these simulation runs, the child-spacing period was placed at 33–37 months, less than the 40 months used previously. A reduction in child spacing could be made as a conscious decision to increase fertility. The child spacing may be reduced further to the natural birth interval but this would entail greater hardship for the mothers, because of greater childbearing, nursing, and rearing effort, especially if the mothers were already malnourished. However, assuming a drop in the child spacing period to the natural birth interval, the population can only replace itself if the age at menarche is no greater than 18 and the average age at death of females is no less than 31 years.

I should like to recall here that although the palaeodemographic data provide an estimate of about 29 years for female adult longevity, ethnographic data (Weiss 1973) provide a basis for assuming an age of 37 years. The effect of undernourishment can be deleterious only if we believe that the palaeodemographic evidence is not underestimated by the method of determining the age of old adults (see discussion in Chapter 7). A case reported by Arsdale (1978) gives an estimate of E_{15} of 27 years, and nubility at age 18–19 years. Using the theoretical model we obtain 3.525

TABLE 8.9

Estimate of Probable Rate of Net Reproduction in Hypothetical Cases of Poorly Nourished Populations at a Birth Interval of 28 Months

Age at menarche (years)	Adolescent sterility (years)	Average age at death of adult females (years)	Number of children per female	Number of daughters per female	Net reproductive rate
18	2	27	3.0	1.46	.67
19	2	27	2.57	1.25	.58
18	2	28	3.43	1.67	.77
19	2	28	3.0	1.46	.67
18	2	29	3.85	1.88	.87
19	2	29	3.43	1.67	.77
18	2	30	4.29	2.09	.96
19	2	30	3.86	1.88	.87
18	2	31	5.14	2.51	1.15
19	2	31	4.26	2.51	.96

surviving children per adult female, compared with an actual figure of 3.5 children. The calculations were based on a spacing interval of 40 months. At that fertility rate the potential rate of growth is 2.71% per year.

It should be also noted here that given the small size of prehistoric populations (see Chapter 4), stochastic fluctuations in population size and changes in the rates of mortality and fertility could have led to periods of population increase or decline if no other mechanisms dampened the effect of such fluctuations. In the next chapter, I will discuss this problem and explore the pattern of population regulation that might have prevailed in prehistoric times.

9

The Regulation of Prehistoric Populations

Desire not a multitude of unprofitable children.

—Eccles.2; Ecclus. 16:1

The potential for population growth in prehistoric times, as I have argued in Chapter 7, was not as great as it is today, because of high levels of mortality; however, it was sufficiently great to allow a very rapid increase in world population. A low estimate of .05% would have allowed a single pair to multiply to 3 billion— the world population today—in no more than 15,000 years and to reach the population density that characterized the end of the Palaeolithic in about 10,000 years. At a rate of 1%, the earth would have been filled to its present capacity in the span of no more than two millennia. The overall Palaeolithic population trend could hardly have approached this inconceivable rate of increase. We must therefore entertain the hypothesis that intervals of rapid growth were infrequent and that they stand out sharply against a background of very slow growth.

Estimates of world population (Chapter 12) indicate that this was indeed the case. By the end of the Palaeolithic there were no more than 8–12 million persons and the average rate of growth during the Pleistocene was well below .01%/year. There are, therefore, compelling reasons to suggest that population controls were exercised by prehistoric populations.

It is my opinion that the practice of population control was common among prehistoric populations (Hassan 1979c). I am aware of the ability of human populations to expand their subsistence base, but, as I will argue in the next chapter, economic growth is not necessarily stimulated by excessive population increase (population pressure). I have also suggested that the limited potential (Hassan

143

1978b) of hunting–gathering subsistence for economic growth places severe limitations on culture change as an alternative to population control. I will concern myself in this chapter with the pattern of population regulation among Pleistocene hunting–gathering peoples. The changes in this pattern during the early period of food production will be dealt with in Chapter 14.

The regulation of hunting–gathering populations, like that of animal populations (Andrewartha 1970; L. Brown 1970; D. E. Davis 1966; Lack 1954; Perrins 1970; Slobodkin 1961; Turk *et al.* 1975), is ultimately a function of available food resources. Animal populations are regulated by behavioral feedback mechanisms that trigger emigration, or by physiological adjustments to reduce birth rate (D. E. Davis 1966). Excluding for the moment man's ability to alter his habitat, the complex and advanced behavioral systems of human populations permit similar responses to overpopulation.

Before I provide a review of the probable role of emigration, and fertility-mortality controls on prehistoric populations, I will discuss the proximate causes of population control that underlie the balance between population and food resources.

A Model of Proximate Causes

Among animals, population controls are in many cases physiological. External circumstances of stress (environmental or social) will activate the hypothalamus, which in turn activates the pituitary, which interferes with reproduction and health. Wynne-Edwards (1965) suggests that behavioral (social) practices are common (see also D. E. Davis 1966). Competition for resources leads to behavioral patterns that influence the survival of existing individuals and the addition of new members. Social rivalry and rank, according to Wynne-Edwards (1965), lead to the exclusion of surplus individuals from the right to share in the resources of the habitat. The competition is especially keen when the population density increases to a level that upsets the existing balance between demand and resources. Competition and rank may not only exclude certain individuals from a share in resources but may also diminish their reproductive success. (See, for example, Drickamer 1974 on rank in *Macaca mulatta.*) In man, behavioral controls are the sole determinants of population regulation (D. E. Davis 1972; Wynne-Edwards 1965).

Among hunting–gathering groups, the proximate causes of population regulation are in my opinion occasioned by (*a*) a desired (optimum) group size, (*b*) the maternal burden of children, and (*c*) a low optimum child-to-adult ratio (Figure 9.1).

Wynne-Edwards (1965) has emphasized the role of territoriality in the behavioral regulation of animal populations. Hayden (1972) rightly dismisses this mechanism for hunter-gatherers because strict territoriality is not common among them. He proposes instead "the optimal size of groups" as an alternative counterpart. Hayden postulates a large group size among the australopithecines for the

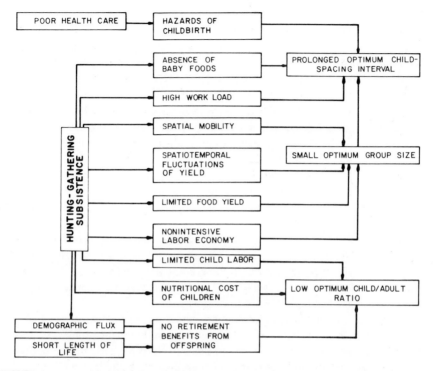

FIGURE 9.1. *A model of the influence of hunting-gathering subsistence on child spacing, group size, and child-adult ratio. A prolonged child-spacing period, a small group size, and a low child-adult ratio are optimal and may thus motivate a damping of fertility.*

purpose of defense against predators, and a nuclear family size once the dominance of man over predators (by tools or weapons) was established. He correlates the first with hierarchical dominance of males over females, maximum work load per female, and an active male role in controlling population density (through "charging displays" by males, as among chimpanzees). In the case of the nuclear family, emerging as a result of the easing of predatorial pressure and the erosion of the basis of large groups, Hayden suggests the emergence of social bonding to ensure group functioning and the creation of a new predator, man himself, to maintain group size.

Although I disagree with certain points in Hayden's model, I share his opinion that optimum group size is a more valid concept for hunting-gathering populations than is territoriality. I have already discussed the adaptive "wisdom" in the formation of small local groups of 15–50 persons bound loosely in regional groups of 500–1000 persons. The reasons are economic, biological, social, and psychological (Chapter 1).

It would be a mistake, however, to equate territoriality with optimum group size among hunter-gatherers, for although the first is fixed, the optimum group size of hunter-gatherers is time-bound, varying with the seasons and with periodic and other variations in resources. The composition of hunting-gathering populations is flexible and fluid. Lee (1968, 1976) notes that among the !Kung Bushmen camp size changes daily. This should bring to our attention one of the most important characteristics of hunting–gathering populations: They are not closed populations. Therefore, a consideration of population size and control must include the fact that natural population increase is always modified by population movements. These include movements of individuals, fission, and migration. According to Lee (1972a), the frequency and kind of movement seem to be dictated mainly by social conflict and the amount of preferred food available for individual consumption (which may not be equally distributed). Woodburn (1968) indicates that individuals may abandon one group and join another because their share of meat is less than what they consider adequate. Hunting success or failure may be another reason for group movement or fission. We must thus recognize the importance of population movement as a mechanism of population regulation. Man is not unique in this regard (Wynne-Edwards 1965:1547).

In short, the limitation of natural abundance, the spatial distribution of resources, and their temporal variability select for a *small* group size. Excessive population growth becomes evident to the group not as much by the occurrence of hunger, but by the greater demands for labor input as yield per capita declines (cf. Glassow 1978:41; Hassan 1978b:75).

Intensification of labor under hunting–gathering conditions, in view of temporal variability in food resources, is not a viable solution to the problem of population increase, since the population would place itself in jeopardy during periods of food scarcity. The limited labor input under hunting–gathering conditions (Lee 1968; Sahlins 1972) is thus not as much a result of "laziness" as it is a means of coping with the ecological conditions of an economy dependent on natural abundance or scarcity. Hunting–gathering communities are thus likely to develop standards of labor that produce a food yield below that of average carrying capacity. These work standards give a margin of safety and monitor overpopulation. I will return to carrying capacity and population in the next chapter.

The burden of children is nutritional and economic. The absence of milk and mushy foods is a dietary fact among hunter-gatherers (N. Howell, according to Coale 1974; Weiss 1976) that commends itself to the question of health in relation to fertility. Infants and young children require a relatively higher proportion of high-quality protein per kilogram of body weight than do adults. An adult needs about 1 gm/kg body weight, whereas an infant needs about 2.2gm/kg (Burton 1976; Dubos 1965). The absence of milk and other mushy foods leads to a greater dependence on mother's milk, and a child thus needs to be nursed for a longer period (Coale 1974). Long spacing intervals therefore ensure adequate nutrition for an already living child (Townsend 1971). The dependence on mother's milk also increases the amount of maternal nutritional drain if children are closely spaced with overlapping nursing periods. Also, hunting–gathering women are responsible for procuring much of the group's food (Hayden 1972; Lee 1968) and must combine this work load with their maternal responsibilities. If they have too many children, their efficiency is reduced and the overall economic welfare of the population is affected (see Nurge 1975 on birth rate and work load).

Lee and DeVore (1968a) Carr-Saunders (1922), Sussman (1972), and Lee (1972) have argued that a long spacing period is also advantageous for hunting–gatherering women because of frequent spatial mobility. Among most hunter–gatherers, a long spacing period (between 3 and 4 years) seems to be the norm (Carr-Saunders 1922; Krzywicki 1934; Lee 1972).

The practice of having a child-spacing period of 3–4 years, which might be prompted by consideration of the health of both mother and child, might inadvertently reduce population growth rate. It may be also suggested that the health hazards that are more frequent for young mothers may be averted by delayed marriage, which would shorten the reproductive span and thus serve as an additional inadvertent population control.

The economic implications of age structure may also have contributed to a certain measure of population control. The ratio of children to adults can be thought of in economic terms as a dependents/producers ratio (Wrigley 1969:24). For hunter–gatherers, this value is generally low because of high infant mortality. The relatively high mortality of adults, however, prevents the child–adult or dependency ratio from being too low. The low child–adult ratio thus is a reflection of "frustrated fertility" where potential fertility cannot be realized because of mortality (Wrigley 1969:22).

If fertility increases as a result of differential relaxation of mortality (a reduction in both infant and adult mortality would not significantly alter the child–adult ratio in a stable population), the dependency ratio may increase, producing a greater work load per producer. This would be an unwelcome development, especially considering the value of children relative to their cost (cf. Spengler 1966). In a hunting–gathering society, there is no need to have as many children as in agricultural communities. Adult women and a few children are enough to procure the amount of plant foods required. Children cannot contribute to the procurement of meat through participation in the hunt, and their value as a part of the labor force is low. In addition, because the optimum group size among hunter–gatherers is small, there will be no high premium on high fertility. Because the life expectancy of adults is low, only a few survive to the age when they would need to be supported by their offspring. As has been mentioned, children's protein needs are proportionately higher than those of adults, and high-quality protein is generally derived from costly animal game. The cost of a child is therefore relatively high. These factors may have contributed to the use of prenatal and neonatal "economic" controls to maintain a low dependency ratio, which serves simultaneously as a "population" control.

Cultural Methods of Population Control

Human populations are known to have practiced a vartiety of cultural methods of population control (Benedict 1970, 1972; Douglas 1966; Hayden 1972; Stott 1962). These methods include fertility controls, mortality controls, and spatial population movements.

Population movement may succeed in redistributing population to take maximum advantage of resources, and migration may siphon away some of the excess population, but, in the long run, other means must be used to hold down group size. The maintenance of a viable human group under such conditions—in part—can be achieved by the fluidity of its population.

Internal migration or demographic shuffle is in fact characteristic of hunter-gatherers. Emigration is a potential solution to overpopulation as long as vacant territories with no environmental or cultural resistance are available. It is, therefore, an option open only for "frontier" populations. The peopling of the world was a slow and gradual process and seems to have been linked with advancements in human adaptiveness (see Chapter 12). Thus, it does not seem, that migration was a viable population-control mechanism for the majority of Pleistocene populations. The peopling of the world was perhaps more a process of nonmigratory expansion rather than purposeful directed migration.

Fertility Controls

The reproductive sequence in humans, as in other mammals, is often quite elaborate and thus can be easily interrupted. In vertebrates, the sequence is long and varied, which permits interference at various stages (Figure 9.2). Therefore, a high degree of population control can be achieved by depressing fertility. In man, the bringing together of mates can be interrupted by social sanctions, delayed marriage, celibacy, elimination of widows from the reproductive pool, polygamy, and age differential between mates. The availability of mates may also be influenced by exogamy or endogamy.

Among mates, the incidence of conception can be inhibited by sexual codes and practices, such as pre-, extra-, and postmarital sex, regularity of intercouse, frequency of intercourse, positions, postpartum abstinence, abstinence during menstruation, ceremonial and religious abstinence, and "deviant" sexuality.

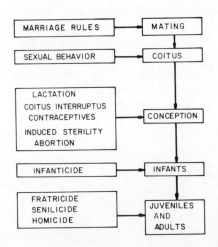

FIGURE 9.2. *Reproductive sequence (right) and factors that can potentially interrupt that sequence and thus reduce fertility or increase mortality leading to a check of population growth (left).*

Successful initiation or completion of pregnancies can be controlled by induced male or female sterility, coitus interruptus, contraceptives, and abortion.

MARRIAGE

Late marriage reduces fertility by shortening the reproductive span. In most nonindustrial societies, including hunter–gatherers, marriage occurs early (Benedict 1972:75; Meggitt 1962:80; Nag 1962:193)—in some cases, before puberty. This would not affect fertility since sexual intercourse would not lead to conception. In other cases, where marriage occurs late, sexual relations and the production of children may precede marriage. Empirical evidence on the age at marriage among prehistoric populations is lacking.

Marriage rules are quite varied. Some of these rules affect fertility. Monogamous marriage, for example, restricts the number of potential mates. Rules against the remarriage of divorcees or widows may also reduce fertility by restricting the pool of potential mates. The impact of polygyny on fertility is controversial (Benedict 1972; Lorimer et al. 1954; Nag 1962, 1975). In many cases it seems to reduce fertility, perhaps through a lower frequency of coitus per female (Nag 1975).

The age of mates may also affect fertility, since there are marked variations in fertility between various age-groups. As a measure for population control, Plato recommended marriage at age 30 for males and 20 for females (Himes 1963:69). The magnitude of promiscuity allowed by the society in the form of premarital, extramarital, or postmarital relations contributes significantly to the fertility rate. In a simulation of the probable impact of certain marriage rules on fertility, Wobst (1975) came up with the results listed in Table 9.1.

The results are based on four sets of rules:

1. There are no limitations on mating.
2. The population is monogamous.

TABLE 9.1

Fertility Rate Required to Maintain Stationary Population with Various Marriage Rules[a,b]

Marriage rules	Fertility rate according to group size				
	100	200	300	400	500
1	4.3%	2.9%	3.3%	2.5%	2.1%
	(5000)	(5000)	(5000)	(5000)	(5000)
2	12.5%	8.3%	5.4%	4.2%	2.9%
	(50,000)	(50,000)	(20,000)	(16,500)	(5000)
3	20.5%	7.7%	5.8%	—	—
	(50,000)	(50,000)	(36,000)	—	—
4	32.0%	10.1%	7.3%	6.3%	3.4%
	(53,000)	(55,000)	(16,000)	(5000)	(5000)

[a] From Wobst 1975.

[b] Values shown are percentages in excess of the stationary life table age-specific fertility rate from model table 25–40 (Weiss, 1973:144). Numbers in parentheses are the censused years on which the mean percentage is based.

3. The population is monogamous and incest taboos disallow mating between individuals sharing a single name in their list of parents, grandparents, or great-grandparents.

4. Rule 3, plus the stipulation that males have to be older than their mates.

The results indicate that for any given population size, the degree of fertility required to maintain a stationary population increases as the limitations imposed on the probability of mating increase. There seems, however, to be a dilution of the effect of these restrictions as the size of the mating group increases.

Small groups are also subject to both positive and negative fluctuations. Wobst (1974) has shown that small groups risk extinction if their mating network does not include other groups. It seems that the continued flux in hunting–gathering group size is not only an advantage from an economic standpoint, as I have argued before, but is also an adaptive mechanism that serves to expand the mating pool without expanding the size of the economic and social unit. Exogamous marriage must be looked upon as a mating pattern that enhances the demographic viability of small hunting–gathering populations. Data by J. W. Adams and A. B. Kasakoff (1975) indicate an increase in the percentage of endogamy as a population increases.

Exogamy, of course, requires a social network of several exogamous groups. The larger social unit, what I have termed the *regional group,* is referred to by others as a *tribe.* The maintenance of a group consisting of 20 to 40 local groups (bands) must be based on amicable social relations among these bands. This kind of social organization is uniquely human. Intergroup behavior in other primates is generally unfriendly and antagonistic.

Exogamy is generally aided by incest taboos. Paradoxically, incest taboos restrict the number of mates potentially available per reproductive individual. However, in a test of the probable impact of incest taboos on fertility, Wobst (1975) undertook a simulation experiment. The results of his simulation indicate that the effect of incest taboos on restricting fertility is negligible when a population of about 500 persons is involved. This is believed to be the size of a small regional group. However, the impact of incest taboos on restricting fertility seems to be considerable when small groups are involved. An exogamous pattern thus would tend to strengthen the social bonds among small local groups for mutual demographic, biological, and economic advantage. It is thus understandable that the congregation of local groups where nubile women and marriageable men are enabled to meet should occasion ceremonial activities, dancing, and feasting (B. G. Campbell 1974).

SEXUAL BEHAVIOR

Any activity that reduces or increases the rate of coitus is likely to affect fertility. However, the effect may in some cases be negligible. The frequency of intercourse, for example, is believed to be more or less similar from one society to another (Pool, comment in Nag 1972; *contra* Ford and Beach 1951), yet Nag (1972:260) feels that fertility level may be affected by some variation. Nag's (1972) own study of a Bengal village reveals a rate of coitus *less* than that among American white women, but this variation does not seem to produce significant differences in fertility.

Nevertheless, from a review of the literature, Nag (1972) suggests that the probability of conception increases as the average frequency of coitus per week increases from less than one to four times and more, because the fertile period of the ovulatory cycle is less than 48 hours. There are no adequate data on the average frequency of intercourse, but a rate of about two to three times per week is common (Katchadourian and Lunde 1972; Pressat 1972). There is also a decrease in frequency of intercourse with age.

Malthus (1826: Vol. I, 37–39) suggested that "hardships and dangers of savage life which take off the attention from sexual passion" lead to lower fertility among hunter–gatherers. Malthus's views reflect the then prevalent exaggeration of the hardships of hunting and gathering. There is little information on the frequency of intercourse among hunter–gatherers, but rates of two to three times per week among the Chiricahua, three to four times a week among the Crow, and the seemingly high figure of three to five times per night among the Arunda (Katchadourian and Lunde 1972:172) do not seem to reflect any abatement of "sexual passion," and does compare well to the rates common among "civilized" peoples.

Abstinence varies in its duration and overt reasons. Postpartum abstinence may vary from weeks to as long as 2 or 3 years. Long periods of abstinence seem to be correlated with a reduction in fertility (Nag 1962). Abstinence during menstruation is unlikely to affect fertility because the ova are not released during that period. Ceremonial or religious rules may account for long periods of abstinence and can thus be effective in reducing fertility. Periodic abstinence (the rhythm method) involves abstinence during the presumed fertile period of the menstrual cycle. However, failure is high because of the frequent irregularity of the cycle; success seems to lie between 15 and 35% (Katchadourian and Lunde 1972:143–144).

Among the wide variety of possible positions during intercourse, the face-to-face position with the man on top seems to be the most common (Katchadourian and Lunde 1972:250). It is also the most likely position to lead to conception, especially if the woman maintains her posture after coitus and the man does not withdraw abruptly.

"Deviant" sexuality may interfere with fertility if it is practiced in lieu of male–female coital activity. Data, however, are scant. Turnbull (1972:294) is of the opinion that homosexuality is a common method of birth control in small societies. He mentions the Indian tribes of South America as the clearest example, where living quarters are divided into male and female sections. The adult males are divided into subgroups and practice homosexual intercourse together. The subgroups hunt together and form warring parties bonded by homosexuality. Homosexuality is encouraged by long weaning periods (up to 3 years). A man may not have intercourse with his wife until the end of that period. However, if lactation retards ovulation, the heterosexual intercourse would not lead to a high risk of conception. Homosexuality then may be mainly a function of postpartum taboos or prohibitions. It may be a by-product of an involuntary method of birth control (Knodel 1977; Nerlove 1974) rather than a birth control method in its own right, unless it is practiced in lieu of heterosexual intercourse.

PROLONGED LACTATION

There is evidence that lactation (breast-feeding) inhibits ovulation (Berman *et al.* 1972; Frisch 1977; R. J. Harrison 1967:122–123; Jain *et al.* 1970; S. H. Katz 1972:361–362). Accordingly, some anthropologists link long child-spacing intervals to prolonged breast-feeding (N. Howell 1976a; Lee 1978; Wolfe 1933). Among the Bushmen, Lee (1972b) notes, mothers nurse their children for 2.5–3.5 years. During the latter half of that period they lead an active sexual life, yet conception does not occur.[1] A long suckling period is also reported by Krzywicki (1934:161) for many hunting–gathering groups and is supported by numerous observations (Hayden 1972). The long nursing period may also be associated with sexual abstinence. Van Ginneken (1974) has concluded that the fertility-reducing effect of lactation lasts less than a year.

COITUS INTERRUPTUS (WITHDRAWAL)

Coitus interruptus is known among many nonindustrial groups (Benedict 1970:72) but is a poor to fair contraceptive, having a success rate of 15–30% (Katchadourian and Lunde 1972).

INDUCED STERILITY

Among hunter–gatherers male sterility may result from certain ceremonial surgical practices (Hayden 1972:208). It is unlikely that female sterilization was ever practiced among prehistoric populations, since it is a major surgical operation.

INDUCED ABORTION

The number of live births can be controlled through prenatal checks including induced abortion (Nurge 1975). Abortion is universal (Devereux 1967) and nonindustrial groups are not an exception (Laughlin 1968). Herbal poisons, heat, irritants, starvation, bleeding, violence, and mechanical techniques are only a few of the means used to induce abortion. Many of these methods are hazardous to the mother. For example, the practice of jumping on the lower abdomen of the mother may abort the fetus but it may also terminate the reproductive role of the mother (see Devereux 1967:27–42, 171–357 for a review of the techniques of abortion).

The practice of abortion during the Pleistocene has been suggested by Nurge (1973) because of the wide use of the practice today and the variety of techniques known. Spontaneous abortion (natural fetal death) is influenced by prenatal care and nutrition (Stott 1962). The probability of miscarriage also increases with the number of pregnancies (Leridan 1977). The age of the mother is still another factor, since the risk of miscarriage rises with age. The probability of miscarriage also is correlated with poor nutrition, heavy work load, and physical hardship (Stott 1962). These factors would indicate that the rate of spontaneous miscarriage among Pleistocene

---

[1]See also R. B. Lee, *Lactation, ovulation, infanticide, and women's work: A study of hunter-gatherer population regulation,* in Biosocial Mechanisms of Population Regulation, R. S. Malpass and H. Goklein (editors), Yale University Press, New Haven, Conn.

women in hunting–gathering groups would have been higher than the rate in present-day industrial societies. In a survey of 16 nonindustrial societies, Nag (1962) reported miscarriages to be in the range of 2.9–23.1% of total pregnancies. The average for all groups was 8%. The rate of induced abortion is less quantitatively known. Nag (1962) reports a "high" incidence of induced abortion in nonindustrial groups. Tietze and Dawson (1973) quote a widely used figure of 24% for abortions out of all live births for the whole world today. Legal abortions, however, in 17 countries provide an estimate of 1.34%. These countries do not include Japan, China, and the U.S.S.R., where a high abortion rate prevails. In some areas of Japan, for example, abortions are over 30% of live births (Nag 1962:136). This frequency is only possible when the practice is widely accepted (Lorimer *et al.* 1954). Nurge (1973:12) suggests a rate of spontaneous abortion among Pleistocene women of 10–25%.

The average rate of abortion that can be tolerated by a stationary and stable population may be calculated from the relationship between fertility rate (f), survivorship to mean childbearing age (l_{15}) and net reproduction rate (R_0). For a stationary population, $R_0 = 1$, and thus:

$$f = \frac{1}{.488 \times l_x} \tag{9.1}$$

where .488 is the ratio of female births to total births. The number of abortions required would be the difference between actual total fertility (f_i) and "stationary" total fertility divided by the actual total fertility rate:

$$\text{Abortion rate} = (f_i - f_0)/f_i$$

Substituting for f from Eq. (9.1) we obtain

$$\text{Abortion rate} = \frac{f_i - \left(\dfrac{1}{.488 \times l_x} \right)}{f_i}$$

Thus, at a total fertility rate of 6.42 and $l_{15} = .50$, the rate of abortion can be estimated as follows:

$$\text{Abortion rate} = \frac{6.42 - \left(\dfrac{1}{.488 \times .50} \right)}{6.42}$$

$$= .36 \text{ or } 36\%$$

This figure assumes a natural birth interval of 28 months (Chapter 7). If prolonged child spacing was practiced, the abortion rate required would be lower. At a child-spacing period of 3–4 years as a result of prolonged lactation, leading to a total fertility rate of 4.5, the rate of abortion (or other methods of controls) required to maintain a stationary population would be about 6%. Abortion, thus, should be considered as a possible population control during the Pleistocene. Its rate was perhaps widely variable, depending on the one hand on the practice of prolonged lactation and its effectiveness as a control, and on the other, on the acceptability of abortion, assuming a need for population control.

Mortality Controls

In contrast to fertility controls, which are oriented toward the reduction of the probability of conception or successful completion of pregnancy, mortality controls involve the removal of an infant, child, or adult from the population. Infanticide, senilicide, and other forms of adult mortality will be dealt with under this heading.

INFANTICIDE

Infanticide is a common practice among many hunter–gatherers (Balicki 1967; Birdsell 1968; Laughlin 1968; Marshall 1960; Neel 1970). Birdsell (1968), Divale (1972), Harris (1977), and Nag (1962) believe that the rate of infanticide has been substantial in the prehistoric past. The practice, however, is not limited to hunter–gatherers.[2] Langer (1972) documents the frequent use of infanticide as a check to population growth in Europe between 1750 and 1850. Kellum (1974) reviews evidence for infanticide in England in the later Middle Ages and concludes that the practice was widespread. In a historical review of infanticide, Langer (1974) notes its occurrence in Hellenistic Greece and Rome. In Christian Europe, the practice continued. Laws and sanctions against infanticide, however, emerged reflecting the new religious attitude.

Among the Australian aborigines, Birdsell (1968) and Krzywicki (1934) indicate that infanticide is responsible for the elimination of 15% of all live births and in some cases 50%. The practice of infanticide is also reported among the !Kung Bushmen (N. Howell 1976b:147; Marshall 1960). Other instances are cited by Dickman (1975). Divale (1972), on the basis of a high male-to-female sex ratio (148 : 100) for the Upper Palaeolithic suggests that female infanticide was common. Weiss (1972a:342) suggests that infanticide eliminates infants who otherwise would have died because of deformities or weakness, or because the mother could not support them or nurse them if she had another child still dependent on nursing. Grantsberg (1973) links twin-infanticide to maternal work load and Carr-Saunders (1922) views infanticide as a response to the difficulty of transporting and suckling. The practice may be linked with certain features of social organization such as preferential kindred endogamy (Riches 1974). Schrire and Steiger (1974: 4) distinguish between infanticide practiced for these reasons and infanticide that involves the systematic elimination of girls at birth.

Schrire and Steiger (1974) attempted also to assess the probable role of infanticide in population control by constructing a simulation model that generates birth and death events according to prescribed mortality and fertility functions. Starting with an initial population, random births and deaths produce the group that enters

[2]In fact other animals practice infanticide. The male *Dicrostonyx* lemming sometimes destroys another male's litter and then mates with the female (Mallory and Brooks 1978:145).

the next time period. The simulation was continued over 500 years and the trajectory of the population was recorded. Rates of infanticide from 10 to 20% were imposed. Their results indicate that even a rate as low as 10% can lead to rapid depopulation. However, the fertility rates and other aspects of the simulation are doubtful (Acker and Townsend 1975).

Calculation of the maximum possible rate of female infanticide for a stationary, stable population, given a reproductive span of 14 years, a survivorship to mean childbearing age of .50, and a natural spacing of 28 months, provides an estimate of 15%. With a maximum total fertility of 8.14 the maximum rate of female infanticide is 25%. Assuming that prolonged lactation, abortion, or other methods are used for population control, the rate of infanticide had to be much lower than these figures. The 15–50% figure suggested by Birdsell (1968:243) may not represent rates that were always common throughout the Pleistocene. It may be noted here that the incidence of malformation identifiable at birth for several populations is about 1%, which would represent a minimum estimate of infanticide if infanticide was motivated by eliminating deformed infants.

The high cost of infanticide could be outweighed at times for a short span by its spontaneous effect on population size (Harpending and Bertram 1975:90). The practice may be necessary if there had been a food shortage due to unpredicted seasonal or periodic fluctuations. It may also have been used to weed out excess females when, because of stochastic processes, the standards of a good life had been threatened (M. M. R. Freeman 1973). Schrire and Steiger (1974) suggest that the inference of female infanticide in some Eskimo populations may have resulted from errors in determining the ages of males and females, since females tended to marry earlier than males. The sex ratio for Palaeolithic and Mesolithic populations (Divale 1972) may also be a function of the difficulty in determining sex and age of fossil populations. The importance of hunters among Eskimos and their frequent accidental death, however, may lead to differential infanticide to balance the ratio of sexes in adulthood. Birdsell (1968:243) notes that in 1929 Birket-Smith reported sex ratios of 145 for children and 80 for adults in five Caribou Eskimo "subtribes." Birdsell suggests that infanticide was practiced to produce an optimum number of hunters.

ADULT MORTALITY

Mortality rates of adults can also be affected by intra- and intergroup aggression (Divale 1972; Divale and Harris 1976; Harris 1977; Hayden 1972). Roper (1969), who made a survey of skeletal evidence of violent death in Pleistocene fossil remains, found consistent evidence for no less than 5% in most samples. Hayden (1972) finds a good match between this figure and that indicated from ethnographic observations. Both Hayden (1972:209) and Divale (1972:231) cite evidence from Upper Palaeolithic cave art for human aggression.

Human aggression is considered by some anthropologists as a population-control mechanism (Divale 1972; Divale and Harris 1976; Harris 1977; Hayden 1972). They fail to consider that aggression is not an effective control if it does not eliminate infants and reproductive females. Warfare and other forms of systematic aggression are not actually as predominant among hunter–gatherers as they are among agricultural and industrial groups (Harris 1971:225; Roper 1975:300). Moreover, it is a practice that is extremely wasteful and uneconomical. It is doubtful that warfare or aggression in general was a deliberate cultural control. Its occurrence, not unlike infanticide, was perhaps infrequent, caused primarily by occasions of extreme stress and competition. It may have served not as a means for controlling population, but as a means for decimating it, and its effect may have had to be combatted by the recruiting of new members. Krzywicki (1934:169), for example, reports that among some of the hunting tribes of North America, captives were adopted to maintain numerical strength.

Overview

It is clear from the foregoing review of cultural population controls that prehistoric populations could have exercised one or more of these controls to maintain a balanced population. It is also clear that, in view of the high reproductive potential given economic conditions of low growth and frequent temporal variability, such practices were essential. A premium was placed on small populations as a result of certain cultural responses to the hunting–gathering economy (cf. M. M. R. Freeman 1970). These practices vary considerably in their effectiveness and efficiency.

Each of these responses can come into play only when it is feasible (cf. M. M. R. Freeman 1970:146–147). The proportional probability of these responses will also be a function of the relative efficiency of these methods. Efficiency as used here includes both energy efficiency and behavioral efficiency. For example, a response that takes more energy and has a small effect on regulating population size will be less favored than response that consumes less energy and promises greater regulatory power. Responses that entail minimum disruption or deviation from preexisting social norms will be also favored over a more disruptive response. Depending on the severity of the environmental impact or the population situation, progressively less efficient responses may be invoked. In certain circumstrances, the regulatory mechanisms could remedy the population–environmental imbalance. In others, the population may have little time to adjust or its regulatory mechanisms can be so that they precipitate unforeseen side effects that may worsen the environmental conditions and/or the population problem.

Fertility controls, such as delayed marriage, restrictive mating rules, and abstinence have no economic cost, but they do bear a certain cost resulting from the denial of sexual pleasure. It is difficult to evaluate the strength of sexual passions and the cost of damping it, but the frequency of mating restrictions seems to suggest that the high benefits of social and economic welfare (e. g., less social conflict between adults, lower labor input, and good food quality) outweigh the cost of sublimating sexual drives. However, since cultural rules are often never strictly observed, a certain amount of "illicit" activity will diminish somewhat the effectiveness of this method as a population-control measure.

Illicit behavior may lead to "unwanted" pregnancies. Such pregnancies can be terminated as they become detectable. Alternatively, unwanted pregnancies may be allowed to become "unwanted infants" who may be dispensed with through infanticide. Abortion under primitive conditions of health care and with crude methods involve high risk for the mother. Risks of trauma, sepsis, tetanus, and infections are high (Dickeman 1975:131). From a "callous," calculating viewpoint, the removal of the infant and the mother may be considered advantageous to the group as a method of population control, since both the unwanted child and the mother, a potential source of fertility, are removed. It is noteworthy that New Guinea sago gatherers have taboos limiting the access of pregnant and lactating women to high-protein foods, thus increasing the probability of miscarriage and infant death. The argument could be also made that women, as in the New Guinea sago gatherer's case, who produce low-protein foods, are less likely to be as economically important as males, who produce high-quality protein foods. Since game is harder to capture, the contributions of meat by weight by males is likely to be far less in quantity than that produced from plant gathering. The Netslingmuit Eskimo, for example, note that they cannot afford to waste several years nursing a girl because the males get old quickly and they must be quick to get a son (Balicki 1967:81). Consequently a reduction in the number of adult women relative to that of males may be economically advantageous. If women produce more plant foods, more animal game has to be procured and males have to work harder. The sex ratio among hunting–gathering populations is quite puzzling. Numerous accounts of female infanticide (Dickeman 1975; Divale 1972) indicate that it leads to a sex ratio of about 125:100 or more in favor of males. One can argue that because of the high incidence of accidental death for the male hunters, the ratio would be corrected at close to 100:100; thus female infanticide can serve as a mechanism for balancing the ratio of females to males in adulthood (Birdsell 1968). However, given the fact that palaeodemographic data and other ethnographic information indicate that there is a high incidence of maternal mortality, the ratio of females to males would be skewed toward males. This would indicate that preferential infanticide may in fact serve as a regulatory mechanism reducing the numbers of neonates, damping the fertility rate of future mothers, and providing an economic balance between adult males and adult females (cf. Denham 1974). As a consequence, however, fewer nubile females are available for adult males, which may lead to limited access of females to young adult males, as among the Australian aborigines, or warfare to secure females as among the Yanomamö. Warfare to secure females may be thus viewed not as a means of limiting population, as Harris (1972, 1977) argues but as a consequence of female infanticide (see also comments by R. W. Howell 1975). It is interesting to note that the high rate of homicide among the Copper Eskimo is also blamed on rivalry over women, who are in short supply because of female infanticide (Rasmussen 1932:17).

The elimination of an adult human being, however, is a terrible waste. Moral

158 | THE REGULATION OF PREHISTORIC POPULATIONS

judgment aside, the energy cost of an adult at ages 19–22 is 14,762,586 cal, compared with 10,800 cal for a newborn infant (Table 9.2). The young adult, using these figures, is worth 137 newborn infants (Figure 9.3). Moreover, the adult is a productive member of the community and has the potential, if he survives to age 45, to contribute about 95,000,000 cal (beginning at age 15 and contributing 8675 calories per day after energy output data by Lee [1968]). In addition to the economic cost of an adult and his potential economic benefits, his social status in the communal life as a parent, friend, and relative endows him with a "social value" that makes his loss even more felt.

In addition to their efficiency and effectiveness, different population-control methods are marked by either immediate or delayed effects. Marriage rules, for example, have a delayed effect. Senilicide or other induced adult mortalities thin the standing population and have both an immediate effect on the size of the population and a delayed effect on fertility if the adults were still reproductive, especially if they are females. Abortion and infanticide also have a short-term effect, as well as a delayed effect, and as I have already noted female infanticide influences future fertility rates.

A population that finds itself growing and manages to decrease its fertility will continue to grow for some time, given a high proportion of potentially fecund

TABLE 9.2
Energy Cost of a Person from Birth to Age 70[a]

Age	Age-specific cost	Cumulative cost	Ratio
		Cumulative calorific cost	
Pregnancy (9 months)	108,000	108,000	1
0–3 months	33,462	141,462	1.3
3–6 months	56,133	197,595	1.83
3–9 months	73,458	271,053	2.50
9–12 months	88,011	359,064	3.32
12–15 months	98,109	457,173	4.23
15–18 months	104,840	562,013	5.2
18–24 months	111,573	673,586	5.23
2–3 years	1,058,500	1,732,086	16.0
4–6 years	1,971,000	3,703,086	34.2
7–10 years	2,628,000	6,331,086	58.6
11–14 years	2,847,000	9,178,086	84.98
15–18 years	2,792,250	11,970,336	110.83
19–22 years	2,792,500	14,762,586	136.79
23–50 years	24,017,000	38,779,586	359.07
50–60 years	7,665,000	46,444,586	430.04
60–70 years	7,665,000	54,109,585	501.01

[a] Energy requirements per person are 400 cal/day during pregnancy, 110 cal/kg/day from birth to age 2, 1300 cal/day for age 3, 1800 cal/day (4–6 years), 2400 cal/day (7–14), 2100 cal/day (15–22), 2000 cal/day (23–50), and 1800 cal/day (51+). The calorific requirements for adults represents an average of male and female requirements. Data from Burton 1976.

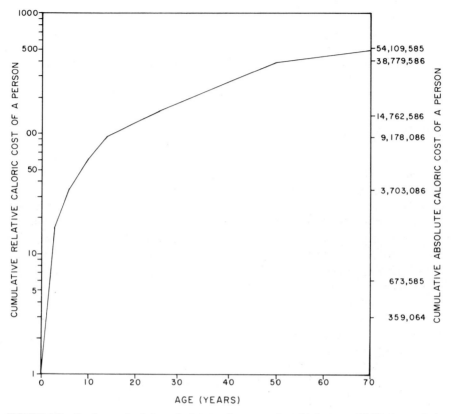

FIGURE 9.3. *Absolute and relative caloric cost of a person from birth to age 70.(Data on caloric requirements by age from Burton 1976.) Relative caloric cost is the ratio of the caloric cost at a specific age to that of a newborn infant.*

women. The lag may be between one generation and nine generations (Pollard and Pollard 1975). This lag, incidentally, applies to the world population problem today. Frejka (1973:14) has indicated that even if we manage to achieve a net reproduction rate of 1 by the middle of the next century, the population would be still 13 billion in 2050 and 15 billion in 2100!

From this discussion, it should be obvious that the question of the motivation and magnitude of population controls is difficult to resolve. Population controls may be a byproduct of other cultural norms and may not reflect a "population policy," but "population problems," actual or potential, are not beyond the comprehension of aboriginal populations. The cues that a problem exists may consist of increasing levels of labor input, consumption of low-quality foods, and social conflicts. Severe population–resource imbalance, resulting from a lack of a behavioral response to excessive fertility rate or to a decline in resource quality or quantity, will manifest itself in greater demands of labor, consumption of yet less desirable foods, and greater social conflict. In addition, nutritional deficiencies can lead to greater rates of miscarriage and infant mortality as a result of inadequate lactation and baby diet. Extreme conditions can create a climate of psychological trauma leading to a reduction in the rates of ovulation, child neglect, fighting, and even cannibalism. It should be noted here that the pathological impact of crowding, as revealed by psychological studies (Calhoun 1962; Freedman 1979) may only be significant under hunting–gathering conditions inasmuch as the concept of crowding is relative.[3] It is perhaps not so much the lack of privacy as the number of people who can subsist with a certain degree of comfort in their habitat.

The high level of behavioral systems in human beings compared to that of other animals leads me to believe that human beings will detect cues for population-resource imbalance before such an imbalance become catastrophic. Crisis, however, will occur when the imbalance is quite sudden, such as under anomalous environmental conditions (e. g., a series of consecutive years of severe drought).

In sum, the great potential for population growth, even under high rates of mortality, for prehistoric hunter–gatherers and the likelihood of fluctuations in the size of small populations suggest that population controls, direct or indirect, must have been responsible for the slow rate of world population growth during the Pleistocene. Population controls under prehistoric hunting–gathering conditions were most probably motivated by the premium placed on a small group, a long child-spacing period to avoid excessive maternal drain, and a low dependents-to-producers ratio in view of the cost of children and their limited value as a labor force or as insurance in old age.

Abortion and infanticide, in addition to other methods of controls, were perhaps common among prehistoric peoples. The practice of breast-feeding and its effect on prolonging the birth interval might have led to a relatively low rate of abortion and infanticide. Female infanticide is more effective than other methods in damping future fertility and may have thus been commonly practiced. Warfare is not likely to have been a common practice among prehistoric hunter–gatherers, and is, in addition, one of the most wasteful and inefficient methods of population control. The infrequent aggressive encounters within or between hunting–gathering groups were most likely related to nondemographic factors.

[3]For many primate species "splitting" and male "takeovers" can occur under conditions of high population density (Eisenberg et al. 1972:868).

10

Carrying Capacity and Population Pressure

If the food is falling short, or a new disease threatens us,
inventions to relieve it must be made before famine and
pestilence have done their work.*

Malthus (1826) contended that population is limited by the means of subsistence and that an increase in population is dependent upon technological advancements. Ester Boserup (1965), in a study of agrarian change, argues that population increase is not a dependent factor and that it leads to a forceful pressure that promotes technological expansion and economic growth. Boserup's ideas were warmly embraced by many archaeologists, and population pressure proved to be one of the most alluring concepts in contemporary archaeology, as witnessed by its wide albeit not always too critical application to the explanation of cultural changes at all stages of human evolution. Notable applications of this concept are to the problems of origins of agriculture and origins of the civilization. These specific applications will be dealt with in Chapters 13 and 14, and the general aspects of the concept will be discussed in this chapter.

Population Pressure: A Critique

Population pressure is a vague and rather ill-defined concept (Hassan 1974). M. G. Smith (1972), one of the leading proponents of the application of this concept

---

*Norbert Wiener, *The human use of human beings,* Houghton Mifflin, Boston, 1954.

to archaeological explanation, regards population pressure as a function of the ratio of actual population size to carrying capacity. This is, in general, the sense of which population pressure seems to be utilized, even when some modifications are made to accommodate its critics, as in the definitions of the concept by Cohen (1977).

Population pressure, with the accent on population, also places the cause of the imbalance between population and carrying capacity on population increase.[1] Population increase, however, cannot be presumed to follow the potential natural rates of population increase, as I have argued in the previous chapter. Except for stochastic fluctuations in group size or naturally induced scarcity of food resources, which can be remedied by population flux or mortality controls, we should assume that human populations were regulated. The occasions during which populations do not show such patterns must be regarded as abnormal. The population problem today is often invoked as a case at hand of unregulated population increase. On the one hand, this view is not universally accepted, and on the other hand, the situation is very recent and represents a transition of socioeconomic rather than demographic origin. It is hardly applicable to long-term patterns of human adaptation.

The other element in the population formula, besides population increase, is carrying capacity, and I will devote this chapter to this intriguing concept, but before I undertake this task, I wish to dispense with some other problems in the application of population pressure as a major cause of culture change (see also Bender 1975; Bronson 1975; G. L. Cowgill 1975; Hassan 1974, 1978b; Hayden 1979):

1. The actual rate of population increase is linked to socioeconomic and other cultural factors and cannot be viewed as a totally independent variable.

2. A cultural change leading to greater productivity is only one of many other responses to an imbalance between economic demands and available resources. Cultural changes, in addition, are not simple responses having foreseeable consequences. Moreover, the changes are often gradual, spanning several generations, and are thus not likely to emerge as short-term strategies against want. Population-pressure models are deterministic so far as population increase is presumed to entail culture change to the exclusion of other alternatives.

3. Population-pressure models reduce culture change to a single cause and are not thus in accord with the multicausal and often nondemographic origins of culture change.

4. Technological innovations that can expand the level of carrying capacity

---

[1] Although Boserup's model is often contrasted with that of Malthus, it should be noted that the Boserupian model is basically Malthusian, since the increase of the population to the limits of its means of subsistence, argued by Malthus (1826:14), is central to the population-pressure model. In addition, Malthus (1826:542) was aware of the economic role of population, as indicated by the following statement: "I should always particularly reprobate any artificial and unnatural modes of checking population, both on account of their immorality and their tendency *to remove a necessary stimulus to industry* [emphasis added]."

cannot always be assumed to be present when a food imbalance occurs. Also, it cannot be assumed that people will readily accept and implement technological innovations, and that these innovations will be integrated in the cultural system without endangering its variability. The probability of the right innovation at the right time is not very high. Cultures as systems do not agglutinize cultural traits. A system consists of coordinated components bound together in a structural framework. An innovation, to become culturally viable, must be integrated into the system. This must be considered in calculating the probability of technological innovations as solutions to demographic crisis.

5. Population-pressure models magnify the role of population increase and underestimate the role of other demographic variables, such as the dependency ratio, the ratio of consumers to producers, and desired family size. The models thus reflect a heavily skewed and biased view of demographic causality.

6. Acceptance of the premise that human populations tend to increase to the limits of the means of subsistence leads us to conclude that population pressure is endemic. At best, thus, population pressure cannot be regarded as a sufficient cause of culture change.

7. The population-pressure models presuppose that carrying capacity is infinitely elastic. This certainly could not be the case under hunting–gathering conditions.

8. The concept of population pressure involves an undue emphasis on population size. The relationship between a population and its resources not only involves the number of people but, especially following the emergence of agriculture, the levels of consumption. A stationary population with rising levels of food or nonfood consumption can create economic demands.

9. Increasing demands must not be confused with population or food crisis. Population-pressure models evoke images of starvation and severe shortages, which are unlikely to occur except under rapid environmental changes affecting resources or sudden failures in the cultural subsystems responsible for the maintenance of the quality of life.

10. The population-pressure model, as often applied, persists in logical vacuity. Cultural changes are attributed to population pressure, even though evidence for "population pressure" may be lacking. The slight evidence of population increase, even though it may be equivocal, is often cited as evidence for population pressure. Even worse, the occurrence of culture change is judged by reference to the general model as evidence of population pressure.

I would like to end this section with the candid remark by P. E. L. Smith (1972:9), a proponent of Boserup's model:

> Admittedly this [presumed increase in population during the Upper Pleistocene] does not explain why the increase in population took place, and it is not clear to what extent we can speak of demographic pressure in the sense oulined earlier. Nevertheless it illustrates a line of thinking that should be followed up.

Carrying Capacity

In 1936, Errington and Hamerston estimated the number of bobwhite quail that wintered in 20 areas in Iowa and Wisconsin during 6 years. They found that each area usually supported a characteristic number of birds. Errington and Hamerston referred to this as the "carrying capacity" of the area (Andrewartha 1963:154). E. P. Odum (1959:182-185) refers to carrying capacity as the maximum population size possible, that is, the upper limit for population growth. This limit, however, is calculated on the basis of long-range survival without damaging the ecological network (H. T. Odum 1971:125). In anthropology the concept has been applied and debated by Birdsell (1958,1971), Brush (1975), Carneiro (1960, 1970), Casteel (1972), Conklin (1957), Dumond (1976a, 1976b), Rappaport (1968), Sherratt (1972), Wilkinson (1972), and Zubrow (1971, 1974).

Carrying capacity represents, theoretically, an upper limit for population growth (Figure 10.1b). A population may overexploit its environment, reaching a level of population density greater than carrying capacity (Figure 10.1a), but in so doing it undermines its resources and is ultimately forced to decline, in some cases to extinction. Extinction under such circumstances may not be unusual for small populations because a reduction in the size of the group endangers its biological viability. We should recall here the figures given by Wobst (1974) from his simulation on the required size of group population (see pp. 149-150).

An initial human population is likely to follow a sigmoid or logistic pattern of growth (Figure 10.1c). The shaded area in the graph may represent a decline in growth due to crowding, greater search time for food, or any other greater competition factors of "environmental resistance" (Boughey 1968). In human populations, as I will suggest later, following a discussion of criticisms of the carrying capacity concept, the stabilized level of the population may occur as a result of perceptions of cues of environmental resistance before the critical levels of the carrying capacity are reached.

Hayden (1975) is critical of the use of the concept for human beings on three accounts:

1. It is almost impossible to calculate, in any accurate way, the amount of potential food in an area usable by a group—especially by hunter-gatherers.
2. It is difficult to calculate the amount of specific potential foods available under various technologies.
3. The variable and cyclical nature of the resource environment makes the use of the concept of carrying capacity as "maximum population size" possibly dubious.

Similar and additional criticisms are voiced by Street (1969), Brush (1975), and Little *et al.* (1976). These criticisms remind us, as sometimes we need to be reminded, that man is not exactly an animal, and that concepts developed in animal

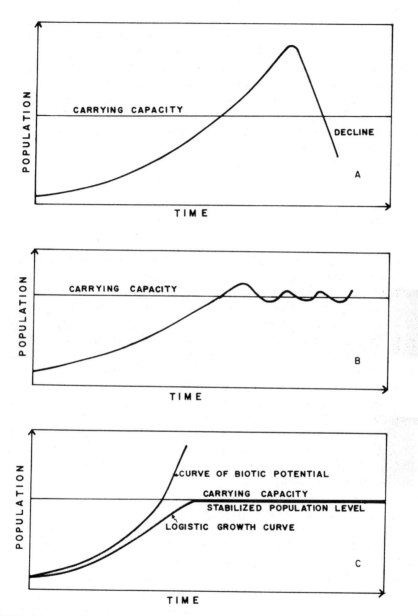

FIGURE 10.1. *Some patterns of population growth relative to carrying capacity: (A) J-shaped exponential growth followed by decline after the population overshoots the carrying capacity; (B) population growth followed by an oscillation of the population around the carrying capacity; and (C) a logistic (sigmoid) growth curve. The population increase diminishes as the population approaches and stabilizes at the carrying capacity level.*

ecology often need slight or significant modification if they are to be applied meaningfully to the human situation (Thomlinson 1965:66). The concept of carrying capacity, however, is a viable concept for human populations. The problem lies in attempting to tailor it to the realities of human existence. Two of the factors that complicate the estimation of carrying capacity for human populations are diet and technology. Thus, in estimating carrying capacity for human populations, these two factors should be taken in consideration. This can be achieved by investigating the dietary habits of the population as evidenced in artifactual and bioarchaeological remains. The efficiency of extractive techniques can be assessed through a comparative study of ethnographically documented cases.

Carrying Capacity: An Alternative Approach

The fact that resources are not constant through time does not threaten the theoretical validity of the carrying capacity concept. In Odum's definition of carrying capacity, the term is used to refer to the maximum population size that can be supported over a long period, thus both short- and medium-range resource fluctuations are taken into consideration. Both Birdsell (1953) and Zubrow (1974) are aware of this problem. They invoke Liebig's rule of the minimum, which states that the "growth of a plant is dependent on the amount of foodstuff which is present in minimum quantity [E. P. Odum 1959]." Birdsell (1953), however, uses Liebig's rule to mean that the maximum population size is dependent on the availability of resources during the leanest season of the year. This perhaps should be expressed as Birdsell's rule rather than as a form of Liebig's rule, since it does not refer to specific resources. Both Birdsell's and Liebig's rules can be combined to state that maximum population size is dependent on the amount of foodstuffs present in minimum amounts at the time these foodstuffs are least abundant.

Both rules make no mention of the kind of resources concerned. I believe that there are certain resources that are critical for human survival and welfare. These are the resources that provide the essential amino acids, vitamins, and certain trace elements, assuming that caloric requirements are satisfied, as they generally are. Townsend (1971) notes, for example, that among the New Guinea sago gatherers, sago can be procured in great amounts, but game—a source of protein—is a limiting factor. Gross (1975) also emphasizes the limiting role of protein foods among the peoples of the Amazon Basin. The new rule may thus be expressed as this: *Maximum human population size is dependent on the quantity of nutritionally critical foodstuffs, which are present in minimum amounts, at the time within the span of a few generations of their least abundance.*

The frequent observations that hunter–gatherers, as well as cultivators, do not live up to the *average* estimate of the number of people that resources could support are explicable in the light of this new rule. Actual population size usually corresponds to as little as 20–30%, and is often about 40–60%, of the average short-term estimate of carrying capacity (Birdsell 1957; Lee and DeVore 1968a). The inflated estimates of carrying capacity based on short-term observations during favorable periods and on averaging methods thus actually measure a *maximum* carrying capacity. Carrying capacity estimates that take into consideration resource fluctuations and the abundance of nutritionally critical resources may be called estimates of *critical* carrying capacity (Hassan 1978b). The critical carrying capacity is not exactly equivalent to the actual average population over a long period. I would think that populations would cushion themselves against occasional severe shortages or stochastic population fluctuation by existing below the critical carrying capacity, at a level that we may refer to as the *optimum* carrying capacity (Figure 10.2). The span of time over which the stability of the environment is perceived, serving as a basis for optimum carrying capacity, is perhaps 60 years or the memory of about three generations. Information on previous environmental conditions suffers from time decay and is also often not perceived to be applicable to present or future conditions because of the subjectivity of human judgment (Hassan 1978b).

It is conceivable that different technologies will not be equally efficient in approaching the optimum level, given a similar spectrum of exploitable resources. Also, areas of the habitat may be left as refuge areas for animal game (Turnbull 1972) or as refuge areas for use during adverse environmental conditions (Wiens 1977). I must also state here that carrying capacity estimates are generally based on consumption at the subsistence level, a level that many groups exceed. Living beyond the subsistence level may not be as common for hunter–gatherers as it is for agricultural groups, and especially modern industrial groups, in which the rate of overconsumption and wastage is sometimes quite high (mainly in certain sectors of the population).

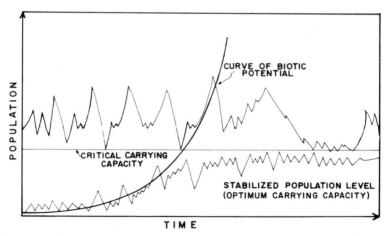

FIGURE 10.2. *Fluctuations in food resources determine a critical level of carrying capacity. An initial population may increase until a level below the critical carrying capicity is reached and then it may stabilize at the "optimum" level, where it is protected from adverse fluctuations in available food resources or occasional upsurges in population size.*

To summarize, the following points are relevant to the relationship between population size and resources:

1. Optimum, critical, and maximum carrying capacity as a function of population and resource fluctuations
2. The dietary choices and the standard of life (levels of consumption and acceptable labor input) and their implications for carrying capacity

Carrying Capacity and Population Regulation

To illustrate the application of these concepts to the mechanisms of population control, let us assume that a hunting–gathering population is subsisting at the critical carrying capacity (Figure 10.3). Now, assuming that the environment becomes degraded because of natural climatic factors, the potential yield per capita (standard of living) will be reduced. As conditions worsen, the standard of living will start to drop below the minimum subsistence level (Figure 10.4). Because of the lag that may exist between the point at which controls are applied and their effect on population growth, life conditions continue to deteriorate, even while population controls are applied. These controls may consist of fertility or mortality damping methods, or both. The effect of fertility damping will not have an immediate effect, and with a deteriorating standard of living, mortality damping (e. g., infanticide) may be exercised. In addition, the deterioration in living conditions may lead to an increase in natural mortality, especially among the vulnerable infants and the young mothers. Similar conditions may occur if stochastic fluctuations lead to overpopulation.

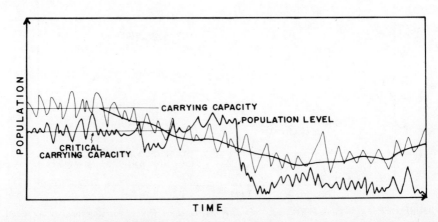

FIGURE 10.3. *A population subsisting at the critical level of the carrying capacity suffers a rapid decline following a lowering of carrying capacity, which may result from climatic changes. The decline in population size is produced by increased morbidity and mortality.*

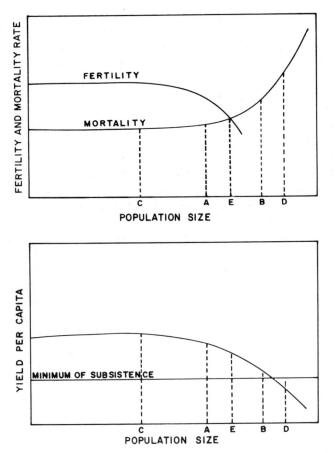

FIGURE 10.4. *A rise in mortality under the conditions indicated in Figure 10.3 (a reduction in carrying capacity for a population at the critical level of carrying capacity) relative to fertility is associated with a reduction in yield per capita to a level below that of the minimum subsistence.*

Under conditions of severe stress, the population may be afflicted by an increase in natural mortality, a drop in fertility as a result of delayed marriage, abstinence, or a greater frequency of miscarriage and induced abortion, and an increase in mortality produced by infanticide and homicide. Changes in the number of conceptions, burials, and marriages similar to those postulated have been noted for three French parishes during a late-seventeenth-century food crisis (Wrigley 1969).

The foregoing model is a "starvation model." It must have occurred occasionally, but it is more likely that cultural patterns that would have eliminated the recurrence of hunger, starvation, and misery would have been selected for. I have already introduced the concept of optimum carrying capacity, and we can now observe the effect of population growth similar to that just discussed on the standard of living and the motivation for population controls. In this case, the population increase affects only the acceptable level of the standard of living. This is unlike the first instance, in which population increase causes the standard of living to drop below the subsistence level. This may thus trigger population controls well before the state of hunger and starvation sets in (Figure 10.5).

This pattern is more adaptive and would have a positive selective value, by comparison to the starvation pattern, which is not only wasteful biologically and in terms of energy, but also culturally disruptive. In the model of optimum living, the population forecasts its coming crisis by the relative scarcity of choice food items, an increase in the work load per producer, or the need to travel farther or schedule its subsistence activity differently. These "anticipatory sensors" avoid a head-on collision between people and resources and provide the population with enough time to reduce its size, and, more important, its growth rate, without bringing the population to the brink of starvation.

A declining standard of living may also lead to the exploitation of secondary food resources, which were previously regarded with less favor. This action would raise the level of the critical carrying capacity and serve as a further safeguard against starvation while the population adjusts its population size and growth rate (Figure 10.6). These secondary resources would generally have been previously known but underexploited because of their disliked taste, tedious preparation, cultural aversion, or the relatively higher cost of extracting them. The "emergency" dietary change is often temporary and disappears as soon as conditions ameliorate. People living at an optimum level, however, will not be subjected to eating what they loathe and what might just be stomach filling without any nutritional value, as a population living at the critical level may be compelled to do. During the Norwegian famine years of the 1740s, the people of Hallingdal washed straw from dunghills to bake a pathetic substitute for bread (Wrigley 1969:66). Cases in which people were

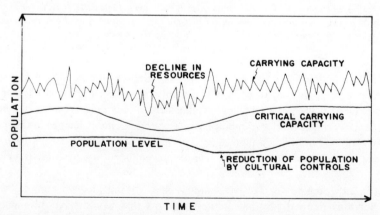

FIGURE 10.5. *A population subsisting at the optimum level of carrying capacity responds to a decline in carrying capacity by damping fertilty. As the population approaches the level of the critical carrying capacity, it regulates its size to maintain its standard of living.*

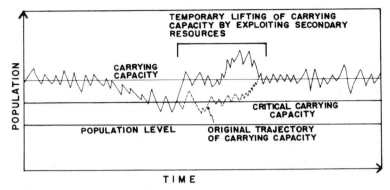

FIGURE 10.6. *A population at the optimum level of carrying capacity responds to a decline in carrying capacity by exploiting secondary resources. A return to "normal" conditions of carrying capacity is associated with abandonment of secondary resources and a return to the previous subsistence regime.*

reduced to eating each other are also not infrequent under extreme starvation (Wrigley 1969).

A demographic crisis, as we have seen, may be relieved by natural and/or cultural fertility or mortality damping. The other possibility is *emigration*. Internal migration and spatial redistribution of the population must be distinguished from emigration, which is the expulsion or departure of a portion of the population from the parent population. I include internal migration within the pattern of local population adjustment to a changing standard of living. These changes may compare with seasonal mobility, except that they could represent rescheduling of subsistence activities or a reorganization of differential exploitation of various resources.

Emigration may occur, in combination with other birth or death controls, as the population starts to exceed its optimum level of living. The excess persons establish a new settlement outside the range of the parent population. Depending on distance, social cohesion, and ecological differentiation between the homeland and the new territory, contact (social, economic, or demographic) with the parent population may be maintained or discontinued. The rate of migration would be largely a function of the resource potentials of bordering territories and the degree of their demographic saturation. Migration is also a function of preexisting technology and subsistence strategy. We should not hesitate to accept the important role of migration in maintaining interregional demographic balance (cf. Cohen 1975), but we should not be tempted to assume that migration was always a viable alternative to birth or death controls or that the rate of migration was constant throughout prehistoric times (see also my discussion of migration in the previous chapter).

Yessner (1977) has suggested that a population that overshoots its carrying capacity would tend to encourage migration into marginal areas where the accumulation of small increments in mortality and reduction in fertility would lead to a reestablishment of previous population status. He remarks that this solution would preclude "the necessity to resort to cultural practices which require genetic wastage and reduction of potential population growth and complexity."

Yessner seems to attach a certain virtue to "population growth and complexity" that should have been apparent to prehistoric hunter–gatherers, and which they were supposed to preserve rather than restrict their numbers and enjoy a comfortable level of existence. Yessner seems to favor this solution of "natural checks" as a basis for a model of continued population fluctuation. As we have seen in the previous chapter, there is no need to posit unchecked population growth as a condition for temporal variations in population size. Both voluntary and involuntary checks cannot lead to a stationary population. This is especially true among hunter–gatherers because of their small size (Ammerman 1975; Kunstadter 1972), the uncertainty in the success of contraceptives or abortion, the low survivorship of infants, which may lead to error on the positive side, as well as to changes in the age and sex structure and thus an uneven population growth pattern. In addition, fluctuations in resources, as much as population fluctuations, are likely to produce similar effects on the economic stability of a group. We should also take note of certain aspects of the sex and age structure of hunter–gatherers. They are generally characterized by a low ratio of children to adults and by differences in the sex ratio related to differences in the mortality pattern of the two sexes. Adult males are more prone to accidental death due to the hazards of hunting. Thus, hunting accidents may deprive a group of its meat producers and would endanger the economic welfare of the group, regardless of whether the general population was increasing or decreasing. Unbalanced sex ratios at birth would be exaggerated in small groups and might lead to differential infanticide or a pooling of mates from various groups. Both population flux and population fluctuations are therefore inherent in the demographic makeup of hunting–gathering populations. The modified model of carrying capacity that I have presented in this chapter dispenses with the need for "population pressure" with its consequences of starvation or serious economic stress. By living at an optimum level, groups can monitor population or resource fluctuations, preventing a slide into catastrophic deprivation. Such signals would fail sometimes, of course, if the fluctuations were quite severe or sudden, which must have occurred at some time. Nevertheless, on the average these signals would have initiated such counterstrategies as (a) changing the diet (e.g., the use of items that had been underrepresented on the menu); (b) expanding the catchment territory; (c) redistributing the population to take advantage of previously underexploited ecological zones; (d) increasing labor input; (e) working with other groups to extract resources that need larger teams; and (f) exercising population control (cf. Dumond 1965). If the fluctuations are a prelude to a long-term increase in population or decline in resources, some of the changes may become institutionalized, but if the fluctuations are ephemeral it is likely that the changes would be reversible.

A population at an optimum carrying capacity would have the time to develop a new technology (under those conditions that would make the adoption and integration of that technology feasible) that might ultimately lift the carrying capacity to a new level (Figure 10.7). The new socioeconomic conditions associated with the

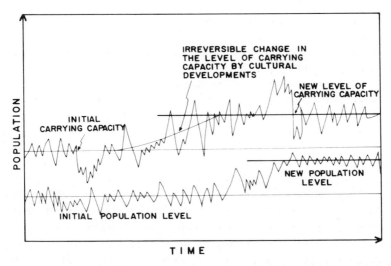

FIGURE 10.7. *A technological achievement leads to an "elastic" carrying capacity with a potential of greater yield per producer and labor intensification stimulates an increase in population size to a higher level.*

new technology may in turn promote population increase. This is, in fact, the basis of my model for agricultural origins, to which I will return in Chapter 13.

Overview

The livelihood of man, like that of any other animal, ultimately depends on the earth's resources. Unlike other animals, however, man can subsist at various levels of extractive efficiency under a wide range of subsistence modes. The record of the human past indicates that man has passed through three major economic periods, each associated with an increase in productivity and a change in economic growth potentials. For most of the prehistoric past, human populations subsisted by a hunting–gathering economy with a limited food productivity and a very limited potential for human growth. By about 9000 years ago, a transition to a food-producing economy took place and at various times since then agriculture became the predominant mode of subsistence. Although agricultural productivity might not have been as great as one might think, the potentials for economic growth were fantastic compared with those of hunting–gathering. Advancements in agricultural economy were capable of lifting the carrying capacity to progressively higher levels. With the emergence of industrial technology, mechanization, application of chemical fertilizers, transportation, use of fossil fuels, and accumulation of capital, even greater carrying capacities were attained. The potential for economic growth under this kind of agroindustry is tremendous and improvements continue to be made.

A concern for the optimum number of people relative to food resources has been expressed by many scholars in antiquity and in more recent times by Malthus and many others since then. The writings of Malthus focused the attention on the relationship between population growth and economic growth. Malthus believed that population increase proceeds at a geometric pace that outruns the mathematical increase in economic productivity. Population increase must be ultimately checked at the cost of considerable human misery. Criticisms of Malthus's theory were based on the potential for cultural population controls and for greater rates of economic growth than those suggested by Malthus. The advent of agroindustry soon after Malthus's work was published led many scholars to discount the Malthusian model of doom. At present, although population growth rates in industrial nations are relatively low, other nations with a traditional agricultural economy are undergoing an upsurge of population growth that seems to threaten the quality of human life. Famines are not unknown and many suffer from undernourishment. What the future holds is uncertain, but the relationship between resources, economy, and population is one of the most pressing issues of this generation.

Under prehistoric conditions, as Wrigley (1969:37) has noted, the hunting-gathering populations were faced by a great discrepancy between their high reproductive potential and a limited yield. As long as they were dependent upon extracting food from wild resources, the potential for economic growth was extremely low.

The limitations on population growth were therefore rigid. Under such conditions, human groups could have been regulated either by natural checks or by cultural means (cf. Skellam 1971). The advanced behavioral system of human populations and the stability of many cultural traditions in the past suggest to me that cultural regulation was more likely. The widespread use of cultural controls among aboriginal populations seems to confirm this view. Small populations, which would have a short decision-making chain and would be in direct contact with the environment, are more likely to perceive resource–population imbalance and act accordingly. As population increases, as the chain of decision making is lengthened, as people who make the decisions are isolated from the natural environment, and as the role of environment becomes unclear in the complex network of complex societies, perception of population—resource imbalance is lessened and the span between perception and action lengthens. This is the situation today. Complex simulations (see Meadows et al. 1972) become a necessity for interpreting the role of environmental change and population trends, and scholarly debates on the validity of the simulation models and the data employed drag on (Cole et al. 1975; Gillette 1972). If there is a serious problem, whether it is a product of overpopulation, economic inequality, fast economic growth, a rising standard of living, or a combination of all of these, the world human population may become extinct before scholars agree on the diagnosis of what is ailing the world. A pessimistic outlook, therefore, may be a successful strategy to cope with the world problem. The world will have to pay a heavy price if the optimists are wrong, but it will be only an embarrassment to the pessimists if their models of doom turn out to be a false alarm.

It is my opinion that prehistoric populations were pessimists toward uncertainty. Environmental fluctuations and stochastic changes in the size of small populations can place a group in serious trouble if it is living at the average level of carrying capacity. Empirical data on hunter–gatherers and people practicing swidden agriculture seem to support this view. In general, no actual populations are more than 20-60% of the maximum carrying capacity. Such levels of population may be called optimum carrying capacity. Although living at such a level will shield the population against more frequent fluctuations, it does not preclude an adverse impact of less common, but more violent events. Such events will lead to a reduction in the standard of living (more work, less food, more social conflict), but the impact would be far less than if the population was at a higher level. Population controls with immediate impact (abortion and infanticide), exploitation of secondary resources, or spatial rearrangement of the population will remedy the situation.

If the situation lasts these adaptive responses may become institutionalized. Adoption of new technology may also occur under such conditions, if the cultural milieu is hospitable for the innovations. The complexity of culture change, however, precludes an invariable causal link between food–resource imbalance and technological developments.

Many archaeologists, influenced by the work of Boserup (1965) on population pressure and agrarian change, argue for a causal link between population increase and a variety of cultural developments, including agriculture, political states, and urban centers. In my opinion and that of many other anthropologists, these explanations are not congruent with actual modes of human behavior, are not sensitive to the complexity of cultural causality, and are in most cases unsupported by empirical evidence.

11

Hunter–Gatherers: Demography and Culture

An empirical approach that extends inquiry from cultural manifestations through processes to ultimate causes may theoretically have great value for reconstructing lines of past evolution. If cultural and environmental factors can be reduced to a limited number of basic functional categories, we should be able within the limitations of prehistoric identification of these factors to infer the nature of society.*

In this chapter I will explore some of the possible relationships between demography and several aspects of culture, namely social organization, technocultural traditions, and language. From an examination of ethnographic hunter–gatherers, it is possible to deduce a number of structural relationships between population and culture that can serve as sources of hypotheses to be tested archaeologically.

The chapter consists of a first section on the impact environmental variables have on the size and mobility of hunting–gathering groups, followed by a discussion of social organization, technocultural traditions, and finally language and dialects.

Environment and Demographic Variability

The relationship between environment and population dynamics under hunting–gathering regimes is of the utmost importance for understanding culture and culture change. Therefore, I propose to examine this relationship in a systematic fashion. The environment of the hunter–gatherer is enclosed within the catchment territory, the area habitually exploited by the group. Within that territory, biotopes

*Julian H. Steward, in *Man the Hunter*, R. B. Lee and I. DeVore, (editors), Aldine, Chicago, 1968, p. 323.

with different resource potentials are often present. From all potentially edible resources, a certain range, often quite large, is the subject of frequent exploitation. None of the resources can be exploited beyond a certain limit, which is set by the biotic potential of the resource. If this is exceeded, the future availability of the resource would be endangered and irreversible ecological changes may follow.

Our concern for the population dynamics of hunter–gatherers must be linked with these aspects of their habitats: (a) biotopic differentiation; (b) species diversity; (c) spatial dispersion or aggregation; (d) seasonality; (e) short-term fluctuations; and (f) yield. The conditions under which a group of hunter-gatherers lives would thus be made up of a specific combination of these aspects, to which their subsistence regime and much that goes with it must be attuned.

Species diversity decreases from tropical to temperate and polar regions. Resources also vary in their spatial dispersion. Evenly distributed resources may be contrasted with resources that occur in clusters or aggregates. Resources also vary in their year-round availability. Some local resources mature or become abundant in a certain season, and other resources, such as waterfowl may be migratory and thus strictly seasonal. In the tropics, seasonal climatic fluctuations are less than those in temperate regions. The productivity of plants and animals, therefore, is maintained for the entire year. This leads to both aseasonal availability of resources and greater productivity. Certain regions, such as deserts or semideserts or exposed seacoasts may be affected by severe short-term fluctuations in climate, which are transmuted into wide variations in the availability of resources.

The environmental conditions under which hunter–gatherers operate are quite distinct from those under which agricultural groups obtain their subsistence. The major differences are in yield, aggregation of resources, biotopic differentiation, species diversity, and type of resources. Both economies are subject to seasonality and short term fluctuations, but agricultural groups simplify their econiches, limit their resources, exploit dense and concentrated foods, enjoy a high yield, and in most cases' subsist on storable products. This permits large local groups, sedentariness, and dense populations, characteristics possible for hunter–gatherers only in exceptional conditions where wild food resources are abundant, concentrated, and storable, such as along the Northwest Coast of North America (Schalk 1977; Suttles 1962, 1968) or along the migration routes of big-game herds (Klein 1973; Mongait 1961).

Among hunter–gatherers living under tropical conditions, the net productivity is high, species diversity is high, and the resources are more or less evenly distributed and aseasonal. The dispersion of the resources leads to small groups, but the high yield and the aseasonality of resources cut down on seasonal long-range mobility. However, the high diversity of the species results in frequent short-range settlement shifts, since no single resource is of sufficiently high yield or aggregation to facilitate localized habitation. In the Malayan rain forest, for example, the Semang obtain their animal protein from small animals such as rats, squirrels, birds, lizards, and grubs. Where rivers are present, fishing provides an additional source of protein and when fish are abundant settlement may be localized (Murdock 1934).

The Andaman (Service 1966), who live under tropical conditions of monsoonal rain, exploit fish, mussels, and the dugong (a large aquatic mammal) in coastal areas. The abundance of these resources makes possible large settlements (villages) and relatively dense occupation (Radcliffe-Brown 1964).

The Congolese forest is much richer in big game than the Malayan forest. This allows larger group size, but the Ituri pygmies nevertheless engage in frequent short-term mobility, as one would expect where resources are evenly distributed and when the game is not concentrated but scattered. Turnbull (1972) notes that the camps are moved within the territory every month. The movement is enhanced by the progressive depletion of resources within a reasonable distance from the camp. It is important to note here that different methods of hunting may lead to different demographic patterns. Among the Ituri pygmies, some groups hunt with bows and arrows, and some hunt with nets. Net hunting requires between 7 and 30 nets. Since nets are possessed by married men only, the net hunting team varies from 7 to 30 families. Thus, the larger the group, the greater the short-term mobility required. The larger the group, the more likely it is for disputes to occur, and disputes are resolved by some segment moving out, which accounts for interband demographic flux. The group splits during the season when honey is available. The archer bands can hunt best in small numbers, which they do for most of the year, congregating once a year for communal hunts that involve about 30 families. The function of the communal hunt seems to lie in maintaining social bonds with other groups (Turnbull 1972).

Animal protein is a major limiting factor for human populations. Thus, despite the high net productivity of tropical forests, the distribution and the low availability of animal game in Asia and South America are quite significant. If Amazonia was once inhabited by hunter–gatherers, the low availability of animal protein would have led to small, dispersed, and shifting groups (Gross 1975). Since tropical fauna are nonmigratory, overexploitation of an area would lead to "permanent" depletion. It is thus advantageous to leave no-man's-lands between exploited territories, as "preserves" where prey species may be replenished (Gross 1975:535). This is actually practiced by the Ituri pygmies (Turnbull 1972:300). No-man's-lands form about 20–30% of all hunting territories.

In the polar regions, conditions are distinctly different. The inland resources are of limited variety (low species diversity), seasonality is marked, and resources are not uniformly available. In addition, the yield from the resources is low. Under these conditions, small groups—even of one or two families—are advantageous. The catchment territory is large and population density therefore low. Long-range mobility allows the group to exploit various widely dispersed resources and to make use of seasonal availability. The relative abundance of such resources would encourage temporary population aggregation. The Caribou Eskimo of Canada provide an excellent example (Damas 1972). In contrast, coastal groups, which have access to varied biotopes and maritime resources and greater diversity of species, can be larger, and may occupy both year round base camps and ancillary camps from which seasonal resources are exploited. There is abundant ethnographic and archaeological evidence from the arctic and subarctic for such a demographic "landscape" (Yessner 1977). The population density is several individuals per square kilometer, groups are from 50 to 100 persons, and year-round base camps are common, with seasonal ancillary encampments (Damas 1968).

In the temperate regions, from which most hunter–gatherers were pushed out by agricultural groups, the species diversity is moderate and seasonality is marked. The net productivity is lower than that of tropical forests, but the biomass of ungulates is very high (see Chapter 2). The biotopic diversity is generally high. This environmental pattern would not require great seasonal long-range mobility. Short-range mobility, however, would be expected to be high and settlement relocation would be frequent. Base camps may be established at certain times of the year in localities where particular resources are concentrated; ancillary satellite camps may also be used. The most probable pattern, however, would consist of small groups with shifting settlements dictated not so much by seasonality as by the need to avoid overexploiting a small area. This pattern has been documented for the Epipalaeolithic Capsian hunter–gatherers of North Africa (Lubell et al. 1976). Because of the biotopic differentiation and the high yield of some resources, different groups may overlap, exploiting various resources and biotopes. There is evidence that this was the case in the Nile Valley during the Terminal Palaeolithic (Wendorf 1968).

In desert habitats, the scarcity and sparse distribution of resources, coupled with low yield and seasonality, are best managed by small groups, with frequent long-range and seasonal movements. The overall density must remain low. Temporary aggregation of groups may occur when certain resources ripen, or when water is scarce during the dry season, which would be followed by disaggregation. This pattern is exemplified by the Australian aborigines (Birdsell 1953) and the Bushmen (Lee 1976; Yellen and Harpending 1972). Coastal and riverine groups, under these conditions, can achieve higher densities as a result of the greater availability of animal protein. Among the Australian aborigines, the population density for riverine groups is 20–30 times that of nonriverine groups (Birdsell 1953).

The foregoing discussion provides the basis for recognizing four types of environmental–demographic patterns. Type I corresponds to tropical conditions; Type II, to temperate conditions; Type IIIA, to inland arctic conditions; Type IIIB, to desert conditions; and Type IV, to coastal and riverine conditions. These are ideal types, and major deviations must be expected. Other types are possible, but I have not intended to present a comprehensive typology of hunting–gathering populations. The types are provided here for subsequent reference to avoid needless repetition of the environmental parameters and their associated demographic patterns.

Demographic Variables and Social Organization

Demographic variables are closely tied with the subsistence regime and economy of hunter–gatherers, as they are among agricultural and industrial groups. They are also tied with the pattern of social organization. The relationship between population and hunting–gathering economy has been discussed in previous chapters. Carneiro (1967) has provided an exemplary analysis of the relationship between population size and the complexity of social organization. He used a list of 205 organizational traits and a total of 100 societies. The relationship between population size and the complexity of social organization proved to be logarithmic, following the general equation

$$N = a P^b$$

where N is the number of organizational traits, P is the population size, and a and b are constants. The results obtained by Carneiro are represented in Figure 11.1. The values of the constants obtained yield the following formula:

$$N = .6P^{.504}, \text{ or approximately } .6 \sqrt{P}$$

These values may vary on the basis of different manipulations of the data, but what is important is that there is a definite relationship between population size and organizational complexity. The number of organizational traits is proportional to the root (or power) of the population size. That the number of organizational traits increases as some root of the population size rather than at the same or a greater rate is reasonable. The addition of several individuals, for example, would not necessitate any organizational changes. A population between 20 and 30 persons may not require more than three organizational traits. The addition of 20 more individuals may not require more than one additional organizational trait.

A significant increase in population brought about by one factor or more would thus encourage the development of a higher level of complexity, if the society is to remain viable. Carneiro (1967:241) gives an example of this process in the social organization of the Plains Indians. During most of the year they lived in small, separate, independent bands. However, for the summer buffalo hunt, numerous

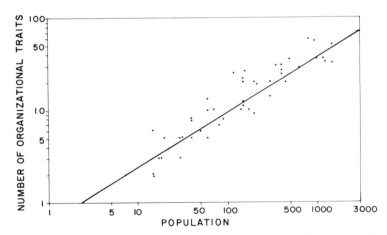

FIGURE 11.1. *Correlation between population size and number of organizational traits. (Data from Carneiro 1967.)*

bands congregated, forming an aggregate of several thousand. An elaborate organization, with a paramount chief, a tribal council, and men's societies, was developed. As Carneiro remarks, however, this complexity was reversible. It continued until the supraband aggregate was broken up again into its primary components. If the aggregation was not ephemeral, the organizational developments would have been irreversible. This seems to be exactly what happened following the adoption of agriculture with the formation of large sedentary populations (Hassan 1977).

The relationship between population and culture is not unidirectional, but rather reciprocal (Dumond 1965). An increase in organizational complexity may enhance further population aggregation. This would represent a positive feedback that enhances cultural evolution (Hassan 1974, 1977). Among hunter–gatherers, the rate of cultural evolution seems low in comparison to agricultural or industrial groups. This is brought about to a great extent as a result of the limitations imposed on the population size that can be attained. These limitations are a function of the very nature of the hunting–gathering economy, particularly the primary dependence on the yield of wild resources (Chapter 2). In addition, the variations in the size of hunting–gathering population through time are too small to permit strong sociopolitical control to develop to the threshold where further increase in population size or organizational complexity would be accelerated at the rate observed among agricultural and industrial populations.

Among hunter–gatherers, the band is formed through loose aggregation of families by kinship extended by marriage alliance (Service 1966:7). Steward (1936, 1955), in a brilliant analysis of the social basis of band societies, concluded that the majority of bands are patrilocal (children are raised in their father's band) and patrilineal (the members of the band are related through the male line). Exogamy (mates are from outside one's band) was also found by Steward to be a common practice. Steward's generalization was preceded by Radcliffe-Brown's recognition of the "patrilocal, patrilineal, territorial, and exogamous horde as the important local group in Australia." Service (1962) called Steward's "patrilineal band" patrilocal and suggested that this was the basic type of band for all hunter–gatherers in the past. Steward (1955:135) proposed the following factors as responsible for the development of the patrilocal, patrilineal bands:

1. Scarce wild foods lead to low population density (less than .4 person/km^2)
2. The principal food is nonmigratory, scattered game
3. Transportation is restricted to human carriers
4. Incest taboos lead to exogamy

Steward (1955:143–150) recognized another type of band, the "composite band," which consists of unrelated nuclear or biological families. According to Steward (1955:149), the factors that would lead to the formation of these bands are (a) the chief food is game that occurs in large herds; and (b) certain social practices that introduce unrelated families into the patrilineal band are exercised. Such practices include adoption, endogamy, matrilocal residence, and a lack of exchangeable women.

Composite bands are a result of the need for cooperation among many families producing a band aggregate of several hundred persons in order to take advantage of the large herds of game. In such large groups, kinship relations are minimized or lost and band endogamy may occur.

However, Service (1966), who is in general agreement with Steward, suggests that patrilocality is a result of the occupation of males in hunting and in warfare. He also suggests that the exchange of women as "gifts" for alliance making is another factor contributing to patrilocality. The composite band, according to Service (1962), was the product of the recent breakdown of hunting–gathering societies.

Williams (1974) has reexamined the band society and suggests that hunter-gatherers possess "economic territories." Families tend to reside most of the time in the band territory of the husband. Thus, the postmarital residence is patrilocal and the associated descent unit is patrilineal. In order to take advantage of what Williams calls "windfall" resources too large to be utilized by a single band, groups of affiliated lineage bands may be linked through matrilineal primary kinship bonds, which Williams calls "matrilineal account." According to Williams, patrilocality results from the association of hunting activities with males. Since hunting, unlike the plant gathering done by females, requires coordination of activities, the males would tend to form the "backbone" of the band and would thus rarely be transferred between autonomous groups. Williams (1974:23) disagrees with Steward on the issue of the composite bands. He believes that they occur only in the case of continuous disruption of the band society.

Gjessing (1975), on the basis of hunting and fishing in the arctic, infers that where there is a need for frequent and instantaneous mobilization of hunting or fishing teams a bilateral system would be advantageous. According to Gjessing, loyalty would be tied to one's own generation. However, Williams (1974:36) points out that a bilateral system may appear to exist among patrilocal and patrilineal groups if an alliance through the female between her husband's group and her natal group is necessary.

Steward (1955:135) has emphasized territoriality as the basis for the patrilineal band.

> Were families to wander at will, hunting the game in neighboring areas, competition would lead to conflict. Conflict would lead to alliance with other families, allies being found in related families. *As the men tend to remain more or less in the territory in which they have been reared and with which they are familiar,* patrilineally related families would tend to band together to protect their game resources. The territory would therefore become divided among those patrilineal bands [emphasis added].

However, if patrilocality results from the need for cooperation among males for hunting and male social dominance (Williams 1974), then there is no need to place much emphasis on territory. Territoriality seems to vary among hunting–gathering groups (Netting 1972:8). Under dense population conditions with evenly distributed resources, localization would be advantageous and territoriality would be well de-marcated with prohibitions against trespass. Territoriality may also develop when resources are sparse and game is small and dispersed, (as in the Ojibwa area when big game declined (Netting 1972). On the other hand, if the total yield is low, seasonality, fluctuations, biotopic differentiation, and moderate species diversity would encourage territorial elasticity and even territorial overlap. Abundance of resources and low population density would also encourage territorial fluidity, as indicated by the Great Basin Shoshone (Steward 1955). Thus, it would seem inap-propriate to generalize about territoriality among hunter–gatherers. We should also distinguish between *territorial attachment* and *territorial exclusion* (territoriality). Hunters tend to reside where they are reared, in the area they are familiar with, but this does not mean that they would prohibit others from sharing their territory. Also, the hunter may be familiar with two or three territories (Turnbull 1972), which would be advantageous if fluctuations are frequent or if spatial mobility is required. Territories are often recognized but rarely defended (Hallowell 1949; Lee, in Lee and DeVore 1968b:157; Steward 1955). The boundaries of a territory are often diffuse, but cases with sharp boundaries based on ecological variations are known, such as in Australia (Pilling, in Lee and DeVore 1968:156–157; Hiatt, in Lee and DeVore 1968:157). In some cases, as among the Australian aborigines, the territory is identified with totemic sites.

Since environmental parameters seem to influence the kinship system of hunter–gatherers through their demographic pattern, it would be advantageous to look closely at the relevant demographic variables in relation to environmental parameters, on the one hand, and kinship, on the other. The demographic variables are as follows:

1. Group size
2. Seasonal or periodic aggregation
3. Population density
4. Localization
5. Overlap

Small groups would tend to encourage exogamy because the unit is not biologically viable and the availability of mates cannot always be guaranteed. Large groups, on the other hand, can permit endogamous marriage, in addition to exogamy. Seasonal and periodic aggregation would tend to encourage matrilineal alliances. Low popu-lation density may or may not be conducive to the maintenance of a strictly pat-rilineal system and endogamous relations may develop, leading to an amorphous kinship system. When density is high, localization of the population would encour-age intergroup alliances, possibly leading to sodalities that may not be kinship based. Intergroup marriage is also likely to occur, which may lead to adoption and "fictitious" kinship. Thus, the four demographic types recognized previously may correspond to the following kinship system:

Type I: Small, no seasonal aggregation, localized residence, exogamy, patrilocality

Type II: Small–large, moderate seasonality, moderate population density; sometimes, under high population density, localized residence and territorial overlap; exogamy, patrilocal, sodalities (associations of men from different residential units)

Type III: Small, nonlocalized, low density, great fluctuations in group size, common periodic aggregation; exogamy, patrilocality with matrilineal alliance, bilateral or amorphous systems

Type IV: Large group size, localized, high density, endogamy possibly supplementing exogamy, locality and lineage indeterminate

These types are only examples of the social implications of certain common combinations of environmental–demographic parameters. It is unfortunate that hunter–gatherers are often forced to fit a specific "stereotype" without any regard for the variability that they exhibit. The patrilocal exogamy model is a general one and serves as a point of departure. Lee (1972a) has criticized the patrilocal model on the basis of his observations of the !Kung Bushmen. Since this group lives in a habitat that leads to a variety of the Type III demographic pattern, his criticisms are only valid in the context of those conditions. It is unlikely that most hunter–gatherers of the Pleistocene were living under such environmental conditions. Since the population was concentrated in temperate regions, the Type II demographic pattern seems more appropriate. If there are great fluctuations in the number of people as a result of severe climatic fluctuations or stochastic demographic oscillations, or if the bands are widely scattered, then endogamy, aggregation of unrelated families, and bilateral or amorphous systems may emerge. If population density is high and territories overlap, nonresidential sodalities are likely to develop as an alternative to intergroup hostilities.

It is important to note here that the small group size of hunter–gatherers, the changing composition of camps, and the imbalance in sex ratio due to stochastic fluctuations or preferential infanticide enhance exogamy as a mechanism to ensure availability of mates (Wobst 1974).

The transition to agriculture was associated with the emergence of large sedentary population units. In a large population, the recruiting of females from outside the population unit diminishes and endogamous marriage patterns can develop. J. W. Adams and A. B. Kasakoff (1975) indicate that the percentage of endogamy increases as population increases.

In addition to bringing about endogamy, the maintenance of a sedentary, large population requires a level of social integration greater than that common among hunter–gatherers (White 1949). Among hunter–gatherers, there is no incentive for strong integrative mechanisms. In fact, such mechanisms would obstruct the demographic flux that is a successful way of coping with shortages [see Kunitz (1976) on the demographic problems of the "sedentarization" of nomadic Indian tribes]. The emergence of formal leaders, the formalization of social rules, and the enforcement of such rules by severe penalities must be viewed as a mechanism of ensuring social coherence and stability for a large population. Occupational differentiation and the demand for a formal policy of sharing would have also enhanced the nucleation of a power structure.

A study by Barry (1973) on the relationship between social complexity and population size for 186 societies indicates that unilinear descent and a large number of levels of political hierarchy are correlated with large populations (see also Naroll 1956). Sedentariness and large population size allow residential kin-based social systems, even among the higher primates (Altman and Altman 1978).

Kinship patterns and various demographic factors such as mobility, fission and fusion, and population growth among agricultural groups are discussed by Fix (1975), Godelier (1975), Hammel (1964, 1977), and Nash and Nash (1963). The trend toward large populations and occupational differentiation was associated with an intensification of labor input (see Chapters 13 and 14 for a discussion of these developments). In part, the demands for labor were created by an increasing ratio of nonfood producers to farmers, a rising level of consumption, especially of nonsubsistence goods, and agrarian changes aimed at stabilizing the simplified ecological system of agricultural subsistence. These developments, which were closely tied with large populations, led to further elaboration in the power structure (for managing labor and capital), leading ultimately to the emergence of rank societies.

Demography and Technocultural Traditions

The implications of these demographic–social patterns are important for understanding spatial distribution and temporal continuity, and discontinuity of cultural traditions. In many cases, artifacts and artifact assemblages constitute the framework of archaeological technological spatiotemporal units. If toolmaking is associated with male artisans, the predominance of a patrilocal residential system and patrilineality would indicate a tendency for the continuation of toolmaking techniques in the residential areas of the band. However, the fission and fusion of allied bands would tend to homogenize the technology of the regional group, which consists of the bands that constitute the interband exogamous pool. The greater the localization, the greater the chance for technological differentiation between neighboring groups. In contrast, if groups are scattered and small, intergroup contact increases the availability of mates and leads to interregional homogenization. The continuity of cultural traditions would be a function of the maintenance of group identity. If conditions are stable and there is limited intergroup interaction, localized technological traditions can be maintained over a long period. Similarly, if the degree of interaction is high and conditions are unstable, the intermixing of groups will lead to a greater interregional homogenization over a long period as a result of the increased demographic flux and nonresidential social relations.

Let us now consider some of the applications of these considerations to concrete archaeological cases. Williams (1974:106–107) suggests that patrilocal bands have been present for the past 40,000–50,000 years. This suggestion is based on the assumption that the rate of local differentiation of cultural artifacts observed during the Upper Palaeolithic may indicate that patrilocality was not previously practiced. Williams, however, fails to note that the acceleration of the rate of artifact technology during the Upper Palaeolithic is primarily a function of increasing population density, localization, and territorial overlap. If patrilocality is basically a function of male dominance, as Williams argues, then it is reasonable to suspect that patrilocality was common in earlier Pleistocene cultures. Male dominance is common in higher primate societies and might indeed have been greatly substantiated during the Basal Palaeolithic times by the need for male defense and antipredatorial vigilance. During the earlier periods of the Pleistocene, because of the relatively moderate density, medium group size, and absence of overcrowding or territorial overlap (modification of Type II), we would expect that patrilocality would not have been inhibited and exogamous relations would have been prevalent. Therefore, there would be a long duration of technological traditions. With greater crowding and territorial overlap during the Late Pleistocene, the rate of innovation would be higher and the cross-cultural transmission of innovations would lead to local differentiation, but the local cultural manifestation would be subject to rapid transformations.

This model fits the archaeological record well. During periods of climatic change and in areas along the margins of major climatic zones or in northern latitudes, severe climatic fluctuations would lead to adverse effects on the economic stability of social groups and their numbers. This disruption would lead to the agglomeration of different groups. This would be reflected in the "mixing" of cultural traditions (if such traditions were previously distinct). Of course, this would be reflected in the archaeological record.

David (1973) provides an example of this kind. The Noaillan, a "culture" dating from the Late Pleistocene between ca. 27,000 and 25,000 B.P., located in the low latitude tundra in France, reveals "acculturation" of Noaillan with another culture, the Perigordian, during two phases of depopulation. In some cases, a population may become so drastically reduced that its fusion with other groups may go totally unnoticed. Mellars (1972) provides a different example based on the Middle–Upper Palaeolithic transition in southwestern France. The transition was associated with an emphasis on reindeer hunting, which may be, in part, related to climatic conditions. This subsistence regime would have encouraged seasonal aggregation of populations for large-scale cooperative hunting of reindeer (Mellars 1972). The large size of many Upper Palaeolithic sites seems to suggest periodic reoccupation with lateral shift leading to sites that are sometimes 10,000 m² in areal spread. This suggests that hunting "villages" of several related bands were formed, and were occupied as long as meat was available. The bands would then disaggregate. This requires further archaeological testing, but if it were the case then a bilateral or patrilineal system with matrilateral "account" would have been favored.

Australian prehistory may be also interpreted in the light of the environmental-demographic–social model outlined. The stone-tool assemblages seem to belong to a single pancontinental core-tool and scraper tradition with some broad stylistic provincial differentiation. The regional stylistic patterns survived for tens of thousands of years (Jones 1973:280). According to the model, this occurrence would have resulted from a sparsely populated region with an overall low density, small group sizes, and high degree of spatial mobility, with little or no localization (Steward 1955:131). This agrees well with the environmental conditions in Australia and the ethnographic–demographic pattern. This, Australia during the Late Pleistocene was much different from other areas in Europe, the Near East, and North Africa, where dense and localized groups were common.

A similar pattern to that of prehistoric Australia is discussed by Yellen and Harpending (1972) who, drawing from ethnographic data on the !Kung Bushmen, for example, infer that the absence of variations in the artifacts of the Wilton—a Late Stone Age industry in Africa—is a result of extreme fluidity in the composition and spatial distribution of population. Yellen (1977) notes that the observed differences between assemblages concentrated around water holes are insignificant, and no greater than differences between sites located around the same water hole or between different stratigraphic units of the same site.

The small size of hunting–gathering populations places severe limits on the frequency of innovation, since the number of potential innovators is minimal. This applies also to the world population at large. The Palaeolithic world population was small, perhaps no more than 10 million at any time.

Innovations are also a function of the magnitude of dissemination of ideas (Barnett 1953:56). The worldwide transmission of ideas today through telecommunication and travel is, of course, unprecedented, and is undoubtedly responsible for the acceleration of cultural evolution.

Among hunter–gatherers the transmission of ideas between populations was limited by social and topographic distances, but in view of the small size of individual groups, the role of intergroup transmission of cultural innovations must have been one of the major mechanisms of cultural evolution during the Palaeolithic. It also provided the impetus for further innovations, which were again incorporated in the "universal innovation pool." The rates of dissemination must have been exceedingly slow, but they were perhaps much faster than the rates of demographic geographic expansion, since innovations can be transmitted independent of population increase and are not restricted, but rather enhanced, by occupied territories. As the overall population density increases the rate of cultural interaction thus increases.

This pattern may explain in part the slight acceleration of cultural evolution during the Pleistocene that has been observed by Isaac (1969). The progressive addition of cultural innovations during the Palaeolithic also would have produced a cumulative effect adding to an increase in the rate of innovations. An overall increase in the density of population over a large region may also lead to localization of individual groups and may thus enhance areal cultural differentiation. The localization of groups, however, may be associated with the development of greater social distances between proximal groups, but it is hardly likely that such distances would overcome the rate of cultural transmission enhanced by geographic proximity. The social mechanisms also could never have been effective in blocking the flow of cultural innovations because of the inherent mobility of hunting–gathering bands and the advantages of a flexible group composition. The relationship between demographic patterns and cultural transmission has been explored by Binford (1963), Owen (1965), and Deetz (1965). Isaac (1972:186–187) provides a similar view, which treats bands or communities as communication systems.

The mechanisms of cultural transmission are based primarily on the flexibility of group composition, dictated by environmental parameters and facilitated by weak group cohesion. In addition the frequent changes in the population size brought about by stochastic resource and/or population fluctuations would also enhance the diffusion of innovations (Ammerman 1975). Thus population processes can contribute to culture change even though no long-term changes in population size are taking place (Ammerman 1975).

It must be realized that since the habitats of hunter–gatherers vary considerably in their environmental parameters, each region would tend to show a distinct pattern of population movement, fluidity, and intergroup contact. Also since climatic variations during the Pleistocene were considerable, the temporal setting of the region is crucial. Within long time segments, it is important to consider periodic fluctuations in climatic conditions, because frequent fluctuations would enhance the unpredictability of the resources and thus increase group mobility.

Demography, Language, and Dialects

The prehistorian working with an unwritten past has no hope of finding direct evidence for the languages and dialects of the peoples who are the subject of his work. However, language cannot be completely ignored, because of its importance in the transmission of culture from one generation to the next and from one group to another. I have been alerted to the potential implications of demographic variables for linguistic phenomena among hunter–gatherers by Jane H. Hill (1972) and much of the material presented here is drawn from her pioneering effort.

Birdsell (1958, 1968, 1970) has used the term *dialectal tribe* to refer to the dialectal uniformity of a unit consisting of a constellation of bands. Hill (1972) suggests that the dialectal tribe is advantageous for the maintenance of a centralized labor pool and a marriage pool. However, Hill realizes that it is extremely difficult to find true "dialectal tribes" and that an exact correspondence between language, technology, and social and cultural units is rare. Therefore she suggests that the "dialectal tribe" model could be used merely as a baseline.

Dialects are difficult to acquire after age 6 or 7. Adults may learn the vocabulary of a new language but can almost never acquire an adequate control over phonemics, retaining a "foreign accent." Anyone who leaves his "tribe" after early adolescence and enters a foreign group would be recognizable and his accent would serve as a potential barrier to full integration.

It would seem, then, that a dialectal tribe would emerge only if the labor pool could be mustered from within the tribe and if the tribe was sufficiently large to provide mates on a long-term basis. An exclusively dialectal tribe is a product of residential stability and large tribal groups. The development of a dialectal affinity among the bands enhances this stability (positive feedback) and ensures mate availability. It appears, then, that a dialectal tribe can hardly be generalized for all hunter-gatherers. In many cases, the development of exclusive dialectal groups may be deleterious rather than advantageous. I will argue that certain environmental-demographic patterns would tend to lead to certain linguistic patterns, one of which is the exclusive "dialectal tribe." Since the development of the dialectal unit is a function of preadolescent learning, residential stability, and large multiband group size, it may be useful to investigate the probability of the development of dialectal and other linguistic aspects in relation to demographic flux. Certain environmental-demographic conditions would tend to lead to localization (Type II and Type IV). Under these conditions, large group size is also feasible. Representatives of groups living under such conditions include the coastal and riverine groups (Type IV). According to Laughlin (1972:381), the Aleuts do exhibit dialectal groups, which play a prominent role in maintaining boundaries. The Northwest Coast Indians are another example (Hulse 1957), but though they had local languages, they also had a pattern of "linguistic exogamy" (Jane Hill, personal communication). Under environmental-demographic conditions that lead to frequent inter-tribal flux (which whould be expected under Types IIIA and IIIB), and under frequent severe short-term climatic and/or demographic fluctuation, the formation of dialectal units would be either inhibited or supplemented by other linguistic forms. These forms include (a) diglossic "high language," (b) sign language, (c) multilingualism, and (d) lexical dialects.

A mutually intelligible diglossic "high language," such as among the Yanomamo, may be used to avoid the intrusion of dialectal differences. Sign languages, a substitute for vocal language, can serve to override language barriers. Hill notes the development of sign language in the Great Plains, where speakers of many languages are gathered. In this case, the horse facilitated rapid long-distance movement so that contact between many languages was more likely (Jane Hill, personal communication). Multilingualism may result from frequent intertribal interaction and exogamy. Owen (1965) and Berndt (1959) believe that multilingual hunter-gatherers are common. Multilingualism may be institutionalized through exogamy, where there would be a tendency to marry outside "father's tongue." This has been reported for the Arnhem Land hunter-gatherers in Australia. Lexical dialects are based on trivial differences that can be easily overridden by adult learners. Lexical dialects are common in the desert areas of Australia. They may thus serve as elastic boundary-maintaining barriers, which can be easily ruptured when necessary.

Certain conditions may favor conservatism. Where the groups are small and relatively distant from each other, they deliberately may attempt to overcome the effect of drift by conservatism, which would facilitate communication and is needed for interband occasional cooperation or for the maintenance of a viable mating pool. Such a conservative pattern is observed in Australia. It is also interesting that phonological conservatism is matched by technological conservatism. However, among the Great Basin Shoshone, where seasonal flux and territorial overlap is great, the groups are phonologically innovative and lack distinct units with areal dialects. According to Hill, this is in part due to the relatively shallow time depth of their language, only about 1000 years.

It may be thus surmised that there would be a general tendency for a dialect to be developed among groups who intermarry and are coresidents of the same territory. However, the development of an areally exclusive dialectal tribe often would be diluted among hunter–gatherers by the demands for extratribal exogamy or seasonal, periodic, or occasional cooperation among different "dialectal" groups. It may thus be suggested that dialectal uniformity over large areas might have prevailed during the earlier part of the Pleistocene. With increasing population density and the development of intensive coastal and riverine adaptations, strongly dialectal units may have developed, but as a result of proximity and the inevitability of cultural seepage, the dialects were perhaps short-lived. This linguistic flux during the Terminal Pleistocene could have been associated with the technological and stylistic differentiation of artifacts. In contrast, the linguistic homogeneity that might have prevailed in earlier Pleistocene times would have accompanied and perhaps facilitated technological uniformity. A pattern of fluid linguistic identity could not have been universal during the Terminal Pleistocene since deserts and tropical areas were inhabited and climatic fluctuations were, in some areas, very severe.

Overview

In this chapter I have explored some of the interrelationships between demography, spatial organization, technocultural traditions, and language. The impact of environmental variables on the size and spatial mobility of hunter–gatherers was viewed as a major, though not the sole, determinant of a number of cultural elements, such as marriage rules, kinship, complexity of social organization, technocultural conservatism, and dialects. Different world biomes exhibit combinations of environmental variables and may thus lead to biogeographic differences in cultural systems. The Eskimos living in arctic areas or the Bushmen in a desert biome thus may not be typical of the majority of the Pleistocene hunter-gatherers, who lived in temperate areas.

12

The Peopling of the World

Relatively few animals press so heavily on their food or are pressed on so heavily by predators. . . . But there are many other causes for the temporariness and the "fluctuation in space" of local populations. Animals need to be constantly dispersing as a normal part of their lives—and those that happen to evolve special patterns of behaviour which speed the processes of dispersal are likely to be favoured by natural selection.*

Changes in population density and rates of growth during the Pleistocene are examined in this chapter. The peopling of the New World and Australia is also discussed. This is followed by an estimation of the carrying capacity of world biomes and an overview of changes in prehistoric subsistence.

The earliest human occupations were in open grasslands or parklands (Butzer 1971). By the end of the Middle Pleistocene, the human population expanded into areas of greater aridity, as well as into forest areas. During the Terminal Pleistocene, settlements were established in yet drier environments and tropical forests. Expansion into the New World is likely to have taken place before 20,000–25,000 years ago; colonization of Australia, at about 40,000–30,000 B.P. The rates of geographic expansion are difficult to estimate, but the average rate of population growth during the Pleistocene does not indicate a fast rate of population expansion. The rates were probably less than 1 km/year during the peopling of Australia and the New World, and perhaps as low as .02 km/year during the Early Pleistocene.

The expansion of human populations into the deserts, arctic areas, and tropical forests would have increased the carrying capacity. These regions would have supported about 800,000 persons in addition to the population supported by the biomes already inhabited. The broad-spectrum adaptation of the Mesolithic/ Epipalaeolithic perhaps permitted about 1 million more.

*H. G. Andrewartha, Introduction to the study of animal populations, University of Chicago Press, Chicago, 1963, pp. 58–59.

The buildup of the world population during the Pleistocene and the relatively rapid increase in world population during the Late Pleistocene were associated with an acceleration in the rate of technocultural differentiation and innovation. This was probably a result of a larger number of regional population units (6000 during the Upper Palaeolithic compared with 1200 during the Middle Palaeolithic, assuming an average regional group size of 1000 persons) a five fold increase, smaller distance between groups allowing for more frequent contact, and increasing territorial attachment.

The stage was by then set for one of the most spectacular achievements of human beings, food production—an achievement that biologists must regard as an evolutionary success because it allowed humans to increase their numbers to a level well beyond that possible under hunting–gathering subsistence (Childe 1936). The transition to agriculture was, however, more than a demographic "explosion." It entailed a transformation of the "essence" of man as a cultural being (Mumford 1956).

Population Expansion during the Pleistocene

Despite an average growth rate that is well below the reproductive potential of hunter–gatherers, and despite the small numbers of the prehistoric world population, the whole world, including the Americas, was populated by the end of the Pleistocene.

The oldest archaeological remains (Oldowan) and human-like (australopithecine) fossil finds, perhaps as old as 3 million years, are mostly from Africa (Isaac and McCown 1976). Outside Africa, the only known archaeological remains resembling the earliest Oldowan artifacts are reported from southern France at Vallonet Cave (.95–.9 million years ago). In this occurrence choppers and flakes were associated with Late Villafranchian fauna (De Lumley 1975). More recent archaeological finds (Developed Oldowan) are reported from Ubeidyia in the Jordan Valley (Bar-Yosef 1975). They are associated with a geological formation with a terminal date of 640,000 years. Early hominid remains, however, are found in Southeast and East Asia. The age of these finds is still uncertain but they seem to range from 1.9 to .5 million years (Pilbeam 1975).

During the Early Pleistocene, the expansion of the advanced hominid populations (*Homo erectus*) outside Africa is documented by numerous skeletal and archaeological finds from the Near East, India, Burma, Thailand, and Malaya, in addition to evidence for continuing occupation in China and Java (Butzer and Isaac 1975).

In Europe, well-documented occurrences are associated with the Elster Glaciation. These include the sites of Torralba and Ambrona in central Spain, Terra Amata in southern France, and Vértesszöllös in Hungary. At Abbeville (Somme Valley) in France, archaeological material is found in river gravel attributed to the

Cromerian. During the Middle Pleistocene, archaeological occurrences extend farther to the north than earlier occurrences (Collins 1969).

Generally, occupations in and outside Africa are located in open vegetation habitats, such as grassland, wooded steppe, and woodland (Butzer 1971; Collins 1969). In Africa, the earliest occupations are restricted to areas that are today subarid to subhumid grassland and park savanna (Clark 1970). Later occupations indicate population spread into areas that are arid today, such as the Kalahari Desert, the Sahara, and Somaliland (Butzer 1971; Clark 1970). It seems also that occupations expanded into the peripheral parts, as well as savanna corridors, of the Congolese forest. In Asia, the setting of the Lantien sites is one of open country (Chow et al. 1965). Similarly, sites in India and Pakistan are found in open hill and plateau country in areas now semiarid to subhumid (Butzer 1971). In Southwest Asia, at Latamne (Syria), the occupations were in wooded steppe and grassland settings (Clark 1975).

The human expansion does not seem to have occurred then beyond the Eurasiatic mountain barrier formed by the Caucasus, the Elbruz, the Hindu Kush, and the Himalayas (Collins 1969). The cold steppes of the Ukraine, the Iranian plateau, and central Asia have not yielded any traces of occupation of Middle Pleistocene age (Butzer 1971:452–453).

During the occupation of the Choukoutien site in northern China (ca. .5 million years ago), pollen evidence suggests cool boreal coniferous forest prevailed (Collins 1969:285).

The distribution pattern of Early and Middle Pleistocene occurrences suggests that earlier stages of population expansion were confined to temperate open grassland and savanna environments (Figure 12.1). Later, new habitats were penetrated, ranging from areas in Africa that are today arid to cold steppe.

During the early part of the Late Pleistocene, the human population continued to expand farther to the north, occupying the cold steppes of the Ukraine, the Iranian plateau, Turkmenia, and Uzbekistan. In Europe, central Germany and southern Poland were penetrated. By the end of the Late Pleistocene, northern Europe as far north as southern Scandinavia and parts of Siberia were colonized. It is also during the terminal part of the Late Pleistocene that Australia was populated (40,000–30,000 years ago). The Americas were settled by 12,000 years ago and were perhaps first infiltrated 25,000 to 20,000 years ago, or earlier.

There is thus a definite indication for progressive geographic expansion of man throughout the Pleistocene. This is an indication of progressive adaptability to varied climatic conditions and habitats (Butzer 1971:454; K. Davis 1974).

Changes in Population Density during Prehistoric Times

As long as human subsistence was based on hunting–gathering, the density of the human population must have been exceedingly low. We can hardly escape this

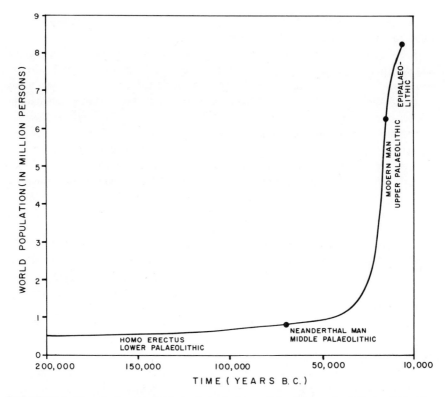

FIGURE 12.1. *Growth of world population from the Lower Palaeolithic to the Epipalaeolithic. (Data from Hassan, this volume.)*

conclusion in view of (*a*) the low population density of living hunter–gatherers, (*b*) the estimates of low density derived from simulation models of resource potentials, and levels of extraction and consumption, and (*c*) the scarcity of archaeological occurrences of prehistoric hunter–gatherers. It is unreasonable, however, to assume that the density of the human population remained unchanged throughout prehistoric times. Deevey (1960) has suggested the levels of population density listed in Table 12.1. Deevey (1960:5) derived his figures from "some figures for modern hunting tribes quoted by Robert J. Braidwood and Charles A. Reed." The figures quoted by Braidwood and Reed appeared in their classic paper, "The Achievement and Early Consequences of Food Production: A Consideration of the Archaeological and Natural–Historical Evidence"(1957). In this paper, Braidwood and Reed classified the whole range of Old World prehistoric culture history in terms of level of subsistence pattern. Estimates of probable population density at each of the levels suggested were given. Of the eight levels mentioned by Braidwood and Reed, the first two are relevant to the present discussion. The first level is one of " 'natural' food-gathering," which is the subsistence pattern of the entire Pleistocene. At this level the "population concentration estimate" is given as .002 person/km^2. At the subsequent level of late glacial and early postglacial times (Upper Palaeolithic and Mesolithic/Terminal Palaeolithic), a pattern of specialized food-collecting (or terminal food-gathering) was associated with a population concentration estimate of .05 person/km².

The estimate of population density at the first level was based on Birdsell's (1953) estimate of .03 person/km² for the Australian aborigines and Kroeber's (1953) estimate of .004 person/km² for Caribou Eskimo. The population density at the second level was determined by analogy with Kroeber's (1953) estimates of .05 person/km² for the Ojibwa, .25 person/km² for seed gatherers of the Great Basin, .004 person/km² for the Montagnais of the Canadian Northeast, and 9.4 person/km² for the Haida of the Northwest Coast.

Deevey's figure for the population density during the Upper Palaeolithic and Mesolithic periods (.04 person/km²) is apparently derived from Braidwood and Reed's .05 person/km² for the same periods. His estimate for the Middle Palaeolithic is equivalent to that of Braidwood and Reed for the level of "natural food-gathering." It is not clear, however, how he derived the estimate for the Lower Palaeolithic.

The population-density estimate given by Braidwood and Reed (1957) has been widely quoted in the past without reservations. Although Braidwood and Reed's pioneering attempt to shed some light on the density of prehistoric populations is commendable, recent data on the population density of hunter–gatherers necessitate a modification of the original figures given in their publication. Baumhoff's (1963) work, for example, indicates that the population density was 1.1 persons/km² among the hunter–gatherers of California, and 1.2 persons/km² for the Lower Klamath fishers, and 3.9 persons/km² for gathering–hunting–fishing peoples of the Sacramento–San Joaquin zone. Eskimos with a caribou and sea mammal hunting economy (e.g., Kivallinquit and Tikiraqmiut) have a population density of .17–.46 person/square mile (.067–.176 person/km²), and those with a caribou hunting and fishing economy (e.g., Kuuvakmiut and Siilvikmiut) have a population density of .11–.49 person/square mile (.042–.19 person/km²; Burch 1972). Eskimos with an almost exclusively caribou hunting economy (e.g., Asiagmuit, Mt. People, Patliqmiut) show a population density of .026–.034 person/square

TABLE 12.1
Estimates of World Prehistoric Population[a]

Period	Population density (persons/km²)	World population (millions)
Lower Palaeolithic	.00425	.125
Middle Palaeolithic	.012	1.00
Upper Palaeolithic	.04	3.34
Mesolithic	.04	5.32

[a] From Deevey 1960.

mile (.011–.18 person/km^2; Burch (1972). Hunter–gatherers in Africa (e.g., Hadza and Bushmen) show a population density of .16–.4 person/square mile (.06–.15 person/km^2; see Lee 1968; Woodburn 1968).

Birdsell (1972) reestimated world population density during the Lower, Middle, and Upper Palaeolithic using the figures for population density and world area occupied in successive periods given in Table 12.2.

The population density estimated for the Lower Pleistocene is slightly higher than the .03 person/km^2 for the Australians and .01 for some groups of the Caribou Eskimo. The estimate for the Middle Pleistocene is based on a figure similar to that for the Australians. The figure should have been higher, because Australia is "a rather unfavored continent for hunters," but the more advanced level of the Australian leads Birdsell to view .03 as a reasonable estimate. The estimates for the Upper Palaeolithic are slightly higher than those for the Australians. They are not too much higher because the population density in the arctic regions must have been rather low.

Birdsell estimates the area occupied during the Lower Pleistocene as 30% of Africa and 10% of Eurasia. He also estimates that 90% of Africa and 20% of Eurasia were occupied during the Middle Pleistocene. During the Upper Palaeolithic the area occupied in Europe and Asia increased to 40%, whereas the area occupied in Africa remained the same.

Birdsell's estimates of world areas occupied throughout the Pleistocene seem reasonable, but his estimates of population density need to be reexamined in the light of the population densities presented in Table 2.1 (p.8), and some estimates of the population density of prehistoric groups.

During the Terminal Pleistocene the population density was perhaps about .2 person/km^2, a figure that is much higher than that for the Australians, who live in arid lands, but closer to that of the Hadza, who live in a woodland savanna environment. The population density in the tundra and desert regions was much lower, perhaps in the neighborhood of .03 person/km^2, whereas in certain coastal areas the density was somewhere between 1 and 2 persons/km^2. However, the population size in coastal areas and the desert regions was not sufficient either to increase or decrease the overall world population density.

During the Upper Palaeolithic, the population density was about .1 person/km^2

TABLE 12.2
Estimates of World Prehistoric Population[a]

Period	Population density (persons/km^2)	Area occupied (10^6 km)	World population (10^6 persons)
Lower Palaeolithic	.015	27.0	ca. .4
Middle Palaeolithic	.032	38.3	ca. 1.0
Upper Palaeolithic	.039	57.5	ca. 2.2

[a] From Birdsell 1972.

in France (Nougier 1954). A similar figure was obtained by Angel (1972) for the eastern Mediterranean. This figure seems more acceptable than the much lower figures quoted for this period. It compares well with the population density of hunting– gathering populations in temperate grassland regions (e.g., the Hadza). With a total area of about 60 million km², the world population may be estimated at about 6 million at this time.

During the Final Palaeolithic, the human population expanded into the tundra (8×10^6 km²) and the deserts (9×10^6 km²). In these areas the population density would have been about .03 person/km² by comparison with living hunter–gatherers (e.g., the Australians and the Caribou Eskimo); the world population would have been increased by about 500,000 persons. In addition, the intensive exploitation of coastal and riverine resources and the advent of a broad- spectrum adaptation should have increased the population density by about 20–40%. The world population during the Epipalaeolithic/Mesolithic period may have thus totaled about 8–9 million.

During the Middle Palaeolithic, the population in France was estimated at one-fifth that of the Upper Palaeolithic, which leads to an estimate of about .03 person/km². This figure is close to that of Birdsell. During the Middle Pleistocene, the population density was perhaps not too much lower, averaging .025 person/km². A figure of about .02 perhaps characterized the Lower Pleistocene. The world population may be thus estimated as listed in Table 12.3. The overall increase in population throughout the Pleistocene (Figure 12.1) was thus rather slow until the advent of *Homo sapiens*. The changes in the rate of increase are shown in Table 12.4.

It is interesting that with the appearance of *Homo sapiens neanderthalensis* the rate of increase was about 70–80 times that of *Homo erectus*. The emergence of *Homo sapiens* was marked initially by a doubling of the Neanderthal's rate. The rate dropped during the Mesolithic/Epipalaeolithic to about one-third the rate of the Upper Palaeolithic. This might have been a function of "environmental resistance," perhaps accentuated by the violent climatic fluctuations of that period.

TABLE 12.3
Estimates of World Prehistoric Population[a]

Period	Area (10^6 km)	Population density (persons/km²)	Approximate world population (10^6 persons)
Epipalaeolithic/Mesolithic	75	.115	8–9
Upper Palaeolithic	60	.100	6.0
Middle Palaeolithic	40	.030	1.2
Lower Palaeolithic	30	.025	.8
Basal Palaeolithic (Oldowan)	20	.020	.4

[a] Data from Hassan, this volume.

TABLE 12.4
*Probable Average Population Annual Growth Rate
during the Palaeolithic Period*

	Growth rate/year
Lower Palaeolithic	.00007%
Middle Palaeolithic	.0054%
Upper Palaeolithic	.011%
Epipalaeolithic/Mesolithic	.0033%

Rates of Population Expansion

The rate of population expansion during the Pleistocene was, on the average, very slow, perhaps amounting to .01 km/year. Birdsell (1957) suggested an expansion rate between 10 and 25 km/year for the colonization of Australia and P. Martin (1973) used a rate of 16–25 km/year for the peopling of the Americas. Such excessively rapid rates, if they ever occurred, were most probably exceptional.

It must be noted that these rates are based on net distance in the direction of expansion. The actual distance traveled is much greater. It is very unlikely that population movements were strictly unidirectional, and more likely that population expansion was a result of increase in population coincident with modest local movements, random in direction. Under such conditions, a wave of population expansion will develop and advance at a constant radial rate (Ammerman and Cavalli-Sforza 1973b). The distribution for migration in two dimensions may be represented as in Figure 12.2. The frequency of individuals located at the beginning at point 0 who are expected to be at a certain point f [defined by the coordinates (x_i, y_i)] after a given time is given by the value on the z-axis. This bidimensional distribution can be transformed into a distribution curve with the distances plotted along one axis. The distance of an individual from the starting point is given by the equation

$$d_i = \sqrt{x_i^2 + y_i^2}$$

The flatness or peakedness of the bidimensional surface and the distribution of distance are both determined by the standard deviation of migration (σ). The rate of advance of the expansion wave front (ρ) is a function of the rate of population increase (ρ) and the standard deviation of migration (σ):

$$\rho = \sigma\sqrt{2r}$$

The standard deviation of migration among prehistoric communities is unknown. The rate among modern "primitive" and peasant populations in Europe during recent historical times averages about 15 km/generation (Ammerman and Cavalli-Sforza 1973b). Since migration occurs in two dimensions, the unit of measurement

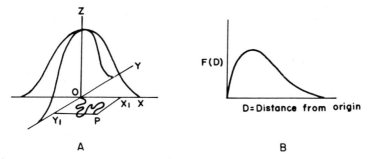

FIGURE 12.2. *Distribution of migration distances, assuming that migration is random in direction, in two dimensions,* x *and* y. *Migration path is shown by* OP. *At a given time* (t), *the frequency of persons expected to be at point* (x, y) *is represented by the value* z = f (x,y). *The curve in B is a transformation of the distribution surface into a unidimensional distribution. The distance from the point of origin is given by* d = x² + y². *(Reproduced from Ammerman and Cavalli-Sforza 1973, by permission of the publisher.)*

should be square kilometers, or in this case $15^2 = 225 \text{km}^2$ for one generation, or $225/25 = 9 \text{ km}^2/\text{year}$ and 3 km/year. If we use this figure and the rate of .5% for population increase we obtain

$$\sigma = 3\sqrt{2 \times .005} = .3 \text{ km/year}$$

At a rate of 2%/year, $P = .6$ km/year. Thus, the rate of advance during periods of population surges was perhaps of this magnitude.

The Peopling of the New World

In an attempt to simulate the peopling of the Americas, P. Martin (1973) postulated a dense wave front, 160 km in depth, with an average population density of .4 person/km² advancing at a rate of 16 km/year and fed by a population increase rate of 3.4%/year. With these specifications, which Martin uses to construct a model of big-game overkill, the invading hunters swept from Canada to the Gulf of Mexico in 350 years, and on to the tip of South America in roughly 1000 years.

Martin, however, uses an intrinsic growth rate that is greater than the potential growth rate of hunter–gatherers, even with the child-spacing interval reduced to its natural limits (see Chapter 8). It is perhaps more realistic to place the maximum rate of increase at about .5%, with an average of .1%. These rates would be comparable to the rates of population increase during the Neolithic and historical times before industrialization (Carneiro and Hilse 1966; G. L. Cowgill 1975; Hassan 1973). At these rates, the time required to "saturate" the Americas may be estimated if the optimum carrying capacity can be estimated. Using the model previously outlined (Chapter 3), this may be estimated from the total animal biomass of wild game in aboriginal times, which was perhaps about 5000 kg/km² (see Table 2.3, p. 13). If 5% of the standing crop of the exploited animals were culled annually, and assuming that the animals exploited represented about 70% of the total mammalian standing crop and that about 10% of the animals hunted were wasted through spoilage or loss, the amount of meat obtainable would be about $5000 \times .7 \times .9$, or 158.3 kg/km². Now, assuming that the hunters were exploiting 40–60% of the maximum carrying capacity and that 50% of the live weight consisted of edible meat, the amount of meat available for consumption would be 31.7–47.6 kg/km². If the population subsisted primarily on meat, a high consumption rate of 1.36 kg/person/day would be likely. At this level of consumption, the population density would be about .06–.1 person/km². On the other hand, if the population supplemented meat with a large intake of plant food, the amount of meat consumed per person per day may be generously placed at about 1 lb or 476 gm. This would correspond to a population density of .18–.27 person/km². These and the afore mentioned densities would suggest optimum population sizes of .47, .78, 1.4, or 2.1 million for the unglaciated United States (7.8 × 10⁶km, after P. Martin 1973:970).

Assuming that the initial population of immigrants was 100 persons, the time required to reach the optimum population size would be 1690–1990 years at a rate of .5% increase per year. At the slower annual rate of .1%, the time required would be 8455–9952 years.

The most crucial factor in these calculations is the rate of increase. For example, if the initial population is increased tenfold to 1000, the time required at a rate of .5% would be 1200–1500 years; if one assumed an optimum population of 5–7 million, the time required would be 2200 years.

Because it is unlikely that these immigrants would have dropped involuntary population controls, I favor a rate of .1% annual increase and thus a period between 8000 and 10,000 years for the peopling of North America. According to Haynes (1969, 1970), the increase in the number of sites from about 12,000 to 7000 B.P. provides a rough estimate of an annual rate of .08%. The people thus inched their way into the continent, increasing gradually in number and expanding into various ecological habitats. The rate of penetration would have been less than 1 km/year and would be thus consistent with the rates assumed elsewhere for population expansion through a wave front (cf. Ammerman and Cavalli-Sforza 1973b).

The implications of a long period of expansion for the peopling of the New World for cultural development in that region are significant. It would indicate that man's entry into the New World occurred between 25,000 to 20,000 years ago, or somewhat earlier. Some recent findings seem to confirm this view (see, for example, Irving and Harington 1973). The number of people would remain low for a considerable time, then as the population reached a certain threshold the increase would become significant. The chances of finding archaeological sites would thus increase, and this may be reflected in the relative abundance of mammoth kill sites from about 11,240 B.P. (Haynes 1970:78–79, 1971). By 8500 B.P. the continent would have been fully saturated and cultural differentiation would have ensued. There is actually evidence for the beginning of regional differentiation of lithic traditions and cultural adaptations by that time (Willey 1966).

The Peopling of Australia

Man was able to reach Australia during the Late Pleistocene by crossing numerous water gaps from the Sunda Shelf to the Sahul Shelf, which at that time joined Australia and New Guinea. Birdsell (1957) constructed a model to estimate the time required to populate Australia. In his model, in which an attempt was made to approximate conditions of the last glacial, he assumed a 240-ft drop in sea level, combined with a 500-mile northward shift of the climatic belt. He estimated about 35 colonizing waves, of which the initial colony (at budding off) was 25 persons and the final size of a regional group was 500 persons. If the colonies were budded off at 60% carrying capacity, at a rate of doubling each generation (3.6%/year), the time required to populate Australia would have been about 2000 years.

According to Jones (1973), humans were well established in Greater Australia by 30,000 to 25,000 years ago. The oldest evidence is from the Lake Mungo region, dated at 32,000 B.P. Mulvaney (1976) suggests that the entry of humans into Australia probably occurred before 40,000 years ago. The rate of expansion along the direction of movement would have been about .34–.5 km/year or less.

To argue that the rate of population increase during periods of population expansion was probably less than that of doubling each generation does not preclude episodes of rapid increase reaching the maximum potential of hunter–gatherers in prehistory. Such episodes are well documented in the initial growth phases of both the Cape Barren Islanders off Tasmania and the inhabitants of Tristan da Cunha (Birdsell, personal communication).

World Biomes and Potential World Carrying Capacity

The impact of environmental parameters on the demographic regime depends in part on the preexisting levels of population density and the level of demographic saturation of the landscape. To assess the latter, an attempt was made to estimate the optimum carrying capacity of different world biomes (Table 12.5). The result, 8.6 million persons, provides a very crude estimate, which is nevertheless useful for the purpose of guessing the relative capacity of different biomes and the upper level of world population size in these biomes.

If the estimate of the optimum carrying capacity is to be trusted, the expansion into the tropical forests, the desert regions, the boreal forests, and the tundra during the Late Pleistocene would have increased the world optimum carrying capacity by

TABLE 12.5
Estimate of Optimum Carrying Capacity of the World under Hunting–Gathering Subsistence

Biome	Area (10⁶⁵ km)	Ungulate biomass (kg/km²)	Ungulate meat consumption (kg/year/person)	Effective level of carrying capacity (%)	Optimum carrying capacity (%)	Optimum carrying capacity (persons)
Tropical forest	20	5.6	50	80	80	106,000
Thorn forest	7	4,900.0	170	60	60	1,430,000
Tropical grassland	15	9,000.0	170	60	60	5,629,000
Temperate grassland	9	1,500.0	170	60	60	536,000
Desert shrub	9	50.0	170	60	60	13,000
Mixed and deciduous Forest	18	750.0	170	60	60	562,000
Boreal forest	12	500.0	170	60	50	285,000
Tundra	8	800.0	350	20	20	43,000
Total						8,600,000

5–10%. However, this represents not more than .25 or .5 million persons. Since the calculations in Table 12.5 do not take into consideration an allowance for fishing, sea mammal hunting, or the exploitation of small game on an intensive basis, the development of such exploitative patterns during the Terminal Pleistocene would have perhaps added another 10–20%. We do not know to what extent the various biomes were saturated before the Late Pleistocene, but it is likely that the invasion of the tropical regions and the tundra was preceded by a saturation of the other world biomes.

Environment, Demography, and the Evolution of Prehistoric Subsistence

Since the majority of the world population was located in grassland, scrubland, and deciduous and mixed forest of temperate and subtropical climate zones during most of the Pleistocene (up to ca. 100,000 years ago), it would be fair to posit a demographic regime of Type II (see previous chapter) as generally representative of that period. The groups would be small to medium, perhaps between 25 and 50, with reasonably large regional units of 1000 persons or more. The short- and medium-range mobility would have been high, with a pattern of rotating settlements rather than a stellar system and with low long-range seasonal mobility. The groups generally would be localized in loosely defined territories of moderate geographic extent. Territorial overlap would be frequent because of high biotopic differentiation and moderate species diversity coupled with a moderate yield. No single resource would be emphasized, but certain groups might limit their efforts to a certain spectrum of species to maximize yield and minimize effort. Geographic expansion was not inhibited in the earlier periods of the Pleistocene when extensive territories were still unoccupied. Thus the dissemination of innovations was relatively fast. The absence of constraints on population dispersal might have been responsible for pronounced technological homogeneity over wide areas. The slow rate of innovation during these periods may be in part a function of the success of the available technology, and perhaps, to a great extent, a function of the psychobiology of *Homo erectus* (cf. Isaac 1969:22). The changing climatic conditions during the Early and Middle Pleistocene certainly were responsible for population readjustments and movements that might have added to the homogenization of the overall technological aspects of these periods.

Although there are definite indications for changes in hunting–gathering technology during the Pleistocene, the antiquity of hunting and gathering is well established. Food remains from the australopithecine sites include elephants, giraffes, buffalo, pigs, antelopes, birds, and lizards. Medium-sized antelopes and pigs are most common. It is not likely that meat was secured primarily through scavenging (Read-Martin and Read 1975), since there is abundant evidence for hunting among chimpanzees today (Teleki 1973). It is also likely that meat was supplemented with roots, stems, mushrooms, blossoms, insects, eggs, resin, honey, and fruits, which are still the major dietary items of the chimpanzees. The procurement of meat, however, is perhaps the most important subsistence pursuit among humans, since it represents a major source of high-quality protein and vitamin B_{12}, which humans cannot synthesize.

There is also abundant evidence for big-game hunting among the hunter–gatherers of the Middle Pleistocene. At Torralba and Ambrona (Freeman 1975; F.C. Howell 1966), for example, bone accumulations of a large number of extinct straight-tusked elephant (*Elephas antiquus*) were found. Remains of horses were found at Ambrona. At Olorgesailie (Isaac 1969) a large number of adult baboons were located. The list of hunted big game during the Middle Pleistocene includes wild cattle, Merck's rhinoceros, stag deer, hippopotamus, and camel (Clark 1967; De Lumley 1969; F. C. Howell 1966). There is also evidence for the consumption of plant foods (e.g., at Choukoutien) and for seasonally specific subsistence activities (e.g., at Terra Amata).

During the Early Pleistocene, the stone tools are dominated by choppers, chopping tools, scrapers, handaxes, and flakes. The tools were used for butchering animals, digging for tubers, and processing plant foods. It is not clear what tools were used during the hunt, but sharpened wooden sticks and stone missiles might have been employed. The site of Ambrona in Spain suggests that animals might have been driven into boggy ground where they were speared and killed. During the subsequent period, in the earlier part of the Late Pleistocene, stone points that qualify as spear heads are abundant. In addition, tools suitable for woodworking (e.g., denticulates), and hide dressing (e.g., endscrapers) appear. Points manufactured of bone are also known from this period. The later part of the Late Pleistocene witnessed the emergence of modern man (*Homo sapiens sapiens*) and with him an array of elaborate points, wood- and bone-working tools (e.g., burins), and in some instances harpoons. Tanged points and arrowheads were numerous in some industries, and small tools were also common toward the end of the Terminal Pleistocene. Many of these small tools and arrowheads were hafted to form arrows. Spearthrowers also appear during this period. By the end of the Pleistocene fishing was emphasized in many localities, as witnessed by the abundance of harpoons and hooks of various styles. Bows and arrows from this period are known and seem to have been used extensively in many regions. It is also during this period that grinding stones became abundant in certain localities, heralding a new era in the processing of plant foods.

It is impossible to estimate the impact of the evolution of Palaeolithic technology on the extractive potentials of hunter–gatherers and thereby on the level of the carrying capacity of their habitats. But the developments must have been rewarding. One of the most salient features of the technological developments is the opening of new frontiers of subsistence. The spear must have increased efficiency in hunting animals that were previously exploited, but the bow and arrow made small mammals, birds, and reptiles more accessible. The use of the dog seems to go back to this period, and dogs would have been an excellent addition for the retrieval of small game. Bows and arrows were also used for fishing, but the developments in fishing technology as a result of the introduction of the harpoon and hook dramatically increased the yield from the sea, rivers, and lakes. Sea hunting also became possible with these developments and with the introduction of boats. The invention of grinding or its application to plant foods must also have made accessible numerous foodstuffs that were previously ignored. We should not underestimate the role of fire as a technological innovation, either for cooking or hunting activities. Cooking by fire made many foodstuffs palatable and digestible, and in some cases destroyed toxic substances present in the food. There is evidence for deliberate fire in the Middle Pleistocene, at Choukoutien, Kalambo Falls, Terra Amata, Torralba and Ambrona, and Hoxne (J. D. Clark 1969, 1971a; Movius 1948), but it was not used extensively until the Late Pleistocene, where, in addition to its use for cooking and perhaps for warmth, it was used in hunting.

In this long evolutionary journey man thus expanded his niche and forced up the ceiling of carrying capacity. Man also forced his presence in a variety of biomes and by the end of the Pleistocene he had left his marks on polar regions and deserts.

We can therefore assume that the world level of carrying capacity was lifted during the Late Pleistocene to progressively higher levels, partly as a result of technological developments and partly as a result of geographic expansion (Fig. 12.3). The two developments are of course linked. The most dramatic lifting of the carrying capacity ceiling seems to have occurred during the Late Pleistocene, especially close to its termination, as a result of very elaborate technology, exploiting multiple biotopes, and almost total geographic conquest of the world geographic biomes. It is not hard to link these developments with the emergence of modern man. The economic advances, however, were modest compared with agriculture.

By the end of the Pleistocene, the climatic fluctuations accompanying the transition from glacial or postglacial conditions were great. These conditions would

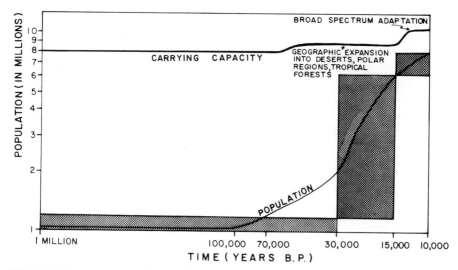

FIGURE 12.3. *Increase in world population and carrying capacity during the Pleistocene. (Data from Hassan, this volume.)*

have enhanced group mobility. However, because the overall population density during the Terminal Pleistocene was much higher than it had been (especially in favorable habitats) and because contiguous groups provided a barrier against territorial expansion or long-range migration, localization of population and regional differentiation was intensified. Localization also enhanced the exploitation of a wide range of resources, which served as a further protection against unpredictable fluctuations.

The fluctuations were worldwide and their effect was therefore global. The resources exploited, however, varied from one area to another depending on what was available, but the exploitation of resources previously ignored or underexploited is a common denominator. In certain areas, the newly exploited or emphasized resources initiated irreversible changes in the size and localization of population units and led ultimately to the emergence of agricultural practices (for an example, see Hassan 1975). It must be emphasized, however, that demographic variables were among many others that precipitated this basic transformation in economy, and that the demographic variables that were most important cannot be reduced to ''population pressure'' or simply to ''unchecked population increase'' (cf. Bindord 1968; Flannery 1969).

Overview

Estimates of the number of persons who could be supported today without lowering the present standards of living vary widely, from 5–7 billion to 50 billion

(Dorn 1966:322). If the present rates of growth continue, that 50 billion figure would be reached in the year A.D. 2116 (Dorn 1966). At present the world teems with about 4.3 billion persons, and as many as 7 million persons are born every *month*. By comparison, the population of the world at the end of the Pleistocene was very small. It may have been 8–9 million, or as many as would be born in a 6-week period today. The New York, Tokyo, and London metropolitan areas are each now inhabited by more people than inhabited the world 10,000 years ago. During earlier periods in the Pleistocene, the world population was even smaller, perhaps about 1.2 million during the Middle Palaeolithic. The average rate of world population growth during the Pleistocene was exceedingly low, about .005%/year during the Middle Palaeolithic, .01% during the Upper Palaeolithic, and .00007% during the Lower Palaeolithic. The acceleration of growth rates from the Lower Palaeolithic to the Upper Palaeolithic perhaps reflects greater evolutionary adaptability and biological developments from *Homo erectus* to *Homo sapiens*.

13

Demography and Early Food Production

*No doubt the reason why the old "law of causality" has so long continued to pervade the books of philosophers is simply that the idea of function is unfamiliar to most of them, and therefore they seek an unduly simplified statement. There is no question of repetitions of the "same" cause producing the "same" effect; it is not in any sameness of causes and effects that the constancy of scientific law consists, but in sameness of relations.**

The transition from hunting–gathering to agriculture is one of the most important economic events in human cultural evolution. It altered man's interaction with his environment and society so radically that a new world view had to emerge to cope with the emerging new ecological and social relations. Two million years of cultural life were transformed over a few millennia to create a new order. Archaeologists have been justifiably fascinated by that momentous transformation and have attempted to clarify the processes that might have triggered such a change and to fathom the consequences of that economic change on the development of a new society.

The archaeological literature abounds with the results of painstaking work in search of the earliest domesticated plants (e.g., Harlan 1971, 1975; Harlan and Zohary 1966; Helbaek 1959; Mangelsdorf 1974; J. M. Renfrew 1973; Trowle 1961; Zohary 1969) and animals (e.g., Clutton-Brock 1976; Reed 1959, 1969; Ucko and Dimbleby 1969; H. Wolf and M. Rohrs 1977; Zeuner 1963). The search for the earliest domesticated remains has been motivated by the need to locate the places where agriculture might have first appeared. Vavilov (1926) believed that domestication of plants emerged in those phytogeographic areas where maximum diversity of species was possible. He distinguished eight centers: China, Southeast Asia, India, the Indus Valley, the Near East, the Mediterranean region, Mesoamerica, and

*Bertrand Russell, *Mysticism and logic*, Penguin, Harmondsworth, England, 1954, p. 184.

South America. Harlan (1971, 1975), 45 years after the publication of Vavilov's work, concluded, from a survey of the data that have accumulated during that span of time, that agriculture originated independently in three different areas, and that in each of these cases agriculture emerged in a center with dispersed domestication activities over distances of 5000 to 10,000 km. The three areas are (*a*) the Near East center, and Africa as a noncenter, (*b*) North China (center), and Southeast Asia (noncenter), and (c) Mesoamerica (center) and South America (noncenter). Harlan notes that the crops did not necessarily originate in the centers, nor did agriculture develop in a geographical center. Although it is not perfectly clear to me what Harlan means by center and noncenter, I think Harlan has distinguished ''belts'' where the domestication of plants emerged. These belts (Figure 13.1) include certain zones (centers) where dozens of crops originated either by domestication of wild plants previously specific to these zones, or by stimulation from the surrounding areas within the same belt. Crops may also have originated in other parts of the belt (noncenter) and were later introduced to the centers.

Recognition of the places where agriculture might have first appeared does not, of course, explain why it appeared there when it did. Childe (1936, 1951), summarizing his views and those by Pumpelly and Newberry before him (according to Bender 1975:24), presented a case for a ''climatic-oasis theory'' of agricultural origins. He noted that food production emerged during a period of climatic desiccation in the arid subtropical regions as a result of the melting of the ice sheets in

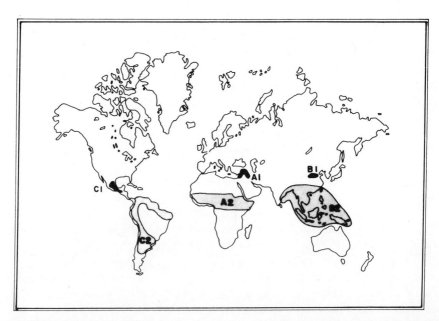

FIGURE 13.1. *Centers (A1, B1, C1) and noncenters (A2, B2, C2) of agricultural origins (Reproduced from* Crops and Man *by Jack R. Harlan 1975, by permission of the American Society of Agronomy and Crop Science Society of America.*

Europe and the contraction of the anticyclones leading to a northward displacement of the rain-bearing depressions. Recurrence of droughts at that time in arid areas changed the landscape from continous grasslands to a sandy desert with occasional oases. People as well as animal game converged on these areas. Agriculture was developed to provide fodder for the "famished beasts." Thus animals were drawn to man and the transition from the hunter to the cultivator and herder was made.

Theories and Models of Agricultural Origins

Childe's theory fails to explain why hunting–gathering was not continued in the oases with perhaps a smaller population and at a low population density. The Bushmen in Africa continue to be hunter–gatherers in a desert environment. In addition, why was agriculture a viable solution at the end of the Pleistocene and not earlier, during similar periods of climatic deterioration? Moreover, in the Near East, for example, changes in rainfall do not seem to have led to the creation of desert conditions as postulated by Childe. My work in the Siwa Oasis (Hassan 1978a) and the Baharia Oasis (1978c,1979a) produced no conclusive evidence of early agricultural communities during the early Holocene. The impact of environmental conditions, however, is not to be totally discarded. It appears again in various models and Childe must be credited for emphasizing the role of the environment in agricultural origins.

Robert Braidwood, to whose stimulating studies a great deal of the current interest in agricultural origins must be credited, proposed a theory of agricultural origins and attempted to test his theory against field evidence. His expedition to the Zagros Mountains was one of the first research projects that recognized the importance of interdisciplinary cooperation. Braidwood's original position (1958), which he later modified (Braidwood 1975), was based on the assumptions that agriculture must have originated in "nuclear areas" where the wild progenitors of domesticated plants were located and that farming was a product of a sequence of cultural developments. Braidwood's recognition of the role played by local habitats and the gradual emergence of agriculture paved the way to further studies and the search for the "cause" or "causes" of agricultural origins.

In 1968 Binford suggested that population increase in the optimal zones for hunting–gathering activities was associated with fission and occupation of marginal areas. According to Binford, the worldwide changes in sea level led to the exploitation of anadromous fish and migratory birds, and encouraged the emergence of sedentary societies with rapid rates of population growth. From these centers daughter colonies became established in less favored habitats, where intensive efforts to increase the means of production led to the emergence of agriculture. (A similar hypothesis was espoused by Flannery in 1969, but was discarded in 1973.)

Binford's hypothesis placed the influences of the environment in the context of demographic change and thus set the stage for other models that employ demographic variables in explaining agricultural origins. Binford's model suffers, however, from several problems. Changes in sea level have occurred repeatedly since the emergence of man, yet agriculture was not invented during any of these earlier periods. In addition, although Binford refers in the same article to the wide application of population controls among hunter–gatherers, he does not provide a reason for the relaxation of such controls among sedentary forager–fishers and especially among the inhabitants of the marginal habitats. Such marginal habitats were also already peopled and would have limited emigration from "optimum" areas. There is no evidence for the emergence of agriculture in those areas adjoining the Northwest Coast of North America and coastal Europe where fishing and sedentary communities were established. The theory advanced by Binford also glosses over the specific processes by which cereals, legumes, and certain animal species were domesticated. The yield of wild cereals was high, as noted by Harlan (1967), who collected 1 kg of grain in 1 hour without even a primitive sickle. Marginal areas might thus have provided previously unexploited resources that would have been sufficient to sustain hunter–gatherers.

Demographic variables were magnified in several models stimulated by the work of Ester Boserup (1965). These models were proposed for various parts of the world by Cohen (1977), Harner (1970), Patterson (1971), P. E. L. Smith (1976), and P. E. L. Smith and Young (1972). Bender (1975), Bronson (1977), G. L. Cowgill (1975a), and Hassan (1974, 1978b, 1979b) among others have been critical of these models (see discussion in Chapter 10). According to these population models, the emergence of agriculture was a response to an increase in population size to a level beyond that of the carrying capacity of the environment. This population pressure was ultimately responsible for the emergence of agriculture. Although there is indeed some evidence for an increase in the density of the human population by the end of the Pleistocene, population increase per se is not a sufficient cause for culture change. Again we may ask why such populations suffering from overpopulation did not limit their population size by one of the methods available (delayed marriage, the use of contraceptives, abortion, and infanticide). Such mechanisms surely existed during the Pleistocene (see Chapter 9).

These models also place undue emphasis on population increase and ignore the role of environmental parameters in changing the amount of yield, spatial location, and seasonal availability of resources.

Other models on agricultural origins include those by H. E. Wright (1977) and Redman (1977). According to Wright, climatic changes by the end of the Pleistocene (ca. 10,000) led to the spread of cereal grasses into the nuclear zones of the Near East, where the domestication of cereals began. In Europe and North America profound climatic changes about 10,000 years ago were not conducive to agricultural origins because cultigens appropriate for domestication were not available. In South America, climatic conditions became warmer about 16,000–10,000 years ago. Man's occupation of the area at that time was accompanied by the extinction of numerous large mammalian species. The extinction of mammals and other environmental changes led to greater dependence on wild plants and finally to cultivation. Although such data on environmental changes are important for understanding why agriculture was established, the incidence of environmental change does not automatically explain the economic transition. What were the effects of such changes on the preexisting economy, and why was agriculture a successful or necessary response to climatic changes?

Redman (1977) emphasized the role of technological developments such as storage facilities. Technological preadaptedness is certainly important, but why were such technological achievements conducive to adoption of agriculture?

In one of the most important contributions to the problem of agricultural origins, Flannery (1968) adopted a "systems approach" to the explanation of agricultural developments in Mesoamerica. Flannery notes that the exploitation of wild grasses grew steadily at the expense of, and in competition with, other resources, and that the increasing complexity in the exploitation of these grasses *necessitated* cultivation. Starting with limited cultivation of maize led to further dependence on maize cultivation (by a positive feedback network). The systems approach applied in this model set the stage for future models, but as it was presented by Flannery it lacked an explanation of the factors that necessitated the cultivation. Why did not the system reach a stage of homeostasis in which wild grasses were exploited with other resources?

In 1973, I developed a model for agricultural origins in Palestine (published 1977). In the same year, MacNeish developed a similar model for Peru (published in the same volume, 1977). Redman (1978), in a study of the rise of civilization from early farmers to urban society in the Near East, presented a model that differs in some details from mine. These models, developed independently, are multicausal, systemic models. They incorporate both environmental and cultural factors and provide a detailed account of the probable processes and mechanisms by which initial changes in the hunting–gathering subsistence–settlement–demographic system were to lead finally to the emergence of agriculture.

The elements of these models may be summarized as follows:

1. Food production emerged in areas where the wild progenitors for domesticated plants or animals were present.
2. Preagricultural hunter–gatherers were already in possession of a technological repertoire that facilitated the transition to a food-producing economy. These groups were already exploiting the wild ancestors of domestic plants and animals.
3. "Sedentary" communities of large residential size had been established prior to the development of agriculture.
4. Environmental changes by the close of the Pleistocene were responsible for changes in the subsistence strategy. Grasses were added to the diet and were ultimately augmented by domestication of plants and animals.

MacNeish (1977) noted the development of seasonally scheduled systems in certain biotopes and concluded that these systems were "sufficient cause" for the domestication of plants and animals. I am not sure why these systems should be a sufficient cause, since seasonal scheduling is an aspect of the economic life of hunter–gatherers that was certainly not unique to Holocene populations.

Redman (1978) attributes to the development of sedentary life by the gatherers of wild grasses a relaxation of population controls, which promoted an increase in population. Larger populations and the development of trade networks enhanced the emergence of innovations including agriculture. Redman does not explain what it was in agriculture that made it more advantageous than the collecting of the high-yield cereal resources. Alternatively, why did not Near Eastern groups continue to live as settled hunter–gatherers, as did the Northwest Coast Indians of the United States?

In my model (1977) for Palestine, I suggested that climatic changes by the close of the Pleistocene in the Near East, a zone susceptible to major and frequent climatic fluctuations during the periods of global climatic changes, were responsible for increasing the seasonal and spatial predictability or previously exploited resources. [For archaeological data on Terminal Pleistocene industries in Palestine, see Bar-Yosef (1970) and D. O. Henry (1973).] The changes in subsistence pattern at that time, referred to as "broad-spectrum adaptation" by Flannery (1969), can be viewed as a strategy to ensure greater survival potential. The change in climatic conditions may on the *average* have been small, but short-term fluctuations over a period of only hundreds of years is sufficient to cause adjustments in the subsistence strategy. "Starvation foods" will be incorporated into the diet in the hope of returning eventually to the preferred diet. If climatic conditions remain unpredictable, these foods become established items of the menu. Wild cereals were thus incorporated in the subsistence base along with snails, small vertebrates, and other previously underexploited resources. The spread of wild cereals into these areas, as Wright (1977) argues, may also explain why such resources became profitable. Scarce, dispersed cereal grasses were less inviting than other dense, and more predictable, resources. The abundance of cereals in wild fields by the end of the Pleistocene would have raised their attraction by reducing the cost of extraction and by the greater yield to be obtained from such fields. It was the high yield of such resources, the need for processing technology to improve the yield for consumption (grinding stones), and their potential for storage that seem likely to have stimulated the emergence of large, sedentary communities. Sedentariness was made possible by the rich yield and storage, as well by the cost of relocating heavy processing equipment (Figure 13.2). Sedentariness also ensured the rights of the people to the fields of wild grasses, and guaranteed that the stored food would not be plundered by others. The increase in yield per capita as more people cooperated during the harvesting of cereals must have encouraged the formation of progressively larger population units. The brittle rachis of the wild cereals meant that as soon as the cereals matured they had to be collected in a short time, before they fell. Flannery (1973) notes that this activity has to be undertaken within 3 days. Aggregation of families to prevent such loss would have been a likely outcome.

The emergence of large, sedentary communities, however, entails a number of

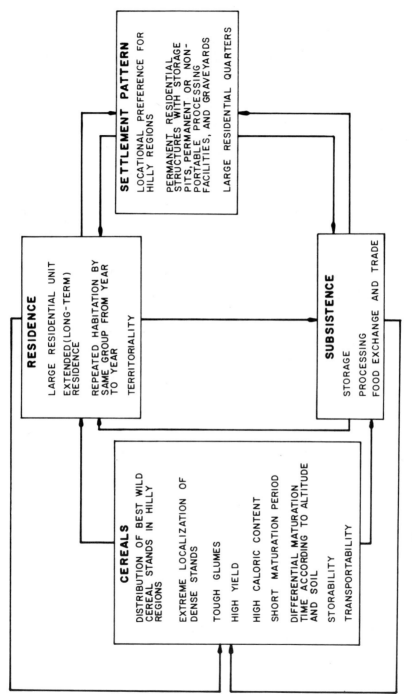

FIGURE 13.2. *Feedback relationship between wild cereals, subsistence, and settlement.*

problems. One of these is the depletion of other local resources, vegetables, pulses, and game animals. Also, larger population units require greater amounts of foodstuffs, especially game, both a source of high-quality protein, and a previously favored food. In addition, periodic changes in rainfall could have at times reduced the yields of cereals. These factors could have led to the reversal of the trend toward sedentariness and to a seasonal round with less emphasis on cereals, or to experimentation with cultivating cereals to ensure greater yield in times of less rainfall. The first solution must have been resisted because of the already established emphasis on cereals and sedentariness, and, most likely, because of social organization that developed to ensure social coherence. Experimentation with domestication did not present any conflict with the preexisting subsistence, settlement, demographic, or social states and would have been welcomed by most groups. Cultivation of pulses to supplement the cereals and domestication of animals to reduce the problems of spatial conflict could have also emerged in that context (Figure 13.3).

Since cereal stands were mostly located in the upland areas where the soils are not the best for cultivating cereals and pulses, and where grazing lands were limited, the next step in the process of domestication would have consisted of relocating to those areas where arable land with year-round moisture or dependable sources of water are available, such as alluvial plains and the neighborhood of major springs.

Agricultural origins, in the light of this model, were a culmination of cultural adjustments to fluctuations in climatic conditions initiated by the end of the Pleistocene in areas where potential domesticates were available. Cultural systems were transformed gradually over thousands of years. In the process, those cultural stages noted by Braidwood (1975) were developed. The cultural responses were aimed at stabilizing the economic base to ensure the continuation of an adequate standard of living. [Hayden (1979) has independently argued along the same lines.] The economic changes were primarily in the pattern of resource use. Exploitation of wild cereals, mussels, snails, and small vertebrates represents an addition of resources of low benefit–cost ratio. The expansion of the cereals into the Near East, however, might have increased their benefit–cost ratio. Cereals had the potential for domestication because of their high yield and storability. Cultivation of cereals in view of droughts might also have served to stabilize the system by expanding the area cultivated or transplanting into areas where there is enough ground moisture from permanent streams or springs. The emergence of agriculture must be, in part, credited to the domesticable qualities of cereals. Other resources, such as snails, were not as domesticable and their utilization could not have led to a food-producing economy based on domesticated herds.

Changes in settlements are likely to have been associated with the changes in resource utilization. In Palestine, the optimum habitat for wild cereals is the well-drained, loamy clay soil where rainfall is between 400 and 1000 mm (Zohary 1969:55–56). This restricts the distribution of the good fields of wild cereals to the upland regions of Palestine. A settlement shift toward these areas is documented for the transition from generalized hunting–gathering during the Kebaran to the period

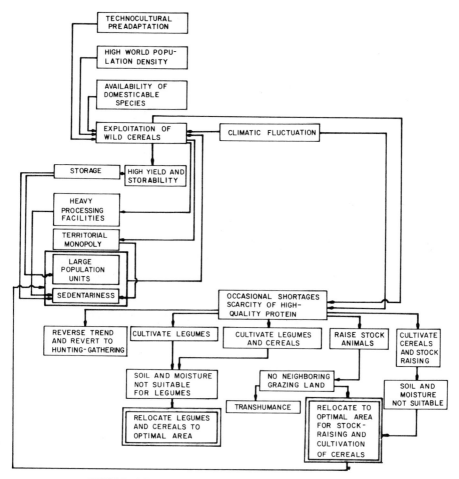

FIGURE 13.3. *A model of agricultural origins in the Near East.*

of intensive cereal utilization during the Natufian (Hassan 1977; D. O. Henry 1973). Many of the Neolithic sites are close to arable lands irrigated by rivers or springs.

The subsistence changes also had some implication for the nutritional adequacy of the diet (Hassan 1976). Cereals lack high-quality protein and have to be supplemented by pulses, nuts, or meat (Dornstreich 1972; Stini 1971). As exploitation of cereals intensified, these high-quality protein resources become a limiting factor. Cultivation of pulses and domestication of animals (Hassan 1976; Saxon 1976) would have removed that obstacle to greater dependence on cereals in a sedentary context.

The demographic changes that seem to have played a significant role in the transition from hunting–gathering to agriculture are those of sedentariness and enlargement of the size of local population units. These were responses to the benefits of sedentariness, as mentioned earlier, and the increase in the size of the optimum economic unit (the group size that provides the greatest yield per producer).

It is uncertain at the moment how this model, developed in this Near Eastern context, applies to other parts of the world. The environmental, demographic, subsistence, settlement, and nutritional changes must be evaluated for the various regions where food production was developed. The model presented by MacNeish (1977) for South America suggests that the processual changes that led to agriculture were not too different from those presented here. For Mesoamerica, Flannery (1973:296) has also noted that the cultivation of *Zea* might have amounted to a deliberate increase in the availability of "emergency" or "relief" food when productivity of wild grasses was low in dry years. Flannery (1973:297) also recognizes the inherent potential for domestication in certain wild species. Both *Setaria* and teosinte were exploited as wild grasses. Experimentation in cultivating both types of grasses could have taken place but teosinte had the potential of responding to cultivation and selection with a series of favorable genetic changes that ultimately led to the emergence of maize.

The situation in Southeast Asia and China is far from clear. Ho (1977) noted that Chinese agriculture has a definite indigenous character. Irrigation was not practiced for the first 4000 years of agriculture, and wheat and barley—characteristic of Southwest Asia—were adopted late in the second millennium B.C., several millenna after the domestication of indigenous plants, and were adapted to dry farming. In north China, an area that includes the Yellow River Valley area of Shensi, Sahnsi, Honan, and Hopei (Chang 1977), millets, including foxtail millet (*Setaria italica*) and broom-corn millet (*Panecum miliaceum*) represented the staple cereals. Rice was apparently domesticated from wild progenitors in the savanna zones of the vast area from India to China (Harlan 1977:371). Wild rice of the annual variety, unlike the perennial floating wild rices of marshy areas, is a good seeder and can be exploited with minimum technology and labor. The marshy areas where floating rice abounds are not suitable for cultivation. Available dates on cultivated rice include 3400 B.C. in north China (Harlan 1977) and 2500 B.C. in India (Higham 1977). Soybean, hemp as a fiber crop, and mulberry (for silkworms) were grown in north China during the Han period (206 B.C.–A.D. 220) according to Chang (1977:119). During that time, pigs and dogs were raised for food.

In Thailand, the study of Banyan Cave, Spirit Cave and Laang Spean has yielded beans, water chestnuts, peas, and cucumbers, as well as carbonized rice. It has been suggested that cultivation was practiced at ca. 5000 B.C. following a period of change from ca. 6000 to 5500 B.C. (Higham 1977) but additional evidence is required. The faunal remains associated with plants indicate that trapping, hunting, and collecting were practiced. At Banyan Cave the fauna include over 20 species.

The causes for indigenous agricultural origins in China and Southeast Asia are as yet conjectural. Chang (1977:117) suggests that the end of the glacial period might have triggered a trend toward domestication by its impact on the productivity of resources. His preconditions for the emergence of agriculture include a diversified natural environment, the availability of potential domesticates, and cultural preadaptation. Climatic changes in the Far East are postulated for 14,000–4000 B.P. (Chang 1970:176).

The onset of the Holocene and the retreat of glaciers marking the termination of the last major glaciation, and the possible impact of such changes on wild resources in climatically unstable areas such as semiarid and subtropical regions, seem to explain the independent emergence of food production in several places of the world beginning with the Holocene. The change in subsistence patterns that ultimately led to agriculture, however, must be sought in the impact of climatic fluctuations associated with the Terminal Pleistocene on cultural systems that were receptive for the transition in areas where the domesticable plants were available. The emergence of various domesticates in different places or in the same place at several points in time from 8000 B.C. to 3000 B.C. may reflect the differential impact of changing climatic conditions and the differential propensity of potential domesticates for cultivation and genetic selection.

Cohen (1977) builds an argument for the emergence of agriculture in the world within several millennia from the end of the Pleistocene on the basis of intensive population pressure resulting from population increase and the equalization of that pressure on a worldwide scale by population flux. Although I agree with Cohen about the increase in the size of world population throughout the Pleistocene (Chapter 12) I do not regard this gradual and slow growth as a case for a buildup of population pressure, nor do I view population pressure as a sufficient argument for technological innovation (Chapter 9). I do, however, think that the increase in world population to 8–10 million persons by the end of the Pleistocene and the colonization of most of the world biomes by the close of the Pleistocene might have served in some cases as a precondition, rather than as a cause or triggering mechanism. Flannery (1973) notes that agriculture emerged in Mesoamerica in areas where population density was low. In the Nile Valley, where population density was high, food production lagged three millennia behind that of Southwest Asia and was in the most part stimulated by outside contacts (J. D. Clark 1971b).

Cohen also confuses the equalization of population pressure, which he assumes to underlie population flux, with internal demographic shuffle in response to periodic fluctuations in the yield of local resources in the region occupied by a multiband population unit. In addition, he oversimplifies the causes for the expansion of the human population in world biomes through time by overemphasizing the role of population increase. Other factors include changes in climatic conditions that facilitated the colonization of new areas, and technological preadaptation to colonizing certain habitats.

The role of demography in the worldwide emergence of agriculture can only be viewed in the context of the impact of climatic conditions on the yield and spatiotemporal predictability of resources that would have altered the relationship between people and the range of resources exploited and the proportional use of resources, as their benefit–cost ratios were altered. The relatively high density of the world population was a favorable condition, but not a sufficient cause.

Sedentariness and large residential population units associated with the shift in the subsistence regime (see for example Jochim (1976) on the relationship between subsistence, settlement, and demography, and Chapters 1 and 9) were more important than population increase or density in stimulating the transition from hunting–gathering to food production.

From a demographic perspective, the spread of agriculture from its nuclear areas was facilitated by contiguity, and in some cases by the overlap of spatial regional population units, which expanded the network of communication. This was not tied with expanding populations under population pressure as Cohen (1977) suggests.

Demography and Agricultural Dispersal

Population movements could have emerged in the later periods of early food production as a result of agricultural geographic expansion. The vulnerability of the agricultural system as a result of the simplification of the ecological system could have led to agricultural expansion associated with intergroup integration of resources or occupation of more land, especially if previously occupied land were

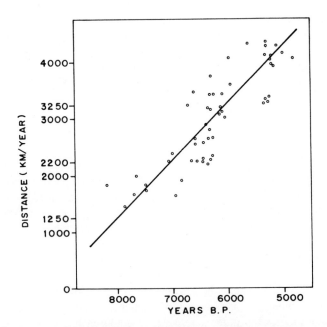

FIGURE 13.4. *Dispersal of agriculture from the Near East to Europe. Radiocarbon dates are plotted against distance from a point of origin in the Near East. (Reproduced from A. J. Ammerman and L.L. Cavalli-Sforza In* The explanation of culture change, *C. Renfrew, editor (1973) by permission of Gerald Duckworth & Co. Ltd.*

rendered waste by decline in soil fertility, salinization, or erosion from deforestation or destruction of the original vegetation cover.

It is not yet clear whether the geographic expansion of agriculture, for example, into Europe from the Near East (Waterbolk 1968) was a result of population movement or diffusion of agricultural innovations (Ammerman and Cavalli-Sforza 1973; Narr 1963). The rate of geographic expansion derived from radiocarbon dates on the earliest Neolithic communities in Eroupe and a Near Eastern point of origin (Ammerman and Cavalli-Sforza 1973), is about 1 km/year (Figure 13.4). Edmonson (1961) provides an estimate of about 2 km/year from the dates on pottery-bearing sites. Regrettably, his procedures and conceptual model of diffusion are questionable (see comments in Edmonson 1961:87–99; Gerald and Binford 1965; Narr 1963).

The Neolithic Population Increase

The impact of food production on world population size has long been recognized by archaeologists. Neither the magnitude of the population increase nor the mechanisms responsible for that increase were adequately known until the attempts made by Carneiro and Hilse (1966), Hassan (1972), and G. L. Cowgill (1975) to determine the probable rate of population growth, and the examination of the likely mechanisms for that increase by Sussman (1972), Polgar (1972), Lee (1972b), and Hassan (1973).

Carneiro and Hilse (1966) focused their attention on the Near East, which they defined as the area from the western end of Turkey to the eastern border of Iran, the Tigris–Euphrates, the Levantine coast and its hinterlands, the entire Arabian peninsula, and Egypt. Assuming that the population in the Near East at the beginning of the Neolithic was about 50,000 to 100,000, and experimenting with various growth rates to arrive at a population of 2–9 million by ca. 4000 B.C., they arrived at a rate of .08–.12% for an initial population of 100,000, and .09–.13% for an initial population of 50,000, or about .1% for those rates on the average. This rate is well below the explosive rates of today, which are often in excess of 1% and 2% in many nations. In 1973, I calculated growth rates for farming communities in various parts of the world on the basis of population estimates based on settlement studies at .1%, a similar figure to that obtained by Carneiro and Hilse (1966).

The significance of these figures may be viewed as follows. At the rate of .5–.7%, an initial population will double its size in 5 to 7 generations, whereas at the rate of .1% doubling would take about 35 generations. We may look at this also from a probable situation where a settlement of 50 persons is undergoing an increase at a rate of .5%. At that rate one additional family of 5 persons will be added in one generation, two by the second, about five by the third generation, and so on. Thus, although these rates are not explosive, as are some present rates, they are sufficiently rapid to alter demographic conditions in a short time. The impact of popula-

TABLE 13.1
*Doubling Time Equivalent to Annual Growth Rates,
.01 to .071.*

Annual growth rate (%)	Doubling time (years)
.01	693
.15	462
.02	347
.30	173
.04	173
.05	138
.06	116
.07	99

tion increase can be shown by considering the time that it would take to double an initial population (Table 13.1).

Mechanisms of Population Increase

Archaeologists have often ignored the demographic mechanisms by which the increase in population during the Neolithic was achieved (Sussman 1972). Many have been satisfied with attributing the growth of Neolithic populations to the increase in food supply. From a demographic perspective, the increase in population could have resulted from the nutritional effects the new diet had on menarche, morbidity, or life expectancy, or from a change in the mechanisms of population regulation under new socioeconomic conditions.

Sussman (1972) and Lee (1972b) attributed the relatively rapid growth of the Neolithic population to the shift from the mobile mode of life of hunter–gatherers to the sedentary life of the cultivators. Child spacing is considered by Lee and Sussman as a function of the ability of the mother to transport and nurse more than one child while moving around in search of food. (This idea was expressed by many others and can be traced to Carr-Saunders 1922:216–217). Thus, under a sedentary mode of life "a woman could have and support a child as soon as one was weaned." Lee (1972b) attempts to strengthen this position by calculating the cost of child transport given various lengths of the spacing period to show the higher cost of closely spaced children under a mobile subsistence regime.

I (Hassan 1972, 1979c) have disagreed with the "sedentariness model" for two reasons: (a) The contrast between the spatial mobility of hunter–gatherers and early farmers is not as sharp or as drastic as one might assume from Lee's and Sussman's treatments of the subject, and (b) child spacing is a function of more than the ability of a mother to transport her children.

The spatial mobility of hunter–gatherers is of two types: long-distance seasonal or periodic movements that take place two or three times a year, and short-range daily movement within say, 10 km from the campsite. During seasonal movements young adults or old adults can relieve the mother, and during daily movement children could be left at camp with those who remain behind. However, since I believe that child-spacing intervals among hunter–gatherers were 3–4 years for other reasons (see subsequent discussion and Chapter 9), this problem did not arise in the first place.

Early farmers were relieved of seasonal relocation, but were not freed from the daily movement from the campsite to the fields, and the gathering of wild plant foods to supplement their diets. The women were not thus freed from the burden of the most common chore of daily mobility.

I have argued for long child-spacing periods among hunting–gathering women because of the heavy work load, the youth of mothers, the hazards of childbearing, and the maternal nutritional drain through nursing in the absence of weaning baby foods (Hassan 1972; Chapters 8 and 9, this volume).

The transition from hunting–gathering to agriculture did not eliminate all of these determinants of a long child-spacing period. The work load was still high, the hazards of childbearing were not diminished, and the mothers entered their reproductive life at a young age. One of the major changes was the availability of cereals that could have provided a substitute for nursing. That by itself would have reduced somewhat the "cost" of children, but I question the assumption that a society maximizes the number of children, that is, that it is desirable to get as many children as possible. The number of children is a function of their "cost" as well as their potential role in improving the economic conditions of the progenitors. In this respect human populations differ from other animal populations. The nature of human adaptation has gone beyond biological survival to "welfare." The cost of children ranges from the nutritional cost of the pregnancies, the food demands before they enter the labor pool, and in more recent times, cost of delivery, "day care," and education. As the quality of life rises and as labor skills demand longer periods of education, the cost of children is likely to continue to increase.

The cost of children is also a function of the potential ratio of food (or other income) that would have to go to them instead of their parents.

The benefits of children, on the other hand, can be viewed as psychological (which are difficult to measure or evaluate), social (they contribute to the "power" of a family), and economic. A subsistence economy that promises more yield per capita if the family or the local cooperative unit is large will encourage the addition of children as potential laborers. Children, in addition, may serve as insurance for their parents' old age (this would have become important with sedentariness). If children could also be employed, this may be another reason for producing them.

Under hunting-gathering conditions, with a limited amount of food and little potential for economic growth, and a small optimum economic population size, many children will be less economical than a few, which would tend to encourage a long child-spacing period, as well as additional controls to remove excess pregnancies and infants. The transition to agriculture provided a definite economic motive for enlarging the size of the family unit and the size of the labor pool. The importance of child labor in agricultural societies is well illustrated by the study of Nag *et al.* (1978).

The increase in population could have been achieved by relaxing some of the previously practiced population controls while maintaining a relatively long spacing period for the reasons discussed earlier. A total lift of population controls and a child-spacing equivalent to that of the natural birth interval would have flooded the population with children and lowered the standard of living. A long child-spacing period is, in fact, observed by many settled, agricultural communities (Birdsell 1972:357; Carr-Saunders 1922:166, 175; Krzywicki 1934:178).

Fertility could also have increased if the age at menarche was reduced, if life expectancy of adult females was prolonged, or if survivorship to adulthood was improved.

There is little indication that survivorship to adulthood was improved, judging by the high infant mortality rate among nonindustrial agricultural populations. In fact, infant mortality might have increased as a result of the impact of the cereal diet (Hassan 1977; Swedlund and Armelagos 1976). Sedentary large populations also provide a host for epidemics (Cockburn 1971; Armelagos and McArdle 1975) and, with agriculture, infestation with malaria can lead to an increase in mortality (Angel 1975). Measles, influenza, and smallpox, however, require a population larger than that of the Neolithic populations, and according to Black (1975) probably do not go back more than 200 generations. The gain in adult life expectancy was minor—that is, if there was any change at all. The Neolithic skeletal series at Catal Hüyük and Nea Nikomedia (Angel 1971) indicate an average age at death of 29.8 years and 30 years, respectively, for adult females (see Chapter 6).

The link between diet and age at menarche is controversial. Sengel (1973) suggested that the increase in the protein intake from cereals could have led to a reduction of the age at menarche and thus to a higher fertility rate. However, the protein from cereals is inferior to that from meat, and would probably have had the effect of delaying the age at menarche (Hassan 1974). It has also been suggested that the greater intake of carbohydrates led to greater body fat, which led to a reduction in the age at menarche (Frisch 1977). The evidence for a link between body fat and age at menarche, however, is inconclusive.

In summary, I suggest that the increase in population concomitant with the advent of agriculture was a function of the change in socioeconomic conditions favoring slight relaxation of the controls damping fertility, without too much reduction of the child-spacing period [see Hawley (1973) for socioeconomic variables and population in an industrial society]. The availability of weaning foods could have reduced the nutritional cost of children. The impact of the diet on survivorship and age at menarche was most probably negligible, but the cereal diet could have increased infant mortality.

Overview

The problem of agricultural origins has preoccupied archaeologists for a long time. I do not pretend to have settled the issue to the satisfaction of all. My aim in this chapter has been to place demographic variables for one part of the world and for a certain kind of agriculture in their proper perspective, neither as omnipotent causes nor as noneffectual dependent elements of cultural determinants. There does not now seem to be any substantial evidence for an increase in the growth rate of Epipaleolithic populations, but there is evidence for an increase in the size of the world population as a result of the cumulative increase in the number of people, which was somewhat accelerated since the advent of modern man. The increase in world population density may be considered as a condition that facilitated the transition to agriculture. It could have hardly forced that transition. I am not sympathetic to explanations of complex cultural changes that hinge on the effect of a single cause, and I am far less sympathetic to explanations that do not clarify the pathways by which external causes lead ultimately to a change in the state of the cultural system. I have opted, in a model for agricultural origins in the Near East, to underline the role of microclimatic fluctuations by the end of the Pleistocene. Such changes occurred before the end of the Pleistocene during periods of glacial–interglacial transition. What made such fluctuations important for culture change at the end of the Pleistocene must be viewed in the light of the associated spread of grasses (Wright 1977), the advanced technocultural and perhaps cognitive level of the Terminal Pleistocene *Homo sapiens,* and the saturation or near-saturation of the world biomes. Each of these conditions has been singled out as a cause for agricultural origins (Braidwood 1975; Childe 1951; Cohen 1977; Wright 1977). I perceive these elements of the cultural systems during the Terminal Pleistocene as necessary conditions, but not as sufficient causes. The climatic fluctuations and their impact on vegetation and fauna, especially in metastable biogeographic zones (e.g., semiarid areas and Mediterranean regions) served as a kicker initiating a variety of responses, which were conditioned by the preexisting state of the cultural system and the specific habitats under exploitation (Figure 13.5). The responses were varied, but seem to have followed simple ecological principles (cf. Hayden 1979). Resources whose cost of capture and processing was higher, or whose taste was less desirable, were incorporated to stabilize the subsistence base. Wild grasses, which were among the resources to be added to the subsistence base, proved to be an ecological trap. The potential high yield of such resources was only to be achieved by the aggregation of people during harvesting time, and by laborious processing. It is interesting to note here that resources of this type "select" for specialization. In a study of natural selection and predator–prey behavior, Smith (1978:121) indicated, on the basis of a mathematical model, that "if resources are abundant but difficult to catch or consume, selection will lead to specialization." This ecological principle not only clarifies the transition from a generalized broad-spectrum adaptation to a

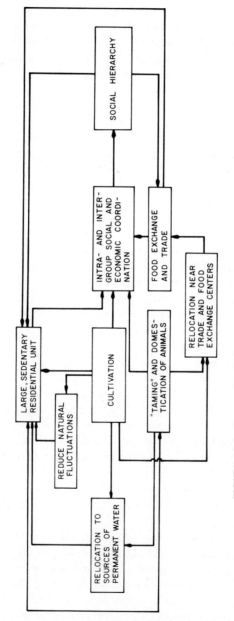

FIGURE 13.5. *Impact of agriculture on settlements, economy, and social organization.*

progressive emphasis on cereals and ultimately to agriculture, but also clarifies the emergence of specialized herding or hunting during the Terminal Pleistocene. The high yield from wild cereals made storage economical. Stored foods and heavy processing technologies allowed populations to reside for much of the year at chosen sites. The trend toward sedentariness was thus initiated, and both sedentariness and large population aggregation served as positive feedback furthering greater exploitation of cereals. The transition to agriculture can only be viewed as a culmination of the evolution of the cultural system under such conditions. Sedentariness and the large size of residential populations are therefore to be highlighted as important demographic elements of the transition from hunting–gathering to agriculture. The emphasis on population increase as the major demographic factor (Cohen 1977), in my opinion, is misplaced.

The emphasis on sedentariness, however, as the cause for reducing the child-spacing period (Lee 1972b; Sussman 1972) is also misplaced. The increase in world population following agriculture was a response to the advantages of a large family and a large group size, and a reduction in child cost as a result of the availability of weaning foods. The value of children was enhanced by opportunities for child labor and the potential security for the elderly in a sedentary setting (Figure 13.6).

The increase in world population during the Neolithic must be viewed as a major demographic transition, as significant as the demographic transition that accompanied industrialization.

The archaeologist should perhaps find some comfort in the fact that demographers and historians, with historical records at their disposal, are still at a loss to "explain" the mechanisms of the industrial demographic transition. The traditional view attributed the transition to falling levels of mortality, but later studies attribute the transition to an increase in fertility probably tied to earlier age at marriage (e.g., Deane 1967; Langer 1963).

The palaeodemographic record does not indicate an improvement in mortality during the Neolithic, but a modest increase in life expectancy for adults is documented for later periods. It must be assumed that the increase in world population was a result of rising fertility. This could have been an involuntary development as a result of dietary changes, perhaps through the effect of carbohydrates on body fat (N. Howell 1976b), as a result of a reduction in infanticide or abortion or the availability of baby foods (Hassan, 1973, 1978b), or perhaps an earlier age of marriage.

The vulnerability of agricultural systems to occasional food scarcities, infestations with malaria from the ecological peculiarities of agriculture, and the incidence of epidemics made possible by large, sedentary populations must have led to frequent fluctuations in population and perhaps greater infant and juvenile mortality. The situation would have been aggravated for children because of the cereal diet.

Prior to agriculture, a state of balance between mortality and fertility rates may be hypothesized (Figure 13.7). This stage was followed by an increase in fertility rate, perhaps associated with an increase in mortality. In a third stage, fertility rates

228

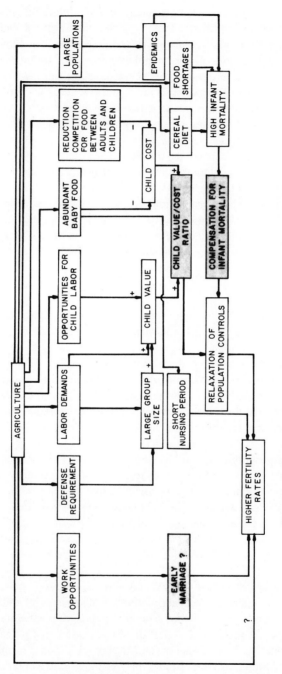

FIGURE 13.6. A model of the impact of agriculture on the determinants of fertility.

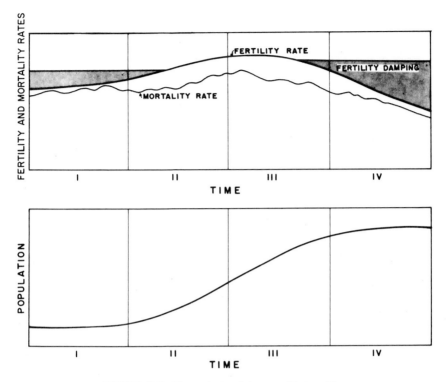

FIGURE 13.7. *The agricultural demographic transition.*

continued to increase and mortality rates begin to decrease. In the fourth stage, mortality rates declined, as did fertility rates, and a new state of limited growth followed. In some instances, the opportunities for labor and agricultural intensification permitted the fertility rates to remain somewhat higher than the mortality rates, allowing for continued increase in population.

14

Demographic Variables and Early Civilizations

He built the wall of Uruk, the enclosure
Of holy Eanna, the sacred storehouse
Behold its outer wall, whose brightness is like copper!
Yea, look upon its inner wall, which none can equal!
Take hold of the threshold, which is from old!

The Gilgamesh Epic, Tablet I/Column i*

Civilization is a state of culture characterized by an advanced level of social and occupational differentiation and a formal, complex, stratified, centralized political–managerial organization (cf. Childe 1950; Redman 1978; Sanders 1968; Service 1975; Willey 1971). Social differentiation is often manifested by social classes based on religious, military, political, and subsistence occupations. Specialization is often associated with differentiation. This basic structural core of civilization is commonly associated with the emergence of large-scale communal works, monumental art, documentation of events and transactions, and an advanced level of science and engineering.

The origins of civilization have been a major concern for archaeologists, philosophers, historians, and other social scientists. I do not intend to provide a comprehensive survey of the theories of the origins of civilization or to detail the characteristics of civilizations of the ancient world (Figure 14.1),[1] but I do intend to examine the probable role of demographic variables in the development of civilization, with reference to southern Mesopotamia as an example. Ancient civilizations did not develop along the same lines, but the major structural transformations are analogous.

*In *The origins of civilization*, W. H. McNeill and J. W. Sedlar, editors, p. 82. Oxford University Press, London, 1968.
[1]The reader may wish to consult R. M. Adams (1966), Lamberg-Karlovsky and Sabloff (1974), Redman (1978), and Service (1975) for an introduction to the origins of civilization.

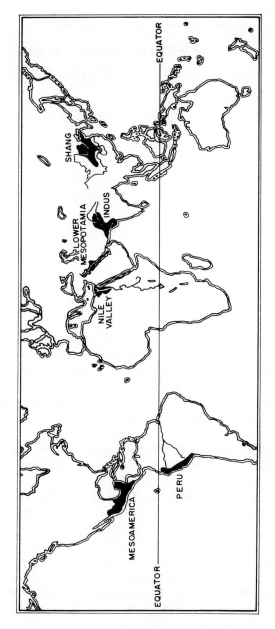

FIGURE 14.1. *Ancient civilizations of the world.*

Theories and Models of the Origins of Civilization

Theories on origins of civilization are based on a variety of causal factors. Warfare has been cited since classical antiquity as a major factor in the origin of civilization (Carneiro 1970:734; Service 1975:270). Herbert Spencer emphasized the role of warfare as an integrative mechanism promoting cooperation and subjugation to command (Carneiro 1970), and Ibn Khaldoun and the "conflict theory of sociologists" attribute the origins of state societies to conquest and the subjugation of the losers (Service 1975:270). Carneiro (1970) has ascribed state origins to warfare resulting from intensified population pressure, which in turn is caused by rapid population increase in geographically circumscribed areas.

Wittfogel (1957) views the origins of the state as a result of the demands of large-scale irrigation, which require centralized management. Childe (1950, 1951) viewed the emergence of food surplus, under an agricultural economy, as a means for supporting craft specialists and as the economic basis for the development of the nonsubsistence aspects of civilization. Long-distance, large-scale trade, according to Sanders (1968) and Rathje (1971), in the context of an agricultural economy, facilitated the emergence of a complex administrative organization for the import, manufacture, and distribution of trade goods (see also Morris and Thompson 1970).

The role of population pressure, which has been taken by Carneiro (1970) as a cause for warfare, is regarded by Young (1972) as a force leading to agricultural intensification and extensification, which were associated with the development of complex managerial organization and urbanization. Gibson (1973) has also considered the role of population pressure in the origins of civilization, but his work focuses more on the environmental context. The negative ecological impact of agriculture on the stability of cultural systems in the formative stages of civilization is thoughtfully considered in his work on the agrarian problems in Mesopotamia (Gibson 1974). The impact of agricultural failures on political evolution from a chief-oriented pattern to a state society is considered in that work and in his discussion of the emergence of Sumer.

Most of the foregoing explanations of the origins of civilization have been received negatively by Service (1975) and Redman (1978), mainly because they underplay the role of other causal factors, and because there are contradictory data from archaeological and ethnographic sources. (See also Butzer [1976] on Wittfogel's model, G. L. Cowgill [1975a, 1975b) and Hassan [1974] on population-pressure models, and Wright and Johnson [1975] on trade.) Multiple causality has been stressed by R. M. Adams (1966), Hassan (1975, 1978b), and Redman (1978), and processual developments, in the framework of general systems theory, were advanced by Flannery (1972) and Hassan (1975)

Redman's model of the origins of civilization in Mesopotamia places an emphasis on the colonization of Mesopotamia as a result of population increase or soil depletion or both followed by the demands for foreign raw materials, irrigation, and specialization in food production. These developments combined with continued population increase led to class stratification, complex administrative organization, and warfare.

Although I agree with Redman on multicausality and the systems approach to the emergence of civilizations, my emphasis is on the vulnerability of the agricultural system, and its potentials for economic growth. I will first examine the problem of population increase and the emergence of urban centers before I present my model of the origins of civilization and my account of the probable role of demographic variables in that process.

Population Increase

The rapid rate of population increase during the Neolithic (.1%/year on the average; see Chapter 13) was perhaps not topped during the succeeding period. Occasional spurts of growth perhaps as high as 1% per year would have been possible, but could not have been sustained over long periods in a regional context (G. L. Cowgill 1975). Data from settlements in the Diyala region (R. M. Adams 1966:41) indicate a rate of growth of .07%/year during the Early Dynastic period (assuming 4 persons/km^2 during the period of dry farming). Estimates by Butzer (1976) on the population of Egypt in Pharaonic times indicate a growth rate of .05%/year from 3000 B.C. to 150 B.C. Data by C. Renfrew (1972a, 1972b) for the Aegean region, including Crete, Cyclades, Messenia, Laconia, Euobia, and central Macedonia, indicate that the growth rate from the Neolithic to the Early Bronze Age was in the range of .04%–.16%/year, with an average of .12%. In Mesoamerica, the average growth rate at Ixtapalapa from 1200 B.C. to A.D. 1520 (Blanton 1972) is estimated at .13%, with rates as high as .59% and .35% during intervals of peak growth.[2]

The continuation of a "rapid" rate of population increase during the early periods of civilization most probably reflects the maintenance of the socioeconomic motives for large families, and large population units (see Chapter 13). Opportunities for labor, feasibility of child work, availability of baby foods, all of which emerged in the context of early agriculture, were not diminished in later periods. There is some evidence for a gain of 1 to 3 years in the duration of the life of adult females (Angel 1972, 1975) during the Bronze Age in the eastern Mediterranean. The wide divergence between the longevity of adult males and females, with the males having a longer life span, as noted for Palaeolithic populations, continued throughout the Neolithic and the periods of urbanization, indicating that childbirth was still hazardous. The greater divergence between the longevity of males and females toward the end of the Bronze Age, where males gained an increase of 6 years as compared with 3 years for females, may be indicative of the change in

---

[2]The average rate of growth of European towns and cities from the sixteenth to the seventeenth centuries was less than .6%; that of the European population as a whole was about .4% (K. Davis 1965).

subsistence activities from the more hazardous hunting to agriculture, specialized crafts, and commerce. Although it could be assumed that under urban conditions a better diet could have led to a prolongation of the life span, it appears that for a large segment of the population the quality of the diet may have deteriorated. In Mesopotamia, fish, which was relatively abundant, would have been emphasized. Herds of sheep and goat were grazed on the fallow land and were kept for milk and wool. Oxen and asses were used for ploughing and fed on barley. We cannot yet determine the composition of the diet of early Mesopotamian farmers to ascertain its adequacy, but if their diet contained what the privileged groups had access to, it could have been highly nutritious. The use of grain, sesame seed, dates, fish, and fruits, as well as beer and wine and vegetables, is recorded from temple magazines (Frankfort 1951). It is unlikely, however, that the population had an equal share of these goods. The temples owned "woods" consisting of date groves, grapes, figs, and pomegranates, which would have provided many of the vitamins that could not be obtained from the cereals. Fresh vegetables are perishable and would have had to be transported daily to the urban center.

In sum, under early urban conditions, the increase in longevity was not suffi- ciently high among females to enhance fertility. The changes in diet were not necessarily for the better among most of the populace. However, a differential between an elite and the peasants may have existed as a result of the former's access to a better diet. Maternal mortality was apparently as high as before. Thus, the negative impact of this factor on population growth was not reduced. The effects of other negative factors related to the ecology of agriculture and high local population density and large group size, such as epidemic diseases and periodic food shortages, were perhaps more pronounced than before. On the whole, the population growth rate would have declined unless infusion of emigrants from other areas was main- tained and cultural methods of fertility control were relaxed. However, in view of the wide discrepancy between the average rate, the maximum reproductive poten- tial, and the actual rate of growth, it must be concluded that cultural checks were not totally lifted.

The Emergence of Urban Centers

One of the major demographic events associated with many civilizations was the emergence of large urban centers. Urbanization is thus often correlated with civilization. However, urbanization is a polythetic concept. The term is derived from *urban*, meaning "of living or situated in a city, or town" (*Concise Oxford Dictionary*). Thus, the term refers to a change in settlement pattern, but it also denotes demographic and sociocultural changes (M. G. Smith 1972). In archae- ology, the term is used in conjunction with state formation as an element in the process of civilization. It appears that urbanization is used commonly among ar- chaeologists to refer to the change from small dispersed villages or hamlets to large cities defined, as in Mesopotamia, on the basis of minimal geographic extent (cf. R. M. Adams 1966; R. M. Adams and H. J. Nissen 1972).

A distinction is thus drawn between civilization with cities and civilization without cities (e.g., Sanders and Price 1968). In Mesopotamia, some of the settlements in the Diyala Plain achieve the proportions of large towns (25–50 ha) but are not regarded as cities. We must not be deluded by this typological distinction, since a structural similarity and a similar sociocultural pattern are shared by other Mesopotamian cities, such as Uruk and large towns such as Ur, Khafajie, and Tell Asmar. Wheatley (1972) has aptly criticized the typological and the trait-list approach to urban phenomena, and suggests that we view cities as centers of dominance. He cites Horace Miner, who describes the "city" as a locus of mediation and control. Actually, Miner did not use the term *city*, but used the phrase *large, urban center*. We may thus refer to both large towns and cities as urban centers.[3] R. M. Adams and H. J. Nissen (1972) already used *small urban center* to refer to what Adams (1966) previously called *large town*. This problem of nomenclature is not trivial. Young, for example, has failed to account for the structural similarity between the large towns of Diyala and the cities of Uruk and Kish. This error led him to speculate that the smaller size of the Diyala urban centers can be interpreted as a result of a lack of intensive population pressure. But without population pressure, the prime mover in Young's model, how would he explain the functional similarity exhibited between the Diyala large towns and the large cities?

The changes in settlements in southern Iraq from Early to Late Dynastic times are treated in detail by R. M. Adams (1965), R. M. Adams and H. J. Nissen (1972), and Gibson (1973). These changes will be reviewed here as a case study of urbanization. Both R. A. Adams and Gibson have communicated to me their strong distrust of the existing data base. Their recent work has led to many changes in the dating of sites, their numbers, and distributions. In view of this I should warn the reader to share the mistrust of the experts. I am heartened by Gibson's statement to me (personal communication) that he would question the reliability of the data base no more than he would question it in his own work, and I am glad that he finds my theoretical formulations very attractive. I should like the reader, however, to treat my manipulation of the data from southern Iraq as an exercise in working with archaeological data from a demographic perspective rather than a documentation of demographic conditions from archaeological data. The model presented in the subsequent section should be regarded as theoretical, to be tested by data to come, and I hope that it will serve as a guide for gathering data in the future.

Agricultural communities appeared in the region during the sixth millennium B.C. Barley and wheat were cultivated. Sheep and goats were herded on fallow land and marsh grasses. Cattle were restricted in number since large pasture areas were not available. Dates and fish were important supplements to the cereal diet. Small-

---

[3]Such early urban centers were predominantly made up of farmers. Perhaps no more than 20% of the population were food nonproducers. Before 1850, no society had more than 25% nonproducers in the total population.

scale irrigation was practiced during the Ubaid period. Trade to secure basic raw material such as flint, wood, bitumen, and basalt seems to have been under way since the Ubaid period (H. T. Wright 1969). It apparently grew in importance during the Protoliterate period. Nonsubsistence imports included copper, gold, coniferous wood, silver, lead, lapis, lazuli, alabaster, carnelian, agate, and obsidian. Sailboats or water transport seem to date back to the Ubaid period, and transport by wheel carts appears in the Protoliterate period. Oxen and perhaps onagers were employed. Craft specialization seems to have become well extablished during the Protoliterate period. Specialist included potters, masons, and stonecutters (R. M. Adams 1955). Ceremonial centers appear at Nippur, Ur, and Eridu during the Ubaid period (including the Eridu and Hajj Muhammed). Settlements during the Ubaid period were generally few, small, and dispersed, but during the Protoliterate period geographic expansion associated with an increase in the number and size of settlements is manifest. Towns and settlement clusters, sometimes with a hierarchical pattern (Gibson 1973), emerged during that period. Direct evidence of social stratification and militarism before the Dynastic period in southern Mesopotamia is restricted to a seal impression from Warka depicting prisoners and a military leader. Evidence for royal authority, on the other hand, is available for the Dynastic period. Vaulted tombs with elaborate and expensive furniture, chariots, and multiple sati burials are known (R. M. Adams 1955). Palaces that rival temples are also known from the Dynastic period. Large settlements and great cities appear. Massive walls surround cities, temples, and sometimes private houses within settlements. Temples, however, were still prominent, both as religious and economic institutions. The land owned by the temple, in one case one-quarter of the area under cultivation, was cultivated by the whole community. Part of the remaining land was allotted to members of the community for their own support and what was left was rented. The temple had stores for grain and magazines for a wide variety of goods. Rations were distributed by the temple regularly and on special occasions. The immense variety of items in the magazines of the temples is indicative of a large volume of trade and food redistribution. The temple also served as a crafts center, where ploughs, chariots, wheel carts, perhaps ships, hides, and woolen textiles were produced. The artisans were organized in guilds. Documents for professional, specialized soldiers are available from the Late Dynastic period.

During the Early Dynastic period, Uruk became a major city, covering more than 400 ha of land, with as many as 30,000 to 40,000 people. None of the settlements in the Diyala Plain grew to this dimension. Khafajie and Tell Asmar were 25 and 20 ha in area. The pattern in the lower Diyala Plain represents, however, a hierarchial network of hamlets and villages.

The archaeological record from the Uruk region for the Ubaid to Late Uruk is scant, consisting of 21 villages and hamlets uniformly dispersed. The Eanna Zuggurat was built during this period at Uruk. To this sanctuary the Kullaba sanctuary was added prior to Jamdet Nasr period. The Eanna, by comparison, was less developed than the Kullaba sanctuary. The two sanctuaries may have belonged to two settlements, according to Nissen (1972). During the Late Uruk period, the number of settlements jumped to 123. But only two towns appeared at that time. They were more or less uniformly spaced within a distance of more than 20 km from Uruk (Figure 14.2).

During the Jamdet Nasr period (Figure 14.3), all the buildings of Eanna were destroyed, apparently deliberately, and a central sanctuary of a different plan was built (Nissen 1972). The number of settlements during the Jamdet Nasr and the

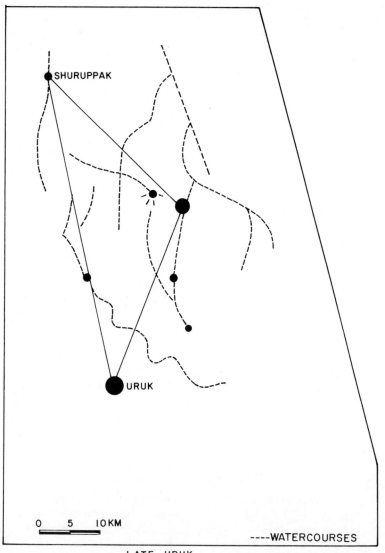

LATE URUK

FIGURE 14.2. *Late Uruk settlements in the Uruk region, southern Mesopotamia. (After R. M. Adams and H. J. Nissen 1972.)*

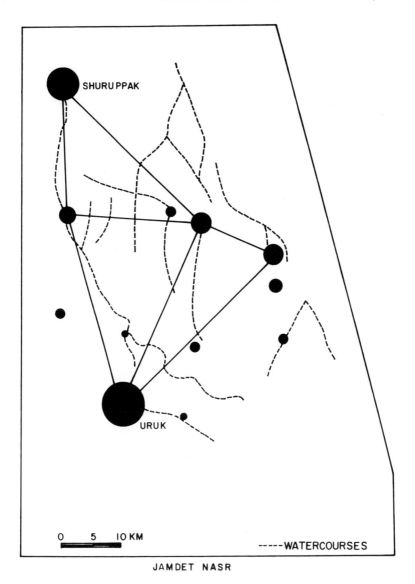

JAMDET NASR

FIGURE 14.3. *Jamdet Nasr settlements in the Uruk region, southern Mesopotamia. (After R. M. Adams and H. J. Nissen 1972.)*

Dynastic I periods was not much higher than during the previous period, totaling 147 settlements. New towns appeared, but the major towns were quasi-equidistant. During the Early Dynastic I period, other cities and towns appeared. The towns were about 7–10 km from each other (Figure 14.4). In Late Dynastic times, the countryside was almost totally abandoned, and in addition to Uruk, which reached a greater magnitude at this time, a cluster of cities and towns dominated the northeast-

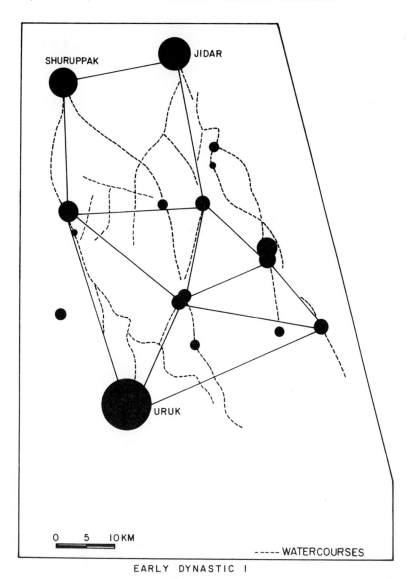

FIGURE 14.4. *Early Dynastic settlements in the Uruk region, southern Mesopotamia. (After R. M. Adams and H. J. Nissen 1972.)*

ern area. Collectively, these settlements covered an area comparable to that of Uruk. The total number of settlements dropped to 33.

Four aspects of settlement change in this region are striking: (*a*) the progress-ive increase in the number of settlements until the Early Dynastic period; (*b*) the deruralization of the countryside beginning with Early Dynastic I; (*c*) the uniformity of a real separation between major settlements; and (*d*) the change in the distance of separation through time and the crowding that appeared during the Early Dynastic II/III in the northeastern area.

Both the progressive increase in the number of settlements and the crowding of settlements are apparently a function of increasing population size. Assuming 100 persons/ha of settled area, the population shows an increase from about 11,000 to 150,000 from the Late Uruk period to the late Early Dynastic period (Figure 14.5). Apparently, this was not solely a result of intrinsic population increase. It is interesting to note that the building of a sanctuary appeared during Late Uruk times, when settlements were scarce and the area was thinly populated, indicating the emergence of incipient theocratic centralization independent of population increase. If we examine the percentage of villages, towns, small urban centers, and cities (Figure 14.6), we find that intensive deruralization appears during the late Early Dynastic period. Unfortunately, the figures on the Early Dynastic I are masked because a combined figure was used for Jamdet Nasr and Early Dynastic I. We may thus envision a steady growth in settlements associated with the emergence of several towns as centers for services, organization, trade, food exchange, and the like. During the Jamdet Nasr period, there was a shift from a diffuse pattern to a pattern closely associated with major water courses, as noted by R. M. Adams (1965). This would reflect a shift in settlement pattern to take advantage of large areas of arable land, a more reliable and permanent water source, and trade. This shift appears to be associated with greater managerial efficiency and large population units. During the Early Dynastic I period, large-scale irrigation was established and small urban centers or small cities became conspicuous. The growth of these centers, their

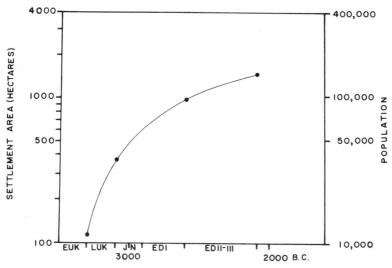

FIGURE 14.5. *Increase in total settlement area and population (assuming 100 persons/ha of settled area) from Late Uruk (LUK) to the end of the Early Dynastic period in the Uruk region, southern Mesopotamia. (Data from R. M. Adams and H. J. Nissen 1972.)*

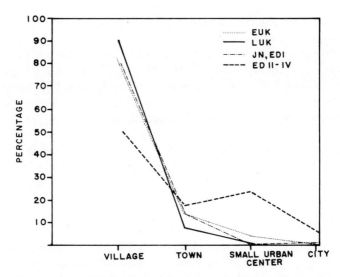

FIGURE 14.6. *Percentage of villages, towns, small urban centers, and large urban centers (cities) in the Uruk region, southern Mesopotamia during successive periods from Early Uruk to Early Dynastic II–IV. (Data from R. M. Adams and H. J. Nissen 1972.)*

location at equal distances along major channel courses, and the practice of large-scale irrigation suggest an organizational threshold associated with large population concentrations having established domains of economic and social dominance. The role of trade in the growth of these centers should not be minimized. During the late Early Dynastic period, the pattern was accentuated. The Umma settlement complex dominated the northeastern area of the region. Earlier settlements in that area seem to have been abandoned, apparently as a result of channel shift and perhaps as a result of the establishment of a trade monopoly by related settlements in this part of the region. Settlements of the Early Dynastic were more or less uniformly spaced, at distances of about 10 km. Apparently this was a function of (*a*) carrying capacity under irrigation agriculture; (*b*) transport pattern; and (*c*) social distance. Since the cultivatable land around Uruk does not seem to have been extensive, the city might have thus achieved its great magnitude because it served as a center of food exchange and trade. The amalgamation of the rural settlements reflects the demands of urban growth. A similar pattern is displayed by the northeastern Umma complex, which could have only achieved this sudden growth as a result of commercial success as a redistributive center, especially after the collapse of the previous settlements caused by channel shift. The network that appeared in this area reflects the more extensive area of the floodplain.

In the Diyala Plain, the settlements during the Ubaid period consisted of a few villages (Figure 14.7). The largest of these villages were uniformly spaced, about 25 km apart in most cases. An incipient linear pattern along watercourses is evident. Some of the small settlements were closely packed within radii of 5–10 km. During the Warka and the Protoliterate periods, sites increased in number (from 22 to 43) and the largest villages of the Ubaid period grew into towns and small urban centers (Figure 14.8). Linear and radial settlement clusters appeared and an interesting pattern of expansion is noticeable. The linear enclave previously occupied by Khafajie alone became crowded, especially along the southern end of the enclave, where there were numerous villages and small towns. Another linear concentration appeared north of Khafajie. Farther north, new small settlements appeared at equal distances from each other. During the Early Dynastic period (Figure 14.9) more settlements appeared in the Khafajie enclave, the southcentral enclave and the northern enclave. A hierarchical pattern is distinct. The major settlements in the northern enclaves were very widely yet uniformly spaced. The wide separation between these northern settlements and the southern settlements seems to indicate

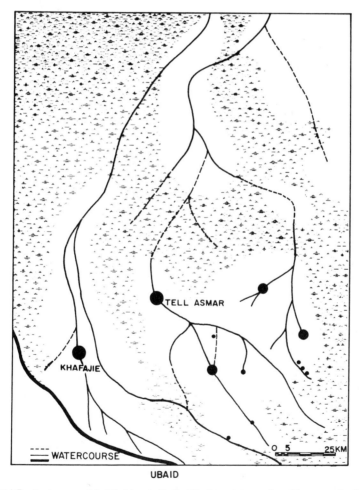

FIGURE 14.7. *Settlements of the Ubaid period in the Diyala region, southern Mesopotamia. (Data from R. M. Adams, 1965.)*

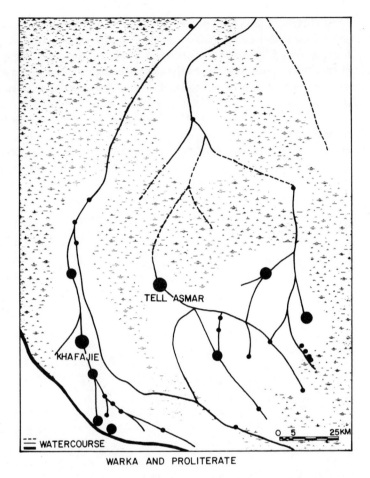

FIGURE 14.8. *Warka and Proliterate settlements in the Diyala region, southern Mesopotamia. (Data from R. M. Adams 1965.)*

that these may represent geographic expansion into the lower Diyala Plain from the north. The new settlements in the Khafajie enclave and the south-central enclave, on the other hand, were very closely spaced. Several towns appeared in intermediate position, between the older major settlements. These may have served as centers for local exchange, but the well-balanced distribution of older settlements and their viability seem to have precluded an exponential growth of such intermediary centers.

The lack of development of a pattern like that which occurred in the Uruk region seems to have been a function of the simultaneous emergence of centers as early as the Ubaid period, forming a balanced network of relations that prevented the emergence of an exceptional gravitational pull of any single settlement. Khafajie, in an enclave by itself, managed to grow to a relatively greater size than the four other towns in the south-central enclave. However, the rank order of settlements in both Uruk and the south-central enclave in the Diyala region was very similar, with slight differences between these two and the Khafajie enclave, which surprisingly shows a very close similarity to the rank order of present world cities (Figure 14.10). For Uruk and south-central Diyala a settlement was half as large as the immediately preceding rank settlement. This empirical find differs from Zipf rank–size rule, which is expressed by the formula $p_n = p_1 (n)^{-1}$, where p_n is the population of the nth town in the series 1, 2, 3, ..., n, in which all towns are arranged in descending order by population, and p_1 is the population of the largest

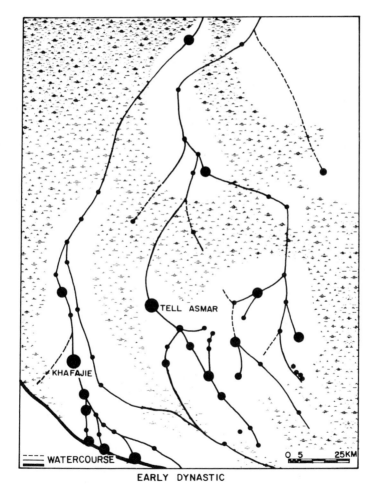

FIGURE 14.9. *Early Dynastic settlement in the Diyala region, southern Mesopotamia. (Data from R. M. Adams, 1965.)*

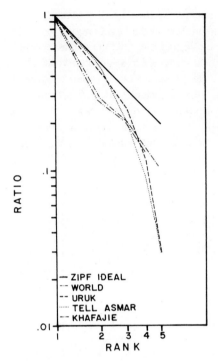

FIGURE 14.10. *Rank order of the settlements of Uruk, Tell Asmar, and Khafajie compared with rank order of the world cities and Zipf ideal. (Data from R. M. Adams 1972; R. M. Adams and H. J. Nissen 1972; and Haggett 1966.)*

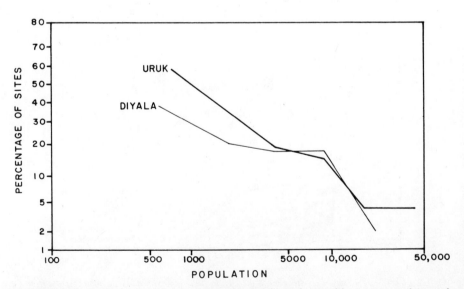

FIGURE 14.11. *Settlement size distribution (normal probability scale is used for percentage of sites and logarithmic scale for population size of settlement). (Data from R. M. Adams 1965 and R. M. Adams and H. J. Nissen 1972.)*

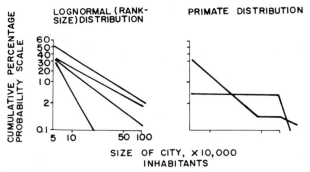

FIGURE 14.12. *Alternative distribution patterns of settlement sizes. (Data from Haggett 1966.)*

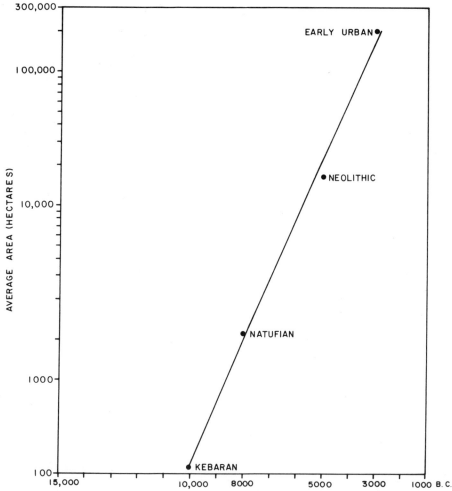

FIGURE 14.13. *Increase in average area settlements from the Epipalaeolithic to the period of early urbanization.*

town. My formula using these symbols is as follows;

$$P_n + 1 = k\,P_n$$

with $k = \frac{1}{2}$ in the case of Uruk and Asmar, and $\frac{2}{3}$ for Khafajie.

Unfortunately, the factors responsible for rank-size order are obscure (Haggett

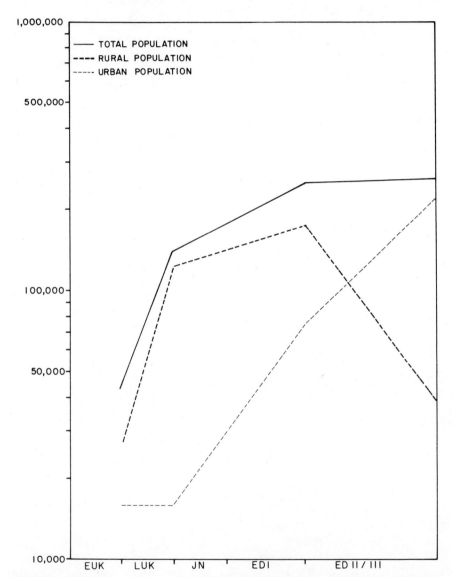

FIGURE 14.14 *Population increase in southern Mesopotamia. Note the decline in rural population relative to the ''urban population'' during Early Dynastic II-III. (Data from R. M. Adams 1965 and R. M. Adams and H. J. Nissen 1972.)*

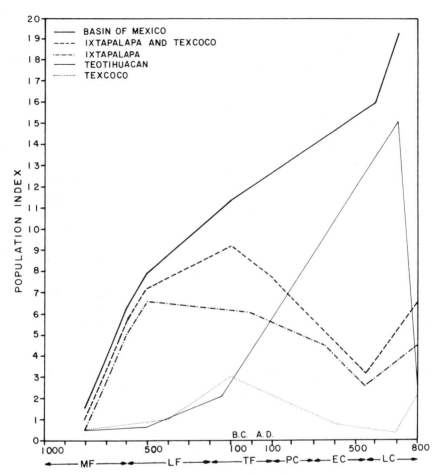

FIGURE 14.15. *Relative increase in various parts of the Basin of Mexico. Note that the increase in the population of Teotihuacán from the Terminal Formative period onward is associated with a decline in the population of other areas. (Data from Sanders 1972 and Blanton 1972.)*

1966). An attempt was made to plot the percentage of settlements against their size using a normal probability scale for percentage and a logarithmic scale for size, a technique devised by Berry (1961). (See Figure 14.11.) An intermediate distribution pattern was obtained for the settlements of the Uruk and Diyala regions indicating a *primate* distribution. This distribution is different from the lognormal distribution (Figure 14.12), which plots as a straight line. The primate pattern shows a marked gap between the largest city or cities and the smaller settlements. Haggett (1966:106) suggests that the primate distribution is the product of urbanization in "countries" that (*a*) are smaller than average; (*b*) have a short history of urbanization; and (*c*) are economically or politically simple. These conditions are in agreement with the characteristics of southern Mesopotamia in Dynastic times.

The preceding discussion clearly indicates that the emergence of large aggregates of populations in cities, with as many as 40,000 in some towns, was a distinct element in the civilization of southern Mesopotamia. The increase in the average area of settlements from the Epipalaeolithic to the Late Dynastic period seems to have followed an orderly growth pattern (Figure 14.13). The progressive trend toward the enlargement of settlements was also accompanied by a hierarchical differentiation of settlements into villages, towns, small urban centers, and large urban centers. The population in the urban centers expanded rapidly at the expense of the inhabitants of the smaller settlements. By the Late Dynastic period, the population in the urban centers was greater than that of the small rural settlements (Figure 14.14). A similar pattern of urbanization can be seen in the Basin of Mexico (Figure 14.15). Sanders (1972) notes that the population in the Texcoco area showed a decline corresponding with the rapid growth of population in the Teotihuacán Valley, indicating a migration to the emerging Teotihuacán city. The data provided by Blanton (1972) for Ixtapalapa show a similar decline in population following the Terminal Formative coincident with the expansion of the population of Teotihuacán. The growth of population during the Late Formative was associated with intensive agricultural techniques and the emergence of large political systems. The Late Formative was a turning point, with expansion of population, irrigation, and the emergence of ceremonial architecture and large population centers. The Teotihuacán city commanded about 15,000 persons and continued to increase to a center of 125,000 persons in the Middle Classic period. The rise of Teotihuacán is attributed by Sanders (1972:114) to irrigation, political unification of the Basin of Mexico, the displacement of population from small settlements to the city, and the expansion of the political and economic influences of the city to outside the basin proper.

The Origins of Civilization: Toward an Explanatory Model

The emergence of civilization was obviously a major cultural transformation, a radical modification of the structural framework of social, economic, and environmental relations. This transformation could have been neither a sudden event nor a quick response to an economic, demographic, or social crisis. On the contrary, this major transformation, as all other such transformations in human history, was the outcome of a sequence of processes involving the reinforcement of certain cultural trends that had been initiated previously. In the case of early urbanization, the emergence of an agricultural economy during the Neolithic led to a number of trends that were ultimately responsible for urbanization. Among these trends, I would emphasize the following:

1. The development of large, year-round sedentary residential units as a successful residential and demographic strategy to maximize yield per capita
2. The emergence of greater and somewhat formally structured intrasocial and

economic coordination (a necessity for maintaining a large, sedentary group and for minimizing social conflict, as well as maximizing communal viability)

3. A structured and more or less formal system of intercommunal food exchange and trade to enhance the economic viability of large, sedentary groups, which lack the adaptive mobility of hunter–gatherers in the face of seasonal or periodic food shortage

4. Incipient social hierarchical differentiation as a result of the development of incipient semiformal leadership to take charge of the responsibilities of social and economic inter- and intracommunal coordination

These trends were mutually interrelated, forming a positive feedback loop (see Hassan 1976 and Chapter 13, this volume).

The ecological changes associated with agriculture must be taken into consideration. Agriculture involves a progressive reduction in the number of food resources and a greater emphasis on a few cultivated staple foods. The crops, moreover, are strongly influenced by changes in soil and climatic conditions. Agricultural systems therefore are metastable systems subject to frequent fluctuations in yield (cf. J. Smith 1978:85, 90–97). The impact of such fluctuations on human agricultural populations is worsened by the sedentariness of the population. The likely response to such devastating fluctuations may consist of storage, communal redistributive mechanisms, and interregional integration of resources. All these measures are stabilizing factors. The course toward civilization may be thus viewed as a result of cumulative changes resulting from progressive intensification of intra- and intercommunal social and economic coordination, agricultural production, centralized management, and social differentiation. A multiplier effect (see C. Renfrew [1972a] for a discussion of this concept) resulted from the development of craft specialization, centralized ritual, extensive trade for basic and sumptuary goods, and perhaps militarism (Figure 14.16). The generative process involved in this course of events has been characterized by Flannery (1972) as one of systemic *linearization* and differentiation or *segregation*. In a sense, linearization is the result of Renfrew's multiplier effect. It involves the development of new control institutions to cement and reinforce high-order controls. New institutions, however, tend to become self-serving, leading to the development of adjunct or supplementary institutions. The multiplication of institutions represents systemic differentiation as described by D. Katz and R. L. Kahn (1969) or segregation as described by Flannery (1972).

The systemic perspective also sheds light on the relationship between increasing productivity, increasing centralization, and differentiation. In an open system, the importation of more energy than is expended can enhance the survivability of the system in periods of low energy input. In an agricultural situation the frequency and great unpredictability of years of low yield will increase the probability of disintegration. As the system's inability to arrest negative entropy increases, the danger becomes more acute, with increasing differentiation requiring greater energy input.

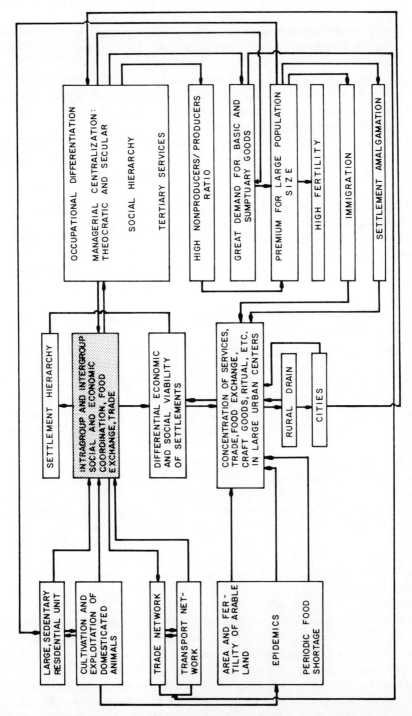

FIGURE 14.16. *A model of the formative processes of early urbanization in southern Mesopotamia.*

The intensification of agriculture and the enlargement of the labor force of primary producers can be seen clearly in this light. The implications of this perspective are illuminating in dealing with the fall of cities and civilization as well. If, on the one hand, the energy input drops below a certain margin sufficient to allow the functional requirements of the system, or if, on the other hand, the energy requirements increase beyond available means of supply, the system will revert to a state of lower organization. Dispersed small settlements may thus appear following the disintegration of a city (cf. Willey and Shimkin [1971] on the collapse of the classic Maya).

The emergence of relatively large settlements and a large local group size is an important aspect of the period of early food production. The localization of dense resources made possible by cultivation and the advantages occurring from a large group size in maximizing agricultural output (Hassan 1976) during the period of early food production led to the emergence of settlements, which reached in some cases an areal extent of 1–2 ha, perhaps with as many as 200 or 400 persons, which was followed by an exponential increase in the size of settlements to as much as about 40,000 persons at Uruk and 150,000 at Teotihuacán.

Long-term regional population increase, as I have suggested, was not more than .1%/year on the average. However, it was characterized most likely by alternation between phases of rapid growth, perhaps as high as .5 and 1%, and phases of very slow growth or even depopulation. These wide fluctuations were also undoubtedly coupled with fluctuations in agricultural yield, which may have been at times, of considerable magnitude. For hunter–gatherers such fluctuations are counteracted by the mobility of the group and the flexibility of group composition. But among sedentary cultivators mobility is prohibited by the mode of production involved, and in the long run a large settlement or a settlement network must be established to guard against population loss and/or food shortage. Small autonomous settlements are not, in the long run, viable because they cannot independently sustain either the impact of an epidemic or an acute food shortage, both not uncommon at that time. The dependence on certain craftsmen for basic agricultural tools would have led to a further reduction in the viability of small settlements. Since the number of craftsmen is usually very small in a village or a hamlet, the chances of losing a craftsman through death or migration to a larger settlement where life is more attractive would definitely lower the chances of the settlement for survival. Thus, the village would have to depend on the larger settlement for services. In some cases, an afflicted settlement may become part of the larger settlement.

The emergence of relatively large settlements in the first place may be a function of access to more fertile land, better management innovations, or their place in the modes of transport, trade, or food exchange. But, even if these conditions were absent, some small settlements may coalesce to form more viable entities. Obviously, this established a kickoff point for a trend-amplifying process.

The periods of rapid population increase also had significant implications for settlement growth and differential enlargement. Rapid population increase, perhaps 1%/year, cannot be sustained over a long period (G. L. Cowgill 1975). A rapid population growth will require an equally rapid rate of economic development and a concomitant change from low-order to high-order controls within very short time spans. At a certain critical threshold, then, individuals or families will leave to join other settlements, especially those that are undergoing economic expansion and are in need of manpower. If there are no nearby centers, the emigrants may settle in satellite hamlets, which by necessity are dependent on the parent settlements for services and economic and biological viability. There are, of course, limitations to this process of fission, expansion, and hierarchical settlement differentiation, based on land availability, organizational efficiency, productivity, and the like.

I propose now to view settlement growth from another angle. Under a given productive regime, there is theoretically an economically optimum population size. This optimum represents the size at which the average output is at a maximum. Beyond it, the addition of new individuals will lower the output per capita and thereby the standard of living. This reduction, of course, cannot exceed a certain tolerable limit beyond which survival would be endangered. Of special importance for us is that the addition of new individuals to the community, either through intrinsic population increase or immigration, is beneficial when the population is below the economic optimum. In dealing with the growth and fission of settlements we sould also keep in mind that population increase is not always associated with a reduction in the standard of living. We should also remember that the economic optimum is a function of the productive regime. Agricultural intensification requires either a large labor force or greater labor input per producer. It can be a result of a variety of factors, such as a decline in the productivity of the land through natural processes or mismanagement, a demand for a better standard of living on the part of the whole population or a segment thereof, an increase in the ratio of nonproducers to producers, and the entrepreneurial ambitions of the temple or wealthy elite. Thus, as occupational differentiations, social hierarchy, and managerial organization increase, the demand for agricultural intensification will grow. One need not place all the weight on the magic of unrestrained population increase. Even without agricultural intensification, an increase in population to meet the demands of the growing numbers of nonproducers will be tolerated as long as a minimal standard of living is not reached. The drop in land fertility as a result of salinization and loss of nutrients (Jacobson and Adams 1958), and the loss of arable land as a result of channel shift (R. M. Adams 1965; R. M. Adams and H. J. Nissen 1972) will enhance both extensification and intensification of agriculture. Large-scale irrigation, for example, can be advantageous. Extensification alone is not a long-term solution, since the area of arable land is very limited and since annual changes in small channels and streams would imply either shifting the settlement or a long commuting distance. Both of these are high-cost measures.

It may be added here that children will be advantageous during these phases of economic expansion because they will provide cheap labor for light but nonetheless essential tasks, as they do today in many agricultural communities, and will relieve adults for other tasks (Nag et al. 1978). This will tend to favor high levels of fertility.

Thus, as the demands for economic growth continue, and such demands would tend to become progressively greater as the size and aspirations of the managerial elite and their capacity for enterprises increase, the enlargement of the settlement will be encouraged. This will maintain the standard of living of the producers, as the standard of living of nonproducers and their numbers increases.

In concluding this section, I wish to make a few remarks on the relation between population, warfare, and urbanization. Steward (1949), Young (1972), and Gibson (1973), among others, have argued that warfare, resulting from competition for scarce resources under conditions of intensive population pressure, was a major cause of the agglomeration of populations in protected urban centers. However, present archaeological data indicate that systematic and organized warfare emerged in Mesopotamia in Late and post-Late Dynastic times. Walls and ramparts surrounding pre-Late Dynastic settlements might have served as defensive measures, and hence may indicate some intergroup military conflict. Roper (1975), for example, suggests that there is evidence for intergroup conflict from the time of early food production. Roper suggests that this conflict may have been related to securing or dominating trade routes and centers. Military conflict, thus, may have had nothing to do with population pressure in many instances. Large-scale, systematic, and organized warfare was more likely to have emerged as a means of aggrandizing power—not by a society on the brink of starvation but by an affluent society that had more to gain from conquest and was sufficiently wealthy to equip and mobilize a military force.[4] Military conflict and warfare may have thus contributed to the emergence of walled and protected settlements. Militarism of this scale seems to date from the earliest part of the Early Dynastic (Gibson, personal communication).

Overview

The primary core of a civilization lies in a formal, complex, hierarchical power structure. My model of the origins of urban civilization views the emergence of such power structures as an outcome of the processes set in motion by the adoption of agriculture, and as a response to the vulnerability of agricultural systems to environmental and cultural perturbations. In essence, I agree with Service (1975:303–308), who views the emergence of civilization as a "managerial" and administrative transformation. The role played by the chiefs as managers in stabilizing the subsistence subsystem by supervising communal storage, redistribution, and food exchange with neighboring groups was crucial for the survival of agricultural systems. The emergence of community leaders does not demand any elaborate explanation, because of the differential aptitude for leadership among people in a society. Under most hunting–gathering conditions certain individuals attain a prestigious position

[4]For refutations of population pressure as a cause of warfare, see Bremer et al. (1973), Fathauer (1954), Murphy (1970), and Sauvy (1969).

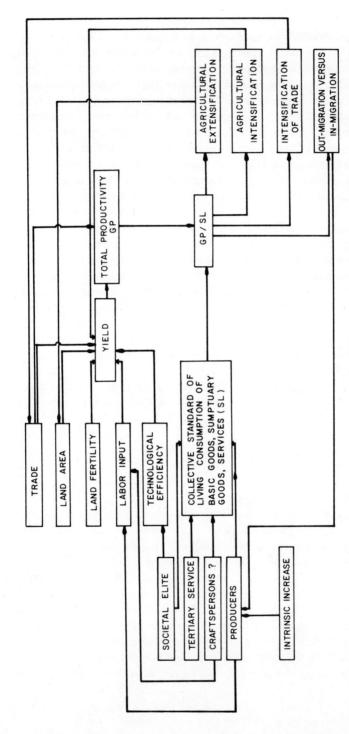

FIGURE 14.17. *A model of the impact of economic and social changes on population. Greater labor demands resulting from a change in the ratio of non-producers to producers and a rising standard of living stimulating agrarian changes encourage population increase and migration.*

(Fried 1960), but because of the changing composition of the group and the low demands for strong integrative mechanisms or managerial organization such individuals do not rise to the status of formal leaders. Even under such conditions of highly productive hunting–gathering where managerial organization may be useful and formal leaders may emerge, as in the Northwest Coast of North America, the limited potential for economic growth under hunting–gathering conditions was not conducive to an escalation of political organization to the level of state structure (see Fried 1960, on the societal mechanics of the transition from egalitarian to stratified societies).

Control of food resources endows leaders in an agricultural community with power, and such power is, in fact, needed to ensure the participation of the community members in the communal economic sector. Informal, voluntary participation is soon replaced by a formal structure. Coercion is only a step away when individuals fail to fulfill their "duties" to the community.

The managerial sector, by its access to power and capital, can initiate communal projects and thus serve as a vehicle for agricultural intensification (cf. Dumond 1972). Management of resources also fosters craft specialization and thus leads to occupational differentiation.

From a demographic perspective, the key variables in the emergence of civilization consist of the large size of agricultural communities, their sedentariness, and the increase in the number of consumers relative to food producers (Figure 14.17). The relationship between population and carrying capacity during the emergence of civilization also undergoes a dramatic change as a result of the demands for nonsubsistence goods. Such goods include tools and facilities for agricultural production, as well as the luxury items that accompany the rise of the elite. "Population pressure," if it was ever a valid concept for hunter–gatherers, is a far less useful concept in this context. Economic demands for nonsubsistence goods can be far greater than those for food.

15

Final Remarks

Happy is the person, who in thinking
Soars, like a lark in a morning sky
And, effortlessly, high above life
Grasps the language of flowers and silent things.*

Charles Baudelaire, Élévation

The demographic history of humanity is closely linked to the cultural transformations that people have experienced in the long journey from the Pleistocene to the present. Throughout most of the past, people subsisted on the natural yield of the wild resources by hunting and gathering, and the population of the world did not surpass 10 million. Neither technological improvements nor greater input of labor could increase the yield to man of natural resources without ultimately destroying them. For 2 or 3 million years, then, the ancestors of modern man and modern man himself lived in small groups, increasing at almost a negligible rate from about 1 million persons during the Lower Pleistocene to about 8–9 million by the end of the Pleistocene. The slow growth was not a reflection of a low level of fecundity. In fact, despite a high infant mortality, a short life expectancy for adults, and a late age of nubility, prehistoric man was capable of rapid growth of .5%/year, even with a child-spacing period of 40 months. The socioeconomic conditions of hunting-gathering did not encourage large families or large population units. Regional population units rarely exceeded 1000 and local cooperative units rarely exceeded 50, with an average of 20–25. The composition of the groups was changeable, in part as a result of the spatiotemporal flux of resource yield, and in part as a result of the small size of the local groups. These small prehistoric populations were subject

---

*In *French symbolist poetry*, University of California Press, Berkeley, 1964, p. 10. English translation by F. A. Hassan.

to pronounced stochastic fluctuations in size and, more important, in age and sex composition; the search for mates encouraged exogamous relationship between groups.

The rate of increase of the world population seems to have been accelerated with the emergence of modern man (*Homo sapiens*). This increase was associated with geographic expansion into previously unoccupied world biomes. Australia and the New World were colonized. Boreal forests, tropical forests, and deserts were invaded. Modern man's greater adaptability might have been responsible for occupying new areas. Watercrafts, sleds, clothing, and fire were adopted in various places and were necessary for colonizing cold regions and traveling over large bodies of water. The ingenuity and the great cognitive abilities of modern man must be credited for the remarkable achievements of the Upper Palaeolithic. These achievements were both technological and intellectual. The fine artistic achievements of Upper Palaeolithic man are perhaps the most direct evidence of the intellectual powers of early modern man.

The end of the Pleistocene brought with it unstable climatic conditions and pronounced fluctuations in the yield of food resources. It also made the spatiotemporal predictability of utilized resources less certain. These conditions could have been alleviated by strict population controls and a reduction of world population to a safe level. Some of the Palaeolithic hunters and gatherers must certainly have taken that route and a few of these people still survive. Certain areas were more subject to fluctuation than others (e.g., Mediterranean and subarid regions) and in some of those areas grasses were becoming abundant as a result of climatic changes. An alternative to population control was present, and some groups found that it was possible to stabilize their subsistence base by adding wild cereals to their food basket. Other foods, previously less emphasized because of the high cost of extraction or preparation for consumption (e.g., snails) were also exploited by many groups at that time.

Wild cereals proved to be the apple that led to man's exit from the world of the hunter to that of the tiller. They were abundant, but they required greater effort for preparation (e.g., parching, grinding, sieving, cooking). The grasses had to be harvested in a short time from the wild fields. These aspects of the wild cereals invited large aggregations of people and ultimately sedentariness, since storage allowed the people to circumvent shortages during lean seasons.

Increasing dependence on wild cereals opened the gate for cultivation. Agriculture allowed the dependence on cereals to continue, and militated against shortages in protein through cultivation of legumes and raising stock.

Agricultural systems, however, are vulnerable to environmental fluctuations, crop failure, and inadvertently adverse agricultural practices. This vulnerability was aggravated by the ecological simplification of the subsistence base. Organizational complexity under such conditions serves as a buffer through storage management, interregional integration of resources, craft specialization, and agricultural extensification and intensification. Organizational complexity fosters the emergence of managerial "specialists," who command the subsistence sector and are endowed accordingly with greater power than the farmers.

In addition to large population size and sedentariness, which are the two major demographic aspects to emerge in the context of early agriculture, population movement and a rise in the ratio of consumers to food producers are among the major aspects of early civilizations. Managers, craft specialists, traders, and other individuals engaged in secondary and tertiary occupations led to greater labor demands. Labor demands were also accentuated by the need to stabilize the agricultural system against crop failure. Such demands for labor sustained the motivation for population increase and in the case of city states led to a population movement from small, vulnerable communities to growing, more stable "urban" centers. In some cases, however, such large centers continued to grow at an exponential rate and thus reached beyond their integrative capability, ultimately leading to their collapse and the subsequent fragmentation of the population.

The population increase during the periods of early agriculture and early civilization cannot be attributed simply to greater availability of food or to a reduction in the long-range spatial mobility characteristic of hunter–gatherers. It is not likely that a long child-spacing period was dropped, because of its advantages for the mother and the children. Opportunities for work and the rise in the optimum economic population as a result of labor-intensifying technological improvements and the increase in the number of nonproducers must have encouraged greater levels of fertility, which could have been achieved by reducing the rates of infanticide or abortion. It is difficult to ascertain the role of age at marriage and the implications of the cereal diet as factors leading to greater fertility. Changes in mortality were not of great magnitude, but they might have contributed to a slight increase in the number of women surviving to the full completion of their reproductive span. Whatever the mechanisms responsible for increase in the world population in post-Neolithic times, the socioeconomic motives for a large labor force must be viewed as the ultimate cause for the increase.

This summary glosses over the details expounded in this book, and is only intended as a general overview of the role of various demographic variables at successive stages of human evolution. Those who are familiar with the literature in demographic archaeology will immediately realize that I have attempted to expand the perspective of that nascent field well beyond a narrow emphasis on population increase and population pressure. I have attempted to present my views with as much empirical data as possible and have tried to place these data within broad demographic, ecological, and economic perspectives. Unfortunately, empirical data on the demography of prehistoric peoples are regrettably scant and of uneven quality. Consequently, I have been discriminatory in my choice of data, but it was a hard choice and I am sure others might be more discriminatory, or perhaps more permissive than I was. I hope, however, that my work will not be regarded as much as a source of demographic statistics on early man, but as a source of insights into the potentials of demographic archaeology and as a stimulus for gathering the kinds of demographic information necessary for an accurate characterization of the demographic conditions of early man and for testing the hypothesis generated throughout this work on the role of demographic variables in social organization, technocultures, subsistence, and settlements.

References

Acker, C. L., and P. K. Townsend
  1975   Demographic models and female infanticide. *Man* *10*:469–470.
Acsádi, G.-Y. and J. Nemeskéri
  1957   Paläodemographische probleme am beispiel des frühmittelalterichen Gräberfeldes von Halimba-Cseres, *Kom. Vezprém1 Ungarn. Homo 8*:133–147.
  1970   *History of human life span and mortality.* Ackademiai Kiado, Budapest.
Acsádi, G.-Y., J. Nemeskéri, *et al.*
  1974   History of human life span and mortality: a book review. *Current Anthropology 15*(4):495–507.
Adams, J. W., and A. B. Kasakoff
  1975   Factors underlying endogamous group size. In *Population and social organization,* edited by Moni Nag. Mouton, The Hague
Adams, R. E. W.
  1977   *The origins of Mayan civilization.* Univ. of New Mexico Press, Albuquerque.
Adams, R. M.
  1955   *Developmental stages in ancient Mesopotamia.* Bobbs-Merrill Reprint Series in European History, No. E-1. Reprinted from *Irrigation civilizations: a comparative study,* edited by J. H. Steward. Pan American Union, Washington, D.C.
  1965   *Land behind Baghdad: A history of settlement on the Diyala Plain.* Univ. of Chicago Press, Chicago.
  1966   *The evolution of urban society: Early Mesopotamia and pre-hispanic Mexico.* Aldine, Chicago.
  1972   Demography and the urban "revolution" in lowland Mesopotamia. In *Population growth: anthropological implications,* edited by B. Spooner, pp. 70–63. MIT Press, Cambridge, Mass.

Adams, R. M., and H. J. Nissen
  1972   *The Uruk countryside: The natural setting of urban societies.* Univ. of Chicago Press, Chicago.
Al-Gihaz al-Markazi lil-Ta'ba' wal'Ihssa'
  1966   The population problem in the U.A.R. *Risalat el-I'lm* 2:94–122 (in Arabic).
Al-Maqrizi, T. A.
  n.d.   *Al-Khitat.* Bulaq 1270 II edition (in Arabic), reprinted by Dar el-Tahrir lil-Tiba' wa'Nashr, Cairo.
Allan, W.
  1949   *Studies in African land usage in northern Rhodesia.* Rhodes-Livingstone Papers, No. 15. The Rhodes-Livingstone Institute, Livingstone, Northern Rhodesia.
  1965   *The African husbandman.* Oliver & Boyd, Edinburgh.
Altman, S. A., and J. Altman
  1978   *Demographic constraints on behavior and social organization.* Paper presented at the Hudson Symposium on Biosocial Mechanisms of Population Regulation, State Univ. of New York, Plattsburgh.
Ammerman, A. J.
  1975   Late Pleistocene population alternatives. *Human Ecology* 3(4):219–233.
Ammerman, A. J., and L. L. Cavalli-Sforza
  1973   A population model for the diffusion of early farming in Europe. In *The explanation of culture change,* edited by C. Renfrew. Duckworth, London.
Ammerman, A. J., L. L. Cavalli-Sforza, and D. K. Wagener
  1976   Toward the estimation of population growth in Old World prehistory. In *Demographic anthropology,* edited by E. B. W. Zubrow, pp. 27–61. Univ. of New Mexico Press, Albuquerque.
Anderson, James E.
  1968a   Late Paleolithic skeletal remains from Nubia. In *The prehistory of Nubia* (Vol. 2), edited by Fred Wendorf, pp. 996–1040. Fort Burgwin Research Center and Southern Methodist Univ. Press, Dallas.
  1968b   Skeletal anomalies as genetic indicators. In *The skeletal biology of earlier human populations,* edited by Don R. Brothwell, pp. 135–148. Symposia of the Society for the Study of Human Biology, Pergamon, London.
Andrewartha, H. G.
  1963   *Introduction to the study of animal populations.* Univ. of Chicago Press, Chicago.
  1970   Population growth and control: Animal populations. In *Population Control,* edited by A. Allison, pp. 43–69. Penguin, Harmondsworth, England.
Angel, J. L.
  1947   The length of life in ancient Greece. *Journal of Gerontology* 2:18–24.
  1969a   The bases of paleodemography. *American Journal of Physical Anthropology* 30:427–437.
  1969b   Paleodemography and evolution. *American Journal of Physical Anthropology* 31:343–353.
  1971   Early Neolithic skeletons from Catal Hüyak: Demography and pathology. *Anatolian Studies*: 77–98.
  1972   Ecology and population in the eastern Mediterranean. *World Archaeology* 4:88–105.
  1975   Paleoecology, paleodemography and health. In *Population, ecology and social evolution,* edited by S. Polgar, pp. 167–190. Mouton, The Hague.
Armelagos, G. J., and A. McArdle
  1975   Population, disease, and evolution. In Population studies in archaeology and biological anthropology: a symposium, edited by A. C. Swedlund, pp. 1–10. *American Antiquity* 40(2), Part 2, Memoir 30.
Arsdale, P. W. Van
  1978   Population dynamics among Asmat hunter–gatherers of New Guinea: data, methods, comparisons. *Human Ecology* 6:435–467.
Asch, D. L.
  1975   *Human evolution* (Second ed.). Rand McNally, New York.

1976   *The Middle Woodland population of the Lower Illinois Valley: A study in palaeodemographic methods.* Northwestern University Archaeological Program, Scientific Papers, No. 1. Evanston, Ill.

1959   A prehistoric population estimate using midden analysis and two population models. *Southwestern Journal of Anthropology 15*:168–178.

Audebeau, M. C.

1919   L'Agriculture Égyptienne à la fin du XVIII siècle. *L'Egypte Contemporaire 10:*132–169.

Balicki, A.

1967   Female infanticide on the Arctic Coast. *Man 2*:615–625.

Banfield, A. W. T.

1954   Preliminary investigation of the barren-ground caribou. *Wildlife Management Bulletin*, Series I, No. 10, A and B.

Bar-Yosef, O.

1970   *The Epi-Palaeolithic cultures of Palestine.* Unpublished Ph.D. dissertation, Hebrew University, Jerusalem.

Bar-Yosef, O., and N. Goren

1973   Natufian remains in Hayonim Cave. *Paléorient 1*:49–68.

Bar-Yosef, Ofer

1975   Archaeological occurrences in the Middle Pleistocene of Israel. In *After the australopithecines,* edited by K. W. Butzer and G. L. L. Isaac, pp. 571–604. Mouton, The Hague.

Barber, W. J.

1967   *A history of economic thought.* Penguin, Baltimore.

Barclay, George W.

1958   Population analysis. Wiley, New York.

Barclay, H. B.

1971   The Nile Valley. In *The central Middle East,* edited by L. E. Sweet. HRAF Press, New Haven, Conn.

Barnett, H. G.

1953   *Innovation: The basis of cultural change.* McGraw-Hill, New York.

Barrett, J. C.

1972   A Monte Carlo simulation of reproduction. In *Biological aspects of demography,* edited by W. Brass. Taylor and Francis, London.

Barry, Herbert, III

1973   *Interrelationships among population size, kinship and societal complexity.* Paper delivered at the 72nd annual meeting of the American Anthropological Association, New Orleans.

Bartholomew, G. A., and J. B. Birdsell

1953   Ecology and the protohominids. *American Anthropologist 55*:481–498.

Baumhoff, M. A.

1963   Ecological determinants of aboriginial California populations. *University of California Publications in American Archaeology and Ethnology 49*(2):155–236.

Bender, B

1975   *Farming in prehistory.* John Baker, London.

Benedict, B.

1970   Population regulation in primitive societies. In *Population control,* edited by A. Allison, pp. 165–180. Penguin, Harmondsworth, England.

1972   *Social regulation of fertility in the structure of human populations,* edited by G. A. Harrison and A. J. Boyce, pp. 73–89. Oxford Univ. Press (Clarendon), London and New York.

Bennett, Kenneth

1973   On the estimation of some demographic characteristics of a population from the American Southwest. *American Journal of Physical Anthropology 39*:223–232.

Berman, M. L., K. Hanson, and I. L. Hellman

1972   The effect of breastfeeding on postpartum menstruation, ovulation, and pregnancy in Alaskan Eskimos. *American Journal of Obstetrics and Gynecology 114*:524–534.

Berndt, R. M.
1959 The concept of "the tribe" in the western desert of Australia. *Oceana 30*:80–107.
Berry, B. J. L.
1961 City size distribution and economic development. *Economic Development and Cultural Change 9*:573–588.
Binford, L. R.
1963 "Red ocher" caches from the Michigan area: A possible case of cultural drift. *Southwestern Journal of Anthropology 19*:98–108.
1968 Post-Pleistocene adaptations. In *New perspectives in archaeology*, edited by S. R. Binford and L. R. Binford, pp. 313–341. Aldine, Chicago.
Binford, L. R., S. R. Binford, R. Whallon, and M. A. Hardin
1970 Archaeology at Hatchery West. *American Antiquity 35*(4): 91, Memoir 24.
Birdsell, J. B.
1953 Some environmental and cultural factors influencing the structuring of Australian populations. *American Naturalist 87*:171–207.
1957 Some population problems involving Pleistocene man. *Cold Spring Harbor Symposium on Quantitative Biology 22*:47–69.
1958 On population structure in generalized hunting and collecting populations. *Evolution 12*:189–205.
1968 Some predictions for the Pleistocene based on equilibrium systems among recent hunter-gatherers. In *Man the hunter*, edited by R. B. Lee and I. DeVore, pp. 229–240. Aldine, Chicago.
1970 Local group composition among the Australian aborigines: a critique of the evidence from fieldwork conducted since 1930. *Current Anthropology 11*:115–131.
1971 Ecology, spacing mechanisms and adaptive behavior in aboriginal land tenure. In *Land tenure in the Pacific*, edited by Ron Crocombe, pp. 334–361. Oxford Univ. Press, Melbourne.
1972 *Human evolution*, Rand McNally, Chicago.
1975 *Human evolution* (second ed.). Rand McNally, Chicago.
Black, Francis L.
1975 Infectious diseases in primitive societies. *Science 187*:515–518.
Blakely, Robert L.
1971 Comparison of the mortality profiles of Archaic, Middle Mississippian skeletal populations. *American Journal of Physical Anthropology 34*(1):43–53.
Blanton, Richard E.
1972 Prehispanic adaptation in the Ixtapalapa region, Mexico. *Science 175*:1317–1326.
Borah, W.
1964 *America as model: The demographic impact of European emphasis upon the non-European world.* XXXV Congreso International de Americanistas, Mexico, 1962. Actas y Memorias, Vol. 3, Mexico, pp. 381–382.
Boserup, Ester
1965 *The conditions of agricultural growth.* Aldine, Chicago.
Boughey, A. S.
1968 *Ecology of populations.* Macmillan, New York.
Bourliére, Francois
1963 Observations on the ecology of some large African mammals. In *African ecology and human evolution*, edited by F. C. Howell and F. Bourlière, pp. 43–54. Aldine, Chicago.
Braidwood, R. J.
1951 From cave to village in prehistoric Iraq. *Bulletin of the American Schools of Oriental Research 124*:12.
1958 Near Eastern prehistory. *Science 127*:1419–1430.
1975 *Prehistoric men* (eighth ed.). Scott, Foresman, Glenview, Ill.
Braidwood, R. J., and C. A. Reed
1957 The achievement and early consequences of food production: A consideration of the archaeolog-

ical and natural–historical evidence. *Cold Spring Harbor Symposium on Quantitative Biology* 22:19–31.

Bremer, S., J. D. Singer, and U. Luterbacher
1973 The population density and war proneness of European nations, 1816–1965. *Comparative Political Studies* 6:329–348.

Briggs, M. S.
1957 Town planning from the ancient world to the Renaissance. In *A history of technology* (Vol. 3), edited by E. J. Holmyard, A. R. Hall, and T. I. Williams, pp. 269–299. Clarendon Press, Oxford.

Bronson, B.
1966 Roots and subsistence of the Ancient Maya. *Southwestern Journal of Anthropology* 22:251–279.
1975 The earliest farming: demography as course and consequence. In *Population, ecology, and social evolution*, edited by S. Polgar, pp. 33–78. Mouton, The Hague.
1977 The earliest farming: demography as cause and consequence. In *Origins of agriculture*, edited by C. Reed, pp. 23–48. Mouton, The Hague.

Brothwell, Don R.
1971 Palaeodemography. In *Biological aspects of demography*, edited by W. Brass, pp. 111–130. Taylor and Francis, London.

Brown, L.
1970 Population control among large mammals. In *Population control*, edited by A. Allison, Penguin, Harmondsworth, England.

Brown, P., and H. C. Brookfield
1963 *Struggle for land*. Oxford Univ. Press, Melbourne.

Brown, P., and A. Podolefsky
1976 Population density, agricultural intensity, land tenure, and group size in the New Guinea Highlands. *Ethnology* 15(3(:211–238.

Brush, Stephen B.
1975 The concepts of carrying capacity for systems of shifting cultivations. *American Anthropologist* 77(4):799–811.

Burch, Ernest S., Jr.
1972 The caribou/wild reindeer as human resource. *American Antiquity* 37(3):339–368.

Burton, Benjamin T.
1976 *Human nutrition* (third ed.). McGraw-Hill (Blakiston), New York.

Butzer, K. W.
1959 Environment and human ecology in Egypt during Predynastic and early Dynastic times. *Extrait du Bulletin de la Société de Geographie d'Egypte* 32:43–87.
1971 *Environment and archaeology* (second ed.). Aldine, Chicago.
1976 *Early hydraulic civilization in Egypt, a study in cultural ecology*. Univ. of Chicago Press, Chicago.

Butzer, K. W., and G. L. L. Isaac
1975 *After the australopithecines: stratigraphy, ecology, and culture change in the Middle Pleistocene*. Mouton, The Hague.

Calhoun, J. B.
1962 Population density and social pathology. *Scientific American* 206(2):139–148.
1970 Population. In *Population control*, edited by A. Allison, pp. 110–130. Penguin, Harmondsworth, England.

Campbell, Arthur A.
1974 Beyond the demographic transition. *Demography* 11(4):549–561.

Campbell, B. G.
1974 *Human evolution* (second ed.). Aldine, Chicago.

Carneiro, R. L.
1960 Slash-and-burn agriculture: a closer look at its implications for settlement patterns. In *Men and cultures: Selected papers from the Fifth International Congress of Anthropological and*

Ethnological Sciences, September 1956, edited by Anthony F. C. Wallace, pp. 131–145. Univ. of Pennsylvania Press, Philadelphia.

1967   On the relationship between size of population and complexity of social organization. *Southwestern Journal of Anthropology 23*:234–243.

1970   A theory of the origin of the state. *Science 169*:733–738.

Carneiro R. L., and Daisy Hilse

1966   On determining the probable rate of population growth during the Neolithic. *American Anthropologist 68*(1):179–181.

Carr-Saunders, A. M.

1922   *The population problem*. Oxford Univ. Press, London.

Casteel, R. W.

1972   Two static maximum-population-density models for hunter–gatherers: A first approximation. *World Archaeology 4*:19–40.

1973   *The relationship between population size and carrying capacity in a sample of North American hunter–gatherers*. Paper presented at the Ninth International Congress of Anthropological and Ethnological Sciences, Chicago.

1976   *Human population estimates for hunting and gathering groups based upon net primary production dates: examples from the Central Desert of Baja California*. Paper presented at the annual meeting of the Southwestern Anthropological Association, San Francisco.

1979a Estimated population density on the island of Hokkaido: A test of the Pmaa(2) model. *Asian Perspectives*, in press.

1979b Relationships between surface area and population size: A cautionary note. *American Antiquity 44*:803–807.

Chang, K. C.

1970   The beginnings of agriculture in the Far East. *Antiquity 44*:175–185.

1977   The continuing quest for China's origins, I. Early farmers in China. *Archaeology 30*:116–123.

Childe, V. G.

1936   *Man makes himself* (first ed.). Watts, London.

1950   The urban revolution. *Town Planning Review 21*:3–17.

1951   *Man makes himself* (third ed.). Watts, London.

Chmielewski, W.

1968   Early and Middle Paleolithic sites near Arkin, Sudan. In *The prehistory of Nubia*, (Vol. 1), edited by F. Wendorf, pp. 110–147. Fort Burgwin Research Center and Southern Methodist Univ. Press, Dallas.

Chorley, R. J.

1964   Geography and analog theory. *Annals of the Association of American Geographers 54*:127–13.

Chow, M. M., C.-K. Hu, and Y.-C. Lee

1965   Mammalian fossils associated with the hominid skull cap of Lantian. *Scientia Sinica 14*:1037–1048.

Clark, G.

1954   *Excavations at Star Carr*. Cambridge Univ. Press, London and New York.

1969   *Archaeology and society*. Barnes and Noble, New York.

1972   *Star Carr: A case study in bioarchaeology*. Addison-Wesley Modular Publications, No. 10, pp. 1–42.

Clark, J. Desmond

1967   The middle Acheulian occupation site at Latamne, northern Syria. *Quaternaria 9*:1–68.

1969   *Kalambo Falls prehistoric site* (Vol. 1). Cambridge Univ. Press, London and New York.

1970   *The prehistory of Africa*. Praeger, New York.

1971a Human behavioral differences in southern Africa during the Late Pleistocene. *American Anthropologist 73*:(5):1211–1236.

1971b A re-examination of the evidence for agricultural origins in the Nile Valley. *Proceedings of the Prehistoric Society 37*:34–79.

1975 A comparison of the late Acheulian industries of Africa and the Middle East. In *After the australopithecines,* edited by K. W. Butzer and G. L. L. Isaac, pp. 605–660. Mouton, The Hague.

Clarke, D. L.
1972 Models and paradigms in contemporary archaeology. In *Models in archaeology,* edited by D. L. Clarke, pp. 1–61. Methuen, London.

Clutton-Brock, Juliet
1976 The historical background to domestication. *International Zoo Yearbook 16:*240–244.

Coale, Ansley
1974 The history of human population. *Scientific American 231*(3):41–51.

Cockburn, T. Aidan
1971 Infectious disease in ancient populations. *Current Anthropology 12:*45–62.

Cohen, M. N.
1975 Population pressure and the origins of agriculture: An archaeological example from the coast of Peru. In *Population, ecology, and social evolution,* edited by S. Polgar pp. 79–121. Mouton, The Hague.
1977 *The food crisis in prehistory.* Yale Univ. Press, New Haven, Conn.

Cole, H. S. D., C. Freeman, M. Jahoda, and K. L. R. Pavitt (editors)
1975 *Models of doom.* University Books, New York.

Collins, Desmond
1969 Culture traditions and environment of early man. *Current Anthropology 10:*267–316.

Colton, H. S.
1932 *A survey of prehistoric sites in the region of Flagstaff, Arizona.* Bureau of American Ethnology, Bulletin No. 104.
1936 The rise and fall of the prehistoric population of northern Arizona. *Science 84:*337–343.
1949 The prehistoric population of the Flagstaff area. *Plateau 22:*21–25.

Conklin, H.C.
1957 *Hanunoo agriculture in the Philippines.* FAO Forestry Development Paper, No. 12. FAO, United Nations, Rome.
1959 Population–land balance under systems of tropical forest agriculture. *Proceedings of the Ninth Congress of the Pacific Science Association, 1957 7:*62.

Cook, S. F.
1946 A reconsideration of shell mounds with respect to population and nutrition. *American Antiquity 12:*51–53.
1972a *Can pottery residues be used as an index to population?* Contributions of the University of California Archaeological Research Facility, No. 14, pp. 17–40.
1972b *Prehistoric demography.* McCaleb Module in Anthropology. Addison-Wesley, Reading, Mass.

Cook, S. F., and R. F. Heizer
1965 The quantitative approach to the relation between population and settlement size. Contributions of the University of California Archaeological Research Facility, No. 64.
1968 Relationship among houses, settlement areas, and population in aboriginal California. In *Settlement archaeology,* edited by K. C. Chang, pp. 79–116. National Press, Palo Alto, Calif.

Cowgill, G. L.
1975 Population pressure as a non-explanation. In Population studies in archaeology and biological anthropology, edited by A. C. Swedlund. *American Antiquity 40*(2):127–131, Memoir 30.

Cowgill, Ursula M.
1962 An agricultural study of the Southern Maya lowlands. *American Anthropologist 64:*273–286.

Damas, D.
1968 The diversity of Eskimo societies. In *Man the hunter,* edited by R. B. Lee and I. DeVore, pp. 111–117. Aldine, Chicago.
1972 The Copper Eskimo. In *Hunters and gatherers,* edited by M. G. Bicchieri, pp. 3–50. Holt, Rinehart and Winston, New York.

David, N.
 1973 On Upper Palaeolithic society, ecology, and technological change: The Noaillian case. In *Man, settlement, and urbanization,* edited by P. J. Ucko, R. Tringham, and G. W. Dimbleby, pp. 277–303. Duckworth, London.

Davis, David E.
 1966 *Integral animal behavior.* Macmillan, New York.
 1972 The regulation of human population. In *Challenging biological problems,* edited by J. A. Behnke, pp. 237–252. Oxford Univ. Press, London and New York.

Davis, Kingsley
 1959 The sociology of demographic behavior. In *Sociology today,* edited by R. K. Merton, L. Broom, and L. S. Cottrell, Jr., pp. 309–333. Basic Books, New York.
 1965 The urbanization of the human population. *Scientific American 213*(2):41–54.
 1974 The migrations of human populations. *Scientific American 231*(3):92–105.

Deane, P.
 1967 *The first industrial revolution.* Cambridge Univ. Press, London and New York.

Deetz, J.
 1965 *The dynamics of stylistic change in Aritcara ceramics.* Illinois Studies in Anthropology, No. 4. Univ. of Illinois Press, Urbana.

Deevey, E. S., Jr.
 1951 Recent textbooks of human ecology. *Ecology 32*(2):347–351.
 1960 The human population. *Scientific American 203*(g):195–204.

DeJong, G. F.
 1972 Patterns of human fertility and mortality. In *The structure of human population,* edited by G. A. Harrison and A. J. Boyce, pp. 32–56. Oxford Univ. Press (Clarendon), London and New York.

De Lumley, H.
 1969 A Palaeolithic camp at Nice. *Scientific American 220*(5):42–50.
 1975 Cultural evolution in France in its palaeoecological setting during the Middle Pleistocene. In *After the australopithecines,* edited by K. W. Butzer and G. L. L. Isaac, pp. 745–808. Mouton, The Hague.

Denham, W. W.
 1974 Population structure, infant transport, and infanticide among Pleistocene and modern hunter-gatherers. *Journal of Anthropological Research 30*:191–198.

Devereux, G.
 1967 *A study of abortion in primitive societies.* Julian Press, New York.

Dickeman, M.
 1975 *Female infanticide and hypergamy.* Paper presented at the 74th annual meeting of the American Anthropological Association, San Francisco.

Dickson, D. B.
 1978 *Tikal, Milpa agriculture and population: A simulation.* Paper presented at the annual meeting of the Society for American Archaeology, Tucson.

Divale, W. J.
 1972 Systematic population control in the Middle and Upper Palaeolithic: Inferences based on contemporary hunter-gatherers. *World Archaeology 4*(2):222–237.

Divale, W. J., and Marvin Harris
 1976 Population, warfare, and the male supremacist complex. *American Anthropologist 78*(3):521–538.

Dobyns, Henry F.
 1966 An appraisal of techniques with a new hemispheric estimate. *Current Anthropology 7*(4):395–416.
 1976 *Native American historical demography. A critical bibliography.* Indiana Univ. Press, Bloomington.

Dorn, H. F.
1966 World population growth: An intentional dilemma. *Science 125*:283-290.
Dornstreich, Mark D.
1972 A comment on Lowland Maya subsistence. *American Anthropologist 74*:776-779.
Douglas, M.
1966 Population control: primitive groups. *British Journal of Sociology 17*:263-273.
Drickamer, L. C.
1974 Social rank, observability, and sexual behaviour of rhesus monkeys (*Macaca mulatta*). *Journal of Reproductive Fertility 37*:117-120.
Dubos, R.
1965 *Man adapting.* Yale Univ. Press, New Haven, Conn.
Dumond, D. E.
1965 Population growth and cultural change. *Southwestern Journal of Anthropology 21*:302-324.
1972 Population growth and political centralization. In *Population growth: Anthropological implications,* edited by B. Spooner, pp. 286-310. MIT Press, Cambridge, Mass.
1973 *Late aboriginal population of the Alaska peninsula.* Paper presented at the 72nd annual meeting of the American Anthropological Association, New Orleans.
1975 The limitation of human population: a natural history. *Science 187*:713-721.
1976a Response to Zubrow. *American Anthropologist 78*:896.
1976b Review of *Prehistoric carrying capacity: A model,* by Ezra B. W. Zubrow. *American Anthropologist 78*:710-711.
Dyson-Hudson, Rada, and E. A. Smith
1978 Human territoriality: an ecological reassessment. *American Anthropologist 80*(1):21-41.
Edmonson, M. S.
1961 Neolithic diffusion rates. *Current Anthropology 2*:71-101.
Ehrlich, P. R., and A. H. Ehrlich
1970 *Population, resources, environment.* Freeman, San Francisco.
Eisenberg, J. F., N. A. Muckenhirn, and R. Rendran
1972 The relation between ecology and social structure in primates. *Science 197*:863-874.
Esche, H., and R. Lee
1975 *Is maximum optimum in human physiology?* Paper presented at the 74th annual meeting of the American Anthropological Association, San Francisco.
Evans, J. D., and C. Renfrew
1968 *Excavations at Saliagos near Antiparos.* Thames and Hudson, London.
Fathauer, G. H.
1954 The structure and causation of Mohave warfare. *Southwestern Journal of Anthropology 10*:97-118.
Fix, A. G.
1975 Fission-fusion and lineal effect: Aspects of the population structure of the Semai Senoi of Malaysia. *American Journal of Physical Anthropology 43*:295-302.
Flannery K.V.
1968 Archaeological systems theory and early Mesopotamia. In *Anthropological archaeology in the Americas,* edited by B. J. Meggers, pp. 67-87. Anthropological Society of Washington, Washington, D.C.
1969 Origins and ecological effects of early domestication in Iran and the Near East. In *The domestication and exploitation of plants and animals,* edited by P. J. Ucko and G. W. Dimbleby, pp. 73-100. Aldine, Chicago.
1971 Archaeological systems theory and early Mesoamerica. In *Man's imprint from the past,* edited by J. Deetz. Little, Brown, Boston.
1972 The cultural evolution of civilizations. *Annual Review of Ecology and Systematics 3*:399-426.
1973 The origins of agriculture. *Annual Review of Anthropology 2*:271-310.

Ford, C. S., and F. A. Beach
1951 *Patterns of sexual behavior.* Harper & Row, New York.
Frankfort, H.
1948 *Kingship and the gods.* Univ. of Chicago Press, Chicago.
1950 Town planning in ancient Mesopotamia. *Town Planning Review 21*:98–115.
1951 *The birth of civilization in the ancient Orient.* Penguin, Baltimore.
Freedman, J. L.
1979 Human reactions to population density. In *Biosocial mechanisms of population regulation,* edited by M. Cohen, R. S. Malpass, and H. G. Klein, Yale Univ. Press, New Haven, Conn.
Freeman, L.
1968 Discussions, Part V. In *Man the hunter,* edited by R. B. Lee and I. DeVore, p. 248. Aldine, Chicago.
1975 Acheulian sites and stratigraphy in Iberia and the Maghreb. In *After the australopithecines,* edited by K. W. Butzer and G. L. L. Isaac, pp. 661–743. Mouton, The Hague.
Freeman, M. M. R.
1970 Not by bread alone: Anthropological perspectives on optimum population. In *The optimum population of Britain,* edited by L. R. Taylor, *Symposia of the Institute of Biology,* No. 19, pp. 139–149. Academic Press, New York.
1973 A social and ecologic analysis of systematic female infanticide. *American Anthropologist 73*(5):1011–1018.
Frejka, Thomas
1973 The prospects for a stationary world population. *Scientific American 228*(3):15–23.
Fried, M. H.
1960 On the evolution of social stratification and the state. In *Culture and history,* edited by S. Diamond, pp. 713–731. Columbia Univ. Press, New York.
Frisch, R. E.
1977 Population, food intake, and fertility. *Science 199*:22–30.
Fussell, G. E.
1958 Growth of food production. In *A history of technology* (Vol. 5), edited by C. Singer, E. J. Holmyard, A. R. Hall, and T. I. Williams, pp. 1–25. London Press, Oxford.
Genovés, S.
1969a Estimation of age and mortality. In *Science in archaeology,* edited by D. Brothwell and E. Higgs, pp. 342–352. Praeger, New York.
1969b Sex determination in earlier man. In *Science in archaeology,* edited by D. Brothwell and E. Higgs, pp. 429–439. Praeger, New York.
Gerald, R. E., and L. R. Binford
1975 On Neolithic diffusion rates. *Current Anthropology 6*:88.
Gibson, McGuire
1973 Population shift and the rise of Mesopotamian civilization. In *The explanation of culture change,* edited by C. Renfrew, pp. 447–463. Duckworth, London.
1974 Violation of fallow and engineered disaster in Mesoptamian civilization, In *Irrigation's impact on Society,* edited by T. E. Downing and McGuire Gibson, pp. 7–19. University of Arizona, Tucson.
1976 By stage and cycle to Sumer. In *The legacy of Sumer,* edited by Denise Schmandt-Besserat, pp. 51–58. Undma Publications, Malibu, Calif.
Gilbert, W. H., Jr.
1944 *Peoples of India.* Smithsonian Institution Publication No. 3767, Washington, D.C.
Gillette, R.
1972 The limits to growth: Hard sell for a computer view of doomsday. *Science 175*:1088–1092.
Gjessing, G.
1975 Socio-archaeology. *Current Anthropology 16*:323–341.

Glass, D. V.
  1965 Introduction, In *Population in prehistory,* edited by D. V. Glass and D. E. C. Eversley, pp.
       1–22. Arnold, London.
Glassow, Michael A.
  1967 Consideration in estimating prehistoric California coastal populations. *American Antiquity*
       32:354–359.
  1978 The concept of carrying capacity in the study of culture process. In *Advances in archaeological*
       method and theory (Vol.1), edited by M. B. Schiffer. Academic Press, New York.
Godelier, M.
  1975 Modes of production, kinship, and demographic structures. In *Marxist analyses and social*
       anthropology, edited by M. Bloch. Wiley, New York.
Gourou, P.
  1966 *The tropical world* (fourth ed.). Ronald Press, New York.
Grantsberg, G.
  1973 Twin infanticide—A cross-cultural test of a materialistic explanation. *Ethos 1*:405–412.
Greene, David Lee, and George Armelagos
  1972 *The Wadi Halfa Mesolithic population.* Research Report No. 11, Department of Anthropology,
       University of Massachusetts, Amherst.
Gross, Daniel R.
  1975 Protein capture and cultural development in the Amazon Basin. *American Anthropologist*
       77(3):526–549.
Hack, John F.
  1942 The changing physical environment of the Hopi Indians of Arizona. *Papers of the Museum of*
       American Archaeology and Ethnology, 35(1).
Haggett, P.
  1966 *Locational analysis in human geography.* St. Martin's, New York.
Hall, Peter
  1966 *The world cities.* McGraw-Hill, New York.
Hall, Richard H.
  1972 *Organizations: Structure and process.* Prentice-Hall, Englewood Cliffs, N.J.
Hallowell, A. I.
  1949 The size of the Algonkin hunting territories: A function of ecological adjustment. *American*
       Anthropologist 51:35–45.
Hammel, E. A.
  1964 Territorial patterning of marriage relationships in a coastal Peruvian village. *American An-*
       thropologist 66(1):67–74.
  1977 The influence of social and geographical mobility on the stability of kinship systems: The
       Serbian case. In *Internal migration: A comparative perspective,* edited by Alan A. Brown and
       E. Neuberger. Academic Press, New York.
Harlan, J. R.
  1967 A wild wheat harves in Turkey. *Archaeology 20*:197–201.
  1971 Agricultural origins: Centers and noncenters. *Science 174*:468–474.
  1975 *Crops of man.* American Society of Agronomy, Madison, Wis.
  1977 The origins of cereals agriculture in the Old World. In *Origins of agriculture,* edited by C. A.
       Reed, pp. 357–384. Mouton, The Hague.
Harlan, J. R., and D. Zohary
  1966 Distribution of wild wheats and barley. *Science 153*:1074–1080.
Harner, Michael J.
  1970 Population pressure and the social evolution of agriculturalists. *Southwestern Journal of An-*
       thropology 26:67–86.

Harpending, H.
1976 Regional variation in !Kung populations. In *Kalahari hunter-gatherers*, edited by R. B. Lee and I. DeVore, pp. 152–165. Harvard Univ. Press, Cambridge, Mass.

Harpending, H., and J. Bertram
1975 Human population dynamics in archaeological time: Some simple models. In Population studies in archaeology and biological anthropology: *A symposium*, edited by A. C. Swedlund, pp. 82–91. *American Antiquity 40*(2), Part 2, Memoir 30.

Harris, Marvin
1971 *Culture, man and nature*. Crowell, New York.
1972 Warfare old and new. *Natural History*.
1977 *Cannibals and kings: The origins of cultures*. Random House, New York.

Harrison, G. A., G. S. Weiner, G. M. Tanner, and N. A. Barnicot
1964 *Human biology*. Oxford Univ. Press, London and New York.

Harrison, Richard J.
1967 *Reproduction and man*. Norton, New York.

Hassan, Fekri, A.
1972 *Population dynamics and the beginning of domestication in the Nile Valley*. Paper read at the 71st annual meeting of the American Anthropological Association, Toronto.
1973 On mechanisms of population growth during the Neolithic. *Current Anthropology 14*(5):535–540.
1974 Population growth and cultural evolution. *Reviews in Anthropology 1:*205–212.
1975a Determinants (erroneously printed as "etermination") of the size, density, and growth rates of hunting-gathering populations. In *Human ecology, and evolution*, edited by Steven Polgar, pp. 27–52. Mouton, The Hague.
1975b *Demographic variables and early urbanization in southern Mesopotamia*. Paper presented at the Cambridge Archaeology Seminar, 1975, Cambridge, Mass.
1976 Diet, nutrition, and agricultural origins in the Near East. In *Origine de l'élevage et de la domestication*, edited by E. Higgs, pp. 227–247. IX ᵉ Congrès Union Internationale des Sciences Préhistoriques et protohistoriques, Nice.
1977 The dynamics of agricultural origins in Palestine: A theoretical model. In *Agricultural origins*, edited by C. Reed. Mouton, The Hague.
1978a Archaeological explorations of the Siwa Oasis. *Current Anthropology 19*(1):146–148.
1978b Demographic archaeology. In *Advances in archaeological method and theory*. (Vol. 1), edited by M. Schiffer, pp. 49–103. Academic Press, New York.
1978c *Prehistoric studies of northern Egypt*. A report to the National Science Foundation, Washington State University, Pullman, Washington.
1978d Sediments in archaeology: Methods and implications for environmental and cultural analysis. *Journal of Field Archaeology 5:*197–213.
1979a Archaeological explorations in Baharia Oasis. *Current Anthropology 20:*806.
1979b Demography and archaeology. *Annual Review of Anthropology 8:*137–160.
1979c Prehistoric settlements along the main Nile. In *The Sahara and the Nile*, edited by M. Marins and H. Faure, pp. 421–450.
1980 The growth and regulation of human populations. In *Biosocial mechanisms of population regulation*, edited by M. N. Cohen, R. S. Malpass, and H. G. Klein, pp. 305–319. Yale Univ. Press, New Haven, Conn.

Haviland, William A.
1972 Family size, prehistoric population estimates and the ancient Maya. *American Antiquity 37*(1):135–139.

Hawley, A. H.
1973 Ecology and population. *Science 179:*1196–1204

Hayden, B.
1972 Population control among hunter/gatherers. *World Archaeology 4*(2):205–221.

1975 The carrying capacity dilemma. *American Antiquity 40*, Mem. 30:205–221.

1979 Research and development back in the Stone Age: Technological transitions among hunter-gatherers. M. on file with author.

Haynes, C. V., Jr.

1969 The earliest Americans. *Science 166*:709–715.

1970 Geochronology of man—mammoth sites and their bearing on the origin of the Llano complex. In *Pleistocene and Recent environments of the central Great Plains*, pp. 77–92. Univ. of Kansas Press, Lawrence.

1971 Time, environment, and early man. *Arctic Anthropology 8*:3–14.

Helbaek, H.

1959 Domestication of food plants in the Old World. *Science 130*:365–372.

Henneberg, M.

1976 Reproductive possibilities and estimation of the biological dynamics of earlier populations. In *The demographic evolution of human populations*, edited by R. H. Ward and K. M. Weiss, pp. 41–48. Academic Press, New York.

Henry, D. O.

1973 The Natufian of Palestine: Its material culture and ecology. Unpublished Ph.D. dissertation, Southern Methodist Univ., Dallas.

Henry, L.

1961 Some data on natural fertility. *Eugenics Quarterly 8*:81–91.

Hickerson, H.

1970 *The Chippewa and their neighbors: A study in ethnohistory*. Holt, Rinehart and Winston, New York.

Higham, C. F. W.

1977 *Economic changes in prehistoric Thailand*. In *Origins of agriculture*, edited by C. A. Reed, pp. 385–412. Mouton, The Hague.

Hill, James N.

1970 *Broken K Pueblo*. Anthropological papers of the University of Arizona, No. 18. Univ. of Arizona Press, Tucson.

Hill, Jane H.

1972 *Language acquisition and ancient human population structures*. Paper presented at the 71st annual meeting of the American Anthropological Association, Toronto.

1978 Language contact systems and human adaption. *Journal of Anthropological Research 34*:1–26.

Himes, N. E.

1963 *Medical history of contraception*. Gamut Press, New York.

Ho, Ping-ti

1977 The indigenous origins of Chinese agriculture. In *Origins of agriculture*, edited by C. A. Reed, pp. 413–484. Mouton, The Hague.

Hole, Frank

1966 Investigating the origins of Mesopotamian civilization. *Science 153*:605–611.

Hole, F., K. V. Flannery, and J. A Neely

1969 *Human ecology of the Deh Luran Plain*. Museum of Anthropology, Univ. of Michigan.

Hole, F., and R. F. Heizer

1973 *An introduction to prehistory*. Holt, Rinehart and Winston, New York.

Hooton, E. A.

1930 *The Indians of Pecos Pueblo*. Yale Univ. Press, New Haven, Conn.

Howell, F. C.

1966 Observations on the earlier phases of the European Lower Palaeolithic. *American Anthropologist 68*:88–201.

Howell, N.

1973 The feasibility of demographic studies in "anthropological" populations. In *Methods and theories of anthropological genetics,* edited by M. H. Crawford and P. I. Workman, pp. 249–262. Univ. of New Mexico Press, Albuquerque.

1976a The population of the Dobe area !Kung. In *Kalahari hunter-gatherers,* edited by R. B. Lee and I. DeVore, pp. 137–151. Harvard Univ. Press, Cambridge, Mass.

1976b Toward a uniformitarian theory of human palaeodemography. In *The demographic evolution of human populations,* edited by R. H. Ward and K. M. Weiss, pp. 25–40. Academic Press, London.

1979a *Demography of the Dobe !Kung.* Academic Press, New York.

1979b Review of Charles D. Laughlin, and Ivan A. Brady, Extinction and survival in human populations. *Science 203*(4386):1235–1236.

Howell, R. W.
1975 Wars without conflict. In *War, its causes and correlates,* edited by M. A. Nettleship *et al.* Mouton, The Hague.

Howells, W. W.
1960 Estimating population numbers through archaeological and skeletal remains. In *The application of quantitative methods in archaeology,* edited by R. F. Heizer and S. F. Cook, pp. 158–180. Viking Fund Publications in Anthropology, No. 28.

1966 Population distances: Biological, linguistic, geographical and environmental. *Current Anthropology 7:*531–535.

Hulse, F. S.
1957 Linguistic barriers to gene flow: The blood groups of the Yakima, Okonagon and Swinomish Indians. *American Journal of Physical Anthropology 15:*235–246.

Irving, W. N., and C. R. Harington
1973 Upper Pleistocene radiocarbon-dated artifacts from the northern Yukon. *Science 179:*335–340.

Isaac, Glynn LL.
1969 Studies of early cultures in East Africa. *World Archaeology 1*(1):1–28.

1972 Early phases of human behaviour: Models in Lower Pleistocene archaeology. In *Models in archaeology,* edited by D. L. Clarke, pp. 167–199. Methuen, London.

Isaac, G. LL., and E. R. McCown
1976 *Human origins—Louis Leakey and the East African evidence.* Benjamin, Menlo Park, Calif.

Jacobsen, T., and R. M. Adams
1958 Salt and silt in ancient Mesopotamia. *Science 128:*1251–1258.

Jain, A. K., *et al.*
1970 Demographic aspects of amenorrhea. *Demography 7:*255–271.

Jamieson, P. L.
1971 A demographic and comparative analysis of the Albany Mounds (Illinois) Hopewell skeletons. In *The Indian mounds at Albany,* edited by E. B. Herold, pp. 107–153. Davenport Museum Anthropological Papers, No. 1., Davenport, Iowa.

Jensen, W. A., and F. B. Salisbury
1972 *Botany: An ecological approach.* Wadsworth, Belmont, Calif.

Jochim, M. A.
1976 *Hunter-gatherer subsistence and settlement—A predictive model.* Academic Press, New York.

Johnson, G. A.
1972 A test of the utility of central place theory in archaeology. In *Man, settlement, and urbanization,* edited by P. J. Ucko, R. Tringham, and G. W. Dimbleby, pp. 769–785. Duckworth, London.

Johnston, F. E., and C. E. Snow
1961 The assessment of the age and sex of the Indian Knoll skeletal population: Demographic and methodological aspects. *American Journal of Physical Anthropology 19:*237–244.

Jolly, A.
1972 *The evolution of primate behavior.* Macmillan, New York.

Jones, Rhys
1973 Emerging picture of Pleistocene Australians. *Nature 246:*278–303.

Katchadourian, H. A., and D. T. Lunde
1972 *Fundamentals of human sexuality.* Holt, Rinehart and Winston, New York.
Katz, D., and R. L. Kahn
1969 Common characteristics of open systems. In *Systems thinking,* edited by F. E. Emery, pp. 59–69. Penguin, Baltimore.
Katz, S. H.
1972 Biological factors in population control. In *Population growth: Anthropological implications,* edited by V. Spooner, pp. 351–369. MIT Press, Cambridge, Mass.
Kees, Herman
1961 *Ancient Egypt: A cultural topography,* edited by T. G. H. James and translated from German by I. F. D. Morrow. Univ. of Chicago Press, Chicago.
Kellum, Barbara A.
1974 Infanticide in England in the later Middle Ages. *History of Childhood Quarterly 1*:367–388.
Kelsall, J. P.
1968 *The caribou.* Department of Indian Affairs and Northern Development, Canadian Wildlife Service, Ottawa.
Kendeigh, S. Charles
1961 *Animal ecology.* Prentice-Hall, Englewood Cliffs, N.J.
Klein, R. G.
1969 *Man and culture in the Late Pleistocene: A case study.* Chandler, San Francisco.
1973 *Ice-age hunters of the Ukraine.* Univ. of Chicago Press, Chicago.
Klepinger, L.
1979 Palaeodemography of the Valdivia III phase at Real Alto, Ecuador. *American Antiquity 44*:305–308.
Knodel, J.
1977 Breast feeding and population growth. *Science 198*:1111–1124.
Kohler, T. A.
1978 Ceramic breakage rate simulation: Population size and the southeastern chiefdom. *Newsletter of Computer Archaeology 14*:1–20.
Kralj-Cercek, L.
1956 The influence of food, body build, and social origin on the age of menarche. *Human Biology 28*:393–406.
Kramer, C.
1978 Estimating prehistoric populations: An ethnoarchaeological approach. Colloque International C.N.R.S. No. 580, *L' Archéologie de l' Iraq du début de l' Époque Néolithique á 33 avant notre Ere-Perspective et limites de l'Interpretation anthropologique des documents.*
Kroeber, A. L.
1939 Cultural and natural areas of native North America. *University of California Publications in American Archaeology and Ethnology 38.*
1953 *Cultural and natural areas of native North America.* Univ. of California Press, Berkeley.
Krzywicki, L.
1934 *Primitive society and its vital statistics.* Macmillan, London.
Kunitz, S. J.
1976 Fertility, mortality, and social organization. *Human Biology 43*:361–377.
Kunstadter, P.
1972 Demography, ecology, social structure, and settlement patterns. In *The structure of human populations,* edited by A. J. Boyce, pp. 851–877. Oxford Univ. Press, London and New York.
Lack, D.
1954 *The natural regulation of animal numbers.* Oxford Univ. Press, (Clarendon), London and New York.
Lamberg-Karlovsky, C. C., and J. A. Sabloff
1974 *The rise and fall of civilizations.* Cummings, Menlo Park, Calif.

Lange, F. W.
1971 Marine resources: Available subsistence alternative for the prehistoric Lowland Maya. *American Anthropologist 73*:619–639.

Langer, W. L.
1963 Europe's initial population explosion. *American Historical Review 69*:1–17.
1972 Checks on population growth: 1750–1850. *Scientific American 226*(2):92–99.
1974 Infanticide: A historical survey. *History of Childhood Quarterly 1*:353–365.

Laughlin, W. S.
1968 Guide to human population studies. *Arctic Anthropology 5*:32–47.
1972 Ecology and population structure—the arctic. In *The structure of human populations*, edited by C. A. Harrison and A. J. Boyce, pp. 379–392. Oxford Univ. Press (Clarendon), London and New York.

Leathem, James H.
1958 The effects of aging on reproduction. In *The endocrinology of reproduction*, edited by Joseph Thomas Belardo. New York.

LeBlanc, Steven
1971 An addition to Naroll's suggested floor area and settlement population relationship. *American Antiquity 36*(2):210–211.

Lee, R. B.
1968 What hunters do for a living, or how to make out on scarce resources. In *Man the Hunter*, edited by R. B. Lee and I. DeVore, pp. 30–48. Aldine, Chicago.
1969 !Kung Bushmen subsistence—an input–output analysis. In *Environment and cultural behavior*, edited by A. P. Vayda, pp. 47–79. Natural History Press, New York.
1972a !Kung spatial organization: An ecological and historical perspective. *Human Ecology 1*:125–147.
1972b Population growth and the beginnings of sedentary life among the !Kung Bushmen. In *Population growth: Anthropological implications*, edited by B. Spooner, pp. 327–350. MIT Press, Cambridge, Mass.
1976 !Kung spatial organization. In *Kalahari hunter-gatherers*, edited by R. B. Lee and I. DeVore, pp. 73–97. Harvard Univ. Press, Cambridge, Mass.
1978 *Lactation, ovulation, infanticide, and women's work: A study of hunter-gatherer population regulation.* Paper presented at the Hudson Symposium on Biosocial Mechanisms of Population Regulation, State University of New York, Plattsburgh.

Lee, R. B., and I. DeVore (editors)
1968a *Man the hunter* Aldine, Chicago.
1968b Problems in the study of hunters and gatherers. In *Man the hunter*, edited by R. B. Lee and I. DeVore, pp. 3–12. Aldine, Chicago.

Lehman, R. S.
1977 *Computer simulation and modeling: An introduction.* Lawrence Erlbaum, Hillsdale, N.J.

Leridon, Henri
1977 *Human fertility, the basic components.* The University of Chicago Press, Chicago.

Little, Michael A., and George E. B. Morren, Jr.
1976 *Ecology, energetics and human variability.* W. C. Brown, Dubuque, Iowa.

Longacre, W. A.
1976 Population dynamics at the Grasshopper Pueblo, Arizona. In *Demographic anthropology*, edited by E. B. W. Zubrow, pp. 169–184. Univ. of New Mexico Press, Albuquerque.

Lorimer, Frank, *et al.* (editors)
1954 *Culture and human fertility.* UNESCO, Paris.

Lovejoy, C. O.
1971 Methods for the detection of census error in paleodemography. *American Anthropologist 73*:101–109

Lubell, David, Fekri A. Hassan, Achilles Gautier, and Jean-Louis Ballais
1976 The Capsian Escargotières. *Science 191*:910–920.

Lumley, H. de
    1969   A Paleolithic camp at Nice. *Scientific American 220*(5):42–50.
Lumley, H. de, M. de Lumley, J.-C. Miskovsky, J. Renault-Miskovsky, and M. Girard
    1976   Grotte du Vallonnet. In *Sites Paléolithiques de la région de Nice et Grottes de Grimaldi,* edited
            by H. de Lumley and L. Banral, pp. 93–103. IXe Congrès Union Internationale des Sciences
            Préhistoriques et Protohistoriques, Nice.
Mabro, Robert
    1974   *The Egyptian economy 1952–1972.* Oxford Univ. Press (Clarendon), London and New York.
McArthur, Norma
    1970   The demography of primitive populations. *Science 167*:1097–1101.
McCarthy, F., and M. McArthur
    1960   The food quest and the time factor in aboriginal economic life. In *Records of the Australian–
            American expedition to Arnhem Land* (Vol. 2), edited by C. P. Mountford. Melbourne Univ.
            Press, Melbourne.
McKinley, Kelton
    1971   Survivorship in gracile and robust australopithecines: A demographic comparison and a pro-
            posed birth model. *American Journal of Physical Anthropology 34*(3):417–426.
McMichael, E. V.
    1960   Towards the estimation of prehistoric populations. *Indiana Academy of Sciences, Proceedings
            69*:76–82.
MacNeish, R. S.
    1977   The beginning of agriculture in Peru. In *Orgins of agriculture,* edited by C. A. Reed, pp.
            753–802. Mouton, The Hague.
Maisel, H., and G. Gnugnoli
    1972   *Simulation of discrete stochastic systems.* SRA, Chicago.
Mallory, F. F., and R. J. Brooks
    1978   Infanticide and other reproductive strategies in the collared lemming, *Dicrostonyx groenlan-
            dicus. Nature 273*:144–146.
Malthus, T. R.
    1826   *An essay on the principle of population* (sixth ed.; first published 1798). London.
Mangelsdorf, P. C.
    1974   *Corn, its origin, evolution and improvement.* Harvard Univ. Press, Cambridge, Mass.
Mann, A. E.
    1974   *Australopithecine demographic patterns.* Paper read at the Conference on African Hominidae
            of the Plio-Pleistocene: Evidence, Problems, and Strategies. Wenner-Gren Foundation for
            Anthropological Research.
    1975   *Some paleodemographic aspects of the South African australopithecines.* Univ. of Pennsyl-
            vania Publications in Anthropology, No. 1.
Maqrizi, T. A.
    n.d.   *Al-Khitat.* Reprinted from original Bulaq text (1270 A.D.) by Dar et-Tahrir lil-Tiba's wa-
            Nashr, Cairo.
Marcus, J.
    1976   The size of the early Mesoamerican village. In *The early Mesoamerican village,* edited by K.
            Flannery, pp. 79–89. Academic Press, New York.
Marks, A. E.
    1968   The Khormusan: An upper Pleistocene industry in Sudanese Nubia. In *The prehistory of Nubia*
            (Vol. 1), edited by F. Wendorf, pp. 315–391. Fort Burgwin Research Center and Southern
            Methodist Univ. Press, Dallas.
Marshall, L.
    1960   !Kung Bushmen bands. *Africa 30*:325–355.
Martin, John F.
    1972   On the estimation of the sizes of local groups in a hunting–gathering environment. *American
            Anthropologist 75*(5):1448–1468.

Martin, P.
1973   The discovery of America. *Science 179:*969-974.
Massat, C.
1971   Erreurs systematiques dans la détermination de l'âge par les sutures craniennes. *Bull. Mém. Soc. Anthropol. Paris,* Sér. 12:85-105.
1973a   La démographie des populations inhumées: essai de paléodemographie. *L'Homme 13:*95-131.
Meadows, D. H., D. L. Meadows, J. Randers, and W. W. Behrens III
1972   *The limits to growth.* University Books, New York.
Meek, R. L.
1971   *Marx and Engels on the population bomb* (second ed.). Ramparts, Berkely, Calif.
Meggitt, J. J.
1962   *Desert people.* Angus and Robertson, Sydney.
Meighan, C. W.
1959   The Little Harbor Site, Catalina Island. An example of ecological interpretation in archaeology. *American Antiquity 24*(4):383-405.
Mellars, P. A.
1972   The character of the Middle-Upper Palaeolithic transition in southwest France. In *Man, settlement and urbanization,* edited by P. J. Ucko, R. Tringham, and G. W. Dimbleby, p. 255. Duckworth, London.
Mobley, C. M.
1980   Demographic characteristics of Pecos Indians. *American Antiquity 45:*518-530.
Mongait, A. L.
1961   *Archaeology in the U.S.S.R.* Penguin, Baltimore.
Mooney, J.
1910   Population. In *Handbook of American Indians north of Mexico,* edited by F. W. Hodge. Bureau of American Ethnology, Bulletin No. 30, pp. 286-287, Part 2.
1928   The aboriginal population of America north of Mexico. In F. R. Swanton (editor), *Smithsonian Miscellaneous Collections 80:*1-40.
Moore, James A., A. C. Swedlund, and George J. Armelagos
1975   The use of life table in paleodemography In Population studies in *archaeology and biological anthropology:* A symposium, edited by A. C. Swedlund. *American Antiquity 40*(2):57-70, Part 2, Memoir 30.
Morris, C., and D. E. Thompson
1970   Huanuco Viejo: An Inca administrative center. *American Antiquity 35:*344-362.
Movius, H. L.
1948   The Lower Palaeolithic cultures of southern and eastern Asia. *Transactions of the American Philosophical Society 38*(4):329-420.
Müller-Beck, Hans
1961   Prehistoric Swiss lake dwellers. *Scientific American 205*(6):138-147.
Mulvaney, D. J.
1976   The Pleistocene occupation of Australia. In *Le premier peuplement de l'archipel Nippon et des iles du Pacifique: chronologie, paléogéographie, industries,* edited by C. Serizawa, pp. 28-29. IXᵉ Congrès, Union Internationale des Sciences Préhistoriques et Protohistoriques, Nice.
Mumford, Lewis
1956   *The transformations of man.* Harper & Row, New York.
Murdock, G. P.
1934   *Our primitive contemporaries.* Macmillan, New York.
Murphy, R. F.
1970   Basin ethnography and ecological theory. In *Language and cultures of western North America,* edited by E. H. Swanson, Jr. Idaho State University, Pocatello.

Nag, Moni

1962 *Factors affecting fertility in non-industrial societies: A cross-cultural study.* Human Relations Area Files Press, New Haven, Conn.

1972 Sex, culture and human fertility: India and the United States. *Current Anthropology 13*:231–237.

1975 Marriage and kinship in relation to human fertility. In *Population and social organization,* edited by Moni Nag. Mouton, The Hague.

Nag, M., B. N. F. White, and R. C. Peet

1978 An anthropological approach to the study of the economic value of children in Java and Nepal. *Current Anthropology 19*:293–306.

Naroll, R.

1956 A preliminary index of social development. *American Anthropologist 68*:687–715.

1962 Floor area and settlement population. *American Antiquity 27*:587–589.

Narr, K. J.

1963 On Neolithic diffusion rates. *Current Anthropology 4*:210–211.

Nash, J., and M. Nash

1963 Marriage, family, and population growth in Upper Burma. *Southwestern Journal of Anthropology 19*(3):251–266.

Neel, J. V.

1970 Lessons from "primitive" people. *Science 170*:815–822.

Nemeskéri, J.

1972 Some comparisons of Egyptian and early Eurasian demographic data. *Journal of Human Evolution 1*:171–186.

Nerlove, Sara B.

1974 Women's workload and infant feeding practices: A relationship with demographic implications. *Ethnology 13*(2):207–214.

Netting, R. M.

1972 *The ecological approach in cultural study.* McCaleb Module. Addison-Wesley, Reading, Mass.

Newell, R. R.

1973 The post-glacial adaptations of the indigenous population of the Northwest European Plain. In *The Mesolithic in Europe,* edited by S. K. Kozlowski. University Press, Warsaw.

Nissen, Hans Jorg

1972 The city wall of Uruk. In *Man, settlement and urbanism,* edited by P. J. Ucko, R. Tringham, and G. W. Dimbleby. Duckworth, London.

Norbeck, Stig

1971 Urban allometric growth. *Geografiska Annaler 32*:54–67.

Nougier, L. R.

1954 Essai sur le peuplement préhistorique de la France. *Population 9*:241–274.

Nurge, Ethel

1973 *Abortion in the Pleistocene.* Paper presented at the Ninth International Congress of Anthropological and Ethnological Sciences, Chicago.

1975 Spontaneous and induced abortion in human and non-human primates. In *Being female: reproduction, power and change,* pp. 25–35. Mouton, The Hague.

Odum, E. P.

1959 *Fundamentals of ecology.* Saunders, Philadelphia.

Odum, H. T.

1971 *Environment, power and society.* Wiley, New York.

Owen, R. C.

1965 The patrilocal band: A linguistically and culturally hybrid social unit. *American Anthropologist 67*:675–690.

Palkovich, Ann M.
   1978   *A model of the dimensions of mortality and its application to palaeodemography.* Unpublished
         Ph.D. dissertation, Northwestern University, Evanston, Ill.
Palmer, L. J.
   1941   *Animals and plant resources of Alaska.* U.S. Department of Fish and Wildlife Resources,
         Wildlife Leaflet No. 176.
Parsons, J. R.
   1971   *Prehistoric settlement patterns in the Texcoco region, Mexico.* Museum of Anthropology,
         Memoirs, No. 3, University of Michigan, Ann Arbor.
Patterson, T. C.
   1971   The emergence of food production in central Peru. In *Prehistoric agriculture,* edited by S.
         Struever, pp. 181–207. Natural History Press, New York.
Pearl, Raymond
   1939   *The natural history of population.* Oxford Univ. Press, London and New York.
Perkins, D., Jr., and P. Daly
   1968   A hunter's village in Neolithic Turkey. *Scientific American 219*(5):96–106.
Perrin, E. P., and M. C. Sheps
   1964   Human reproduction: A stochastic process. *Biometrics 20:*28–45.
Perrins, C.
   1970   Bird populations. In *Population control,* edited by A. Allison, pp. 70–92. Penguin, Har-
         mondsworth, England.
Peterson, William
   1975   A demographer's view of prehistoric demography. *Current Anthropology 16*(2):227–246.
Phillips, Patricia
   1972   Population, economy and society in the Chassey Cortaillod-Lagozza cultures. *World Archae-
         ology 4*:41–56.
Pilbeam, D. R.
   1975   Middle Pleistocene hominids. In *After the australopithecines,* edited by K. W. Butzer and G.
         L. L. Isaac, pp. 809–856. Mouton, The Hague.
Plog, Fred
   1975   Demographic studies in southwestern prehistory. In Population studies in archaeology and
         biological anthropology: A symposium, edited by A. C. Swedlund. *American Antiquity
         40*(2):94–103, Memoir 30.
Polgar, S.
   1972   Population history and population policies from an anthropological perspective. *Current An-
         thropology 13*:203–211, 260–262.
Pollard, Helen P., and Gordon C. Pollard
   1975   *A perspective on the nature of demographic systems and cultural change.* Paper presented at
         the 74th annual meeting of the American Anthropological Association, San Francisco.
Pounds, N. J. G., and R. Roome
   1971   Population density in fifteenth-century France and the Low Countries. *Annals of the Associa-
         tion of American Geographers 61*:116–130.
Pressat, Roland
   1971   *Population.* Penguin, Baltimore.
   1972   *Demographic analysis.* Aldine-Atherton, Chicago.
Puleston, D.
   1968   *Brosimum alicastium as a subsistence alternative for the classic Maya of the central lowlands.*
         Unpublished M.A. thesis, Department of Anthropology, Univ. of Pennsylvania, Philadelphia.
Puleston, D. E., and O. S. Puleston
   1971   An ecological approach to the origins of Maya civilization. *Archaeology 24*:330–337.
Radcliffe-Brown, A. R.
   1964   *The Andaman Islanders.* Glencoe, New York.

Rappaport, R. A.
  1968 *Pigs for the ancestors: Ritual in the ecology of a New Guinea people.* Yale Univ. Press, New Haven, Conn.
Rasmussen, Kund
  1932 *Intellectual culture of the Copper Eskimos.* Report of the Fifth Thule Expedition, 1921-1924, g, Cy/dendaiske Boghandel, Copenhagen.
Rathje, W. L.
  1971 The origin and development of Lowland classic Maya civilization. *American Antiquity* 36:275-285.
Read, D. W.
  1978 Towards a formal theory of population size and area of habitation. *Current Anthropology* 19(2):312-317.
Read-Martin, C. E., and D. W. Read
  1975 Australopithecine scavenging and human evolution: An approach from faunal analysis. *Current Anthropology* 16:359-368.
Redman, C. L.
  1977 Man, domestication, and culture in southwestern Asia. In *Origins of agriculture,* edited by C. A. Reed, pp. 523-542. Mouton, The Hague.
  1978 *The rise of civilization: From early farmers to urban society in the ancient Near East.* Freeman, San Francisco.
Reed, C. A.
  1959 Animal domestication in the Near East. *Science 130*:1-11.
  1969 The pattern of animal domestication in the prehistoric Near East. In *Domestication and exploitation of plants and animals,* edited by P. J. Ucko and G. W. Dimbleby, pp. 361-380. Duckworth, London.
Renfrew, Colin
  1972a *The emergence of civilization.* Methuen, London.
  1972b Patterns of population growth in the prehistoric Aegean. In *Man, settlement, and urbanization,* edited by P. J. Ucko, R. Tringham, and G. W. Dimbleby. Duckworth, London.
Renfrew, J. M.
  1973 *Palaeoethnobotany, the prehistoric food plants of the Near East and Europe.* Columbia Univ. Press, New York.
Rice, Don S.
  1978 Population growth and subsistence: Alternatives in tropical lacustrine environment. In *Prehispanic Maya agriculture,* edited by P. D. Harrison and B. L. Turner, pp.35-61. University of New Mexico Press, Albuquerque.
Riches, David
  1974 The Netsilik Eskimo: A special case of selective female infanticide. *Ethnology 13:*351-361.
Rivet, P.
  1924 Langues Ameraines. In *Les Langues du Monde,* edited by A. Meillet and M. Cohen, pp. 597-712. Collection Linguistique, La société de Linguistique de Paris.
Roper, M. K.
  1969 A survey of the evidence for intrahuman killing in the Pleistocene. *Current Anthropology* 10(4): 427-450.
  1975 Evidence of warfare in the Near East from 10,000 to 4300 B.C. In *War, its causes and correlates,* edited by M. A. Nettleship *et al.,* pp. 299-343. Mouton, The Hague.
Rosenblat, A.
  1945 La publication indigena de América desde 1492 nasta la actualidad. Institución Cultural Española, Buenos Aires.
Rostlund, E.
  1952 Freshwater fish and fishing in native North America. *University of California Publications in Geography 9.*

Russell, J. C.
1958 Late ancient and medieval populations. *Trans American Philosophical Society 48*:1–152.
Sahlins, Marshall
1972 *Stone age economics.* Aldine-Atherton, Chicago.
Sanders, W. T.
1965 *Cultural ecology of the Teotihuacán Valley.* Mimeographed Report, Pennslvania State Univ., Department of Sociology and Anthropology, University Park, Pennsylvania.
1968 Hydraulic agriculture, economic symbiosis, and the evolution of states in central Mexico. In *Anthropological archaeology in the Americas,* edited by B. G. Meggers, pp. 88–107. Anthropological Society of Washington, Washington, D.C.
1972 Population, agricultural history, and societal evolution in Mesoamerica. In *Population growth: Anthropological implications,* edited by B. Spooner, pp. 101–153. MIT Press, Cambridge, Mass.
Sanders, W. T., and B. J. Price
1968 *Mesoamerica: The evolution of a civilization.* Random House, New York.
Sapper, C.
1924 Die Zahl und Die Volksdichte der Indianischen Bevölkerung in Amerika vor Der Conquista und in Der Gegenwart. *Proceedings of the 21st International Congress of Americanists,* Part 1, The Hague.
Sauvy, Alfred
1969 *General theory of population* (trans.). Basic Books, New York.
Saxon, E. C.
1976 The evolution of domestication: A reappraisal of the Near Eastern and North African evidence. In *Origne d'Élevage et de la domestication,* edited by E. Higgs, pp. 180–226. IX^{e}Congrès, Union Internationale des Sciences Préhistoriques et Protohistoriques, Nice.
Schalk, R. F.
1977 The structure of an anadromous fish resource. In *For theory building in archaeology,* edited by L. Binford. Academic Press, New York.
Schaller, G. B.
1963 *The mountain gorilla: Ecology and behavior.* Univ. of Chicago Press, Chicago.
Schiffer, M. B.
1976 *Behavioral archaeology.* Academic Press, New York.
Schrire, C., and W. L. Steiger
1973 Population control among hunter–gatherers. *Centre de Recherches Mathematique, Tech. Report 351.* Université, de Montréal, Montréal.
1974 A matter of life and death: An investigation into the practice of female infanticide in the arctic. In *Man 9*:161–184.
Schwartz, Douglas W.
1956 Demographic changes in the early periods of Cohonina prehistory. In *Prehistoric settlement patterns in the New World,* edited by G. R. Willey. Viking Fund Publications in Anthropology, No. 23.
Sengel, R. A.
1973 Discussion and criticisms. *Current Anthropology 14*(5):540–542.
Service, E.
1962 *Primitive social organization: An evolutionary perspective.* Random House, New York.
1966 *The hunters.* Prentice-Hall, Englewood Cliffs, N.J.
1975 *Origins of the state and civilization, the process of cultural evolution.* Norton, New York.
Shannon, R. E.
1975 *Systems simulation.* Prentice-Hall, Englewood Cliffs, N.J.
Shantis, S. B., and W. W. Behrens III
1973 Population control mechansims in a primitive agricultural society. In *Toward global equilib-*

rium: Collected papers, edited by D. L. Meadows and S. H. Meadows. Wright-Allen Press, Cambridge, Mass.

Shawcross, Wilfred
1967 An investigation of prehistoric diet and economy on a coastal site at Galatea Bay, New Zealand. *Proceedings of the Prehistoric Society 33*:107–131.

Sherratt, A. G.
1972 Socio-economic and demographic models for the Neolithic and Bronze Ages of Europe. In *Models in archaeology,* edited by D. Clarke, pp. 479–542. Methuen, London.

Skellam, J. G.
1971 Human population dynamics considered from an ecological standpoint. In *Biological aspects of demography,* edited by W. Brass, pp. 131–146. Taylor and Francis, London.

Slobodkin, L. B.
1961 *Growth and regulation of animal populations.* Holt,, Rinehart and Winston, New York.

Slobodkin, L. B., and S. Richman
1960 Calories per gram in species of animals. *Nature 191:*299.

Smith, J. M.
1978 *Models in ecology.* Cambridge Univ. Press, London and New York.

Smith, M. G.
1972 *Complexity, size and urbanization.* Reprint 185. Reprinted from *Man, settlement and urbanism,* edited by P. J. Ucko, R. T. Tringham, and G. W. Dimbleby. Duckworth, London.

Smith, P. E. L.
1976 *Food production and its consequences.* Cummings, Menlo Park, Calif.

Smith, P. E. L., and T. C. Young
1972 The evolution of early agriculture and culture in greater Mesopotamia: A trial model. In *Population growth: Anthropological implications,* edited by B. Spooner, pp. 1–59. MIT Press, Cambridge, Mass.

Sohary, Daniel
1969 The progenitors of wheat and barley in relation to domestication and agricultural dispersal in the Old World. In *The domestication and exploitation of plants and animals,* edited by P. J. Ucko and G. W. Dimbleby, pp. 47–66. Aldine, Chicago.

Spengler, Joseph G.
1966 Values and fertility analysis. *Demography 3*(1):109–131.

Spooner, Brian (editor)
1972 *Population growth: Anthropological implications.* MIT Press, Cambridge, Mass.

Spuhler, J. N.
1959 Physical anthropology and demography. In *The study of population,* edited by Philip M. Hauser and O. D. Duncan, pp. 728–758. Univ. of Chicago Press, Chicago.

Steward, J. H.
1936 The economic and social basis of primitive bands. In *Essays in honour of A. L. Kroeber.* Univ. of California Press, Berkely.
1937 Ecological aspects of southwestern society. *Anthropos 32:*87–104.
1938 Basin–plateau sociopolitical groups. Bureau of American Ethnology, Bulletin No. 120.
1945 The changing American Indian. In *The science of man in the world crisis,* edited by R. Linton, pp. 282–305. Columbia University Press, New York.
1949 *Cultural causality and law: a trial formulation of the development of early civilizations.* Bobbs-Merrill Reprint Series in Social Sciences, No. A-216. Reprinted from *American Anthropologist 51*:1–27.
1955 *Theory of culture change.* Univ. of Illinois Press, Urbana.

Stewart, T. D.
1962 Comments on the reassessment of the Indian Knoll skeletons. *American Journal of Physical Anthropology 20*:143–148.

1973 *The people of North America.* Scribner's, New York.
Stini, William A.
1971 Evolutionary implications of changing nutritional patterns in human populations. *American Anthropologist 73*:1019–1030.
Storey, Rebecca
1980 *Chiefdom society in demographic perspective.* Paper presented at the 45th annual meeting of the Society for American Archaeology, Philadelphia.
Stott, D. H.
1962 Cultural and natural checks on population growth. In *Environmental and cultural behavior: Ecological studies in cultural anthropology,* edited by Andrew P. Vayda, pp. 90–115. Natural History Press, New York.
Street, John
1969 An evaluation of the concept of carrying capactiy. *Professional Geographer 21*:104–107.
Sussman, Robert W.
1972 Child transport, family size, and increase in human population during the Neolithic. *Current Anthropology 13*:258–259.
Suttles, W.
1962 Variations in habitat and culture on the Northwest Coast. *Proceedings of the 34th International Congress of Americanists.* Verlag Ferdinand Berger, Horn-Vienna, Austria.
1968 Coping with abundance: Subsistence on the Northwest Coast. In *Man the hunter,* edited by R. B. Lee and I. DeVore, pp. 56–68. Aldine, Chicago.
Swedlund, A. C., and G. J. Armelagos
1976 *Demographic anthropology.* W. C. Brown, Dubuque, Iowa.
Tanner, J. M.
1955 *Growth at adolescence.* Thomas, Springfield, Ill.
Teleki, Geza
1973 The omnivorous chimpanzee. *Scientific American 228*(1):33–42.
Thomas, D. H.
1973 An empirical test for Steward's model of Great Basin settlement patterns. *American Antiquity 38*:155–177.
Thomlinson, Ralph
1965 *Population dynamics.* Random House, New York.
Thompson, F. M. L.
1968 The second agricultural revolution 1815–1880. *Economic History Review 21*:62–77.
Thompson, H. P.
1966 A technique using anthropological and biological data. *Current Anthropology 7*:417–424.
Tietze, Christopher, and Deborah A. Dawson
1973 *Induced abortion: A factbook.* Reports on Population Family Planning, No. 14. Population Council, New York.
Todd, T. W.
1927 Skeletal records of mortality. *Scientific Monthly 24*:481–496.
Townsend, Patrica K.
1971 New Guinea sago gatherers. *Ecology of Food and Nutrition 1*:19–24.
Trowel, M. A.
1961 *The ethnobotany of pre-Columbian Peru.* Aldine, Chicago.
Truswell, A. D., and J. D. L. Hansen
1976 Medical research among the !Kung. In *Kalahari hunter–gatherers,* edited by R. B. Lee and I. DeVore, pp. 166–194. Harvard Univ. Press, Cambridge, Mass.
Turk, Jonathan, Janet T. Wittes, Robert Wittes, and Amos Turk
1975 *Ecosystems, energy, population.* Saunders, Philadelphia.
Turnbull, C. M.
1972 Demography of small-scale societies. In *The structure of human populations,* edited by G. A.

Harrison and A. J. Boyce, pp. 283–312. Oxford Univ. Press (Clarendon), London and New York.

Turner, B. L., II
1974 Prehistoric intensive agriculture in the Maya lowlands. *Science 185*:118–124.

Turner, C. G., and L. Lofgren
1966 Household size of prehistoric Western Pueblo Indians. *Southwestern Journal of Archaeology 22*(1):117–132.

Ubelaker, D. H.
1976a Prehistoric New World population size: Historical review and current appraisal of North American estimates. *American Journal of Physical Anthropology 45*:661–666.
1976b The sources and methodology for Mooney's estimates of North American Indian populations. In *The native populations of the Americas in 1495,* edited by W. M. Denevan, pp. 243–288. Univ. of Wisconsin Press, Madison.
1978 *Human skeletal remains.* Aldine, Chicago.

Ucko, P. J., and G. W. Dimbleby (editors)
1969 *The domestication and exploitation of plants and animals.* Aldine, Chicago.

Vallois, H. V.
1937 La durée de la vie chez l'homme fossile. *L'Anthropologie 47*:499–532.
1960 *Vital statistics in prehistoric population as determined from archaeological data. Quantitative methods in archaeology.* Viking Fund Publications in Anthropology, No. 28, pp. 186–222.

Van Ginneken, J. K.
1974 Prolonged breast feeding as a birth spacing method. *Studies in Family Planning 5*:201–208.

Vavilov, N. I.
1926 *Studies on the origin of cultivated plants.* Inst. Appl. Bot. Pland Breeds, Leningrad.

Vita-Finzi, and E. S. Higgs
1970 Prehistoric economy in the Mount Carmel area of Palestine. Site catchment analysis. *Proceedings of the Prehistoric Society 36*:1–37.

Ward, R. H., and K. M. Weiss (editors)
1976 *The demographic evolution of human populations.* Academic Press, London.

Waterbolk, H. T.
1968 Food production in prehistoric Europe. *Science 162*:1093–1102.

Watt, Kenneth E. F.
1968 *Ecology and resource management, a quantitative approach.* McGraw-Hill, New York.

Weidenreich, F.
1939 The duration of life of fossil man in China and the pathological lesions found in his skeleton. *Chinese Medical Journal 55*:34–44.
1943 The skull of *Sinanthropus pekinesis,* a comparative study on a primitive hominid skull. *Palaeontologia Sinica* n.s., No. 10, Peiping.
1951 Morphology of Solo Man. *American Museum of Natural History, Anthropology Papers 43*:205–290.

Weiss K. M.
1972a A general measure of human population growth regulation. *American Journal of Physical Anthropology 37*:337–344.
1972b On the systematic bias in skeletal sexing. *American Journal of Physical Anthropology 37*:239–250.
1973 Demographic models for anthropology. *American Antiquity 38*(2), Part 2, Memoir 27.
1976 Demographic theory and anthropological inference. *Annual Review in anthropology 5*:351–381.

Wendorf, Fred (editor)
1968 *The prehistory of Nubia* (two vol.). Fort Burgwin Research Center and Southern Methodist Univ. Press, Dallas.

Wendorf, F., R. Said, and R. Schild
  1970 Egyptian prehistory: Some new concepts. *Science 169:*1161–1171.
Wendorf, F., and R. Schild
  1976 *Prehistory of the Nile Valley.* Academic Press, New York.
Wenke, R. J.
  1975 *Imperial investments and agricultural developments in Parthian and Sussanian Khuzistan: 150 B.C. to A.D. 640.* Unpublished, Ph.D. dissertation, Univ. of Michigan, Ann Arbor.
Wheat, J. W.
  1972 *The Olsen-Chubbuck site: A Paleo-Indian bison kill.* Memoirs of the American Society for American Archaeology, No. 26.
Wheatley, Paul
  1972 The concept of urbanism. Warner Modular Publication, Reprint 12. Reprinted from *Man, settlement, and urbanism,* edited by P. J. Ucko, R. Tringham, and G. W. Dimbleby. Duckworth, London.
White, Carmel, and Nicholas Peterson
  1973 Ethnographic interpretations of the prehistory of western Arnhem Land. Warner Modular Publication, Reprint 540, pp. 1–23.
White, Leslie
  1949 *The science of culture.* Grove, New York.
White, T. E.
  1953 A method of calculating the dietary percentage of various food animals utilized by aboriginal peoples. *American Antiquity 4:*396–398.
Wiens, John A.
  1977 On competition and variable environment. *American Scientist 65:*590–597.
Wiessner, P.
  1974 A functional estimator of population from floor area. *American Antiquity 39*(2):343–350.
Wilcox, W. F.
  1931 Increase in the population of earth and the continents since 1650. In *International migrations* (Vol. 2), edited by W. F. Wilcox, pp. 33–82. National bureau of Economic Research, New York.
Wilkinson, P. F.
  1972 Ecosystem models and demographic hypotheses: Predation and prehistory in North America. In *Models in archaeology,* edited by David L. Clarke, pp. 543–576. Methuen, London.
Willey, G. R.
  1966 *An introduction to American archaeology* (Vol. 1). Prentice-Hall, Englewood Cliffs, N.J.
  1971 *Commentary on the emergence of civilization in the Maya lowlands.* Contributions of the California Archaeological Research Facility, No. 11, pp. 97–111.
Willey, G. R., and D. B. Shimkin
  1971 The collapse of classis Maya civilization in the southern lowlands: A symposium summary statement. *Southwestern Journal of Anthropology 27:*1–18.
Williams, B. J.
  1974 A model of band society. *American Antiquity 39*(4), Part 2, Memoir 29.
Winter, M. C.
  1972 *Tierras Largas: A formative community in the Valley of Oaxaca, Mexico.* Unpublished Ph.D. dissertation, Department of Anthropology, University of Arizona, Tucson.
Wittfogel, K. A.
  1957 *Oriental despotism: A comparative study of total power.* Yale Univ. Press, New Haven, Conn.
Wobst, H. Martin
  1974 Boundary conditions for Paleolithic social systems: a simulation approach. *American Antiquity 39*(2):147–178.
  1975 The demography of finite populations and the origins of the incest taboo. In Population studies in archaeology and biological anthropology: A symposium, edited by A. C. Swedlund, pp. 74–81. *American Antiquity 40*(2), Part 2, Memoir 30.

Wolf, E.
  1959   *Sons of the shaking earth.* Univ. of Chicago Press, Chicago.
  1966   *Peasants.* Prentice-Hall, Englewood Cliffs, N.J.
Wolfs, H., and M. Röhrs
  1977   Zoological considerations on the origins of farming and domestication. In *Origins of agriculture,* edited by C. Reed, pp. 245–279. Mouton, The Hague.
Wolfe, A. B.
  1933   The fecundity and fertility of early man. *Human Biology 5*:35–60.
Woodburn, J.
  1968   An introduction to Hadza ecology. In *Man the hunter,* edited by R. B. Lee and I. DeVore, pp. 49–55. Aldine, Chicago.
Wright, H. E., Jr.
  1977   Environmental change and the origin of agriculture in the Old and New World. In *Origins of agriculture,* edited by C. A. Reed, pp.218–318. Mouton, The Hague.
Wright, H. T.
  1969   *The administration of rural production in an early Mesopotamian town.* Museum of Anthropology, University of Michigan Anthropological paper, No. 38.
Wright, H. T., and G. A. Johnson
  1975   Population, exchange, and early state formation in southwestern Iran. *American Anthropologist 77:*267–289.
Wrigley, E. A.
  1969   *Population and history.* McGraw-Hill, New York.
Wynne-Edwards, V. C.
  1965   Self-regulating systems in population of animals. *Science 147*:1543–1548.
Yellen, J.
  1976   Settlement pattern of the !Kung Bushmen: an archaeological perspective. In *Kalahari hunter-gatherers,* edited by R. B. Lee and I. DeVore, pp. 47–72. Harvard Univ. Press, Cambridge, Mass.
  1977   *Archaeological approaches to the present.* Academic Press, New York.
Yellen, J, and Henry Harpending
  1972   Hunter–gatherer populations and archaeological inference. *World Archaeology 4*(2):244–253.
Yengoyan, A. A.
  1968   Demographic and ecological influences on aboriginal Australian marriage sections. In *Man the hunter,* edited by R. B. Lee and I. DeVore, pp 185–199. Aldine, Chicago.
Yessner, D. R.
  1977   Resource diversity and population stability among hunter–gatherers. *Western Canadian Journal of Anthropology 3*(2):18–59.
Young, Cuyler T.
  1972   Population densities and early Mesopotamian urbanism. In *Man, settlement, and urbanism,* edited by P. J. Ucko, pp. 827–842. Duckworth, London.
Zeuner, F. E.
  1963   *A history of domesticated animals.* Hutchinson, London.
Zubrow, Ezra, B. W.
  1971   Carrying capacity and dynamic equilibrium in the prehistoric Southwest. *American Antiquity 36*(2):127–138.
  1974   *Population, contact, and climate in the New Mexican pueblos.* Anthropological papers of the University of Arizona, No. 24. Univ. of Arizona Press, Tucson.
  1975   *Prehistoric carrying capacity: A model.* Cummings, Menlo Park, Calif.

Index

STUDIES IN ARCHAEOLOGY

Consulting Editor: Stuart Struever

Department of Anthropology
Northwestern University
Evanston, Illinois